TOKYO, LONDON, NEW YORK, LOS ANGELES, AND MANY MORE

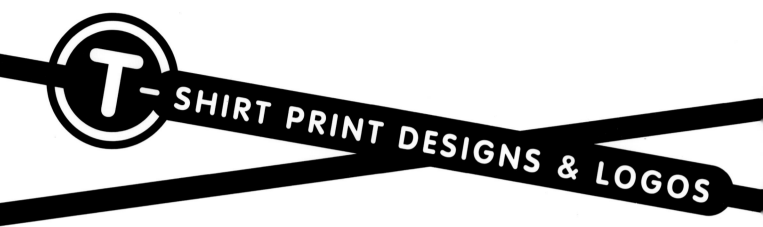

T-SHIRT PRINT DESIGNS & LOGOS

AN UPBEAT COLLECTION OF T-SHIRTS, TOGETHER WITH ALL SORTS OF LOGOS,

ILLUSTRATIONS AND PHOTOS USED ON T-SHIRTS

PIE BOOKS

T-SHIRT PRINT DESIGNS & LOGOS

First published in Japan in 1994 by: P·I·E BOOKS

Villa Phoenix Suite 407, 4-14-6 Komagome,

Toshima-ku, Tokyo 170 Japan

Tel: 03-3949-5010 Fax: 03-3949-5650

ISBN 4-938586-61-4

First published in Germany in 1994 by:Nippan

Nippon Shuppan Hanbai Deutschland GmbH

Krefelder Str.85 D-40549 Düsseldorf, Germany

Tel: 0211-5048080 Fax: 0211-5049326

ISBN 3-910052-49-5

Printed in Hong Kong

CONTENTS

は じ め に

Tシャツは移動するメディアである。街がショップ、広告、カルチャー等、渦巻く情報をクロスオーバーしながら発信する一つのメディアだととらえるのと同様に、そこに集まる人々は街を形成していくファクターであり、彼らの行動や興味、それを反映させる美意識、音楽やファッション傾向、趣味嗜好等に今やTシャツは密接に結びついている。目を引くTシャツを着て歩く行為は、小さな看板やポスターと類似するパワーを持っている。Tシャツの魅力はたくさんある。まずは、ノンセックス、ノンシーズン、ノンエイジ、ノンルールという点で、あらゆるカジュアルウエアの代表として多目的に楽しむことができるアイテムであるということ。そしてシンプルなフォルムだからこそ、キャンバスにした際にひとつのヴィジュアルを生き生きと表現することが、プリントという手法において可能になってくる面白さ。しかも、素材及び製品としてはカット＆ソーに総称されていて、これは簡便でローコスト、つまりライトで実用的という長所をもっている。

ファッションのカジュアル化は過去10年程前に顕著な傾向として現れてきた。それは社会現象やライフスタイルの変化等に伴い、自由時間の増大と関連した結果であったことは言うまでもないが、やがて消費の多様化が商品供給側と消費者ニーズにおいての双方の側それぞれで進行していくようになる。'90年に入って、メーカーや工場が在庫処分の為に行うアウトレットの出現とバーゲンの常態化、また無店舗販売やディスカウントシステム等が派生し、それによってブランドイメージのダウンが引き起こされた。ちなみに欧米ではノン・ブランドという実用的衣服の新しいグループが台頭してきている。このような現状的に難しい構造のアパレル業界であるが、各メーカーは今のところ毎シーズン、商品としてTシャツを提案している。シーズンのテーマやコンセプトに沿ってデザインされる衣服の中でもTシャツは、比較的手間やコストをかけずに制作されるだろうが、メーカーが打ち出すイメージをよりストレートなヴィジュアルで表現できるアイテムである。そして前述のように多様化や個性化、また衣料知識のレベルが向上した消費者にもまた、自分の共感するデザイナーのセンスを気負わず最もラフに取り入れて自由な着こなしができる嬉しさが備わっている。

アパレルやスポーツメーカーが制作するTシャツの他に、グラフィックデザイナーやイラストレーターがTシャツの為にデザインを起こして販売している流通がある。こういったプロデュースを担うクライアントが多くなっていることは、アーティスティックな作品を身につける機会が増えた喜ばしい現実としてとらえることができる。企業や団体がプロモーションとして制作するTシャツも多岐に渡ってあるが、イベントやセールス、CI目的のプレゼンテーションの際に登場するものは、そのほとんどが限定や記念版である。一つの共有する出来事や意識を体感した限られた人々のみのTシャツは、制作する側の意欲や姿勢と着る側の連帯感が一体となって、また格別の付加価値を持ったものとなるであろう。

今、国際的な諸問題としてクローズアップされているものにエイズ問題、人種差別問題、環境・動物保護問題等があるが、それらに対しての強烈なメッセージの入ったTシャツも次から次へと作り出されている。社会問題と関連して世の中の文化は、物質至上主義から精神志向へ移行している。スピリチュアルな世界にある関係の深いトレンド・モチーフとして幾つかを挙げてみよう。まずボーダーレスを象徴するものとして、天使、悪魔、アンドロジナス、宇宙人etc‥‥。宗教的なものとして、十字架、ブッダ、キリスト、ジャンヌ・ダルクetc‥‥。精神トリップ的なものとして、ドラッグ、CGのパターンやステレオグラム、ヒッピー・エフェクトetc‥‥。本書でも、これらのモチーフをフィーチャーしたTシャツ・プリントを数多く掲載している。

Tシャツは常に多種多様なデザインが登場して、簡単に生まれて即消えていく短命のもの、また長く愛用されるものと消費も多様である。いずれのシチュエーションでもその時代時代の中で広がる文化にぴたりとマッチするのがTシャツの魅力だ。このようなTシャツ特有の性質や実情をふまえて、本書は企画構成された。今を感じとれる新鮮なデザインはもちろん、過去にあった素晴らしいデザインまでをTシャツにおけるプリントという切り口で集約している。Tシャツのためのオリジナル・ロゴやイラスト、コラージュ等の原版までコレクションに加えた。本書を御覧になる方に、登場する約700点ものTシャツそれぞれのデザインの発想やクリエイション、主張やメッセージにおいて、時代のリアリティを感じていただけたら幸いである。最後に本書にご協力いただいた皆様に感謝を申し上げます。

ピエ・ブックス編集部

PREFACE

T-shirts are a mobile medium. The urban environment as a whole can be regarded as a medium generating a maelstrom of information in messages projected through retailing, advertising and popular culture. The urban population is one element making up that environment, and the T-shirts people wear these days relate closely to their interests and activities, and the esthetic values, trends in music and fashion, and individual tastes that underlie them. The simple act of walking around in an eye-catching T-shirt puts over the same kind of powerful message as a small advertisement or poster. T-shirts are attractive for several reasons. First of all, they can be worn free of any constraints by people of either sex and any age, and are not limited to any particular season. So people enjoy wearing T-shirts because they are the ultimate in all-purpose casual clothing. The T-shirt's ultra-simple shape gives it an added point of interest: it provides a canvas for the expression of highly visual, fresh, lively images which can be readily printed on. Furthermore, the fabric is, as the industry term 'cut and sew' suggests, easy to handle, and the finished product is quick and inexpensive to produce, and light and practical to wear.

Fashion has become noticeably more casual over the last ten years or so, no doubt partly due to the increased amount of leisure time that people now have, as lifestyles and social circumstances have changed. The diversification of consumption patterns can be seen both in the products offered and in the requirements of consumers. The 1990s saw the advent of 'outlets' for manufacturers to clear their old stock, regular bargain sales and such new ideas as armchair shopping and discount systems. All this has undermined the hold of designer brands over the retail market. In North America and Europe new fashion groups are putting out practical clothing with no brand name. With the apparel industry finding survival tough in these changing times, all the manufacturers are now promoting T-shirts as fashion items every season. Of the clothing designed to a specific fashion concept for each season, T-shirts are the one item that can be produced relatively quickly and inexpensively, but they also can express that concept in a very direct, and highly visual way. And for present-day consumers, who are better informed and, as I have said, have more diversified tastes and greater individuality of style, T-shirts offer the fun of a new freedom in dressing, as they identify only very loosely with a particular designer's look.

Besides the T-shirts produced by clothing and sporting goods manufacturers, there is now a separate retail distribution of T-shirts designed by graphic designers and illustrators. The fact that there are enough buyers to support this particular output points to a welcome new trend: people are increasingly ready to wear something that is first and foremost good art. There is also a wide range of T-shirts manufactured to the specific requirements of business or other organizations. Used for sales or event promotions, or to project corporate image, they are often only produced in limited editions or to commemorate one specific occasion. Those T-shirts produced for a limited number of people attending a particular event or sharing a common interest bring together the aspirations of the those producing the T-shirt with the sense of rapport felt by the wearers, and thus they provide a distinctive added extra.

Recently, we are seeing more and more T-shirts that convey passionate messages about current issues of global concern, such as AIDS, human rights, protection of the environment, endangered species, and so on. At the same time, our cultures all around the world are shifting away from ultra-materialism towards a more spiritual orientation. More and more motifs are reflecting this new emphasis on the spiritual. Images that symbolize exceeding the bounds include angels, demons, aliens from space, and androgynous forms. More specifically religious motifs are the crucifix, Christ, Buddha, Joan of Arc and so on. Psychedelic imagery is conveyed in computer-generated patterns, holograms and so-called 'hippie art'. These motifs appear time and again on the T-shirts featured in this book.

Designs for T-shirts are enormously varied. The lives of T-shirts as consumer items also vary: some appear very suddenly and disappear just as quickly, while others become long-term favorites. The attraction of T-shirts is that they offer a crisp, concise reflection of the culture of the times, wherever and whenever. This book was created to underline these particular characteristics and the place of T-shirts in our society. We have collected all manner of T-shirt print designs, from those that convey the latest ideas of modern design as it evolves, to the long-surviving quality designs from the past. To these we have added some original logos, illustrations and collages produced to be printed on T-shirts. In total, the book contains almost 700 T-shirt designs. We hope that the inspiration behind the creation of these T-shirts, and the messages they convey, will give readers a closer feel of the realities of our times.

Finally we would like to take this opportunity to thank everyone who assisted in the production of this book.

P·I·E BOOKS Editorial Department

VORWORT

T-Shirts sind ein bewegliches Kommunikationsmedium. Faßt man die Straße als eines der Medien auf, die unter Verknüpfung einer Flut von Informationen aus Läden, Werbung, Kultur usw. Eindrücke vermitteln und ausstrahlen, sind die Menschen, die dort zusammentreffen, der Faktor, der das Straßenbild prägt. Mit den Aktivitäten und Interessen dieser Akteure, mit ihrem Schönheitsempfinden, das diese widerspiegeln, mit Musik-, Modetendenzen und Freizeittrends sind T-Shirts heute eng verbunden. Sich in einem auffälligen T-Shirt auf die Straße zu wagen, erzielt eine ähnliche Wirkung wie eine Reklametafel oder ein Poster. Viele Dinge machen den Reiz des T-Shirts aus. Zunächst einmal ist es ein Stück Stoff, das man unter dem Aspekt seiner Unabhängigkeit von Geschlecht, Jahreszeit, Alter oder irgendwelchen Regeln als das lässige Kleidungsstück schlechthin zu allen möglichen Gelegenheiten tragen kann. Dazu kommt, daß es sich - gerade weil es eine so simple Form hat - bestens als neutrale Grundlage eignet, um ein einzelnes Motiv frech in Szene zu setzen, möglich geworden durch die Textildrucktechnik. Weitere Vorzüge liegen, wie sie in der Branchenbezeichnung "cut&saw" für Material und Ware zum Ausdruck kommen, in der Unkompliziertheit und den niedrigen Kosten der T-Shirts, oder mit anderen Worten in seiner Leichtigkeit und seinen praktischen Eigenschaften.

Casual Wear ist seit etwa 10 Jahren ein ernstzunehmender Modetrend. Man braucht nicht zu betonen, daß dies auf ein Mehr an freier Zeit in Verbindung mit veränderten Sozialstrukturen und einem Wandel im Lebensstil zurückzuführen ist und im Endeffekt für die Bereicherung der Modepalette beide Seiten verantwortlich sind, also sowohl die Anbieter, die mit ihrem Warenangebot Wünsche wecken als auch die Kunden, die nach entsprechender Ware verlangen. Seit Beginn der neunziger Jahre entzaubern Geschäfte, die die Hersteller und Fabriken nur zur Räumung ihrer Lager eröffnen, ständige Sonderverkäufe, Versandhandel und Discountläden das Image der Markenmode. In den USA und Europa hat sich beispielsweise bereits eine neue Kategorie von Alltagskleidung, sog. "non-brand"-Mode, herausgebildet. In dieser sich gegenwärtig in einem schwer durchschaubaren Umwälzungsstadium befindlichen Branche verzichtet kein Couturier darauf, zu jeder Saison T-Shirts als Bestandteil der Kollektion zu entwerfen. Passend zur Saison und zum Thema der Kollektion sind T-Shirts im Vergleich zur übrigen Designerkleidung schnell und ohne hohe Kosten herzustellen und doch ein Mittel, das vom Hersteller beabsichtigte Image pur zum Ausdruck zu bringen. Der Käufer, der sich, wie oben gesagt, durch größere Individualität, Differenziertheit und ein gestiegenes Modebewußtsein auszeichnet, kann auf der anderen Seite mit dem T-Shirt den Charme "seines" Designers, unexaltiert und unverfälscht übernehmen und zwang- und problemlos tragen.

Neben den T-Shirts von Bekleidungs- und Sportartikelherstellern entwerfen und verkaufen heute auch Grafik-Designer und Illustratoren Designs für T-Shirts. Die Nachfrage nach solchen Designs nimmt zu, da ein hübsches Bild als Bekleidung erfreulicherweise bei mehr und mehr Gelegenheiten hoffähig wird. Viele Firmen und Künstler verteilen T-Shirts in allen Variationen, die sie zu Werbezwecken anfertigen lassen. Diejenigen T-Shirts, die bei Veranstaltungen, zur Verkaufsförderung oder als Bestandteil von Corporate Identy verschenkt oder verkauft werden, sind meist in ihrer Auflage limitiert und zur Erinnerung an ein bestimmtes Ereignis gedacht. Ein solches T-Shirt begrenzt den Empfängerkreis auf ein gemeinsames Erlebnis oder Anliegen. Es steht so am Kreuzungspunkt der Interessen der ausgebenden Seite und der T-Shirt-Träger und weist damit auch einen über den eigentlichen Wert hinausgehenden auf.

Als Probleme, die heute international Beachtung finden, sind vor allem Aids, Rassendiskriminierung, Umwelt- und Naturschutz zu nennen und zu diesen Komplexen werden in schneller Folge T-Shirts mit eindringlichen Botschaften hergestellt. In Zusammenhang mit den gesellschaftlichen Problemen wendet man sich weltweit vom Primat des Materialismus ab und einer stärker spirituell geprägten Weltanschauung zu. Dies zeigt sich in spirituell angehauchten Trendmotiven wie solchen, die sich mit dem Phänomen des Grenzenlosen befassen, z.B. Engel, Teufel, Androgyne, Außerirdische etc. Daneben sind religiöse Motive zu finden wie Kreuz, Buddha, Christus, Jeanne d'Arc etc. Zu den Psychomotiven gehören Drogen, Computergrafiken und Stereogramme, Hippie-Effekte etc. Der vorliegende Band enthält eine Vielzahl von T-Shirtdrucken zu all diesen Motiven.

So unterschiedlich wie die vielen Arten und Formen der T-Shirts sind auch ihre Träger. Bei dem einen hat das einfach hergestellte Produkt nur ein kurzes Leben, bei dem anderen hält es sich liebevoll gepflegt über Jahre. Es macht den Reiz des T-Shirts mit seiner nicht vorhersehbaren Zukunft und seiner, wenn man so will, Vergänglichkeit aus, daß es jeweils genau zum jeweils herrschenden Zeitgeist paßt. Unter diesen Aspekten, mit Blick auf Charakteristik und die gegenwärtige Verwendung der T-Shirts wurde dieses Buch konzipiert. Zusammengefaßt sind als "Druckmotive auf T-Shirts" natürlich Beispiele jüngsten Designs, dessen Aktualität man spürt, aber auch beeindruckendes Design der Vergangenheit. Daneben finden sich Sammlungen von Original-Logos und Illustrationen, Collagen usw. für T-Shirts. Es wäre in unserem Sinne, wenn der Leser beim Betrachten gut 700 abgebildeten T-Shirts durch die jeweiligen Motive, Creationen, dargestellten Ideen und Botschaften etwas von der Atmosphäre der jeweiligen Zeit spürt. Zum Schluß möchte der Verfasser allen Beteiligten, die am Zustandekommen dieses Buchs mitgearbeitet haben, seinen Dank aussprechen.

Die Herausgeber Von P·I·E BOOKS

EDITORIAL NOTES:

CD:Creative Direction

AD:Art Direction

D:Design

P:Photography

I:Illustration

CW:Copy Writing

DF:Design Firm

CL:Client

IR:Importer,Retailer

The Title given for each entry

is the brand name or

main title of the artwork,

and any other title provided

by the contributor is given in quotes.

The country indicated is

the country where

the artwork was produced.

本文クレジット中、タイトルは

ブランド名または作品名を、

その他固有のタイトルは " "で表記しています。

国名は制作国を表記しています。

FASHION FASHION FASHION FASHION FASHION FASH

T-SHIRTS FOR RETAIL SALES

SPORTS SPORTS SPORTS SPORTS SPORTS SPORTS

OTHERS OTHERS OTHERS OTHERS OTHERS OTHER

FASHION FASHION FASHION FASHION FASH

SPORTS SPORTS SPORTS SPORTS SPORTS SPO

OTHERS OTHERS OTHERS OTHERS OTH

HYSTERIC GLAMOUR
JAPAN 1991 D:Nobuhiko Kitamura CL:Ozone Community Corporation

HYSTERIC GLAMOUR
JAPAN 1989 / 1993 D:Nobuhiko Kitamura
CL:Ozone Community Corporation

 T-SHIRTS FOR RETAIL SALES
FASHION FASHION FASHION FASHION FASHION FASHION FASHION FASHION FASHION FASHION FASHION FASHIO

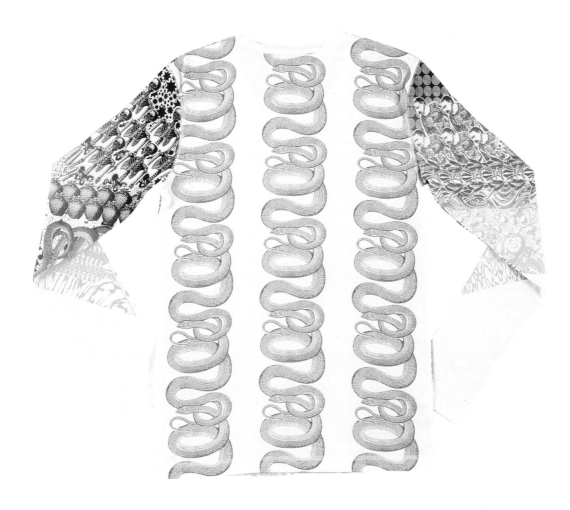

HYSTERIC GLAMOUR
JAPAN 1991 D:Nobuhiko Kitamura
CL:Ozone Community Corporation

T-SHIRTS FOR RETAIL SALES
FASHION FASHION FASHION FASHION FASHION FASHION FASHION FASHION FASHION FASHION FASHION FASHION

OZONE COMMUNITY
JAPAN 1988 CL:Ozone Community Corporation

HYSTERIC GLAMOUR
JAPAN 1988 D:Nobuhiko Kitamura CL:Ozone Community Corporation

T-SHIRTS FOR RETAIL SHION FASHION FASHION FASHION FASHION FASHION **014** FASHION FASHION FASHION FASHION FASHION FASHION FASHION FOR RETAIL SALES

OZONE COMMUNITY
JAPAN 1989 CL:Ozone Community Corporation

HELMUT LANG
JAPAN 1994 D:Helmut Lang CL:Toalady's Co.,Ltd.

OZONE COMMUNITY
JAPAN 1994 CL:Ozone Community Corporation

HELMUT LANG
JAPAN 1993 D:Helmut Lang CL:Toalady's Co.,Ltd.

JEAN PAUL·GAULTIER

JAPAN 1994 D:Jean Paul·Gaultier CL:Onward Kashiyama Co.,Ltd.

THE NEW PARADISE

GARAGE

HARLEM

?

VELVET OVERHIGH'M
JAPAN 1991 D:Couichi Hirayama CL:Shige Design Office Co.,Ltd.

VELVET OVERHIGH'M
JAPAN 1991 AD:Naomi Machida D:Couichi Hirayama CL:Shige Design Office Co.,Ltd.

T-SHIRTS FOR RETAIL SALES SPORTS SPORTS SPORTS SPORTS SPORTS SPORTS **018** SPORTS FOR RETAIL SPORTS SPORTS SPORTS SPORTS SPOR

ARCHAIC SMILE
USA 1993 D:Jeff Gladhart / Rachel Williams
CL:Archaic Smile

ANARCHIC ADJUSTMENT
USA 1992 D:Nick Philip CL:Anarchic Adjustment

ARCHAIC SMILE
USA 1993 D:Jeff Gladhart / Rachel Williams CL:Archaic Smile

ARCHAIC SMILE
USA 1993 D:Jeff Gladhart / Rachel Williams CL:Archaic Smile

ARCHAIC SMILE
USA 1992 D:Jeff Gladhart / Rachel Williams CL:Archaic Smile

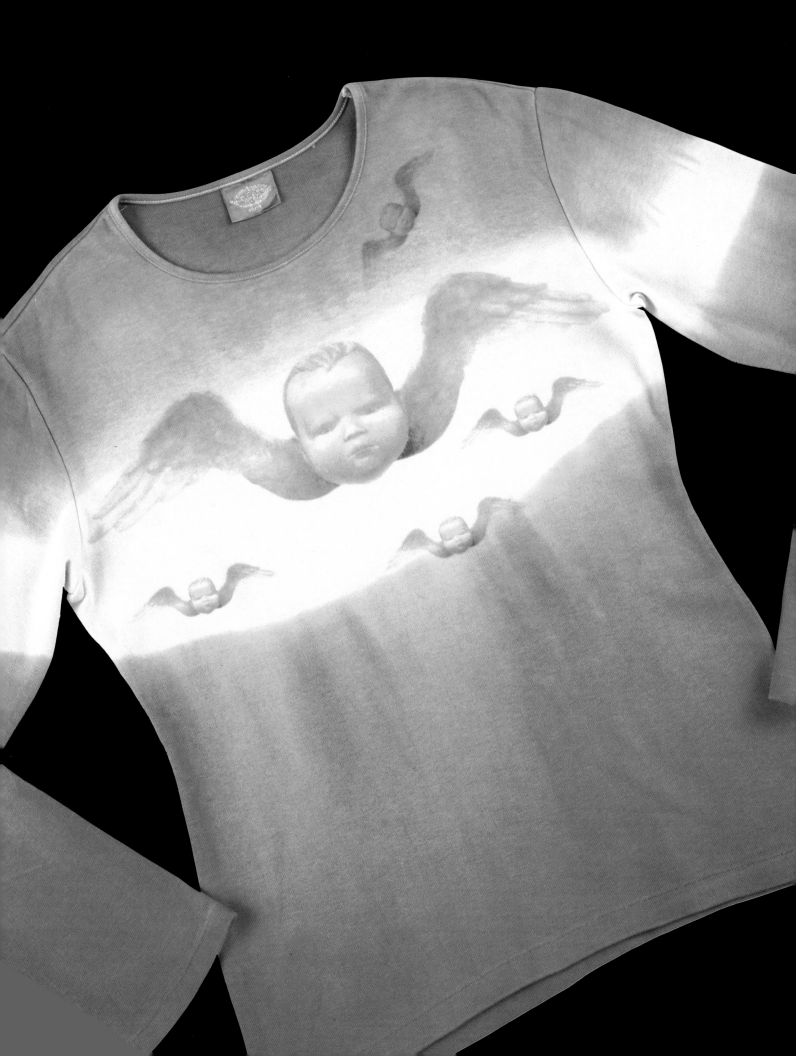

OZONE COMMUNITY
JAPAN 1993 CL:Ozone Community Corporation

BACK

FRONT

BACK

FRONT

OZONE COMMUNITY
JAPAN 1993 CL:Ozone Community Corporation

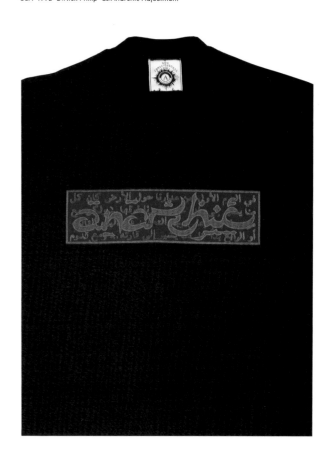

T-SHIRTS FOR RETAIL SALES

FASHION FASHION FASHION FASHION FOR FASHION FASHION FASHION FASHION FASHION FASHION FASHION FASHION FASHION

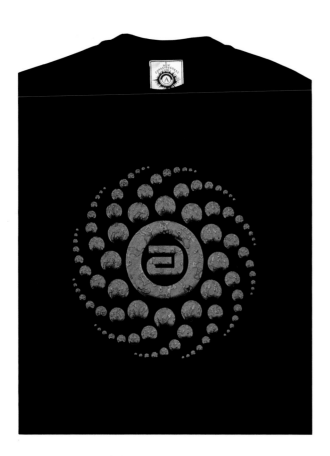

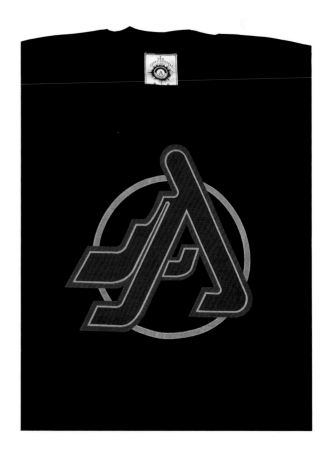

AZTEC SKULL
UK 1993 CD:Ms. Dot D:Brian Gurtler / Guy Hazell
CL:Dot Productions

RED OR DEAD
UK 1992 CL:Red or Dead

FRONT

BACK

HYSTERIC GLAMOUR
JAPAN 1989 D:Nobuhiko Kitamura CL:Ozone Community Corporation

D.BROOKS
USA 1994 D:David Brooks DF:D.Brooks Design

D.BROOKS
USA 1993 D:David Brooks DF:D.Brooks Design

FASHION FASHION FASHION FASHION FASHION FASHION **T-SHIRTS FOR RETAIL SALES** 027 FASHION FASHION FASHION FASHION FASHION FASHION

ARCHAIC SMILE
USA 1992 D:Jeff Gladhart / Rachel Williams
CL:Archaic Smile

BODY-RAP
UK 1993-1994

FRONT

BACK

FRONT

BACK

BODY-RAP
UK 1993-1994

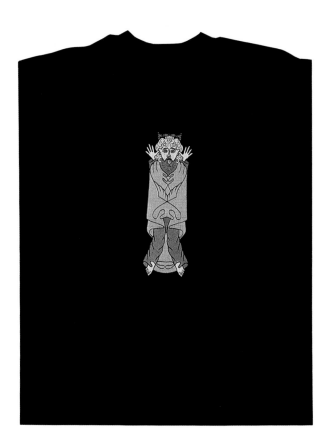

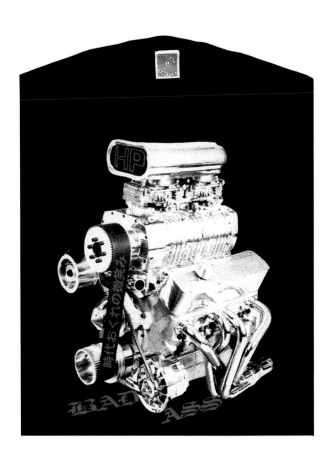

ARCHAIC SMILE
USA 1993 D:Jeff Gladhart / Rachel Williams CL:Archaic Smile

ARCHAIC SMILE
USA 1993 D:Jeff Gladhart / Rachel Williams CL:Archaic Smile

BODY-RAP
UK 1993-1994 P:Don Conningham

BODY-RAP
UK 1993-1994 P:Don Conningham

BABY DOLL BABY DOLL BABY DOLL BABY DOLL

T-SHIRTS FOR RETAIL SALES
SHION FASHION FASHION FASHION FASHION FASHION FOR RETAIL SALES ⓪③⓪ FASHION FASHION FASHION FASHION FASHION FASHION

MILK BOY
JAPAN 1994 CL:Milk Inc.

MILK BOY
JAPAN 1994 CL:Milk Inc.

HYSTERIC GLAMOUR
JAPAN 1988 AD:Nobuhiko Kitamura D:Couichi Hirayama
CL:Ozone Community Corporation

"EAT FASHION!"

DESIGNER PIG

FASHION FASHION FASHION FASHION FASHION RETAIL SALES FASHION FASHION FASHION FASHION FASHION FASHIC

T-SHIRTS FOR RETAIL SALES 031 T-SHIRTS FOR RETAIL SALES

goo-goo-eyes
velvet
overhigh'm
d m x

VELVET OVERHIGH'M
JAPAN 1989 AD:Naomi Machida D:Couichi Hirayama
CL:Shige Design Office Co.,Ltd.

RED OR DEAD
UK 1993 CL:Red or Dead

RED OR DEAD
UK 1993 CL:Red or Dead

TRUTH
JAPAN 1993 CD:Takumi Matsuda P:Bun Shaka I:Kazushige Miida (Kad's) CL:Beatniks

COOL COUNTER
JAPAN 1993 CD:Takumi Matsuda I:Kazushige Miida (Kad's) CL:Beatniks

COOL COUNTER
JAPAN 1993 CD:Takumi Matsuda I:Kazushige Miida (Kad's) CL:Beatniks

RED OR DEAD
UK 1993 CL:Red or Dead

FASHION FASHION FASHION FASHION FOR FASHION RETAIL FASHION · T-SHIRTS FOR FASHION FASHION FASHION FASHION FASHION

BEATNIKS
JAPAN 1993 D:Takumi Matsuda CL:Beatniks

NINE TOO ZERO
JAPAN 1993 CL:Nine Too Zero

BETTY'S BLUE
JAPAN 1993 CL:Lemon Co.,Ltd.

BACK

T-SHIRTS FOR RETAIL SALES

FASHION FASHION FASHION FASHION FASHION FASHION FASHION FASHION FASHION FASHION FASHION FASHION

T-SHIRTS FOR RETAIL SALES ...SHION FASHION FASHION FASHION FOR FASHION RETAIL SALES T-SHIRTS FOR FASHION FASHION FASHION FASHION FASHION

T-SHIRTS FOR RETAIL SALES
FASHION FASHION FASHION FASHION FASHION FOR RETAIL SALES FASHION FASHION FASHION FASHION FASHION FASHION

BETTY'S BLUE
JAPAN 1993 I:Nishi Tokyo Illustrators CL:Lemon Co.,Ltd.

HYSTERIC GLAMOUR
JAPAN 1991 D:Nobuhiko Kitamura CL:Ozone Community Corporation

VELVET OVERHIGH'M
JAPAN 1988 D:Couichi Hirayama CL:Taps

T-SHIRTS FOR RETAIL SALES ③⑨ T-SHIRTS FOR RETAIL SALES

HYSTERIC GLAMOUR
JAPAN 1988 AD:Nobuhiko Kitamura D:Couichi Hirayama
CL:Ozone Community Corporation

WILD DANCER
JAPAN 1993 D:Couichi Hirayama CL:Wild Dancer

HYSTERIC GLAMOUR
JAPAN 1990 D:Nobuhiko Kitamura CL:Ozone Community Corporation

T-SHIRTS FOR RETAIL SALES

FASHION FASHION FASHION FASHION FOR FASHION RETAIL SALES **041** T-SHIRTS FOR FASHION FASHION FASHION FASHION FASHION FASHIC

MILK
JAPAN 1994 CL:Milk Inc.

BETTY'S BLUE
JAPAN 1994 CL:Lemon Co.,Ltd.

T-SHIRTS FOR RETAIL SALES SPORTS SPORTS SPORTS SPORTS SPORTS SPORTS SPORTS SPORTS SPORTS SPORTS SPORTS SPORTS SPORTS FOR RETAIL SALES

HYSTERIC GLAMOUR
JAPAN 1993 D:Nobuhiko Kitamura CL:Ozone Community Corporation

HYSTERIC GLAMOUR
JAPAN D:Nobuhiko Kitamura CL:Ozone Community Corporation

HELTER SKELTER
JAPAN 1993 CL:Bic Company Co.,Ltd.

RED OR DEAD
UK 1990 CL:Red or Dead

T-SHIRTS FOR RETAIL SALES SPORTS SPORTS SPORTS SPORTS SPORTS SPORTS

HELTER SKELTER
JAPAN 1993 CL:Bic Company Co.,Ltd.

HELTER SKELTER
JAPAN 1993 CL:Bic Company Co.,Ltd.

BEATNIKS
JAPAN 1993 D,I:Takumi Matsuda CL:Beatniks

MILK
JAPAN 1994 CL:Milk Inc.

BETTY'S BLUE
JAPAN 1994 CL:Lemon Co.,Ltd.

NICO NICO FACTORY
JAPAN 1993 CD:Masato Masuoka AD:Mie Hoshino I:Makoto Osanai
DF:I'mage Inc. CL:Nagoya Craft,Inc.

HELTER SKELTER
JAPAN 1993 CL:Bic Company Co.,Ltd.

HELTER SKELTER
JAPAN 1993 CL:Bic Company Co.,Ltd.

T-SHIRTS FOR RETAIL SALES

FASHION FASHION FASHION FASHION FASHION FASHION FASHION FASHION FASHION FASHION FASHION FASHIO

T-SHIRTS FASHION FASHION FASHION FASHION FASHION FASHION ⓞ48 FASHION FASHION FASHION FASHION FASHION FASHION FOR RETAIL SALES

T-SHIRTS FOR RETAIL SALES
FASHION FASHION FASHION FASHION FASHION FASHION 049 FASHION FASHION FASHION FASHION FASHION FASHION FASHIO

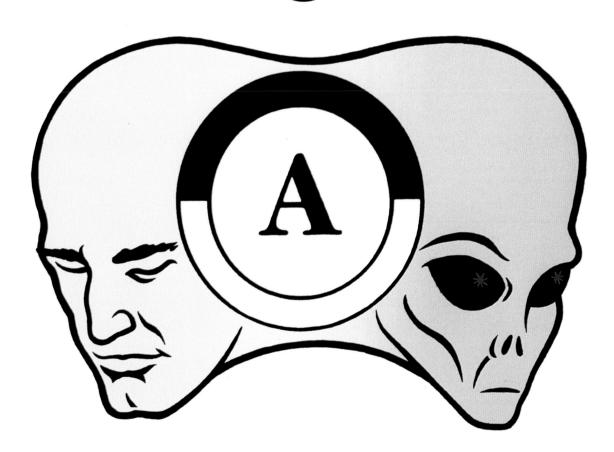

DUFFER

UK 1993 D Brian Griver CL Duffer of St George

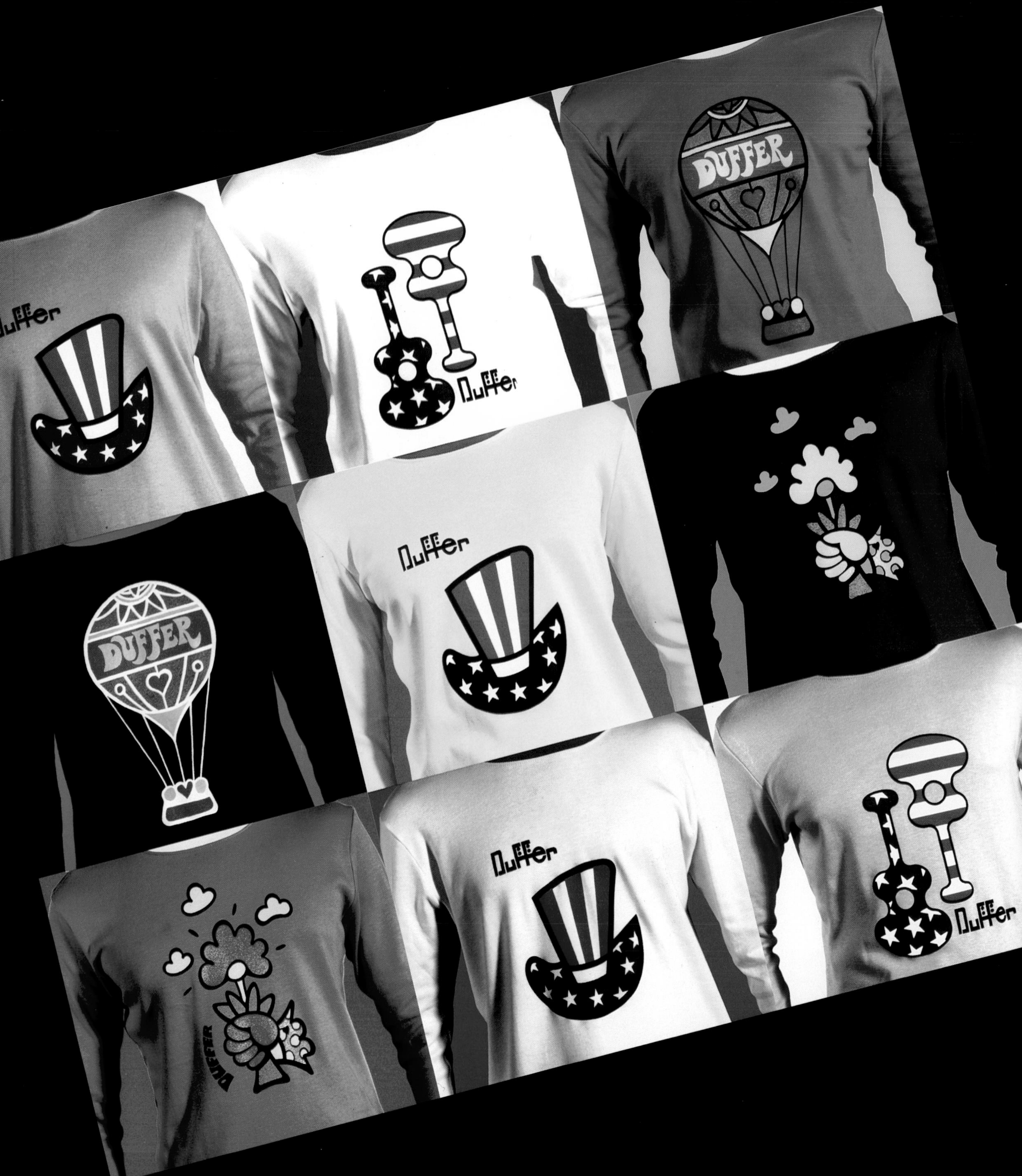

ACE
"KING O'DIAMONDS" UK 1993 AD,D,I,CW:The Designers Republic
DF:The Designers Republic CL:Ace Clothing

ACE
"JACK O'CLUBS" UK 1993 AD,D,I,CW:The Designers Republic
DF:The Designers Republic CL:Ace Clothing

T-SHIRTS FOR RETAIL SALES
FASHION FASHION FASHION FASHION FASHION FASHION FASHION **051** FASHION FASHION FASHION FASHION FASHION FASHION

ACE
"TARGET" UK 1993 AD,D,I,CW:The Designers Republic
DF:The Designers Republic CL:Ace Clothing

ACE
"FUNKY QUEEN" UK 1993 AD,D,I,CW:The Designers Republic
DF:The Designers Republic CL:Ace Clothing

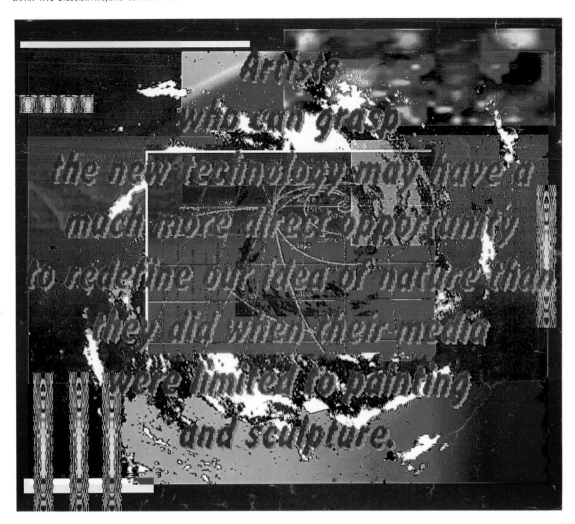

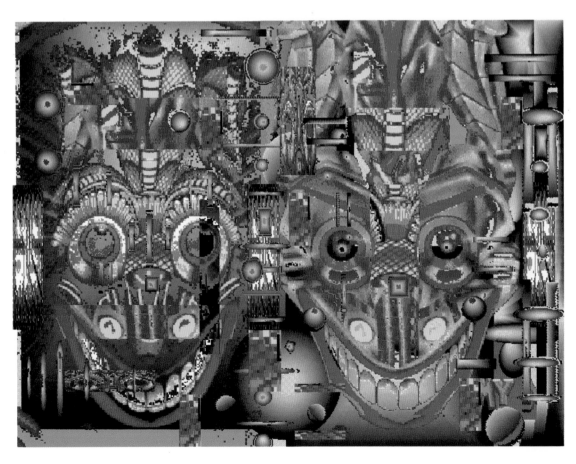

TRENTE ET DEUX
JAPAN 1993 D:Couichi Hirayama CL:Trente et Deux

DEUX IGUREGU
JAPAN 1989 D Couichi Hirayama CL Awase Co Ltd

FOR DAMNED INTELLECTUALS GRAPHIX ANTHOLOGY
A National Invitational Sculpture Exhibition

T * A * P * S *

KEEP PACE WITH ART IN NEW YORK

VELVET OVERHIGH'M

FRONT

BACK

FRONT

BACK

PAUL SMITH

BOY LONDON
HONG KONG 1993 AD,D:Eric Chiang DF:Cheval Design Ltd.
CL:Boy London International Ltd.

MAMBO SPECS
UK 1993 AD,D,I:Trevor Jackson DF:Bite It! CL:Mambo

MAMBO SOFTWEAR
UK 1993 AD,D,I:Trevor Jackson DF:Bite It! CL:Mambo

GTV
UK 1993 AD,D,I:Trevor Jackson DF:Bite It! CL:Good Enough

GOOD ENOUGH
UK 1993 AD,D,I:Trevor Jackson DF:Bite It! CL:Good Enough

T-SHIRTS FOR RETAIL SALES

WEIRD ONE
UK 1993 AD,D,I:Trevor Jackson DF:Bite It! CL:Weird Wear

MAMBO GRIFFIN
UK 1993 AD,D,I:Trevor Jackson DF:Bite It! CL:Mambo

MAMBO HARDWEAR
UK 1993 AD,D,I:Trevor Jackson DF:Bite It! CL:Mambo

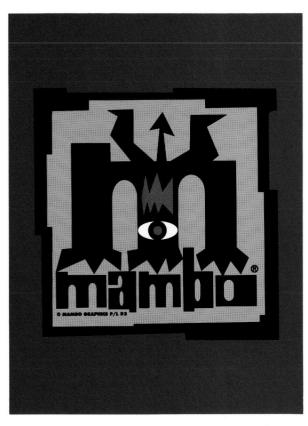

MAMBO GOTHIC 2
UK 1993 AD,D,I:Trevor Jackson DF:Bite It! CL:Mambo

MAMBO GOTHIC 3
UK 1993 AD,D,I:Trevor Jackson DF:Bite It! CL:Mambo

T-SHIRTS FOR RETAIL SALES
FASHION FASHION FASHION FASHION FASHION FASHION 060 FASHION FASHION FASHION FASHION FASHION FASHION

T-SHIRTS FOR RETAIL SALES
FASHION FASHION FASHION FASHION FOR FASHION RETAIL FASHION **061** FASHION FASHION FOR FASHION FASHION FASHION FASHION

CROSS
UK 1993 CD:Ms. Dot D:Brian Gurtler / Guy Hazell CL:Dot Productions

MEN'S BA-TSU
JAPAN 1993 CL:Ba-tsu Co.,Ltd.

BOY LONDON
HONG KONG 1993 AD,D:Eric Chiang DF:Cheval Design Ltd.
CL:Boy London International Ltd.

T-SHIRTS FOR RETAIL SALES

SHION FASHION FASHION FASHION FASHION FASHION FASHION **062** T-SHIRTS FOR FASHION FASHION FASHION FASHION FASHIO

BOY LONDON
HONG KONG 1993 AD,D:Eric Chiang DF:Cheval Design Ltd.
CL:Boy London International Ltd.

OWN COMPANY
UK 1994 AD,D:Howie Jeavons DF:Fake London Ltd
CL:Own Company

OWN COMPANY
UK 1994 AD,D:Howie Jeavons DF:Fake London Ltd
CL:Own Company

PAUL SMITH
JAPAN 1994 D:Paul Smith CL:Joi'x Corporation

PAUL SMITH
JAPAN 1994 D:Paul Smith CL:Joi'x Corporation

T-SHIRTS FOR RETAIL SALES
FASHION FASHION FASHION FASHION FOR FASHION RETAIL FASHION FASHION FASHION FASHION FASHION FASHION FASHIO

PAUL SMITH
JAPAN 1994 D:Paul Smith CL:Joi'x Corporation

PAUL SMITH
JAPAN 1994 D:Paul Smith CL:Joi'x Corporation

FRONT

56cm

72cm

60cm

56cm

SIZE
FREE
by Men's Ba-tsu

52cm

25cm

SIZE FREE
bust : 120cm
length : 72cm
sleeve : 56cm

by Men's Ba-tsu

2

BACK

BACK

FRONT

BACK

FRONT

Ba-tsu Company.

SPECIALTY

Ba-tsu Company.

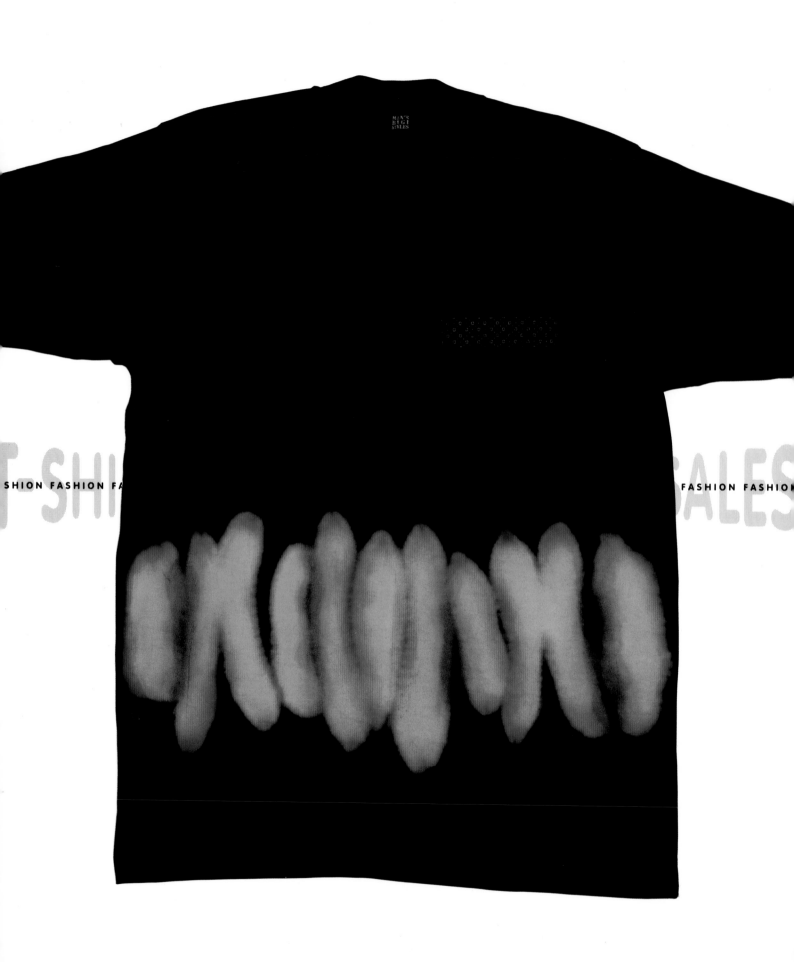

PAUL SMITH
JAPAN 1994 D:Paul Smith CL:Joi'x Corporation

BEATNIKS
JAPAN 1993 D:Takumi Matsuda CL:Beatniks

PAUL SMITH
JAPAN 1994 D:Paul Smith CL:Joi'x Corporation

PAUL SMITH
JAPAN 1994 D:Paul Smith CL:Joi'x Corporation

PAUL SMITH
JAPAN 1994 D:Paul Smith CL:Joi"x Corporation

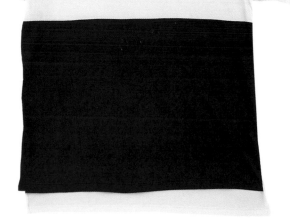

SHION FASHION FASHION FASHION FASHION FASHION FASHION FASHION FASHION FASHION FASHION FASHIO

FRONT

HEARD

PAUL SMITH
JAPAN 1994 D:Paul Smith CL:Joi'x Corporation

BACK

FRONT

T-SHIRTS FOR RETAIL SALES
ASHION FASHION FASHION FASHION FASHION FASHION 071 T-SHIRTS FASHION FASHION FASHION FASHION FASHION FASHIO

PAUL SMITH
JAPAN 1994 D:Paul Smith CL:Joi'x Corporation

PAUL SMITH
JAPAN 1994 D:Paul Smith CL:Joi'x Corporation

Men's Ba-tsu Original ®

T-SHIRTS FOR RETAIL SALES
FASHION FASHION FASHION FASHION FASHION FASHION FASHION FASHION FASHION FASHION FASHION FASHI

Men's Ba-tsu Div.
I don't think
people should be
judged by
their appearance.

BMC

BENETTON UOMO
ITALY 1994 CL:Benetton

012 BENETTON
ITALY 1994 CL:Benetton

012 BENETTON
ITALY 1994 CL:Benetton

T-SHIRTS FOR RETAIL SALES

ASHION FASHION FASHION FASHION FOR FASHION RETAIL SALES FASHION FASHION FASHION FASHION FASHION FASHIO

BENETTON FORMULA 1
JAPAN 1994 CL:Benetton

BENETTON FORMULA 1
JAPAN 1994 CL:Benetton

BENETTON
ITALY 1994 CL:Benetton

BENETTON
ITALY 1994 CL:Benetton

MILK BOY
JAPAN 1994 CL:Milk Inc.

012 BENETTON
ITALY 1994 CL:Benetton

VENICE UNDERGROUND
USA 1994 IR:Nine Too Zero

FRONT

BACK

MILK
JAPAN 1994 CL:Milk Inc.

BENETTON FORMULA 1
JAPAN 1994 CL:Benetton

BENETTON FORMULA 1
JAPAN 1994 CL:Benetton

BENETTON FORMULA 1
JAPAN 1994 CL:Benetton

T-SHIRTS FOR RETAIL SALES FASHION FASHION FASHION FASHION FASHION FASHION FASHION FASHION FASHION FASHION FASHION FASHION

BENETTON UOMO
ITALY 1994 CL:Benetton

BENETTON UOMO
ITALY 1994 CL:Benetton

SCOOP MAN
JAPAN 1993 D:Yukiko Honda / Daisuke Suzuki CL:Scoop Inc.

BORN TOBE LOUD
JAPAN 1993 CL:Nine Too Zero

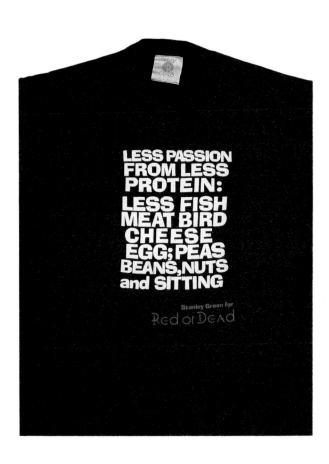

RED OR DEAD
UK 1993 CL:Red or Dead

MEN'S BA-TSU
JAPAN 1993 CL:Ba-tsu Co.,Ltd.

T-SHIRTS FOR RETAIL SALES
SHION FASHION FASHION FASHION FASHION FASHION RETAIL FASHION (082) FASHION FASHION FASHION FASHION FASHION FASHIO

SCOOP MAN
JAPAN 1993 D: Yukiko Honda CL:Scoop Inc.

MEN'S BA-TSU
JAPAN 1993 CL:Ba-tsu Co.,Ltd.

PERSON'S
JAPAN 1994 CL:Person's Co.,Ltd.

WILD DANCER
JAPAN 1993 D:Couichi Hirayama CL:Wild Dancer

DEUX IGUREGU
JAPAN 1989 D:Couichi Hirayama CL:Awase Co.,Ltd.

T-SHIRTS FOR RETAIL SALES

SHION FASHION FASHION FASHION FASHION FASHION FASHION FASHION FASHION FASHION FASHION FASHION

BLUE ON PINK
JAPAN 1989 D:Couichi Hirayama CL:Shige Design Office Co., Ltd.

BA-TSU CLUB
JAPAN 1993 CL:Ba-tsu Co.,Ltd.

MEN'S BA-TSU
JAPAN 1993 CL:Ba-tsu Co.,Ltd.

T-SHIRTS FOR RETAIL SALES

SHION FASHION FASHION FASHION FASHION FASHION FASHION FASHION FASHION FASHION FASHION FASHION

MEN'S BIGI
JAPAN 1994 CL:Men's Bigi Co.,Ltd.

MEN'S BA-TSU
JAPAN 1993 CL:Ba-tsu Co.,Ltd.

my idea of who I am changes every ten minutes

ESPRIT

ESPRIT
UK 1992 CD:Nice AD,D:Neil Edwards / Stephen Male
DF:Nice CL:Esprit (Europe)

this is your

ESPRIT

ESPRIT
UK 1992 CD:Nice AD,D:Neil Edwards / Stephen Male
DF:Nice CL:Esprit (Europe)

ESPRIT

the rhythm of life

ESPRIT
UK 1992 CD:Nice AD,D,I:Neil Edwards / Stephen Male
DF:Nice CL:Esprit (Europe)

HOLLYWOOD RANCH MARKET
"LABEL FLAG" "SMOKE ALICE" JAPAN 1991/1990 CL:Seilin & Co.

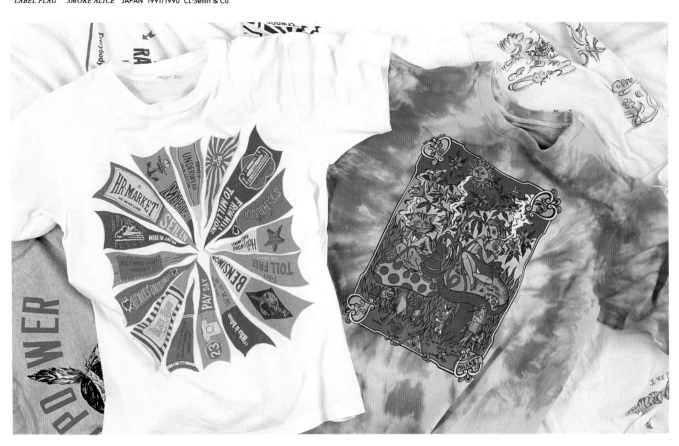

HOLLYWOOD RANCH MARKET
"PACHAMAMA" "KASEKI OJISAN" JAPAN 1990/1989 CL:Seilin & Co.

**HOLLYWOOD
RANCH MARKET**
"WORLD CHAMP" "SWEET HEART"
JAPAN 1989/1992 CL:Seilin & Co.

**HOLLYWOOD
RANCH MARKET**
"BUTTERFLY" "HEART FLAG"
JAPAN 1991/1990 CL:Seilin & Co.

**HOLLYWOOD
RANCH MARKET**
"HEART TRAIN" "WONDERFUL HEART"
"FLOWER WAPPEN"
JAPAN 1986/1990/1990 CL:Seilin & Co.

MELROSE
JAPAN 1994 CL:Melrose Co.,Ltd.

MELROSE
JAPAN 1994 CL:Melrose Co.,Ltd.

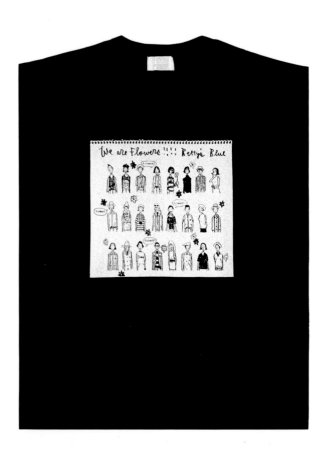

FLOWERS
JAPAN 1993 I:Nishi Tokyo Illustrators CL:Lemon Co.,Ltd.

JUNKO SHIMADA PART 2
ANIMAL COLLECTION
JAPAN 1993 D:Junko Shimada CL:Lecien Planning Corporation

BA-TSU CLUB
JAPAN 1993 CL:Ba-tsu Co.,Ltd.

POU DOU DOU
JAPAN 1994 CL:Galerie de Pop Co.,Ltd.

PAINT SET
JAPAN 1993 AD:Toshiaki Ichihara I:Yukiko Ei DF:atelier NEU!! CL:Takihyo Co.,Ltd.

MEN'S BA-TSU
JAPAN 1993 CL:Ba-tsu Co.,Ltd.

NORTH MARINE DRIVE
JAPAN 1993 AD,D,P,I:Joji Yano CL:45RPM-Studio Co.,Ltd.

45RPM STUDIO
JAPAN 1993 AD,D,P,I:Joji Yano CL:45RPM-Studio Co.,Ltd.

T-SHIRTS FOR RETAIL SALES
SHION FASHION FASHION FASHION FOR FASHION FOR RETAIL FASHION FASHION FASHION FOR FASHION FASHION FASHION FASHION FASHION

45RPM STUDIO
JAPAN 1993 AD,D,P,I:Joji Yano CL:45RPM-Studio Co.,Ltd.

NORTH MARINE DRIVE
JAPAN 1993 AD,D,P,I:Joji Yano CL:45RPM-Studio Co.,Ltd.

NORTH MARINE DRIVE
JAPAN 1993 AD,D,P,I:Joji Yano CL:45RPM-Studio Co.,Ltd.

NORTH MARINE DRIVE
JAPAN 1993 AD,D,P,I:Joji Yano CL:45RPM-Studio Co.,Ltd.

FASHION FASHION FASHION FASHION FASHION FASHION FASHION FASHION FASHION FASHION FASHION FASHION

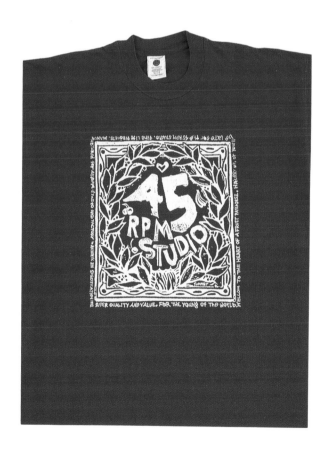

HOW TO?
JAPAN 1993 AD,I:Naoaki Akiyama DF:St.Evans Co.,Ltd. CL:Bizazz

45RPM STUDIO
JAPAN 1993 AD,D,P,I:Joji Yano CL:45RPM-Studio Co.,Ltd.

5351 POUR LES HOMMS
JAPAN 1994 CD:Hideshi Maruya I:Satsuki Hosoi
CL:Abahouse International Company

5351 POUR LES HOMMS
JAPAN 1994 CD:Hideshi Maruya I:Motomu Oyama
CL:Abahouse International Company

5351 POUR LES HOMMS
JAPAN 1994 CD:Hideshi Maruya I:Hiroshi Nagai
CL:Abahouse International Company

5351 POUR LES HOMMS
JAPAN 1994 CD:Hideshi Maruya I:Junko Sakuraba
CL:Abahouse International Company

powder
JAPAN 1993 AD,D:Hideki Shimosako CL:powder Co.,Ltd.

powder
JAPAN 1993 AD,D:Hideki Shimosako CL:powder Co.,Ltd.

POU DOU DOU
JAPAN 1994 CL:Galerie de Pop Co.,Ltd.

POU DOU DOU
JAPAN 1994 CL:Galerie de Pop Co.,Ltd.

EN PRIVÉ MARINA DE BOURBON
JAPAN 1994 CL:Orizzonti Co.,Ltd.

EN PRIVÉ MARINA DE BOURBON
JAPAN 1994 CL:Orizzonti Co.,Ltd.

JUST BIGI
JAPAN 1993 CD:Michiyo Handa AD:Kumi Motomatsu I:Kaoru Hironaka
CL:Bigi Co.,Ltd.

JUST BIGI
JAPAN 1993 CD:Michiyo Handa AD:Kumi Motomatsu I:Kaoru Hironaka
CL:Bigi Co.,Ltd.

HOW TO?
JAPAN 1993 AD,I:Naoaki Akiyama DF:St.Evans Co.,Ltd. CL:Daiei / Ito Yokado

FELIX THE CAT
JAPAN 1993 AD,I:Naoaki Akiyama DF:St.Evans Co.,Ltd. CL:Felix the Cat

T-SHIRTS FOR RETAIL SALES FASHION FASHION FASHION FASHION FASHION FASHION 097 FASHION FOR RETAIL SALES

BASSETT WALKER
JAPAN 1992 AD,D:Toshiiku Uzuka I:Keiko Habara DF:atelier NEU!! CL:Jun Co.,Ltd.

MEN'S BA-TSU
JAPAN 1993 CL:Ba-tsu Co.,Ltd.

FRONT

BACK

powder
JAPAN 1993 AD,D:Hideki Shimosako CL:powder Co.,Ltd.

powder
JAPAN 1993 AD,D:Hideki Shimosako CL:powder Co.,Ltd.

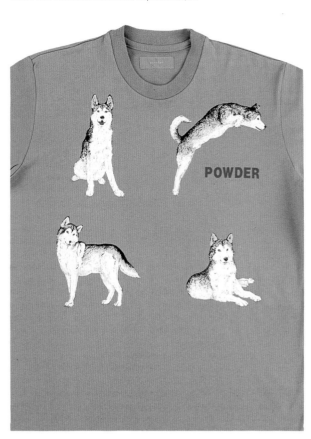

T-SHIRTS FOR RETAIL SALES

FASHION FASHION FASHION FASHION FASHION RETAIL SALES 099 FASHION FASHION FASHION FASHION FASHION FASHIO

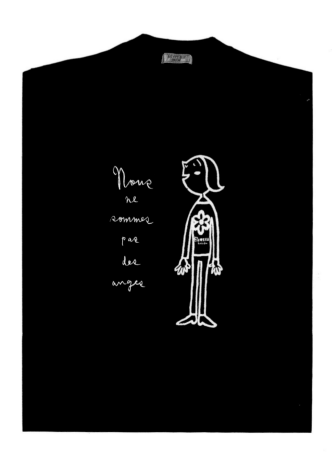

HELTER SKELTER
JAPAN 1993 CL:Bic Company Co.,Ltd.

FLOWERS
JAPAN 1993 I:Nishi Tokyo Illustrators CL:Lemon Co.,Ltd.

SNOOPY SPORTS
JAPAN 1993 CD:Mineko Oshima D:Keiko Kijima I:Keiko Habara
DF:N Studio Aoyama Office CL:Ōsaka Nishikawa Co.,Ltd.

SNOOPY SPORTS
JAPAN 1993 CD:Mineko Oshima D:Keiko Kijima I:Keiko Habara
DF:N Studio Aoyama Office CL:Ōsaka Nishikawa Co.,Ltd.

SNOOPY SPORTS
JAPAN 1993 CD:Mineko Oshima D:Keiko Kijima I:Keiko Habara
DF:N Studio Aoyama Office CL:Ōsaka Nishikawa Co.,Ltd.

SNOOPY SPORTS
JAPAN 1993 CD:Mineko Oshima D:Keiko Kijima I:Keiko Habara
DF:N Studio Aoyama Office CL:Ōsaka Nishikawa Co.,Ltd.

SALEM
USA 1992
IR:World Sports Plaza 2

102

CONVERSE
Its what's inside that counts

NIKE
USA 1993 CD:Angela Snow AD:Todd Van Horne D:Jodi Dahlager
I:Mark Ryden CL:Nike

NIKE
USA 1993 CD:Angela Snow AD:Todd Van Horne D:Jodi Dahlager
I:Mike Benny CL:Nike

FRONT

BACK

NIKE
USA 1993 CD:Angela Snow AD:Todd Van Horne D:Jodi Dahlager
I:Tim Gabor CL:Nike

SALEM

USA 1992-1993 IR:World Sports Plaza 2

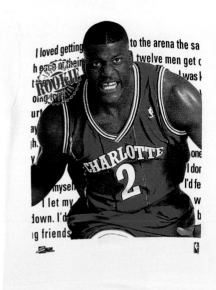

FRONT

FRONT

BACK

NIKE

USA 1993 IR:World Sports Plaza 2

NIKE
USA 1992 CD:Angela Snow AD:Todd Van Horne
D:Peter Kramer CW:Bruce Crawford CL:Nike

BACK

FRONT

NIKE
USA 1993 IR:World Sports Plaza 2

NIKE
USA 1993 IR:World Sports Plaza 2

NIKE
USA 1993 CD:Angela Snow AD:Todd Van Horne D,I:Jodi Dahlager CL:Nike

NIKE
USA 1993 CD:Angela Snow AD:Todd Van Horne D,I:Jodi Dahlager CL:Nike

T-SHIRTS FOR RETAIL SALES SPORTS SPORTS SPORTS SPORTS SPORTS SPORTS SHIRTS FOR RETAIL SALES SPORTS SPORTS SPORTS SPORTS SPORTS SPORT

NIKE
USA 1993 CD:Angela Snow AD:Todd Van Horne D:Jodi Dahlager
I:Alex Gross CL:Nike

NIKE
USA 1993 CD:Angela Snow AD:Todd Van Horne D:Jodi Dahlager
I:Harvey Chan CL:Nike

SALEM
USA 1992 IR:World Sports Plaza 2

NIKE
USA 1993 CD:Angela Snow AD:Todd Van Horne D,I:Peter Kramer CL:Nike

NIKE
USA 1993 IR:World Sports Plaza 2

NIKE
USA 1992 CD:Angela Snow AD:Todd Van Horne D:Peter Kramer
CW:Nike Design CL:Nike

NIKE
USA 1993 CD:Angela Snow AD:Todd Van Horne D:Peter Kramer CL:Nike

FRONT

BACK

NIKE
USA 1993 CD:Angela Snow AD:Todd Van Horne D:Peter Kramer CW:Nike CL:Nike

NIKE
USA 1993 CD:Angela Snow AD:Todd Van Horne D,I:Peter Kramer CL:Nike

SALEM
USA 1993 IR:World Sports Plaza

JOHNNY TOCCO
CANADA 1993 IR:World Sports Plaza

T-SHIRTS FOR RETAIL SALES
ORTS SPORTS SPORTS SPORTS SPORTS SPORTS SPORTS T-SHIRTS FOR RETAIL SALES SPORTS SPORTS SPOR

SALEM
USA 1993 IR:World Sports Plaza

JOHNNY TOCCO
CANADA 1993 IR:World Sports Plaza

SALEM
USA 1993 IR:World Sports Plaza

BACK

FRONT

RTS SPORTS SPORTS SPORTS SPORTS SPORTS SPORTS SPORTS SPORTS SPORTS SPORTS SPORTS SPORTS SPORT

CHAMPION
USA 1992-1993 IR:World Sports Plaza 2

HOME BOY
USA 1993 IR:World Sports Plaza

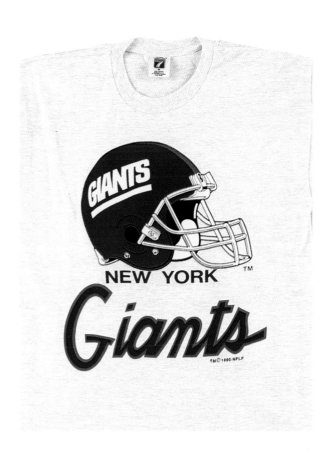

JOHNNY TOCCO
CANADA 1993 IR:World Sports Plaza

NIKE
USA 1993 IR:World Sports Plaza

NIKE
USA 1992 CD:Angela Snow AD:Todd Van Horne D,I:Peter Kramer CL:Nike

NIKE
USA 1993 CD:Angela Snow AD:Todd Van Horne
D,I:Shawn Wenzel CL:Nike

T-SHIRTS FOR RETAIL SALES SHIRTS FOR RETAIL SALES

ORTS SPORTS SPORTS SPORTS SPORTS SPORTS SPORTS 113 SPORTS SPORTS SPORTS SPORTS SPORTS SPORTS SPOR

NIKE
USA IR:World Sports Plaza 2

MONSTER SKATE BOARD
USA 1992 IR:World Sports Plaza

T-SHIRTS FOR RETAIL SALES
ORTS SPORTS SPORTS SPORTS SPORTS SPORTS SPORTS SHIRTS FOR RETAIL SPORTS SPORTS SPORTS SPORTS SPOR

ORTS SPORTS SPORTS SPORTS FOR RETAIL SALES 015 T-SHIRTS FOR RETAIL SPORTS SPORTS SPORTS SALES SPORTS SPOR

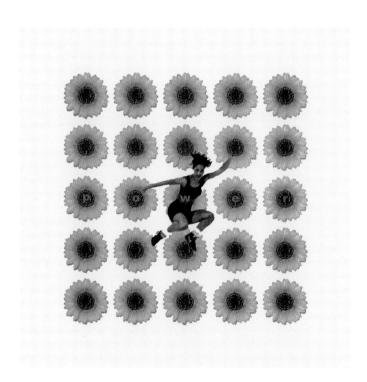

ORTS SPORTS SPORTS SPORTS SPORTS SPORTS SPORTS SPORTS SPORTS SPORTS SPORTS SPORTS SPORTS SPOR

T-SHIRTS FOR RETAIL SALES FOR RETAIL SALES

BASIC
ITALY 1993 IR:World Sports Plaza Campione

NOTMEG
USA 1993 IR:World Sports Plaza Campione

FRONT

BACK

CYRK
USA 1993 IR:World Sports Plaza Campione

NIKE
USA 1993 CD:Angela Snow AD:Todd Van Horne D:Peter Kramer
I:Patty McNally CL:Nike

BASIC
ITALY 1993 IR:World Sports Plaza Campione

CATEGORY-1
IAPAN 1993 CL:World Sports Plaza Campione

CATEGORY-1
JAPAN 1993 CL:World Sports Plaza Campione

ADIDAS
USA 1993 IR:World Sports Plaza Campione

Ruy RAMOS

 119

PORTS SPORTS SPORTS SPORTS SPORTS SPORTS SPORTS ⬤ 119 ⬤ T-SHIRTS FOR RETAIL SALES

FOCUS

CATEGORY-1
JAPAN 1993 CL:World Sports Plaza Campione

NOTMEG
USA 1993 IR:World Sports Plaza Campione

MOONEYES
JAPAN 1993 CL:Moon of Japan Co.,Ltd.

FRONT

BACK

MOONEYES
JAPAN 1992 CL:Moon of Japan Co.,Ltd.

MOONEYES
JAPAN 1993 CL:Moon of Japan Co.,Ltd.

T-SHIRTS FOR RETAIL SALES
ORTS SPORTS SPORTS SPORTS SPORTS SPORTS SPORTS SPORTS FOR SPORTS SPORTS SPORTS SPORTS SPO

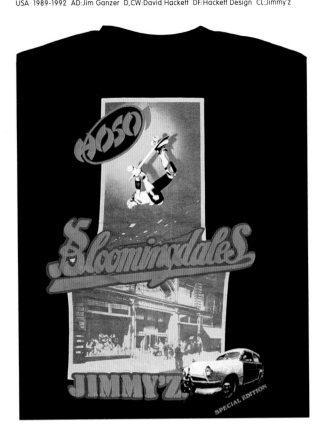

NIKE
USA 1993 CD:Angela Snow AD:Todd Van Horne D:Ted Jacobs CL:Nike

NIKE
USA 1993 CD:Angela Snow AD:Todd Van Horne D:Ted Jacobs I:Alex Gross CL:Nike

JIMMY'Z

USA 1989-1992 AD:Jim Ganzer D,CW:David Hackett DF:Hackett Design CL:Jimmy'z

JIMMY'Z

USA 1989-1992 AD:Jim Ganzer D,CW:David Hackett DF:Hackett Design CL:Jimmy'z

T-SHIRTS FOR RETAIL SALES OTHERS OTHERS OTHERS OTHERS OTHERS OTHERS OTHERS OTHERS OTHERS OTHERS OTHERS OTHERS OTHERS OTHERS OTHERS OTHERS OTHERS OTHERS OTH

BERGER

JAPAN 1993 AD,D:Hiroyoshi Shimizu D:Koichi Hirayama
DF:Thêas Co.,Ltd. CL:Phenix Co.,Ltd.

BERGER

JAPAN 1993 AD,D:Hiroyoshi Shimizu D:Koichi Hirayama
DF:Thêas Co.,Ltd. CL:Phenix Co.,Ltd.

BERGER
JAPAN 1993 AD,D:Hiroyoshi Shimizu D:Koichi Hirayama
DF:Thēas Co.,Ltd. CL:Phenix Co.,Ltd.

BERGER
JAPAN 1993 AD,D:Hiroyoshi Shimizu D:Koichi Hirayama
DF:Thēas Co.,Ltd. CL:Phenix Co.,Ltd.

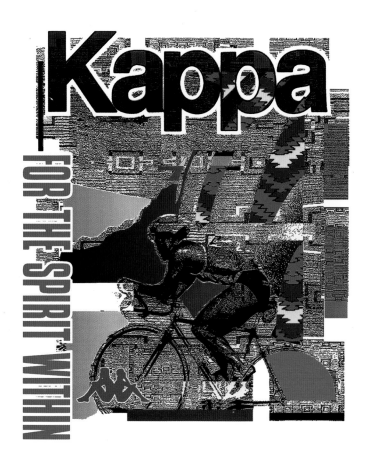

BOWLIN GAL
USA 1993 AD:Howie Idelson DF:Urban Image Studio CL:Style Kings

PRO CIRCUIT
USA 1994 AD:Howie Idelson DF:Urban Image Studio CL:Pro Circuit

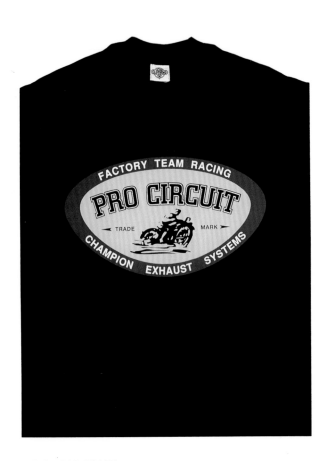

PRO CIRCUIT
USA 1994 AD:Howie Idelson DF:Urban Image Studio CL:Pro Circuit

PRO CIRCUIT
USA 1994 AD:Howie Idelson DF:Urban Image Studio CL:Pro Circuit

BODYBOARDING DUDE
USA 1990 AD:Dave T.Parmley D:Sandy Gin CL:O'Neill,Inc.

CALIFORNIA BEACH
USA 1986-1990 AD:Richard Sawyer D,I:Tracy Sabin
DF:Tracy Sabin,Illustration & Design CL:California Beach Co.

DIFFERENT WAVE,SAME PLANET
USA 1989 AD:Dave T.Parmley D:Sandy Gin CL:O'Neill,Inc.

PAISLEY O'NEILL
USA 1990 AD:Dave T.Parmley D:Sandy Gin CL:O'Neill,Inc.

JIMMY'Z
USA 1989-1992 AD:Jim Ganzer D,CW:David Hackett DF:Hackett Design CL:Jimmy'z

ZONK
USA 1990-1991 AD:Greg Sabin D,P,I:Tracy Sabin
DF:Tracy Sabin,Illustration & Design CL:Zonk,Inc.

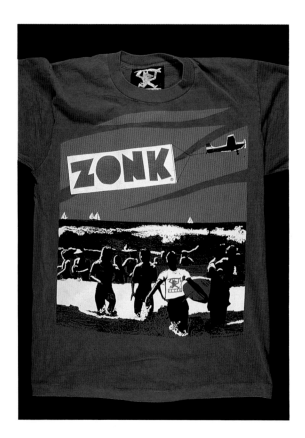

ZONK
USA 1990-1991 AD:Greg Sabin D,P,I:Tracy Sabin
DF:Tracy Sabin,Illustration & Design CL:Zonk,Inc.

ZONK
USA 1990-1991 AD:Greg Sabin D,P,I:Tracy Sabin
DF:Tracy Sabin,Illustration & Design CL:Zonk,Inc.

ZONK
USA 1990-1991 AD:Greg Sabin D,P,I:Tracy Sabin
DF:Tracy Sabin,Illustration & Design CL:Zonk,Inc.

ZONK
USA 1990-1991 AD:Greg Sabin D,P,I:Tracy Sabin
DF:Tracy Sabin,Illustration & Design CL:Zonk,Inc.

ZONK
USA 1990-1991 AD:Greg Sabin D,P,I:Tracy Sabin
DF:Tracy Sabin,Illustration & Design CL:Zonk,Inc.

ZONK
USA 1990-1991 AD:Greg Sabin D,P,I:Tracy Sabin
DF:Tracy Sabin,Illustration & Design CL:Zonk,Inc.

GRAPHIC MANIPULATOR
JAPAN 1991 AD,D:Sumio Takemoto DF:Graphic Manipulator IR:Thirty Three Co.,Ltd.

GRAPHIC MANIPULATOR
JAPAN 1992 AD,D:Sumio Takemoto DF:Graphic Manipulator IR:Thirty Three Co.,Ltd.

GRAPHIC MANIPULATOR
JAPAN 1992 AD,D:Sumio Takemoto DF:Graphic Manipulato IR:Thirty Three Co.,Ltd.

GRAPHIC MANIPULATOR
JAPAN 1993 AD,D:Sumio Takemoto DF:Graphic Manipulator IR:Thirty Three Co.,Ltd.

GRAPHIC MANIPULATOR
JAPAN 1992 AD,D:Sumio Takemoto DF:Graphic Manipulator IR:Thirty Three Co.,Ltd.

GRAPHIC MANIPULATOR
JAPAN 1992 AD,D:Sumio Takemoto DF:Graphic Manipulator IR:Thirty Three Co.,Ltd.

FAKE CHILDREN
JAPAN 1993 I:Kunihiko Kanao CL:Thirty Three Co.,Ltd.

T-SHIRTS FOR RETAIL SALES
OTHERS OTHERS OTHERS OTHERS OTHERS OTHERS OTHERS OTHERS OTHERS OTHERS OTHERS OTHERS OTHE

BODY PARTS
JAPAN 1993 D:Kiminari Kamiyama CL:Thirty Three Co.,Ltd.

BODY PARTS
JAPAN 1993 D:Kiminari Kamiyama CL:Thirty Three Co.,Ltd.

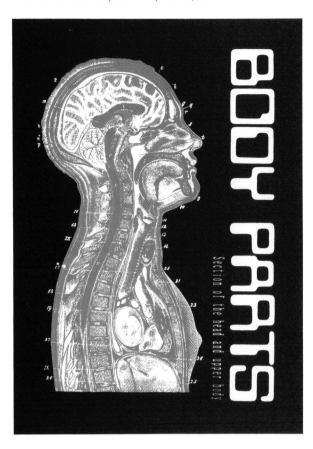

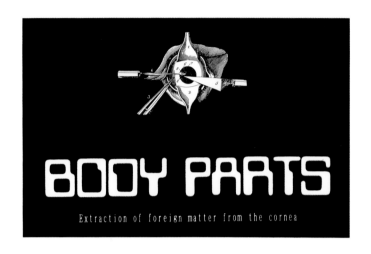

GRAPHIC MANIPULATOR
JAPAN 1992 / 1990 AD,D:Sumio Takemoto DF:Graphic Manipulator IR:Thirty Three Co.,Ltd.

DISCO UNIVERSE
UK 1992 AD,D,I,CW:Joern Kroeger DF:Design by Joern Kroeger
CL:Design by Joern Kroeger

RIDE
UK 1993 AD,D,I,CW:Joern Kroeger DF:Design by Joern Kroeger
CL:Design by Joern Kroeger

QEWGO
JAPAN 1993 D:Takeshi Suzuki CL:Thirty Three Co.,Ltd.

TAR COMMUNICATIONS
JAPAN 1993 D:Toshiyuki Seki CL:Thirty Three Co.,Ltd.

GRAPHIC MANIPULATOR
JAPAN 1994 AD,D:Sumio Takemoto
DF:Graphic Manipulator IR:Thirty Three Co.,Ltd.

GRAPHIC MANIPULATOR
JAPAN 1994 AD,D:Sumio Takemoto
DF:Graphic Manipulator IR:Thirty Three Co. Ltd.

BM HAND
UK 1993 AD,D,I:Trevor Jackson DF:Bite It! CL:Black Market International

BM MAN
UK 1993 AD,D,I:Trevor Jackson DF:Bite It! CL:Black Market International

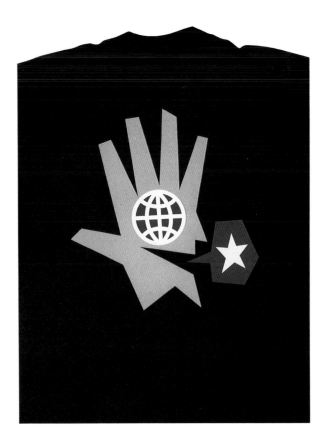

FUNKY PEACE
UK 1992 AD,D,I:Trevor Jackson DF:Bite It! CL:Funky Peace Productions

QEWGO
JAPAN 1993 D:Takeshi Suzuki CL:Thirty Three Co.,Ltd.

NATURAL CYCLE CLUB
USA 1993 AD,D:Jay Vigon CL:Natural Cycle Club

AR / AT
USA 1992 D:Jay Vigon DF:Jay Vigon Studio CL:AR / AT

OTHERS OTHERS OTHERS OTHERS OTHERS OTHERS OTHERS OTHERS OTHERS OTHERS OTHERS OTHERS OTHERS OTHE

OTHERS OTHERS OTHERS OTHERS OTHERS OTHERS OTHERS FOR RETAIL SALES 139 OTHERS OTHERS OTHERS OTHERS OTHERS OTHERS OTH

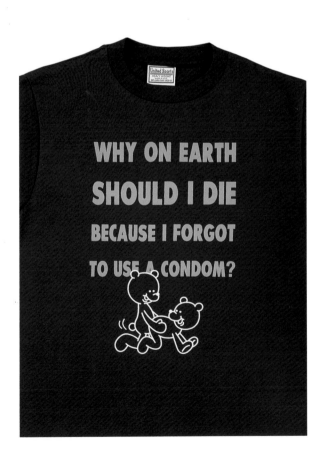

T-SHIRTS AS MEDIA
"HIP-HOP-WORLD" JAPAN 1993 D:Takashi Chiba CL:Club King Co.

T-SHIRTS AS MEDIA
"WHY ON EARTH SHOULD I DIE BECAUSE I FORGOT TO USE A CONDOM?"
JAPAN 1993 D:Seijiro Kubo CL:Club King Co.

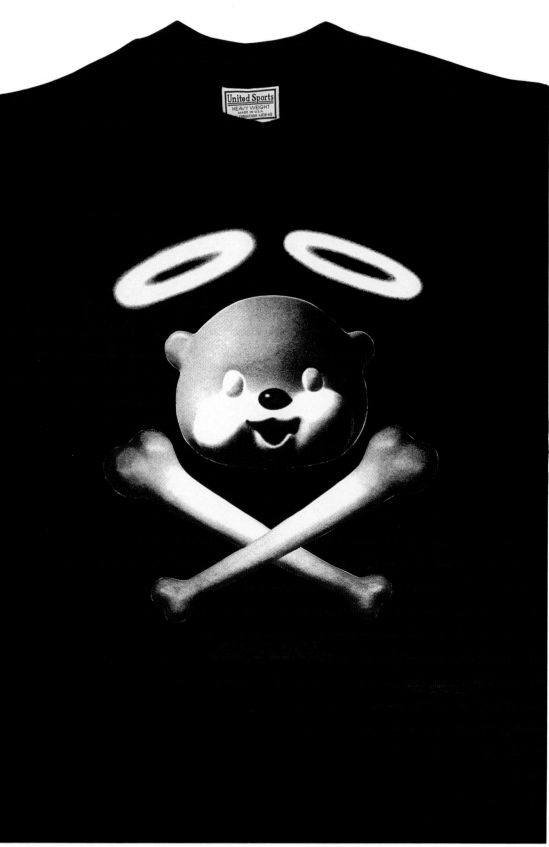

T-SHIRTS AS MEDIA
"THE BIKINI HUNTER" JAPAN 1993 D:Spark CL:Club King Co.

T-SHIRTS AS MEDIA
"COMPUTER BEAR" JAPAN 1991 D:Ito Gabin CL:Club King Co.

T-SHIRTS AS MEDIA
"HI-END-AUDIO" JAPAN 1992 D:Takashi Chiba CL:Club King Co.

T-SHIRTS AS MEDIA
"VA-BONE-CHAN" JAPAN 1993 D:Spark CL:Club King Co.

T-SHIRTS AS MEDIA

"SARU BRUNEI" JAPAN 1993 D:Gento Matsumoto CL:Club King Co.

PERLE

JAPAN 1993 D:Yukiko Yamaguchi CL:Thirty Three Co.,Ltd.

T-SHIRTS FOR RETAIL SALES
OTHERS OTHERS OTHERS OTHERS OTHERS OTHERS OTHERS 142 T-SHIRTS FOR RETAIL SALES OTHERS OTHERS OTHERS OTHERS OTHERS OTHE

CRAZY CAT LADY

USA 1992 D:Jay Vigon DF:Jay Vigon Studio CL:Crazy Cat Lady

T-SHIRTS AS MEDIA
"I'M FINE!!" JAPAN 1993 D:Tycoon Graphics CL:Club King Co.

GRAPHIC MANIPULATOR
JAPAN 1994 AD,D:Sumio Takemoto DF:Graphic Manipulator IR:Thirty Three Co.,Ltd.

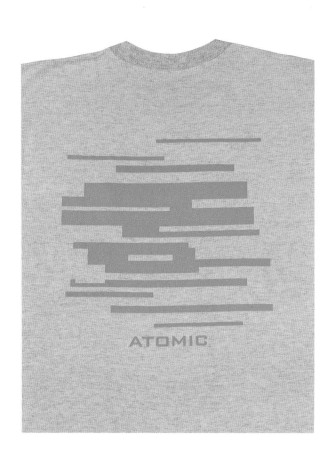

T-SHIRTS AS MEDIA
"ATOMIC" JAPAN 1993 D:Akihiro Tomobe CL:Club King Co.

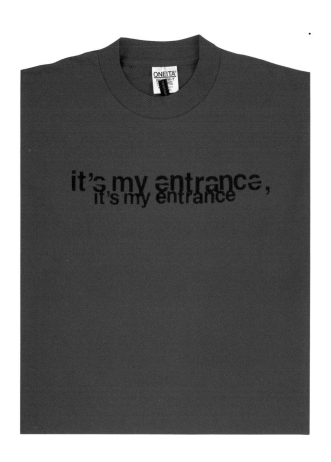

ISOTOPE BOOTLEG
JAPAN 1993 D:Hodaka Hamada CL:Thirty Three Co.,Ltd.

OTHERS OTHERS OTHERS OTHERS OTHERS OTHERS   144   OTHERS OTHERS OTHERS OTHERS OTHERS OTHERS OTHE

T-SHIRTS FOR RETAIL SALES

**COASTAL
PRINTWORKS,INC.**
USA 1993 AD,D:Fat Fish CL:Tattoo-Santa Barbara

T-SHIRTS AS MEDIA
"MIDNIGHT SISTER" JAPAN 1993 D:Wataru Komachi CL:Club King Co.

FABRIC ART
USA 1993 CD:Steve Lutz D,CW:Tom Prochaska P:David Lutz CL:Fabric Art Inc.

THE ORIGINAL AMERICAN
UK 1992 CL:Brave Design

COASTAL PRINTWORKS,INC.
USA 1993 AD,D:Patricia CL:Bowers Museum

T-SHIRTS FOR RETAIL SALES 146 T-SHIRTS FOR RETAIL SALES
OTHERS OTHERS OTHERS OTHERS OTHERS OTHERS OTHERS OTHERS OTHERS OTHERS OTHERS OTH

MEDIUM RARE
"SAFE·GUN" JAPAN 1993 CL:Club King Co.

MEDIUM RARE
"LOVELY DAYS" JAPAN 1993 CL:Club King Co.

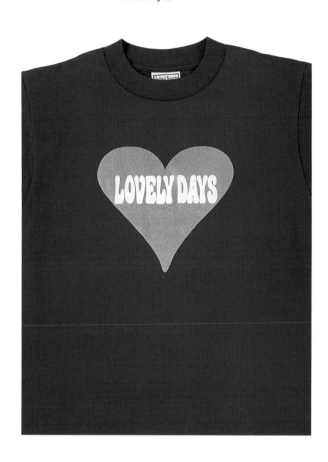

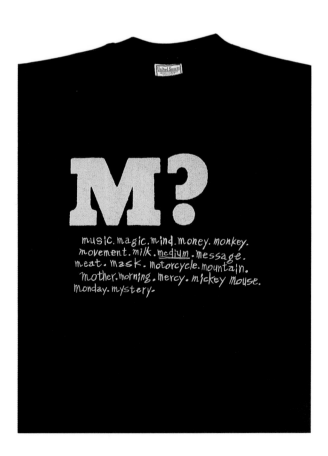

MEDIUM RARE
"M? R?" JAPAN 1993 CL:Club King Co.

T-SHIRTS AS MEDIA
"M·O·T LABEL COMPILATION" JAPAN 1993 CL:Club King Co.

ARTS RUSH
JAPAN 1994 AD:Newton D:ACCA International Ltd. I:Chips / CLS
CL:Cohwa International Co.,Ltd.

ARTS RUSH
JAPAN 1994 AD:Newton D:ACCA International Ltd. I:Hiroyuki Yamada / CLS
CL:Cohwa International Co.,Ltd.

FABRIC ART
USA 1992 CD:Steve Lutz D,CW:Michele Maynard P:David Lutz CL:Fabric Art Inc.

COASTAL PRINTWORKS,INC.
USA 1993 AD:Douglas Kim CL:Watermind

OTHERS OTHERS OTHERS OTHERS OTHERS OTHERS OTHERS **49** OTHERS OTHERS OTHERS OTHERS OTHERS OTHERS OTH

T-SHIRTS FOR RETAIL SALES OTHERS OTHERS OTHERS OTHERS OTHERS OTHERS 150 OTHERS T-SHIRTS FOR RETAIL SALES OTHERS OTHE

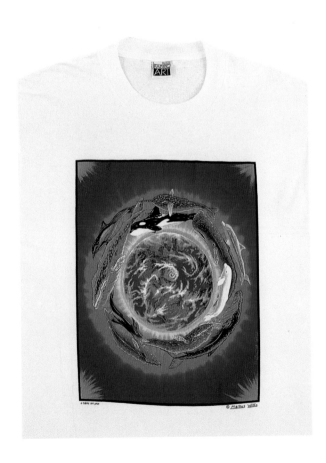

FABRIC ART
USA 1993 CD:Steve Lutz D,CW:Rebecca Baldwin P:David Lutz CL:Fabric Art Inc.

COASTAL PRINTWORKS,INC.
USA 1993 AD,D:Pamela Pease CL:Oliver Pease

T-SHIRTS FOR RETAIL SALES
OTHERS OTHERS OTHERS OTHERS OTHERS OTHERS OTHERS OTHERS OTHERS OTHERS OTHERS OTHERS OTHERS OTHERS OTHERS OTH

COASTAL PRINTWORKS,INC.
USA 1993 AD,D:Andre Miripolsky CL:Andre Miripolsky

FABRIC ART
USA 1992 CD:Steve Lutz D,CW:Sharon Bronzan P:David Lutz CL:Fabric Art Inc.

ARTS RUSH
JAPAN 1994 AD:Newton D:ACCA International Ltd. I:Atsushi Kaneko / CLS
CL:Cohwa International Co.,Ltd.

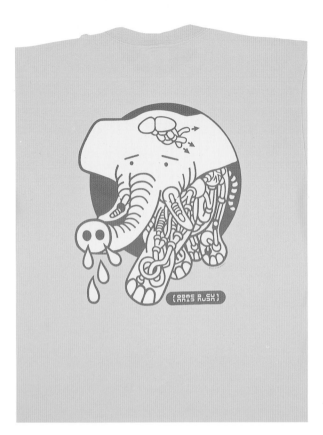

ARTS RUSH
JAPAN 1994 AD:Newton D:ACCA International Ltd. I:Atsushi Kaneko / CLS
CL:Cohwa International Co.,Ltd.

T-SHIRTS FOR RETAIL SALES

ERS OTHERS OTHERS OTHERS OTHERS OTHERS OTHERS OTHERS OTHERS OTHERS OTHERS OTHERS OTHERS OTHE

T-SHIRTS AS MEDIA
"DRIVING DOG" JAPAN 1993 D:Atsushi Kaneko CL:Club King Co.

T-SHIRTS AS MEDIA
"BAMBI" JAPAN 1991 D:Yuri Shimojo CL:Club King Co.

T-SHIRTS AS MEDIA
"BACK TO THE NATER" JAPAN 1992 D:Toshio Nakanishi CL:Club King Co.

T-SHIRTS AS MEDIA
"AMBIENT BEAR" JAPAN 1991 D:Toshio Nakanishi CL:Club King Co.

T-SHIRTS FOR RETAIL SALES

HERS OTHERS OTHERS OTHERS OTHERS OTHERS OTHERS (153) OTHERS OTHERS OTHERS OTHERS OTHERS OTHERS OTH

PERLE
JAPAN 1993 D:Yukiko Yamaguchi CL:Thirty Three Co.,Ltd.

T-SHIRTS AS MEDIA
"I'M COOL ARE YOU?" JAPAN 1993 D:Toshio Nakanishi CL:Club King Co.

KANUDOR NUBIANS
UK 1992 CL:Private Client (Dot Productions)

T-SHIRTS AS MEDIA
"FREEDOM RABBIT" JAPAN 1990 D:Mick Itaya CL:Club King Co.

T-SHIRTS AS MEDIA
"DON'T MOVE" JAPAN 1993 D:Atsushi Kaneko CL:Club King Co.

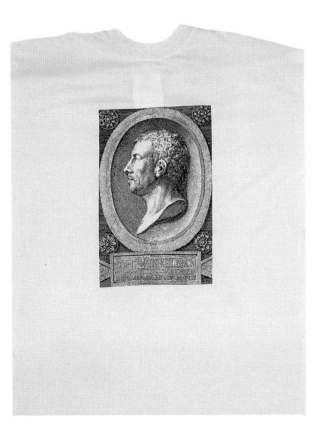

WINCKELMANN DESIGN
UK 1993 CD:Biri Fay CL:Winckelmann Museum

T-SHIRTS AS MEDIA
"MONKEY" JAPAN 1993 D:Akihiro Tomobe CL:Club King Co

ARTS RUSH
JAPAN 1994 AD:Newton D:ACCA International Ltd. I:Yasushi Nakayama / CLS
CL:Cohwa International Co.,Ltd.

ARTS RUSH
JAPAN 1994 AD:Newton D:ACCA International Ltd. I:Yasushi Nakayama / CLS
CL:Cohwa International Co.,Ltd.

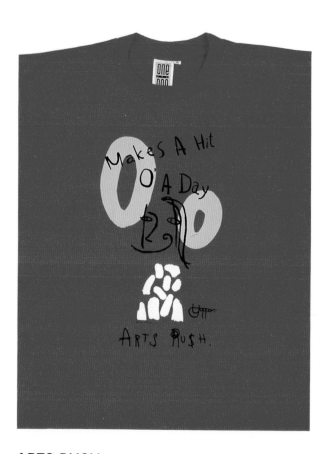

ARTS RUSH
JAPAN 1994 AD:Newton D:ACCA International Ltd. I:Motomu Oyama / CLS
CL:Cohwa International Co.,Ltd.

ARTS RUSH
JAPAN 1994 AD:Newton D:ACCA International Ltd. I:Yoshitaka Maeda / CLS
CL:Cohwa International Co.,Ltd.

T-SHIRTS AS MEDIA
"YOU NEVER ESCAPE" JAPAN 1993 D:Hirosuke Ueno CL:Club King Co.

MINORITY
JAPAN 1993 D:Hironori Ichinose / Hirokazu Miura CL:Thirty Three Co.,Ltd.

MINORITY
JAPAN 1993 D:Hironori Ichinose / Hirokazu Miura CL:Thirty Three Co.,Ltd.

MEDIUM RARE
"HARD DUB VERSION" JAPAN 1993 CL:Club King Co.

CLUB KING
"FACE IS A PERSONAL HISTORY ?!" JAPAN 1990 CD:Moichi Kuwahara
AD,D,I:Hirosuke Ueno CL:Club King Co.

CLUB KING
"WHICH DO YOU WANT?" JAPAN 1993 CD:Moichi Kuwahara AD,D,I:Hirosuke Ueno
CL:Club King Co.

Face is a Personal History ?!

WHICH DO YOU WANT ?

T-SHIRTS FOR RETAIL SALES 159 T-SHIRTS FOR RETAIL SALES

OTHERS OTHERS OTHERS OTHERS OTHERS OTHERS OTHERS OTHERS OTHERS OTHERS OTHERS OTHERS OTHERS OTH

HYPE
UK 1990 AD,D,I:Nice DF:Nice CL:Barnsley

CLUB KING
JAPAN 1991 CD:Moichi Kuwahara AD,D,I:Hirosuke Ueno CL:Club King Co.

T-SHIRTS FOR MESSAGE COMMUNICATION

ATION IDENTITY   ORGANIZATION IDENTITY   ORGANIZATION IDENTITY   ORGAN

ICAL STATEMENTS   POLITICAL STATEMENTS   POLITICAL STATEMENTS   POLITIC

PRODUCT, EVENT PROMOTION   PRODUCT, EVENT PROMOTION   PRO

MIGHTY
THINGS

ATION IDENTITY   ORGANIZATION IDENTITY   ORGANIZATION IDENTITY   ORGA

STATEMENTS   POLITICAL STATEMENTS   POLITICAL STATEMENTS   POLITICAL S

CAPP STREET
USA 1992 AD,D:Jennifer Morla D:Sharrie Brooks P:Holly Stewart
DF:Morla Design CL:Capp Street Project

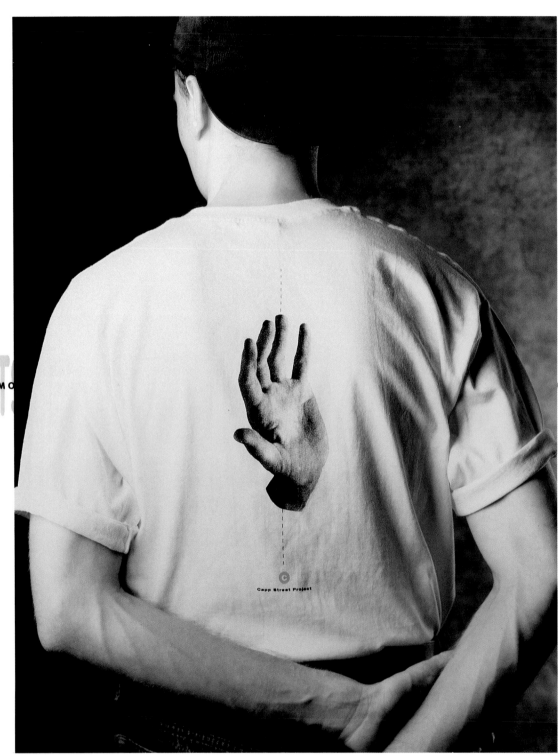

Capp Street Project

**PETER GABRIEL-
COME TALK TO ME**

UK 1992-1993 CD:Michael Coulson
AD,D:Martha Ladly ARTIST:David Mach
DF:Real World CL:Peter Gabriel Ltd.

WOMAD '93-COLLAGE

UK 1993 CD:Thomas Brooman AD:Martha Ladly
D:Tristan Manco DF:Real World CL:Womad / Bravado

PETER GABRIEL
"STEAM" UK 1992-1993 CD:Michael Coulson AD,D:Martha Ladly ARTIST:Ian Hughes
DF:Real World CL:Peter Gabriel Ltd.

Steam

Ian Hughes

© 1992 Peter Gabriel Ltd

TROUBLE
UK 1993 D:Daniel Holliday / Andrew Holland CL:Trouble

T-SHIRTS FOR MESSAGE COMMUNICATION
UCT, EVENT PROMOTION PRODUCT, EVENT PROMOTION 165 PRODUCT FOR MESSAGE COMMUNICATION PRODUCT, EVENT PROM

FRONT

BACK

DR SOKKA
"FOUL" UK 1992 AD,D,I,CW:The Designers Republic DF:The Designers Republic
CL:Pop Will Eat Itself

PWEI
"SKATE OR DIE" UK 1992 AD,D,I,CW:The Designers Republic
DF:The Designers Republic CL:Pop Will Eat Itself

THE ORB
"MISSION '92" UK 1992 AD,D,I,CW:The Designers Republic DF:The Designers Republic
CL:Pop Will Eat Itself

PETER GABRIEL-US
UK 1992 CD:Michael Coulson AD:Martha Ladly D:Malcolm Gardett (Assorted Images)
DF:Real World CL:Peter Gabriel Ltd.

FRONT

BACK

BLACK
"HAPPY FACE" USA 1993 D:Art Chantry DF:Art Chantry Design
CL:Art Institute of Seattle / Tom Dyer

PWEI
"LIVE" UK 1992 AD,D,I,CW:The Designers Republic DF:The Designers Republic
CL:Pop Will Eat Itself

PWEI
"PHO-KU PWEINIX" UK 1993 AD,D,I,CW:The Designers Republic
DF:The Designers Republic CL:Pop Will Eat Itself

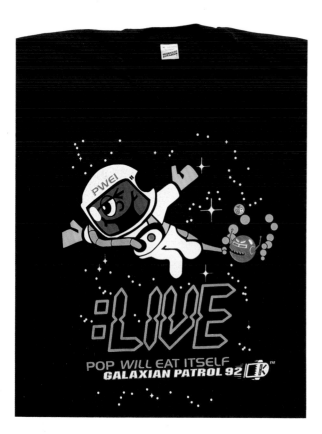

SHIRTS FOR MESSAGE COMMUNICATION

CT, EVENT PROMOTION PRODUCT, EVENT PROMOTION PRODUCT, EVENT PROMOTION PRODUCT, EVENT PROMOT

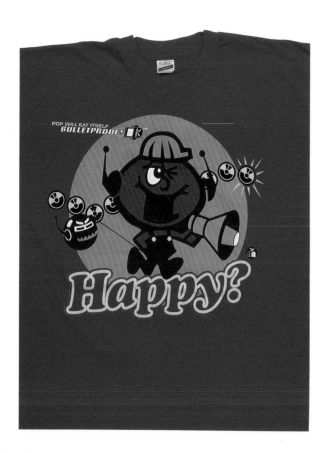

PWEI
"HAPPY ?" UK 1992 AD,D,I,CW:The Designers Republic DF:The Designers Republic
CL:Pop Will Eat Itself

PWEI
"HOME FIXTURE" UK 1992 AD,D,I,CW:The Designers Republic
DF:The Designers Republic CL:Pop Will Eat Itself

PWEI AFC '93
UK 1993 AD,D,I,CW:The Designers Republic DF:The Designers Republic
CL:Pop Will Eat Itself

PWEI COMMUNICATIONS
UK 1993 AD,D,I,CW:The Designers Republic DF:The Designers Republic
CL:Pop Will Eat Itself

PWEI
"GALAXIAN PATROL" UK 1992 AD,D,I,CW:The Designers Republic
DF:The Designers Republic CL:Pop Will Eat Itself

PWEI
"GUN '93" UK 1992 AD,D,I,CW:The Designers Republic DF:The Designers Republic
CL:Pop Will Eat Itself

PWEI
"RELAX JUST BLOW" UK 1992
AD,D,I,CW:The Designers
Republic
DF:The Designers Republic
CL:Pop Will Eat Itself

DR SOKKA
"I LIKE BEER,ME" UK 1992
AD,D,I,CW:The Designers Republic
DF:The Designers Republic CL:Pop Will Eat Itself

JIMMY HENDRIX
UK 1991 CD:Nice AD,D,I:Stephen Male DF:Nice CL:Wrangler UK

MEN FROM U.N.K.L.E. PIECE KLUB

2

KICKS MORE FUNK THAN A SHAOLIN MONK

1

100% BLUNTED SWIFTIES

FAVOURITE GEARS — HIGHLY INFLAMMABLE TYPOGRAFIX

3

100% BLUNTED
SWIFTIES
FAVOURITE GEARS

4

1. **MO'WAX**
   "KICKS MORE FUNK THAN SHADU'N MONL" UK 1993 AD,D:Swifty
   DF:Swifty Typografix CL:Mo' Wax-James Lavelle

2. **MO' WAX PIECE KLUB**
   UK 1993 AD,D:Swifty DF:Swifty Typografix CL:Mo' Wax-James Lavelle

3. **SWIFTIES-100% BLONTED**
   UK 1993 AD,D:Swifty DF:Swifty Typografix CL:Swifty

4. **SWIFTIES-100% BLONTED**
   UK 1992 AD,D:Swifty DF:Swifty Typografix CL:Swifty

MO'WAX
"MEN FROM UNKLE PIECE KLUB" UK 1993
AD,D:Swifty DF:Swifty Typografix
CL:Mo' Wax-James Lavelle

A MEN FROM

U.N.K.L.E.

PRODUCTION

THE WINKY WAGON
UK 1992 CD:Nice AD,D,I:Neil Edwards / Stephen Male
DF:Nice CL:Rapido Television

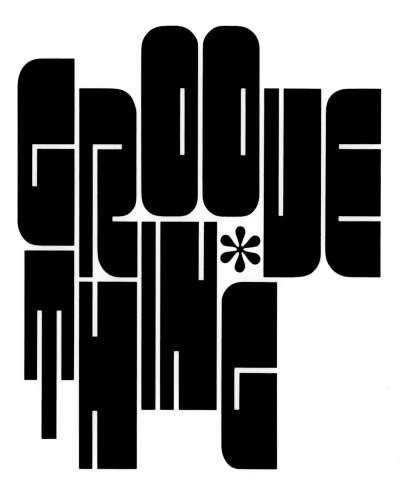

GROOVE THING LOGO
USA 1993 CD:Alex Kaplan AD,D:Christy Trotter
DF:The Ministry of Fun CL:e / Eightball Records

PWEI
"HOME FIXTURE" UK 1992 AD,D,I,CW:The Designers Republic
DF:The Designers Republic CL:Pop Will Eat Itself

PWEI
"GUN '93" UK 1992 AD,D,I,CW:The Designers Republic DF:The Designers Republic
CL:Pop Will Eat Itself

GET A LIFE
UK 1992 AD:Nice DF:Nice CL:Time Out Magazine

MIRO
UK 1993 CD:Nice AD:Richard Bonner-Morgan DF:Nice CL:Vincon

LAFORET
JAPAN 1993 AD:Takuya Onuki D:Yuichi Shimabayashi
P:Shintaro Shiratori CL:Laforet Harajuku

LAFORET
JAPAN 1993 AD:Takuya Onuki D:Yuichi Shimabayashi
P:Shintaro Shiratori CL:Laforet Harajuku

UCT, EVENT PROMOTION FOR MESSAGE COMMUNICATION PRODUCT, EVENT PROMOTION PRODUCT, EVENT PROMO

LAFORET
JAPAN 1993 AD:Takuya Onuki D:Yuichi Shimabayashi
P:Shintaro Shiratori CL:Laforet Harajuku

LAFORET
JAPAN 1993 AD:Takuya Onuki D:Yuichi Shimabayashi
P:Shintaro Shiratori CL:Laforet Harajuku

1

2

3

3

EDWARD TSUWAKI'S

1. *"DESIGNED FOR FLYING KIDS"* JAPAN 1992 AD:Edward Tsuwaki's
P:Toshikazu Oguruma COURTESY:Big O / Takarajima Sha,Inc.
2. *"DESIGNED FOR HANNA BARBERA'S-MUTLEY"* JAPAN 1993 AD:Edward Tsuwaki's
P:Masaya Kikuchi MODELS:Yue Nishihashi / Kaoru Koizumi / Makiko Watanabe
COURTESY:100idée / Cizna Inc.
3. *"DESIGNED FOR MARINA WATANABE"* JAPAN 1991 AD:Edward Tsuwaki's
P:Hajime Tachibana COURTESY:Sony Music Stars / Shinchosha Company /
Karen Kirishima / Hajime Tachibana

4

3

2

1

EDWARD TSUWAKI'S

"EDWARDROBE '94-SNOW CRYSTALS" JAPAN 1994 AD:Edward Tsuwaki's
P:1.Masaya Kikuchi / 2.3.4.Yasuyuki Takagi
MODELS:Yutaka Saino / Mariko / Dave / Mika Ichinohe
HAIR & MAKE UP:Hisano Komine (SASHU) COURTESY:Amazone / Now Fashion Agency

T-SHIRTS FOR MESSAGE COMMUNICATION

UCT, EVENT PROMOTION FOR PRODUCT, EVENT PROMOTION PRODUCT, EVENT PROMOTION PRODUCT, EVENT PROMO

ROGER AND ANGELICA
JAPAN 1986 AD,D,I:Tadanori Yokoo CL:Private Art Class

KUMANO SPARK
JAPAN 1993 AD,D:Tadanori Yokoo CL:Kumano International Art Festival

WITH 2 PEOPLE
JAPAN 1979 AD,D:Tadanori Yokoo CL:Setouchi Butsudan

HAIZUKA
JAPAN 1979 AD,D:Tadanori Yokoo CL:Haizuka Printing Co.

T-SHIRTS FOR MESSAGE COMMUNICATION PRODUCT, EVENT PROMOTION PRODUCT, EVENT PROMOTION PRODUCT, EVENT PROMOTION PRODUCT, EVENT PROMO

WITH 2 PEOPLE
JAPAN 1979 AD,D:Tadanori Yokoo CL:Setouchi Butsudan

HAIZUKA
JAPAN 1979 AD,D:Tadanori Yokoo CL:Haizuka Printing Co.

I'M NOT ARTIST
JAPAN 1981 AD,D,I:Tadanori Yokoo CL:Private Art Class

FRONT

BACK

-SHIRTS FOR MESSAGE COMMUNICATION

CT, EVENT PROMOTION PRODUCT, EVENT PROMOTION 182 PRODUCT, EVENT PROMOTION PRODUCT, EVENT PROMOT PRODUCT, EVENT PROMOTION PRODUCT, EVENT PROMOTION MESSAGE COMMUNICATION

FRONT

BACK

A LAUGH FOR LUNCH 1993

LAUGH FOR LUNCH
AUSTRALIA 1993 AD,D:Sophie Bartho DF:Sophie Bartho and Associates Pty Limited
CL:2 Day FM Australia

WELCOME SHIKOKU VILLAGE
JAPAN 1979 AD,D,I:Tadanori Yokoo CL:Shikoku Village

HAIZUKA
JAPAN 1979 AD,D:Tadanori Yokoo CL:Haizuka Printing Co.

THE ROCKET
USA 1992 AD,D:Art Chantry I:Peter Bagge CW:Gerry Roslie
DF:Art Chantry Design CL:The Rocket

YELTSIN JOKE
UK 1993 CD:Katherine Sorrell CL:The Cartoonist Magazine

BO DEANS
USA 1993 AD,D:Ken Hanson D:Shawn Doyle I:Jon Hargreaves
DF:Hanson / Dodge CL:Bo Deans

ANDERSON REUNION
USA 1992 AD,D,I:John Sayles DF:Sayles Graphic Design
CL:Anderson Family

BEING SINGLE IS FOR
THE BIRDS
USA 1993 AD,D,I:John Sayles DF:Sayles Graphic Design
CL:Teri & Andy TeBockhorst

PASSION FRUITS

JAPAN 1993 CD:Nobukazu Fukui AD:Yoshihiko Uchio
I:Noboru Itani CL:Takisada & Co.,Ltd.

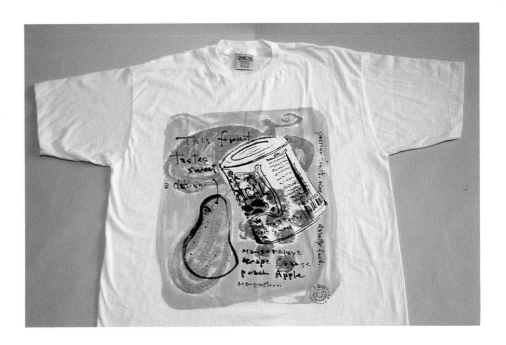

JAZZ BAR MOON WATER

JAPAN 1993 CD:Nobukazu Fukui AD:Yoshihiko Uchio
I:Noboru Itani CL:Takisada & Co.,Ltd.

CIGARETTE

JAPAN 1993 CD:Nobukazu Fukui AD:Yoshihiko Uchio
I:Noboru Itani CL:Takisada & Co.,Ltd.

ENJOY A MOTT'S CLAMATO

CANADA 1992 D,I:Andy Ip DF:TDH Marketing Communications Ltd.
CL:Cadbury Beuerages Canada Inc.

JOSE CUERVO GOLD SLAM 1993

AUSTRALIA 1993 AD,D:Sophie Bartho DF:Sophie Bartho and Associates Pty Limited
CL:Swift and Moore Pty Limited

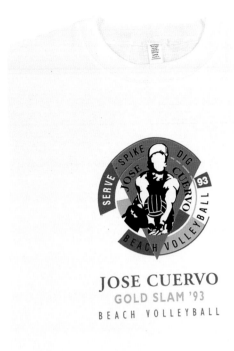

SHIRTS FOR MESSAGE COMMUNICATION CT, EVENT PROMOTION PRODUCT, EVENT COMMUNI 186 PRODUCT, EVENT PROMOTION PRODUCT, EVENT PROMOT

WIZARDS OF OZ

AUSTRALIA 1992 AD,D,I:Sophie Bartho DF:Sophie Bartho and Associates Pty Limited
CL:Sony Music Australia

AJINOMOTO MUSIC MEETS ART

JAPAN 1993 CD:Etsufumi Umeda AD:Yutaka Ota D:Koichi Kurenuma
DF:Genet Associates Inc. CL:Ajinomoto Co.,Ltd.

DIADORA
USA 1986 AD,D,I:Jack Anderson D:Cheri Huber
DF:Hornall Anderson Design Works CL:Diadora USA

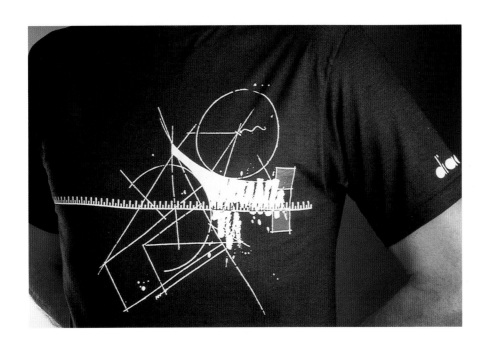

USTA / CELLULAR ONE
USA 1990 AD,D:Jack Anderson D:David Bates
I:Julia LaPine / Brian O'Neill DF:Hornall Anderson Design Works
CL:Cellular One

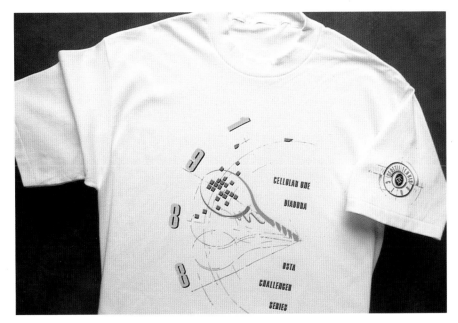

SEATTLE-TO-PORTLAND
USA 1989 AD,D,I:Jack Anderson D:Jani Drewfs D,I:David Bates
DF:Hornall Anderson Design Works CL:Cascade Bicycle Club

DINASAUR
USA 1992 CD:Gro Frivoll D,I:Mike Quon DF:Mike Quon Design Office
CL:American Museum of Natural History

SCOTT MAYEDA
USA AD,I:Scott Mayeda CL:Scott Mayeda

MILWAUKEE BALLET

USA 1993 CD:John Constable AD:Ken Hanson D:Cory DeWalt
I:Jon Hargreaves DF:Hanson / Dodge CL:Mikwaukee Ballet

SEATTLE ART MUSEUM

USA 1988 AD,D:Jon Hornall
D:Mike Courtney / Brian O'Neill / David Bates
DF:Hornall Anderson Design Works CL:Seattle Art Museum

VIOLENT FEMMES

USA 1993 AD,D:Ken Hanson D:Shawn Doyle I:Jon Hergreves
DF:Hanson / Dodge CL:Violent Femmes

JALAPEÑO HENRY'S

USA 1993 CD,D,I:Keith Sasaki DF:Honblue Inc. CL:Honblue Inc.

POST-INDUSTRIAL 5TH ANNIVERSARY

USA 1993 CD:Skip Jensen D:Art Chantry DF:Art Chantry Design
CL:Post-Industrial Stress+Design

T-SHIRTS FOR MESSAGE COMMUNICATION UCT, EVENT PROMOTION PRODUCT, EVENT PROMOTION PRODUCT, EVENT PROMOTION PRODUCT, EVENT PROMO

RENOWN FASHION WEEK

JAPAN 1992 AD:Nobuo Hara D:Yumiko Kitagawa I:Mariko Abe CL:Renown Inc.

RENOWN FASHION WEEK

JAPAN 1992 AD:Nobuo Hara D:Yumiko Kitagawa I:Mariko Abe CL:Renown Inc.

DINO IN PARIS
JAPAN 1992 I:Kaoru Hironaka

P-SANTA!
JAPAN 1992 I:Kaoru Hironaka

T-SHIRTS FOR MESSAGE COMMUNICATION
DUCT, EVENT PROMOTION PRODUCT, EVENT PROMOTION 191 PRODUCT, MESSAGE PROMOTION PRODUCT, EVENT PROM

SURGICAL
USA 1992 AD,I:Mike Quon DF:Mike Quon Design Office CL:CHC / MED

CUERVO
AUSTRALIA 1993 AD,D,I:Sophie Bartho DF:Sophie Bartho and Associates Pty Limited
CL:Swift and Moore Pty Limited

VARSITY RUSH
USA 1989 AD,D,I:John Sayles DF:Sayles Graphic Design CL:Villanova University

WEEKEND
USA 1991 CD:Ted Eyes D,I:Mike Quon DF:Mike Quon Design Office CL:HBO

MARUI O'NEILL WORLD TOUR
USA 1990 AD:Dave T.Parmley D:Sandy Gin CL:O'Neill,Inc.

PEPSI COLLEGIATE VOLLEYBALL CHALLENGE
USA 1989 AD:Dave T.Parmley D:Sandy Gin CL:O'Neill,Inc.

THE LEGEND LIVES
USA 1992 CD,D,I:John Sayles AD:Val Thunder
DF:Sayles Graphic Design CL:Sun Microsystems

BACK

FRONT.

T-SHIRTS FOR MESSAGE COMMUNICATION

MENTS POLITICAL STATEMENTS POLITICAL STATEMENTS 194 POLITICAL MESSAGE COMMUNICATION STATEMENTS POLITI

FRONT

BACK

SERRA DO MAR,SÃO PAULO E PANTANAL

BRAZIL 1993 D:Silvio Silva Junior DF:Studio Lúmen CL:Fernando Chignone

AERO KING

USA 1993 AD:Howie Idelson DF:Urban Image Studio CL:Style Kings

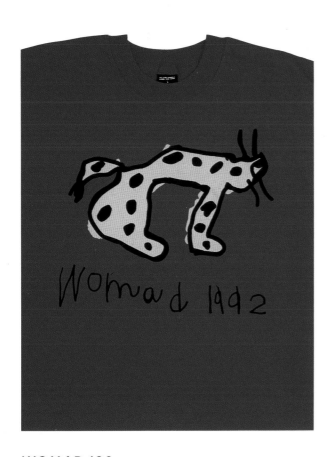

WOMAD '92

UK 1991 CD:Thomas Brooman AD:Vicki Anderson I:Thomas Gray (Aged5)
DF:Real World CL:Womad / Bravado

CHICAGO LUNG ASSOCIATION

USA 1992 AD,D:Carlos Segura I:Mary Flock Lempd DF:Segura Inc.
CL:Chicago Lung Association

TERROR
USA 1993 AD:Howie Idelson DF:Urban Image Studio CL:Malibu Boardriders Club

MALIBU SURF CLASSIC
USA 1993 AD:Howie Idelson DF:Urban Image Studio CL:Malibu Boardriders Club

MUDHONEY
USA 1992 AD,D:Art Chantry I:Edwin Judah Fotheringham DF:Art Chantry Design
CL:Warner Bros. / Reprise Records

THE ROCKET
USA 1992 AD:Art Chantry I:Scott McDougall DF:Art Chantry Design CL:The Rocket

DARE MIGHTY THINGS
USA 1993 CD:Charles Hively AD:Tom Cleveland CL:The Hively Agency,Inc.

T-SHIRTS FOR MESSAGE COMMUNICATION
DUCT, EVENT PROMOTION FOR PRODUCT, EVENT PROMOTION 197 PRODUCT, EVENT PROMOTION PRODUCT, EVENT PROMO

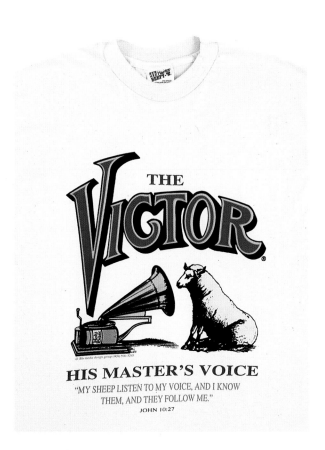

THE VICTOR
USA 1993 AD;Steve Burgoon D,I:Rex Morache DF:IHS Media Design Group
CL:IHS Media Design Group

GRUNTRUCK
USA 1992 D:Art Chantry DF:Art Chantry Design CL:Art Institute of Seattle / Tom Dyer

5TH WESTERN REGIONAL TRIATHLON
CLUBS CHAMPIONSHIP
USA 1992 AD,D:Mark Palmer D:Patricia Kellogg DF:Mark Palmer Design
CL:American Red Cross

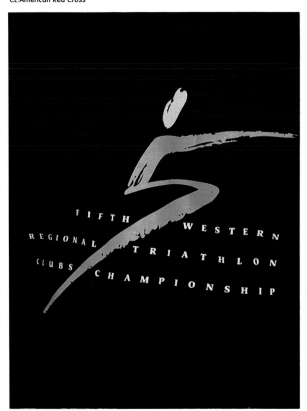

RIVERWALK
USA 1993 AD,D,I:Ruth Wyatt DF:Good Design CL:Family Health Centers

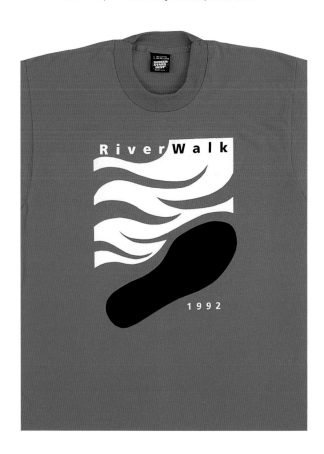

MEET ME FOR BREAKFAST
USA 1992 CD:Charles Hively AD:Laura Tolar CL:Administaff

WE'LL HAVE FOLKS
USA 1992 CD:Charles Hively AD:Tom Cleveland CL:Moody Gardens

MUCH ADO ABOUT NOTHING

USA 1992 AD,D,I:Kevin Wyatt CW:Shakespeare DF:Good Design
CL:Kentucky Shakespeare Festival

OTHELLO

USA 1992 AD,D,I:Kevin Wyatt CW:Shakespeare DF:Good Design
CL:Kentucky Shakespeare Festival

THE IMAGE BANK

"VARIOUS" USA D,I:Mike Quon DF:Mike Quon Design Office CL:The Image Bank

GANG OF SEVEN
USA 1992 AD,D:Jack Anderson D:Brian O'Neill DF:Hornall Anderson Design Works CL:Gang of Seven

TIP TOP DESIGN
USA 1993 AD,D,I:John Sayles DF:Sayles Graphic Design
CL:Sayles Graphic Design

801 STEAK & CHOP HOUSE
USA 1993 AD,D,I:John Sayles DF:Sayles Graphic Design
CL:801 Steak & Chop House

CHEMICAL FREE-WHEELIN'
USA 1992 AD,D,I:John Sayles DF:Sayles Graphic Design CL:Ragbrai XX

K2 8.3 EXTREME

USA 1991 AD,D:Jack Anderson D:Denise Weir / Julia LaPine / Brian O'Neill
DF:Hornall Anderson Design Works CL:K2 Corporation

K2 EURO PLUS, ACTION PLUS, BASE PLUS

USA 1990 AD,D,I:Jack Anderson D:Denise Weir / Julie Tanagi-Lock I:Jani Drewfs
DF:Hornall Anderson Design Works CL:K2 Corporation

TEAM UNIX

USA 1993 AD,D,I:John Sayles DF:Sayles Graphic Design CL:Team UNIX

ATOMIC GRAPHICS

USA 1993 AD,D:Greg Stevenson I:Kevin Mahoney
DF:Atomic Graphics CL:Atomic Graphics

FRONT

BACK

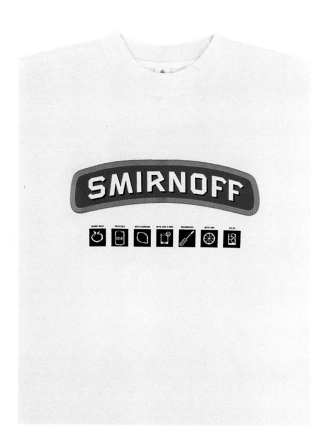

SMIRNOFF VARIETY

AUSTRALIA 1993 AD,D:Sophie Bartho DF:Sophie Bartho and Associates Pty Limited
CL:Swift and Moore Pty Limited

SMIRNOFF-THE WORLDS FINEST VOOKA

AUSTRALIA 1993 AD,D:Sophie Bartho DF:Sophie Bartho and Associates Pty Limited
CL:Swift and Moore Pty Limited

ARCADE RENEGADE-FISTS
UK 1993 D:Antony Wallis / Martin Ward CW:Patrick Barnes / Robin Woodhouse
CL:Future Shooter

ARCADE RENEGADE-DRIVER
UK 1993 D:Antony Wallis / Martin Ward CW:Patrick Barnes / Robin Woodhouse
CL:Future Shooter

ARCADE RENEGADE-JOYSTICK
UK 1993 D:Antony Wallis / Martin Ward CW:Patrick Barnes / Robin Woodhouse
CL:Future Shooter

ARCADE RENEGADE-SHOOTER
UK 1993 D:Antony Wallis / Martin Ward CW:Patrick Barnes / Robin Woodhouse
CL:Future Shooter

RAVER
UK 1993 D:Antony Wallis / Martin Ward CW:Patrick Barnes / Robin Woodhouse
CL:Sega

GEEZA
UK 1993 D:Antony Wallis / Martin Ward CW:Patrick Barnes / Robin Woodhouse
CL:Sega

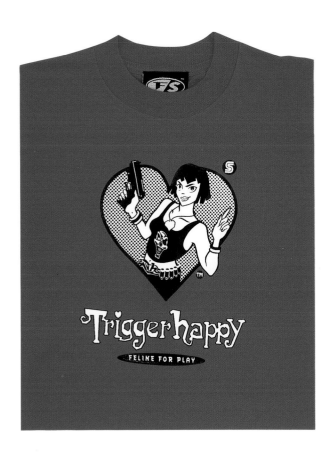

TRIGGER HAPPY
UK 1993 D:Antony Wallis / Martin Ward
CW:Patrick Barnes / Robin Woodhouse CL:Sega

FUTURE SHOOTER
UK 1993 D:Antony Wallis / Martin Ward CW:Patrick Barnes / Robin Woodhouse
DF:Future Shooter CL:Sega

SIX SIGMA
USA 1993 AD,D:Jack Anderson D:Heidi Hatlestad DF:Hornall Anderson Design Works CL:Six Sigma

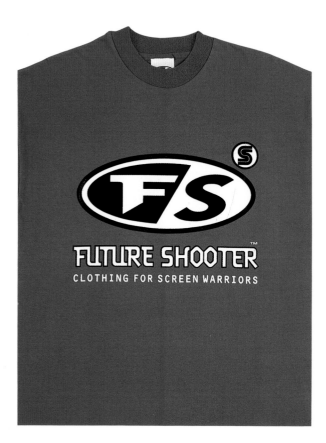

FUTURE SHOOTER
UK 1993 D:Antony Wallis / Martin Ward
CW:Patrick Barnes / Robin Woodhouse CL:Sega

TRIGGER HAPPY
UK 1993 D:Antony Wallis / Martin Ward
CW:Patrick Barnes / Robin Woodhouse CL:Sega

PARADIGM PHILADELPHIA
USA 1993 D:Joel Katz DF:Paradigm Design CL:Paradigm Design

PICAROS
JAPAN 1992 AD:Takeshi Yamamoto CL:Picaros

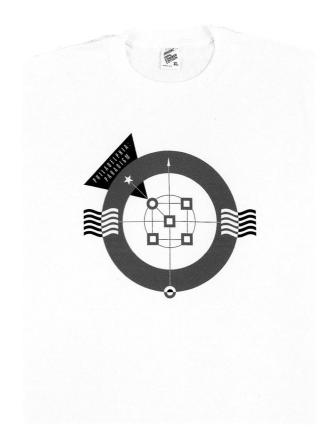

PALM STREET
JAPAN 1991 D:Nobuo Abe DF:Gong CL:All Japan Glass Chain

DRAGON FLY
USA 1993 CD:Kevin Millis AD:Ralph Beach
D:Peter Kramer P:Rick Garcia
I,CW:Masaaki Hatsumi CL:Bujinkan Millis Dojo

T-SHIRTS FOR MESSAGE COMMUNITY ORGANIZATION IDENTITY ORGANIZATION IDENTITY ORGANIZATION IDENTITY 210 ORGANIZATION MESSAGE COMMUNICATION IDENTITY ORGANIZATION IDENTITY ORG

CAFFE LUNA
USA 1990 AD:H.Red Lefkowitz
D,I:Claire Lorain / Boyd Hetrick
DF:First in Fasion,USA CL:Caffe Luna

GONG
JAPAN 1988 D:Nobuo Abe DF:Gong CL:Gong

T-SHIRTS FOR MESSAGE COMMUNICATION

'Well behaved dance music!'

ZOO DE BUENOS AIRES
ARGENTINA 1993 CL:Zoo De Buenos Aires

GOODBOY RECORDS
UK 1993 D:The Cooler I:K.O.F. CL:Goodboy Records

WE HAVE BUT ONE WORLD

USA 1986 AD,D,CW:Mary Lynn Sheetz
DF:Mary Lynn Sheetz Graphics CL:Ute・T's

CARPE DIEM

USA 1992 AD,D,I:Mary Lynn Sheetz CW:Martin G.Taylor
DF:Mary Lynn Sheetz Graphics CL:Ute・T's

COLUMBUS DIDN'T DISCOVER AMERICA
USA 1991 AD,D,CW:Mary Lynn Sheetz DF:Mary Lynn Sheetz Graphics CL:Alterni-T's

WILL WORK FOR FOOD
USA 1992 AD,D:Mary Lynn Sheetz DF:Mary Lynn Sheetz Graphics CL:Alterni-T's

IF YOUR ONLY TOOL IS A HAMMER
USA 1992 AD,D:Mary Lynn Sheetz DF:Mary Lynn Sheetz Graphics CL:Alterni-T's

PERSIAN GULF
USA 1991 AD,D:Mary Lynn Sheetz DF:Mary Lynn Sheetz Graphics CL:Alterni-T's

KOKOPELLI
USA 1990 AD:Mary Lynn Sheetz D,I,CW:Doug Smith DF:DS Design CL:Ute・T's

PIECE IT TOGETHER
USA 1993 AD,D,CW:Mary Lynn Sheetz DF:Mary Lynn Sheetz Graphics CL:Alterni-T's

POLITICAL STATEMENTS POLITICAL STATEMENTS POLITICAL STATEMENTS POLITICAL STATEMENTS POLITIC

NIGHT FLIGHT
USA 1989 AD,D,CW:Martin G.Taylor I:Mary Lynn Sheetz DF:MT Graphics CL:Ute・T's

ANGELS
USA 1993 AD,D,I,CW:Mary Lynn Sheetz DF:Mary Lynn Sheetz Graphics CL:Ute・T's

SPEAK OUT!
USA 1989 AD,D:Mary Lynn Sheetz DF:Mary Lynn Sheetz Graphics CL:Alterni-T's

CHIEF SEATTLE
USA 1989 AD,D,I:Mary Lynn Sheetz DF:Mary Lynn Sheetz Graphics
CL:Ute・T's / Alterni-T's

FIRST THEY CAME FOR THE JEWS, BUT I WASN'T A JEW, SO I
DIDN'T REACT ● THEN THEY CAME FOR THE COMMUNISTS, BUT I
WASN'T A COMMUNIST, SO I DIDN'T OBJECT ● THEN THEY
CAME FOR THE HOMOSEXUALS BUT I WASN'T HOMOSEXUAL,
SO I DIDN'T STAND UP ● THEN THEY CAME FOR THE
POLITICAL ACTIVISTS BUT I WASN'T A POLITICAL
ACTIVIST, SO I DIDN'T PROTEST ● THEN THEY CAME
FOR ME...AND BY THAT TIME NO ONE WAS LEFT TO

SPEAK OUT

THIS WE KNOW:
THE EARTH DOES NOT
BELONG TO US,
WE BELONG
to the
EARTH.

MAN DID NOT
WEAVE THE
WEB OF LIFE-
HE IS MERELY A
STRAND IN IT.
WHATEVER HE DOES
TO THE WEB, HE DOES
TO HIMSELF.

CHIEF SEATTLE

A GENEROUS HELPING
USA 1993 AD,D,I:John Sayles DF:Sayles Graphic Design CL:The Boys and Girls Club of Central Iowa

VISUAL AID
USA 1990 AD,D:Jennifer Morla D:Sharrie Brooks DF:Morla Design CL:Visual Aid

CONTRIBUTORS' INDEX

T-SHIRT PRINT DESIGNS & LOGOS

ART DIRECTOR
Kazuo Abe

DESIGNER
Yutaka Ichimura

EDITOR
Kaori Shibata

PHOTOGRAPHER
Kuniharu Fujimoto

COORDINATORS
Chizuko Gilmore (San Francisco)
Sarah Phillips (London)

ENGLISH CONSULTANTS
Sue Herbert
Clive Avins

TRANSLATORS
Triscope Corporation
Write Away Co.,Ltd.

BUSINESS MANAGER
Masato Ieshiro

PUBLISHER
Shingo Miyoshi

PRINTING AND BINDING
Everbest Printing Co.,Ltd.

SPECIAL THANKS TO
Kaoru Endo
Naomi Sakuma
Rie Okada
Koei Systematic Co.,Ltd.

1994年 8月11日初版第 1 版発行

発行所 ピエ・ブックス
〒170 東京都豊島区駒込4-14-6-407
TEL: 03-3949-5010 FAX: 03-3949-5650

©1994 P·I·E BOOKS

ISBN 4-938586-61-4 C3070

P·I·E Books, as always, has several new and ambitious graphic book projects in the works which will introduce a variety of superior designs from Japan and abroad. Currently we are planning the collection series detailed below. If you have any graphics which you consider worthy for submission to these publications, please fill in the necessary information on the inserted questionnaire postcard and forward it to us. You will receive a notice when the relevant project goes into production.

REQUEST FOR SUBMISSIONS

A. Postcard Graphics

B. Advertising Greeting Cards

C. Brochure & Pamphlet Collection

D. Poster Graphics

E. Book Cover and Editorial Design

F. Corporate Image Design

G. Business Card and Letterhead Graphics

H. Calendar Graphics

I. Packaging and Wrapping Graphics

ピエ・ブックスでは、今後も新しいタイプのグラフィック書籍の出版を目指すとともに、国内外の優れたデザインを幅広く紹介していきたいと考えております。今後の刊行予定として下記のコレクション・シリーズを企画しておりますので、作品提供していただける企画がございましたら、挟み込みのアンケートハガキに必要事項をご記入の上お送り下さい。企画が近づきましたらそのつど案内書をお送りいたします。

作 品 提 供 の お 願 い

A. ポストカード・グラフィックス

B. アドバタイジング・グリーティングカード

C. ブローシュア ＆ パンフレット・コレクション

D. ポスター・グラフィックス

E. ブックカバー＆エディトリアル・デザイン

F. コーポレイト・イメージ ＆ ロゴマーク・デザイン

G. ビジネスカード＆レターヘッド・グラフィックス

H. カレンダー・グラフィックス

I. パッケージ＆ラッピング・グラフィックス

Comme toujours, P·I·E Books a dans ses ateliers plusieurs projets de livres graphiques neufs et ambitieux qui introduiront une gamme de modèles supérieurs en provenance du Japon et de l'étranger. Nous prévoyons en ce moment la série de collections détaillée cidessous. Si vous êtes en possession d'un graphique que vous jugez digne de soumettre à ces publications, nous vous prions de remplir les informations nécessaires sur l'étiquette à renvoyer située à la carte postale questionnaire insérée et de nous la faire parvenir. Vous recevrez un avis lorsque le projet correspondant passera à la production.

DEMANDE DE SOUMISSIONS

A. Graphiques pour cartes postales

B. Cartes de voeux publicitaires

C. Collection de brochures et de pamphlets

D. Graphiques sur affiche

E. Designs de couverture de livre et d'éditorial

F. Designs de logo d'image de société

G. Graphiques pour en-têtes et cartes de visite

H. Graphiques pour calendrier

I. Graphiques pour emballage et paquetage

Wie immer hat P·I·E Books einige neue anspruchsvolle Grafikbücher in Arbeit, die eine Vielzahl von hervorragenden Designs aus Japan und anderen Ländern vorstellen werden. Momentan planen wir eine Serie mit den nachfolgend aufgeführten Themen. Wenn Sie grafische Darstellungen besitzen, von denen Sie meinen, daß sie in diese Veröffentlichung aufgenommen werden könten, geben Sie uns bitte die nötigen Informationen auf der entsprechenden Antwortseite am füllen Sie die beigelegte Antwortkarte aus und schicken Sie sie an uns. Wir werden Sie benachrichtigen, wenn das entsprechende Projekt in Arbeit geht.

AUFFORDERUNG ZU MITARBEIT

A. Postkarten-Grafik

B. Werbe-Grußkarten

C. Zusammenstellung von Broschüren und Druckschriften

D. Postergrafik

E. Bucheinbände und redaktionelles Design

F. Corporate-Image-Logo-Design

G. Visitenkarten und Briefkopf-Grafik

H. Kalendergrafik

I. Grafik auf Verpackungen und Verpackungsmaterial

ADVERTISING GREETING CARDS 1
Pages: 224(144 in color) ¥15,000
業種別ダイレクトメールの集大成
A collection of more than 500 direct mail
pieces selected from thousands used
throughout Japan. Cards were selected
for their distinctive design and include
3-D pop-ups, special die-cuts, folds and
embossings.

BROCHURE & PAMPHLET COLLECTION 1
Pages: 224(144 in color) ¥15,000
業種別カタログ・コレクション
Here are hundreds of the best brochures
and pamphlets from Japan.
This collection will make a valuable
sourcebook for anyone involved in
corporate identity advertising and
graphic design.

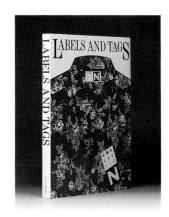

LABELS AND TAGS
Pages: 224(192 in color) ¥15,000
ファッションのラベル&タグ・コレクション
Over 1,600 garment labels representing
450 brands produced in Japan are
included in this full-color collection.

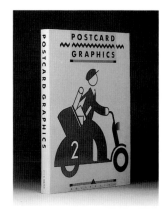

POSTCARD GRAPHICS 2
Pages: 240(208 in color) ¥16,000
好評！業種別ポストカードの第2弾
Here are 1,500 promotional postcards
created by Japan's top design talent.
A wide range of clients are represented
including 120 fashion houses and 90
major retailers. Presented in striking full
color.

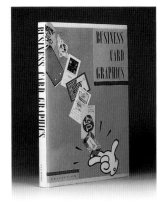

BUSINESS CARD GRAPHICS 1
Pages: 256(160 in color) ¥16,000
世界の名刺&ショップカード集大成
Over 1,200 business cards are presented
in this international collection.
Created by 500 of the world's top design
firms, designers will discover a wealth of
new ideas in this remarkable collection.

FASHION INSIGNIA
Pages: 224(208 in color) ¥16,000
ファッションのワッペン・コレクション
One thousand full-color emblems have
been gathered in this beautiful and
sometimes playful collection.
The great variety of color and shape
demonstrates the versatility of
embroidery art.

ADVERTISING GREETING CARDS 2
Pages: 224(176 in color) ¥16,000
世界のダイレクトメール・コレクション
500 visually remarkable works
representing a variety of businesses.
Pieces include new product
announcements, invitation cards and
direct mail envelopes. An excellent image
bank for graphic designers.

BROCHURE DESIGN FORUM 1
Pages: 224(192 in color) ¥15,000
世界のカタログ・コレクション
A large collection of international
brochures from a variety of business
categories. Showcases more than 250
eye-catching works.

COVER TO COVER
Pages: 240(176 in color) ¥17,000
世界のブック&エディトリアル・デザイン
The latest trends in book and magazine
design are illustrated with over 1,000
creative works by international firms.

BUSINESS STATIONERY GRAPHICS 1
Pages: 224(192 in color) ¥15,000
世界のレターヘッド・コレクション
Creatively designed letterheads,
business cards, memo pads, and other
business forms and documents are
included this international collection.

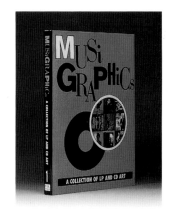

MUSIGRAPHICS 1
Pages: 224(192 in color) ¥16,000
世界のLP&CDグラフィックス
A collection of more than 600 of the
world's most outstanding CD and LP
covers, featuring design for all musical
genres.

BROCHURE & PAMPHLET COLLECTION 2
Pages: 224(192 in color) ¥15,000
業種別カタログ・コレクション、第2弾
Features a selection of 1,000 brochures
and pamphlets covering a wide range of
products from Japan. The value of
brochures in visual communication is
demonstrated in this dazzling collection.

CORPORATE IMAGE DESIGN
Pages: 336(272 in color) ¥16,000
世界の業種別CI・ロゴマーク
This collection presents the best
corporate identity projects from around
the world. Creative and effective designs
from top international firms are featured
in this valuable source book.

POSTCARD GRAPHICS 3
Pages: 232(208 in color) ¥16,000
世界の業種別ポストカード・コレクション
Volume 3 in the series presents more
than 1,200 promotional postcards in
dazzling full color. Top designers from
the world over have contributed to this
useful image bank of ideas.

GRAPHIC BEAT London / Tokyo 1 & 2
Pages: 224(208 in color) ¥16,000
音楽とグラフィックのコラボレーション
1,500 music-related graphic works from 29
of the hottest designers in Tokyo and
London. Features Malcolm Garrett, Russell
Miles, Tadanori Yokoo, Neville Brody,
Vaughn Oliver and others.

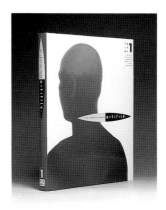

The Creative Index ARTIFILE 1
Pages: 224(Full color) ¥12,500
実力派プロダクション104社の作品集
Showcases the best works from 104
graphic studios in Japan and abroad.
A variety of fields included such as
advertising design, corporate identity,
photography and illustration.

CALENDAR GRAPHICS
Pages: 224(192 in color) ¥16,000
世界のカレンダー・グラフィックス
An exciting collection of creatively
designed calendars from around the
world. A wide variety of styles included
such as poster, book and 3-D calendars.
Clients range from large corporations to
retail shops.

BUSINESS CARD GRAPHICS 2
Pages: 224(192 in color) ¥16,000
世界の名刺&ショップカード、第2弾
This latest collection presents 1,000
creative cards from international
designers. Features hundreds of cards
used in creative fields such as graphic
design and architecture.

T-SHIRT GRAPHICS
Pages: 224(192 in color) ¥16,000
世界のTシャツ・グラフィックス
This unique collection showcases 700
wonderfully creative T-Shirt designs from
the world's premier design centers.
Grouped according to theme, categories
include sports, casual, designer and
promotional shirts among others.

DIAGRAM GRAPHICS
Pages: 224(192 in color) ¥16,000
世界のダイアグラム・デザインの集大成
Hundreds of unique and lucid diagrams,
charts, graphs, maps and technical
illustrations from leading international
design firms. Variety of media
represented including computer graphics.

SPECIAL EVENT GRAPHICS
Pages: 224(192 in color) ¥16,000
世界のイベント・グラフィックス特集
This innovative collection features design
elements from concerts, festivals, fashion
shows, symposiums and more.
International works include posters,
tickets, flyers, invitations and various
premiers.

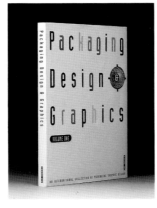

PACKAGING DESIGN & GRAPHICS 1
Pages: 224(192 in color) ¥16,000
世界の業種別パッケージ・デザイン
An international collection featuring 400
creative and exciting package designs
from renowned designers.

RETAIL IDENTITY GRAPHICS
Pages: 208(176 in color) ¥14,800
世界のショップ・グラフィックス
This visually exciting collection
showcases the identity design campaigns
of restaurants, bars, shops and various
other retailers. Wide variety of pieces are
featured including business cards, signs,
menus, bags and hundreds more.

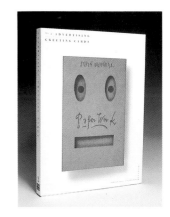

ADVERTISING GREETING CARDS 3
Pages: 224(176 in color) ¥16,000
世界のダイレクトメール集大成、第3弾
The best-selling series continues with
this collection of elegantly designed
advertising pieces from a wide variety of
categories. This exciting image bank of
ideas will interest all graphic designers
and direct mail specialists.

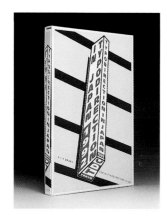

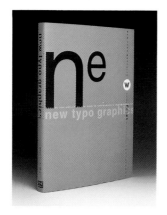

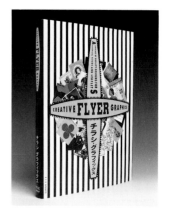

TYPODIRECTION IN JAPAN 4
Pages: 254(183 in color) ￥17,000
年鑑 日本のタイポディレクション '92
314 award-winning works of outstanding
typographical art from Japan and abroad.
Included, you will find up-to-the-minute
examples of concept-development works
and previously unpublished typefaces
from top art dirctors and graphic designers.

NEW TYPO GRAPHICS
Pages: 224(192 in color) ￥16,000
世界の最新タイポグラフィ・コレクション
New and innovative typographical works
gathered from top designers around the
world. A wide variety of type applications
are shown including posters, brochures,
CD jackets, calendars, book designs
and more.

The Production Index ARTIFILE 2
Pages: 244(240 in color) ￥13,500
活躍中！最新プロダクション年鑑、第2弾
A design showcase featuring the best
works from 115 graphic design studios,
photographers, and creators in Japan.
Works shown include print advertisements,
corporate identity pieces, commercial
photography and illustration.

CREATIVE FLYER GRAPHICS
Pages:224(176 in color) ￥16,000
チラシ・グラフィックス
Features about 500 rigorously screened
flyers and leaflets. You see what superior
graphics can accomplish on a single
sheet of paper. This is an invaluable
reference to all your advertising
production for years to come.

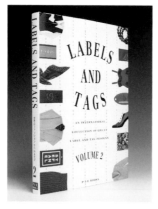

1·2 & 3 COLOR GRAPHICS
Pages:208(Full Color) ￥16,000
1・2・3色 グラフィックス
See about 300 samples of 1,2 & 3 color
artworks that are so expressive they
often surpass the impact of full 4 color
reproductions. This is a very important
book that will expand the possibilities of
your design works in the future.

LABELS AND TAGS 2
Pages:224(192 in color) ￥16,000
世界のラベル＆タグ・コレクション　2
This long-awaited second volume
features 1500samples representing 400
top name-brands from around the world.

BROCHURE DESIGN FORUM 2
Pages:224(176 in color) ￥16,000
世界の最新カタログ・コレクション　2
Features 70 businesses and 250
reproductions for a complete overview of
the latest and best in brochure design.

カタログ・新刊のご案内について
総合カタログ・新刊案内をご希望の方は、はさみ込みのアンケートはがきを
ご返送いただくか、７２円切手同封の上、ピエ・ブックス宛にお申し込み下さい。

A BOOK IS A PRESENT

YOU CAN OPEN AGAIN AND AGAIN

© Mary Engelbreit

8256

This Book Belongs To

The Turner Family

GREATER Philadelphia

"Greater Philadelphia's Enterprises"
by
Susan Gurevitz
and
Margaret O. Kirk

Windsor Publications, Inc.
Chatsworth, California

GREATER

Philadelphia

INTO THE FUTURE

A Contemporary Portrait by Belinda Hulin-Salkin

Windsor Publications, Inc.—Book Division
Managing Editor: Karen Story
Design Director: Alexander D'Anca
Photo Director: Susan L. Wells
Executive Editor: Pamela Schroeder

Staff for *Greater Philadelphia: Into the Future*
Manuscript Editor: Douglas P. Lathrop
Photo Editor: Robin Mastrogeorge Sterling
Senior Editor, Corporate Profiles: Jeffrey Reeves
Senior Production Editor, Corporate Profiles: Una FitzSimons
Proofreader: Michael Moore
Customer Service Manager: Phyllis Feldman-Schroeder
Editorial Assistants: Elizabeth Anderson, Dominique Jones,
Kim Kievman, Michael Nugwynne, Kathy B. Peyser,
Theresa J. Solis
Publisher's Representatives, Corporate Profiles: Hannah Dresser,
Steve Nafe
Layout Artist, Corporate Profiles: Christopher L. Murray

Designer: Christina L. Rosepapa

Windsor Publications, Inc.
Elliot Martin, Chairman of the Board
James L. Fish III, Chief Operating Officer
Mac Buhler, Vice President/Acquisitions

Library of Congress Cataloging-in-Publication Data
Hulin-Salkin, Belinda, 1954-
Greater Philadelphia : into the future : a contemporary portrait /
by Belinda Hulin-Salkin.—1st ed.
p. 272   cm. 23x31
Includes bibliographical references and index.
ISBN 0-89781-387-1 : $36.95
1. Philadelphia Metropolitan Area (Pa.)—Economic conditions.
2. Philadelphia Metropolitan Area (Pa)—Economic conditions
Pictorial works.   I. Title
HC108.P5H85 1991
330.9748'11043—dc20   90-27587
CIP

Previous spread: Philadelphia's skyline illuminates the evening sky along the banks of the majestic Delaware River. Photo by Rich Zila

This spread: Picturesque Logan Circle, one of the four parks originally designed by founder William Penn, offers a quiet respite in the heart of the city. Photo by George Adams Jones

Contents

To Richard,
without whom I might never
have discovered Philadelphia

When I moved to Philadelphia in 1980, the city was punch-drunk from nearly two decades of economic battering. The decline of manufacturing and heavy industry in the Northeast, high energy costs, and a soaring prime interest rate all had taken a toll on the local psyche. As a business writer, I spent a lot of time listening to tales of woe from area economists and business leaders. As a new resident of Philadelphia, I marveled at the museums, the orchestra, the lush landscape, and the rich architectural legacy of the city. How, I wondered, could a place with so much to offer fail to thrive?

During the next decade Greater Philadelphia rebounded. Abandoned buildings gave way to skyscrapers, flashy restaurants and boutiques opened in old storefronts, and new settlers came to embrace the city's cultural treasures. Attitudes have shifted, and today there's an air of celebration about town. I've been lucky enough to witness this transformation firsthand, and even luckier to have the chance to tell the story.

Many people contributed to this book. Unfortunately, I have space to credit only a few. Virtually every aspect of Greater Philadelphia life has been chronicled in a book, an article, a brochure. I'd like to thank the writers and editors whose myriad works I consulted, and the librarians and public information specialists who guided me through the great maze of available research. Special thanks to Doug Lathrop and Pam Schroeder of Windsor Publications for giving me the opportunity to write about my adopted hometown, and for offering encouragement and advice along the way. Ken Finkel of the Library Company of Philadelphia also merits special attention.

Not being a native Philadelphian, I leaned heavily on friends while writing this book, tapping their memories and their contacts. I'd like to thank Robin Warshaw, Gail Greenberg, Sandra McCaffrey, Nancy Wagman, Howard Gibson, Emily Lysinger, Polly Hurst, Selma Rudnick, and Meg Miller for their invaluable assistance. Long-distance moral support and general cheerleading for this project was very capably and lovingly provided by A.J. and Audrey Hulin and Elinor and Robert Bleyer.

Finally, my deepest gratitude to Richard A. Salkin, my first and best editor, for his love, support, and patience during the many months that "the Philadelphia book" dominated our lives.

—Belinda Hulin-Salkin

Acknowledgments

Glass-adorned office towers rise to the challenge of Philadelphia's vibrant business community. Photo by George Adams Jones

Part One

Into the
Future

O n warm spring nights the sounds of horse-drawn carriages echo through the cobblestone streets of Old City, Philadelphia. History—and aspiration—are palpable here. A few blocks away skyscrapers dominate the cityscape and streets hum with traffic and contemporary chatter. But in the shadows of Independence Hall, strolling visitors become part of an evolving, dramatic tableau—a living portrait of America carved from its past.

The United States was born in Philadelphia, and the character of the country today reflects that origin. Within the eighteenth-century halls, shops, and townhouses that still grace the city, men and women once gave passionate voice to their ideals and demanded a free, sovereign nation. But a nation of what mold? Wealthy landowners, merchants, craftsmen, immigrants, and scholars, the pious and the impoverished—all clamored to be heard in those Philadelphia assemblies. Each offered a separate vision for the new land, based on their respective wants, talents, and goals.

The struggle to accomodate such diverse interests while building on common ground is the history of America. It's also the spirit and guiding force that created Philadelphia. More than 300 years ago William Penn founded this city on the

The signing of the Constitution of the United States on September 17, 1787, was a triumphant moment in the history of our country. Captured by artist Howard Chandler Christy, this historic gathering was the culmination of America's battle for independence. Courtesy, National Park Service

The Birthplace of the Nation

Delaware River as an oasis of religious tolerance. Since that time the city has flourished as a center of commerce, industry, and individual enterprise. For thousands the city's landmarks stand as symbols of freedom and opportunity.

Today, Greater Philadelphia remains a microcosm of America, buffeted by national social and economic trends, bolstered by a vast network of natural and human resources. Nearly 5 million people live and work in the small towns, airy suburbs, and bustling city neighborhoods of the Delaware Valley. The region boasts a vibrant social mix of academic and aristocratic elite, dynamic entrepreneurs, and feisty working-class heroes. Fifth-generation Philadelphians share orchestra box seats with upwardly mobile transferees. At Veterans Stadium Main Line matrons sit alongside shipyard mechanics, both hurling insults at the field with equal vehemence. Every year thousands of newcomers move here.

The American dream still thrives in Philadelphia. It's the kind of city where a bricklayer's daughter can grow up to become a princess, and the next mayor might be a former cop or a sharecropper's son.

A City of Firsts

In 1682 William Penn stepped onto the banks of the Delaware River at the site that would become Philadelphia. Before he ever laid eyes on the place, Penn had already given his New World capital the Greek name meaning "city of brotherly love." The move reflected both Penn's Quaker belief in "that of the Divine in every man" and his hope that, as proprietor of the newly chartered colony of Pennsylvania, he could create a religious refuge where men and women of all faiths might worship and prosper.

An admiral's son and a landed gentleman, young Penn had managed to provoke British authorities with his vocal, dissident views on God and government. As an observant member of the Society of Friends (commonly known as the Quakers), he preached pacifism, refused to take oaths, and would not bear arms. For following his conscience and generally irritating King Charles II, Penn suffered government fines and periodic jailings. When he approached the king for repayment of a debt that the monarch owed Penn's father, the king happily granted Penn the New World charter as recompense, at once absolving the debt and removing a likely agitator from the court.

Almost immediately Penn set about designing a liberal government for his colony—one that would guarantee freedom of religion, trial by jury, taxation only by law, and the right of taxpayers to vote. He sold parcels of land in Pennsylvania and its anchor city to some 750 "first purchasers," mostly Quaker merchants, shopkeepers, and craftsmen from the British Isles. Then he began to plot the dimensions of Philadelphia—the New World's first planned city.

Penn was a sophisticated man and a world traveler who had visited the great capitals of Europe. But he favored the country life of his estate in Sussex, and he feared the corruption, poor health conditions, and fire hazards of congested urban centers. He wanted Philadelphia to be a "greene countrie towne which will never be burnt and always be wholsome." His design, carried out with surveyor Thomas Holme, called for a 1200-acre rectangle fronting both the Delaware and the Schuylkill Rivers, with wide streets, symmetrically placed houses, room for orchards and gardens, several green public squares, and a suburban farm belt surrounding the developed area.

The Philadelphia Museum of Art rises over the banks of the scenic Schuylkill River. Photo by David H. Wells

Although many elements of Penn's grand scheme fell through as citizens squabbled over riverfront lots and prime commercial sites, his original gridiron street layout remains largely unchanged, with Broad Street as the city's north-south axis and High (now Market) Street stretching east-west from river to river. The four public parks he decreed—now known as Washington Square, Rittenhouse Square, Franklin Square, and Logan Circle—still afford pedestrians a green respite from city life. A central 10-acre square at the intersection of Broad and Market now accomodates Philadelphia's landmark City Hall, one of the country's preeminent examples of the Second Empire style in architecture.

Modern-day Philadelphians point to the city's tree-shaded, uniform streets and credit Penn's foresight. In the late seventeenth century, however, many of Philadelphia's prime thoroughfares were in fact open sewers where hogs, goats, and assorted other livestock roamed at will. Early residents, in a crude and largely unintentional attempt at landfill, used the streets as garbage dumps. Tree stumps studded most roads well into the eighteenth century.

In spite of such inauspicious beginnings, Philadelphia grew rapidly in size and sophistication. Most of the first citizens were well-to-do Quakers of an entrepreneurial bent who saw in Penn's colony a

chance to prosper without political harassment. By 1700 that initial cadre had been augmented with carpenters, bricklayers, weavers, tailors, brewers, clockmakers, coppersmiths, tavernkeepers, shipbuilders, and traders—more than 2,500 settlers in all. Most were Quakers, many of very modest means, recruited by Penn from depressed areas of England. With the investment capital provided by Philadelphia's affluent early settlers, and the service and trade skills offered by later arrivals, the city had sown the seeds for an effective commercial economy and a well-rounded community.

Of course, well-rounded is a relative term. Philadelphia's Quaker emphasis on serenity and modest deportment gave the town a dour facade and a stodgy reputation that the city has tried to live down ever since. Early Philadelphia law emphasized a moral code based on the Ten Commandments, which meant that swearing, respect for one's parents, and observing the Lord's Day got nearly as much attention as sex crimes, murder, and theft. Stage plays, dice, cards, masques, revels, bullbaiting, cockfighting, gossiping, and dueling were prohibited as acts "which excite people to rudeness, cruelty, looseness and irreligion" and which were otherwise detrimental to an atmosphere of brotherly love.

Penn's colony was not completely homogeneous.

Eighteenth-century life in Philadelphia revolved around the city's port, which carried on a profitable trade with other early American colonies, as well as the British Isles and the West Indies. Courtesy, National Park Service

The Quaker community attracted a few pietist sects from other parts of Europe, chiefly Dutch Quakers and German Mennonites, who eventually settled the city's Germantown section. There they established a near-independent economy based on linen weaving, milling, and an open marketplace. Penn emphasized peaceful coexistence with the native Lenni Lenape Indians, and shortly after his New World arrival paid the tribe 1,000 pounds for their lands. The Quakers also maintained good relations with a small colony of Swedish and Dutch settlers that came to the Delaware Valley before them.

This theologically idyllic, if somewhat dull, utopia did not last long. From the beginning Penn imagined his colony to be a hospitable harbor for the industrious and righteous of all faiths. It is doubtful whether his Quaker brethren shared that vision, but by the early eighteenth century Philadelphia had in fact become the primary port of entry for European immigrants to the colonies. Wars, famine, repressive monarchs, and religious persecution drove thousands of Irish, Germans, and Central Europeans to the rich farmlands around Philadelphia and to the profitable craft and shipping trades within the city.

The prosperity of Philadelphia's port, which carried on a lucrative trade with the British Isles, the West Indies, and the other colonies, also attracted a number of well-heeled English Anglicans and Presbyterians, many the second or third sons of British land barons. These gentrified pioneers brought to the city their Old World sensibilities: an appreciation of grand country homes, elegant dress, fine furniture and art, carriages, great books, and such leisure pursuits as horse breeding and gracious parties. Ancestors to

Leading citizen Benjamin Franklin was a pivotal figure in the early development of Philadelphia. Printer, inventor, statesman, scientist, and scholar, Franklin was responsible for establishing the first volunteer fire department in the colonies, served as Philadelphia's postmaster, and founded the first fire insurance company. Courtesy, National Park Service

Philadelphia's legendary, buttoned-down Main Line WASPs (a term, incidently, coined by Philadelphia sociologist E. Digby Baltzell), the new arrivals scandalized old-line Quakers with their penchant for revelry and ostentatious displays of wealth.

The Philadelphia Dancing Assemblies, private balls founded for the amusement of Philadelphia's young Protestant elite, were among the offending social contributions of this burgeoning upper class. Subscribers to the first assembly, held in 1748, included a who's who of Philadelphia's non-Quaker establishment. Shippens, Allens, Willings, McCalls, Hamiltons, Peterses, Biddles, and Bonds all joined hands with each others' cousins and sisters and neighbors at these affairs. Intermarriage and business dealings among the families solidified their power base in the city. Some would say their descendents still wield extraordinary social and economic clout. At the very least the Philadelphia Assemblies continue to reign as the most exclusive of the city's social events.

If Philadelphia's rising fortunes attracted Europeans from all trades and classes, they also served as a magnet for entrepreneurs and fortune-seekers from other American colonies. Philadelphia's most famous citizen, Benjamin Franklin, was actually a Boston-born lad who arrived in the city in 1723. His published experiments with electricity were the sort of work that established Philadelphia as an important academic hub, and ensconced Franklin as one of the world's premier scientists.

Although Franklin earned many titles in his lifetime—statesman, inventor, scholar, publisher, entrepreneur—he usually described himself as a printer. In 1729, at the age of 23, he opened the New Printing Shop on High Street and quickly became a favored source for legal documents and handbills. He gained influence in the colony by taking over *The*

Pennsylvania Gazette and eventually secured a contract for all government printing, including Pennsylvania's paper money. He protected the colony's specie against fraud with a distinctive tree-leaf trademark.

During his lifelong career as pundit and sage, Franklin gave Philadelphia many of its distinctive "firsts." He organized the first volunteer fire company in the colonies, the first fire insurance company (the Philadelphia Contributorship), and the first subscription library (the Library Company of Philadelphia). He was instrumental in founding Pennsylvania Hospital, which still thrives today, and in founding the College of Philadelphia, a forerunner to the University of Pennsylvania.

It might also be said that Franklin was the country's first serious networker. He had a fondness for starting organizations—the American Philosophical Society being one of the best known—and freely admitted that these associations provided him with contacts which advanced his business and civic interests.

Franklin astutely observed that in Philadelphia it was not who you were but what you could do that counted. Although eighteenth-century Philadelphia society had begun to suffer from class-based elitism, such drawing-room snobbery still left plenty of room for men and women of ideas and ingenuity to leave their mark on the community. Well before the centennial of its founding, the city had taken on the air of a cosmopolitan port, and was a focal point of the intellectual, cultural, and economic life of the American colonies. In 1776 Robert Morris, Philadelphia merchant, banker, and statesman, described the city's critical role in the emerging nation: "You will consider Philadelphia from its centrical situation, the extent of its commerce, the number of its artificers, manufactures and other circumstances, to be to the United States what the heart is to the human body in circulating the blood."

Come the Revolution

In May 1774 Paul Revere, silversmith and renowned horseman, rode into Philadelphia with a plea for solidarity with the people of Boston. In retaliation for the Boston Tea Party a few months earlier, the British Parliament had decreed that the port of Boston be shut down. That action made all the colonies vulnerable to such repressive measures, and cut off some of Philadelphia's valuable colonial trade. In September select Philadelphians joined with other colonists to fashion a response to the king.

Delegates to the First Continental Congress met in Philadelphia's new Carpenters' Hall. Between proclamations and speeches to rouse anti-British sentiment, the colonial radicals enjoyed the hospitality of Philadelphia homes and hostelries. Many were boarded in the well-appointed townhouses and sumptuous estates of the city's most prominent citizens and sampled the cuisine of local taverns and kitchens. The City Tavern—reconstructed and in business today on Second Street—was a favorite watering hole.

In letters home delegates appeared suitably impressed with their hosts' Chippendale furnishings, fine china, and silver place settings, as well as the intricately carved and paneled interiors of their homes. John Adams gave some idea of the delegates' lot in Philadelphia when he wrote, "We go to Congress at nine and we stay there until three in the afternoon; then we adjourn, and go to dine with some of the nobles of Pennsylvania at four o'clock and feast upon a thousand delicacies, and sit drinking Madeira, claret and Burgundy until six or seven and then go home fatigued to death with business, company and care."

Founder of the Democratic party, fourth president of the United States, and coauthor of the *Federalist* papers, James Madison is perhaps best-known as the Father of the Constitution of the United States. Courtesy, National Park Service

A symbol of America's struggle for independence, the Liberty Bell was first cast in London in 1752, but cracked soon after its arrival in Philadelphia. It was successfully recast by local foundrymen and rang out with other city bells on July 8, 1776, to celebrate the Declaration of Independence. Now on public display at Independence National Historic Park, the current crack in the 2,080-pound iron bell is said to have appeared while the bell was being tolled during the 1835 funeral of Chief Justice John Marshall. Photo by George Adams Jones

The first congressional delegates may have been graciously received, but they were not universally admired in Philadelphia. The city population, with its residual Quaker pacifists and high-born British loyalists, gave the meeting mixed reviews. Prior to the Second Continental Congress meeting in 1775, however, colonial irregulars in Massachusetts encountered the British at Lexington and Concord. At the news of that bloody event, Philadelphia troops began to mobilize against the British. On May 10, 1776, the Congress authored a resolution for colonial independence from the British crown. In spite of a Pennsylvania Assembly order forbidding Pennsylvania delegates from supporting such a measure, a majority from the state—including Philadelphia's Benjamin Franklin—pushed it through. On July 4, 1776, in the assembly room of the Pennsylvania State House (now Independence Hall), "The unanimous Declaration of the Thirteen United States of America" was adopted by the delegates. The inkwell used to sign the Declaration still stands in the Hall, as does the Rising Sun chair in which George Washington sat during the Constitutional Convention.

Lore has it that the State House bell—now known as the Liberty Bell—was rung to proclaim liberty throughout the land that July 4. That's a nice idea, but no one really knows if it's true. According to David Dutcher, chief historian at Independence National Historic Park, the bell more likely rang out on July 8, along with all the other bells in the city, when the Declaration was announced and read to the general population. About 1 million people a year now visit the Liberty Bell, originally ordered to celebrate the 50th anniversary of William Penn's 1701 charter for the city. Cast in London, the bell cracked on its first trial in Philadelphia and had to be recast by local foundrymen. The disabling crack occurred when the bell was rung in 1835 to mark the funeral of Chief Justice John Marshall.

During the Revolutionary War the Liberty Bell was moved north to Allentown for safekeeping when Philadelphia was occupied by the British. Washington engaged British troops at Germantown and again at nearby Whitemarsh in 1777, before settling in for the winter at Valley Forge—now a historic park in one of the city's fastest-growing suburbs. Washington reclaimed the city in June 1778. It seems doubtful that Philadelphia's civilians, who accomodated the British, suffered much under their authority. Various memoirs recount a lively social season that winter, with an extravagant ball called the Meschianza, dining, and dancing.

In spite of Philadelphians' seemingly fickle nature, General George Washington remained a hero to them. Following the liberation of New York in 1783, Washington passed through the city on his way home to Virginia. He was feted in the streets by cheering crowds and saluting cannons. It was the first of many enthusiastic receptions Washington would receive in the City of Brotherly Love. In 1787 he returned to take his place at the Constitutional Convention, site of the celebrated "Miracle at Philadelphia" that gave the U.S. its government and led to Washington's tenure as first President. Philadelphia served as capital of the fledgling democracy until 1800.

The Rise of Industry

In the early nineteenth century Philadelphia boasted paved, tree-lined streets, gracefully carved fountains and statuary, museums, theaters, and a thriving academic community. Life in the city was culturally rich, economically prosperous, and for some, socially genteel. A newspaper reporter of the time observed, "Philadelphia is a city to be happy in . . . Delightful cleanliness everywhere meets the eye . . . Everything is well conditioned and cared for." Visitors to the city remarked on the gracious life-style of its citizens and its amenities.

But change is rarely decorous. By midcentury the industrial revolution had hit Philadelphia with a force that shattered its well-ordered complacency. By 1838 Philadelphia was a steam-driven city with factories, foundries, and mills lining the city's waterways (and shortly thereafter, its inland highways). Textile mills, carpet weaving factories, glass works, sugar refining operations, shipyards, iron works, and flour mills dominated many neighborhoods.

The city's proximity to Pennsylvania's rich anthracite coal deposits literally fueled its growth as a manufacturing center. Railroad connections to Pennsylvania farmlands and mining towns boosted the city's stature as a transportation hub and shipping depot. Throughout the nation, Philadelphia-built locomotives and steam engines by Matthias Baldwin and other makers were in use. Philadelphia-area textiles, domestic furnishings, and industrial machines became world-renowned.

The labor to drive Philadelphia's stoked-up factories and terminals came from an explosion of immigration to the city. Prominent citizens and newly minted industrial barons enjoyed the comforts of a still-vibrant, cultured metropolis. But in the crowded back alleys of the city's smokestack neighborhoods, poverty,

Inaugurated as the first president of the United States in 1789, General George Washington led the Continental Army to victory during the American Revolution, and was well-loved by the patriotic citizens of Philadelphia. This famous portrait of Washington was painted by renowned artist Charles Willson Peale. Courtesy, National Park Service

Second Street was a busy thoroughfare in early nineteenth-century Philadelphia. Courtesy, National Park Service

crime, and disease festered, breeding discontent. The
American labor movement got its start in Philadelphia. In 1835 coal heavers, bricklayers, painters, carpenters, masons, and other tradesmen—many of them
unskilled immigrants—walked off their jobs, striking
for a 10-hour workday.

Labor and social unrest often erupted into violence
during that time, with members of newly arrived ethnic groups setting upon each other and upon passersby.
Neighborhood gangs flourished, and anti-Catholic
and anti-Negro riots regularly scarred the city's civi-
lized image. Philadelphia Quakers sometimes risked
their lives, standing between intemperate mobs and
the targets of their anger.

Prominent local Quakers, Unitarians, and others
established Philadelphia as a center of abolitionist
activity prior to the Civil War. It must be noted, however, that most of the city had little heart for that
fight. As the southernmost of America's major northern cities, Philadelphia had many social and economic
ties to the South. Although African-Americans had
settled in the area prior to William Penn's arrival, they
lived segregated lives and most were relegated to me-
nial jobs. When the Civil War came, many of the
city's political elite urged peace and reconciliation
with the South at whatever cost.

Nevertheless, Philadelphia's munitions factories,
foundries, and shipbuilding enterprises prospered dur-

ing the Civil War. And, as the threat of a Confederate invasion of Philadelphia loomed larger, local residents became a little less charitable toward their Southern neighbors. In 1864 a great gathering of Philadelphians pledged support for the Union army hospitals at a benefit fair held at Logan Square. Abraham Lincoln made an appearance at the festival, bonding public sentiment to the Union cause. If nothing else, Philadelphians were proud of their city's role in founding the nation, and they were unwilling to give up on the United States too quickly.

After the war Philadelphia tended its own interests, developing public lands and creating decent housing for working-class families. Thousands of the two- and three-story brick row houses that today characterize Philadelphia neighborhoods were built during the late nineteenth century. The subtly posh red-brick and brownstone Union League building at Broad and Sansom opened its doors in 1865, and a few years later the architecturally fanciful Masonic Temple, built at a cost of one million dollars, went up at Broad and Filbert. As part of the expanding Fairmount Park, the Philadelphia Zoological Gardens opened in 1876—just in time for the national Centennial.

The United States Centennial of 1876 showcased American history and Philadelphia ingenuity. Put together over four years at a cost of nearly $10 million, the exposition dominated much of West Fairmount Park. Its Main Building, a temporary iron-and-glass structure, covered 21 acres. In all, 249 structures dotted the fair grounds. The exhibit at Machinery Hall, where the 56-ton Corliss Engine powered some 800 machines, drew huge crowds. Other popular attractions included Alexander Graham Bell's telephone, the torch and hand of the as-yet-unassembled Statue of Liberty, an elevated train around the grounds, and hundreds of artworks. Aside from President Ulysses Grant and his entourage, the fair attracted Russian

dukes, European monarchs, representatives from
Japan, and a bevy of international socialites.

The Centennial put Philadelphia's industrial might
on display and secured its position as the Iron Age
capital of America. The Pennsylvania and Reading
Railroads serviced area iron and steel mills, and eventually dominated inland transportation on the East
Coast. "Railroading" in one form or another figures
prominently in the roots of many Philadelphia families, and the wealthy suburban commuter enclaves of
the Main Line were actually developed by Pennsylvania Railroad executives. City landmarks include numerous turn-of-the-century railroad stations and
terminals. The Reading Terminal Building at Twelfth
and Market, now being incorporated into a new Convention Center, still houses one of the finest and oldest farmers' markets in the country.

As the city's locomotives chugged and factory furnaces smoked, Philadelphia's commercial community
thrived. John Wanamaker, the father of American
advertising and a legendary retailer, opened his first

"Grand Depot" department store in a renovated
freight depot across from City Hall in 1876, before
rebuilding the expanded store. Gimbel Brothers,
which founded its retail empire in Philadelphia in
1865, opened a store at Eighth and Market. Strawbridge & Clothier—still a thriving local institution—
also built nearby. For its expansion needs, Lit Brothers
took over a full city block of buildings with cast-iron
and terra-cotta facades. The store is now out of business, but the historic structures have been reclaimed
and restored by Mellon Bank.

Perhaps the greatest monument to Philadelphia's
industrial-age bounty and optimism today rises over
the intersection of Broad and Market streets. City Hall
was begun in 1872 and finally completed in 1899 at a
cost of $10 million. The ornate, French Renaissance-
inspired hall covers a 486-by-470-foot site and
includes a central courtyard. Upon its completion the
massive building was the largest single structure in
America. City Hall tower, which stands 548 feet, is
topped by a 37-foot statue of William Penn carved by

Alexander Milne Calder. Until 1987 the top of Penn's hat reigned as the tallest peak in Philadelphia.

Into the Twentieth Century

Philadelphia's rail, shipping, and manufacturing concerns carried the city triumphantly into the twentieth century. The Chamber of Commerce dubbed the city the "Workshop of the World." By 1920, however, some of the region's mass-production manufacturers had already begun to move elsewhere in search of cheaper labor. Commentators of the time characterized the city as conservative to the point of being dull and lacking in innovation. Essayist Agnes Repplier, a Philadelphian, described the city as "Oh, so tepid." Others were less kind. During that period Philadelphia gained a reputation for political corruption which led journalist Lincoln Steffens to dub it the "worst-governed city in the country." Steffens' description of the city as "corrupt and contented" would be resurrected by its detractors for years to come.

Philadelphia's political woes stemmed largely from the city's long-standing traditions of factional, ward-based politics and patronage, and a consensus among the city's upper classes that holding public office was an unseemly occupation. (Given that one of the city's early ward leaders, William McMullin, began his polit-

ical career leading a neighborhood gang called the Killers, it's easy to understand how that idea took hold.) Evidence of vote fraud, kickback schemes, payroll padding, bribery, and outright theft by public officials regularly came to light in the city, with occasional halfhearted calls for reform. Only after the watershed of World War II did Philadelphia finally summon the will and the leadership to scour City Hall.

In 1947 returning war hero Richardson Dilworth—a lawyer from a wealthy Pittsburgh family—ran for mayor on a ticket that included several idealistic, well-born young men. Despite his genteel origins, Dilworth played politics like a contact sport, exposing political corruption, naming names, and rousing public sentiment. He lost the 1947 election, but kept on campaigning under the slogan "Sweep the rascals out!" In 1949, after Dilworth's campaign charges resulted in several arrests, indictments, and a few suicides in the city administration, he ran for city treasurer and supported his friend Joseph Clark for controller. Both won their seats and went on to distinguished public service careers in the city and state. Each served a term as mayor, and the period from 1950 to 1962 ranks as a turning point in Philadelphia municipal government.

Above: This friendly checkers match on 17th Street in 1938 is indicative of the spirit of Philadelphia's tight-knit neighborhoods, where friends and neighbors would gather together for conversation, laughter, and fellowship. Courtesy, Pennsylvania State Archives

Left: Philadelphia has been a hub of political activity since it was founded in the late seventeenth century, and recent times have proved to be no exception. Here, members of the city's 43rd Ward gather to support Bill Green, Jr., the Democratic congressional candidate of 1965. Courtesy, Pennsylvania State Archives

Dilworth and Clark's credits include leading the fight for a new Philadelphia city charter, which was drawn up in 1950 and approved by voters in 1951. Although the zealous reform spirit of the time has subsided considerably, Philadelphia City Hall has since been spared the rampant corruption of the late nineteenth and early twentieth centuries. Observers credit the city charter, which features a strong Civil Service merit system, citizens' commissions, and a decentralized administration, with keeping the bureaucracy in line.

Economically, Philadelphia's industrial base survived the early twentieth century largely by supplying the country's insatiable war machine. The city's shipyards, mills, and factories were kept busy during World War I, and cranked to capacity during World War II. European immigrants and refugees flooded the city, providing a ready supply of labor as Philadelphia men—and in some cases women—signed on for military duty. After World War II a citywide housing shortage and various public works projects kept people employed and the economy rolling through the 1950s.

But time and national economic trends began to take a toll on Philadelphia's once-proud smokestack industries. By the 1970s foreign imports and a nationwide decline in domestic manufacturing had left many Delaware Valley factories idle. Without sufficient business, plant owners lacked the capital to modernize aging, cumbersome facilities. The energy crisis dealt a final blow to many local industries. High fuel and labor costs made the operation of already inefficient factories prohibitive. The era's great sunbelt migration of industry—and jobs—is reflected in Philadelphia population figures: From 1950 to 1980 the city lost nearly 20 percent of its residents.

Social unrest fomented during the postwar years. Like most large urban areas, Philadelphia suffered an exodus of white middle-class families to the suburbs. Neighborhood racial tensions increased, and by the late 1960s race riots broke out in several parts of the city. Nervous citizens turned to then-Police Commissioner Frank Rizzo to calm their fears and quiet their streets. Rizzo's controversial law-and-order tactics made him a repressive caricature in some circles, a hero in others.

The South Philly native's supporters probably outnumbered his detractors; in 1971, and again in 1975, Rizzo was elected mayor of Philadelphia. Passionate in his views, vocal, and visible, Rizzo remained a contro-

versial figure. His public call for federal military assistance during the Bicentennial, ostensibly to protect visiting dignitaries from out-of-town agitators, made would-be tourists uneasy. Twenty million people had been expected to descend on the city in 1976, pumping much-needed revenue into the local economy. When only half that number showed up, many of Philadelphia's business leaders blamed Rizzo's overzealous crowd-control plans. In 1979 Rizzo tried to change the city's Home Rule Charter so he could run for a third term as mayor. Voters defeated that proposition by a two-to-one majority, and William J. Green, Jr., a former U.S. congressman from Philadelphia, was elected to lead city government. Despite a combative relationship with the Philadelphia press, Green proved to be a far more businesslike and less colorful figure than Rizzo. He served one term of office and was succeeded by W. Wilson Goode, a black sharecropper's son who gained recognition as the city's managing director during the Green administration. Elected largely by virtue of his government-as-business posture, Goode reflected the no-nonsense, back-to-work mood of the city.

Goode's record as mayor, however, is blighted by the events of May 13, 1985. On that date Philadelphia police, responding to complaints from residents of threats and harassment by members of a radical group called MOVE, surrounded a fortified West Philadelphia row house occupied by the group. When MOVE members responded to police demands with gunfire, police fired 10,000 rounds at the house in the next 90 minutes, and munitions experts used a helicopter to drop a powerful military explosive on top of the MOVE bunker. In a fateful decision, city, police, and fire officials allowed the fire to burn beyond the ability of firefighters to contain the blaze. Neighbors were evacuated, but once the conflagration had subsided, 61 homes had been destroyed. Eleven MOVE members, including five children, died in the blaze.

Public hearings followed the incident, and an independent commission investigated the role of city officials, police, and firefighters. No criminal charges were filed against anyone involved. Since that time the razed row houses have been rebuilt at city expense, and a sense of community is gradually being restored. Memories of that scorched neighborhood still haunt many Philadelphians. But in spite of the MOVE disaster, Goode was reelected mayor of Philadelphia in

1987, defeating challenger Frank Rizzo, then running on the Republican ticket.

Goode's second term in office has been marked by fiscal crises. Although economists say the Greater Philadelphia area should remain financially secure into the 1990s, the city of Philadelphia has had to face tough economic hurdles. Increased costs for social services and the city court system, combined with lower-than-expected tax revenues and state aid, contributed to a budget deficit of more than $200 million in 1990. The city government's fiscal difficulties were compounded in June 1990 when Standard & Poor's Corporation gave Philadelphia its lowest acceptable bond rating and Moody's Investors Service, Inc., dropped the rating to junk-bond status. These high-risk designations, plus the city's ongoing financial difficulties, scared off a number of potential investors. A planned short-term note sale in September 1990 had to be cancelled, severely limiting Philadelphia's operating funds.

At this writing a consortium of Philadelphia banks has plans to buy a large block of municipal notes. States and local officials have begun mapping out a financial rescue-and-reform program expected to include the creation of a fiscal oversight committee and private sector control over some city services. State aid, spending cuts, and a sales tax increase would round out the package.

Although the city government currently is in difficult financial straits, most observers take an optimistic view of Philadelphia's future. Says one business leader, "This is a temporary situation. The important thing to know is that we're putting together safeguards to keep it from happening again."

Going the distance

Rocky Balboa triumphantly running up the Art Museum steps—that's the image many Americans have of Philadelphia. It's a particularly good metaphor for the modern metropolis. Old Philadelphia—symbolized by the city's classic architecture, culture, art, and educational institutions—endures. Traditional values anchor the city. But at the same time, something new and fresh has evolved from the brawny, industrial backbone of this 300-year old commercial center. Never inclined to give up a fight, Philadelphians have reshaped their old rustbelt haven into a world-class economic contender.

Building on the city's perennial strengths—the port, road and rail access, affordable land, skilled labor, and a high quality of life—Philadelphia boosters have attracted a variety of new high-tech, service, and distribution businesses to the Delaware Valley. There's a building boom going on in Center City as blue-chip corporations stake their claim on this strategic regional hub. New office and research parks unfold across the suburbs. Small manufacturing firms have blossomed and unemployment is at a thirteen-year low. New restaurants, boutiques, clubs, and cabarets enliven city neighborhoods and enrich the local economy.

When asked for a suitable epitaph for his tombstone, Philadelphia native W.C. Fields once quipped, "On the whole, I'd rather be in Philadelphia." That barbed reference has come full circle. People who live in Philadelphia today often can't imagine living anywhere else. No longer cloaked in Quaker gray or recession rust, Philadelphia heads into the future as an exciting, vibrant city.

Historic Elfreth's Alley, situated off Second Street, has remained mostly untouched by modern development and has been continuously occupied since 1700. Photo by Mary Ann Brockman

For nearly 100 years the statue of William Penn atop City Hall tower dominated the Philadelphia skyline. The city founder's image reigned by "common consent": that is, by a general agreement among public and private interests that no new building would rise higher than the crown of Penn's hat—a 548-foot peak.

The unwritten rule harkened to Philadelphia's Quaker roots and its commitment to public interest over private grandeur. Supporters say the custom made Philadelphia a human-scale city, with commercial buildings that topped out at a modest 41 stories. Detractors insist that the height limitation inhibited growth and kept city real estate values artificially depressed. Either way, the "Penn's hat" rule became, in the minds of many, a symbol of Philadelphia's conservatism—some would say, its dearth of individual initiative.

A New Attitude

Today Philadelphia has a new symbol: the 61-story blue glass and granite Liberty Place tower rising high above the Center City skyline. Completed in 1987, the silver-spired structure was conceived by one man, developer Willard G. Rouse III, but it is a private endeavor that makes a strong public statement, signifying a major shift in local attitudes

Home of the nation's first bank, Philadelphia and its surrounding counties now host the headquarters or major regional offices of more than 60 financial institutions. Photo by Rebecca Barger

Reaching for the Sky

toward business and economic growth. "It was the right time for that project," says Rouse. "People either loved us or hated us for pressing the issue, but it was the right time. Before, the city probably couldn't have absorbed anything taller."

Six additional high-rises—each reaching more than 600 feet—have since joined One Liberty Place, giving Philadelphia a bold new profile. The emerging cityscape reflects Greater Philadelphia's commitment to progress, and the region's promising future. According to a 1987 report by Wharton School economists Anita A. Summers and Thomas F. Luce, "the economy of the Philadelphia area is increasingly robust in relation to the nation—its rates of employment growth are higher and its unemployment rates lower than for the United States as a whole."

That trend continues. Philadelphia Industrial Development Corporation (PIDC) figures show that from 1985 to 1988, 61 companies (including a dozen foreign-owned firms) moved operations to the city from other locations. New corporate settlements in the eight-county metropolitan area have added more than 290,000 non-farm jobs to the Greater Philadelphia market over the last 10 years. Those jobs have cut across all standard industrial categories.

Just over a decade ago Greater Philadelphia was in decline, seemingly bound to its heritage of smokestacks and heavy manufacturing. Today the region boasts a thriving, diversified economy. Statistics from local Federal Reserve Bank economists show that manufacturing accounts for only 18 percent of jobs in the area. Business and personal services employment claim 28 percent of the Greater Philadelphia work force, and financial services employment tops 7 percent. Trade industry jobs—a sector targeted for future growth—now stand at 23.2 percent. High-tech employment, both in light manufacturing and in services, is well represented in the area marketplace.

"We're in the middle of the longest, continuing peacetime expansion that this city has ever seen," says Webster M. Christman III, vice president of research and planning at PIDC. "The sheer length of it has made some people nervous. But it's important to note that this hasn't been a one-shot, across-the-board boom. Instead we've had individual business sectors each taking their turn, growing, then holding steady. When one subsector hits a recession, another one compensates, and the overall economy just gets stronger."

Surging international demand for "brain-intensive" products and services bodes well for Greater Philadelphia's future. The city and environs harbor the second highest per-capita assemblage of colleges and universities in the nation. The synergy between area academic institutions and local companies has been a boon both to high-tech start-up firms such as Rabbit Software and such industry giants as Unisys Corp. Biotech, pharmaceutical, and medical services companies like Eastman Pharmaceuticals, Shared Medical Systems, and Mediq, Inc., enjoy close ties to Philadelphia's prestigious medical schools and hospitals.

Executives who have relocated business operations to the area or have founded new ventures here say Philadelphia's enticing mix of business incentives and life-style amenities is what won them over. The metropolitan area offers a good labor climate, a cost-effective business environment, strong government cooperation, available land, an unbeatable transportation network, and a bounty of recreation sites and cultural attractions.

The city's strategic advantages have helped Philadelphia survive hard times, and have contributed to its postindustrial-age renaissance. Current business and economic indicators predict strong, steady growth for the future. After years of struggle, transition, and transformation, the City of Brotherly Love stands ready to stake its claim on the 1990s.

Raising the Rafters

Center City Philadelphia is in the throes of a multibillion-dollar building boom that's changing the face of this historic city. Spurred by the Liberty Place development, a glittering palisade of skyscrapers now borders Market Street West. Two Liberty Place—the 58-story companion to Rouse's standard-bearer—houses the 290-room Ritz Carlton Hotel, a posh retail arcade, and the national headquarters of Cigna Corp.

Facing page: This dramatic look at the changing Philadelphia skyline shows three of the city's new high-rise structures. Clockwise from left are One Penn Tower, Two Liberty Place, and the Provident National Bank building. Photo by Rich Zila

Above: Spurred by Philadelphia's excellent quality of life and strong business climate, corporate relocations have prompted a new infusion of workers to the city and surrounding counties. Photo by Rich Zila

Bell Atlantic's $200-million terraced monolith of coral granite and gray glass overlooks Logan Square, and the partially completed twin towers of Commerce Square at 20th and Market Street house the new offices of Blue Cross of Philadelphia and the future offices of Conrail. Long emulated by America's urban planners, the city is once again setting standards. Architects to the New Philadelphia include a virtual who's who of twentieth-century urban designers: Helmut Jahn; I.M. Pei; Skidmore, Owings & Merrill; Kling-Lindquist.

Philadelphia's glittering new business bowers have given the city a physique well suited to its growing prominence as an East Coast commercial hub. As of 1989 Center City boasted 35 million square feet of office space—an increase of nearly 30 percent over 1984. Proposed new buildings will boost that total to

Facing page: In addition to office space for the city's ever-developing business community, Philadelphia's downtown building boom has provided jobs for thousands of skilled construction workers. Photo by Rich Zila

Left: Local companies find the brainpower generated by the Philadelphia academic community a valuable asset to their challenging business needs. Photo by Rich Zila

45 million by the mid-1990s. A solid, continuing demand for first-class business accomodations in the center of town has fueled the explosion of steel, glass, and granite. Most of the buildings recently completed, or currently under construction, have been pre-leased. Tenant logos now etched into the fabric of the city include SmithKline Beckman, Rohm and Haas, Conrail, Mellon Bank, Pennwalt Corp., and a full slate of other blue-chip companies.

In the wake of expanding corporate enterprise, service businesses have proliferated. Fast-growing consulting firms, data processing centers, and marketing and advertising agencies have reclaimed office suites vacated by upwardly mobile corporate tenants. Once-sedate, prosperous old-line law firms and "big eight" accounting shops have seen their billable hours

Access to high-speed transportation and extensive commuter rail lines makes the Penn Center complex an ideal Center City location for the headquarters of service professionals, whose clients are based throughout the mid-Atlantic region.
Photo by George Adams Jones

swell and personnel rosters multiply.

Not all new business emanates from the city itself. Center City Philadelphia has become the nerve center of a well-muscled regional marketplace. U.S. Census Bureau figures show that from 1980 to 1986, 21,851 companies moved to or began operations in the eight-county metropolitan area. Service professionals headquartered in the city serve clients across the Mid-Atlantic region. Several firms have set up branch offices in Greater Philadelphia's suburban corporate centers, giving employees greater access to suburban clients like Campbell Soup Co., Commodore International, and Subaru of America.

In March 1990 Pennsylvania opened its doors to nationwide banking, adding to Greater Philadelphia's strengths as a regional financial center. According to economists Luce and Summers, the region is a hotbed of finance, insurance, and real estate activity, stoked both by local market growth and by the buoyant economy of the Northeast. Home to the nation's first insurance company and its first bank, Greater Philadelphia now hosts headquarters or major subsidiary offices for more than 60 banks and savings and loans and a half-dozen investment banking houses. Most major insurance carriers in the U.S. are represented here, and a few, like Cigna, Penn Mutual, and Reliance, direct international operations from the area.

Philadelphia's reputation on the world financial scene has been enhanced by the aggressive innovations of the Philadelphia Stock Exchange—the oldest securities exchange in the U.S. Known for its timely introduction of creative new products, the exchange is oft-courted as a potential merger candidate by other major trading posts. Foreign currency options trading originated in Philadelphia, as did cash index participations (CIPs). The exchange operates from 4:30 a.m. to 10:00 p.m., giving it the longest trading day of any exchange in the world.

New Faces for Old Places

Regional business growth has brought fresh young faces to Philadelphia. Lured by job opportunities and Philadelphia's relaxed, yet sophisticated demeanor, these bright, dynamic transplants have teamed up with an assertive new generation of city natives. Together—working with existing civic groups and city agencies—they have given Philadelphia an infectious can-do air. Whereas the city once embraced stodginess like a badge of honor, it now roars with new ideas, lively diversions, and creative enterprise.

Philadelphia's bricks-and-mortar transformation stands as a testament to the power of new blood and well-invested capital.

Of course, there's an old adage that says the last person to move to the neighborhood is the most vocal about preserving its character. Philadelphia natives have always loved the city's historic monuments and its graceful architectural treasures—even if they've been somewhat slow to fund restoration. Newcomers to the city, on the other hand, have been positively passionate about renovating these landmarks. In the shadows of frenzied skyscraper construction, Philadelphia's colonial and Victorian gems are being reborn.

Visitors and suburban commuters enjoy the benefits of this "face-lift fever" whenever they step onto the platform at Philadelphia's grand 30th Street Station railroad terminal. The 50-year-old neoclassical structure recently underwent $75 million in renovations, including the addition of underground parking, shops, a food court, and refurbished office space. A proposal to develop 66 acres of air rights adjoining the site, just west of Center City, could spark the next wave of new construction in town. According to plans, the spruced-up terminal would serve as the centerpiece of a 30-million-square-foot entertainment-residential-office complex.

Perhaps the most celebrated restoration in the city, Mellon Independence Center, stretches across a full block of Market Street East. Formerly the home of Lit Brothers department store, the complex consists of 15 buildings sporting terra-cotta and cast-iron facades, all built between 1859 and 1918. The store closed in 1977, leaving the site—and an entire city block—deserted. Several developers attempted to revive the complex, but abandoned the idea of restoration as too costly and the hope of finding tenants as too slim. As the site became more and more blighted, it very nearly

Above: The Philadelphia Stock Exchange is the oldest securities exchange in the United States. Frenzied trading at this 1900 Market Street facility can be observed by the public during regular work hours. Photo by David H. Wells

Left: The creation of Mellon Independence Center at Market Place East in 1987 rescued the old Lit Brothers' department store complex, which had stood vacant for nearly 10 years. Characterized by elegant marble floors, cast-iron facades, and many other details from an earlier era, the buildings were converted into mixed-use office and retail space. Photo by Linda Zila

succumbed to the wrecker's ball despite protests from preservationists. In 1987, in an eleventh-hour reprieve, U.S. Managers Realty (a California-based developer) spent $95 million converting the buildings into a mixed-use office and retail complex. Their heroics were made possible through Mellon Bank, then new to Philadelphia, which put up money for the project and leased 650,000 square feet of space in the buildings for its computer and research operations. Today the old Lit Brothers complex looks like an ornate wedding cake, the centerpiece of the Market Street East retail district. The city recently spent $14 million improving that section of Market Street, adding new curbs, brick sidewalks, and decorative light fixtures, as well as repaving much of the street from City Hall to Independence Mall.

A few blocks west of Lit's, John Wanamaker's department store—which was dedicated by President William Howard Taft in 1911—recently got an overhaul. Wanamaker's store now occupies the first five floors of the 12-story building; the top floors have been converted to office space. The store's vaulted Grand Court is now a four-story atrium at the center of the building.

Across from Independence Mall, The Curtis Center has been carved from the former offices of the Curtis Publishing Company. Known by most Philadelphians for the exquisite 49-foot Tiffany glass mosaic in the lobby, the building was intended to be a corporate showplace for Cyrus H.K. Curtis' publishing empire. Built in 1916, the classically designed structure features an entrance colonnade of 32-foot Vermont marble columns, Palladian windows, and massive bronze doors. The refurbished building retains the original architectural grace notes—like corner offices with Italian walnut and hand-carved oak paneling—and adds a few modern amenities. The old loading dock has been transformed into a lush atrium anchored by a seven-color marble fountain, surrounded by shops and offices.

The Bellevue Stratford Hotel, a sentimental favorite among locals, has been renovated and put back into service as a luxury hotel-cum-office complex. Kings and presidents stayed at the Bellevue during its reign as the grand hotel of Philadelphia. Now managed by Cunard Hotels, the 173-room Hotel Atop the Bellevue attracts corporate chiefs and heirs to the boardroom. The hotel occupies the top seven

Facing page: The view from Logan Circle clearly shows Philadelphia's new direction as symbolized by its expanding skyline. Long the tallest structure in Center City, the statue of William Penn atop City Hall now stands dwarfed by modern skyscrapers. Photo by James Blank

The gracious grande dame of Philadelphia department stores, John Wanamaker's has long served residents as a favorite shopping institution and a gathering place for friends. Photo by Rebecca Barger

Above: Designers of the Hotel Atop the Bellevue, Sara Tomerlin Lee and Roger Danforth of Tom Lee Limited helped to restore the 1906 Beaux-Arts styling of the Bellevue Stratford Hotel. They retained many of the hotel's original features, including the stunning grand staircase pictured here. Photo by Rich Zila

Right: According to *Philadelphia* magazine's "Best of Philly" issue, Founders Restaurant in the Hotel Atop the Bellevue offers the best view in town. Photo by Rich Zila

Facing page: When the Curtis Center was created out of the old Curtis Publishing Company building, architects Oldham and Slez turned the former loading dock into the Fountain Court. Now a magnificent 12-story atrium with a vaulted glass roof, the Court is in constant demand for cultural and charitable events, and also provides a serene haven from the hectic work day. Photo by Rich Zila

floors of the 19-story building, which was completed in 1904. Lower floors house exclusive retail shops and public rooms, with 10 floors of offices in between. Developers put $150 million into the project, restoring the hotel's original ballrooms—rooms that held many of the city's society weddings and gala receptions—and instituting such contemporary niceties as tea service and a fitness center.

Convention City of the Future

While Philadelphia wins kudos as a great place to live and work, it's also gaining stature as a fine place to visit. Some 3 million people tour the city each year, taking in historic sights and sampling the city's acclaimed restaurants, museums, and musical events.

So far, only a small percentage of visitors come to Philadelphia as part of a convention assembly. According to Tom Muldoon, president of the Philadelphia Convention and Visitors Bureau, that situation should change dramatically after 1992—the date scheduled for the unveiling of the new Pennsylvania Convention Center. After years of political and financial wrangling, construction on the $500-million, 450,000-square-foot facility is under way. The state-of-

the-art meeting and exhibition facility will rise above and behind historic Reading Terminal on Market Street at North 12th Street. The site is within walking distance of Independence Mall and the Delaware Riverfront, as well as Center City restaurants, theaters, and office towers.

The Convention Center promises to attract 700,000 convention delegates a year to the city, spurring construction of several new hotels to accomodate the surge—including a 1,000-room hotel adjacent to the center. The 140-room Omni Hotel at Fourth and Chestnut streets—in the heart of Society Hill—opened in 1990, as did the Ritz Carlton at Two Liberty Place. The recent additions augment the city's existing community of first-class hostelries, including The Four Seasons, The Rittenhouse, The Wyndam Franklin Plaza, and the Hershey Hotel.

From History to Haute Couture

The historic sights of Philadelphia beckon tourists and schoolchildren, but these days many locals prefer to peruse more contemporary landmarks. Highbrow boutique shopping has arrived in Philadelphia, and after years of languishing behind other East Coast markets,

Its strategic location in the city's Historic District makes the Sheraton Society Hill a popular choice for tourists and business travelers. Photo by David H. Wells

the city has established itself as a sophisticated retail mecca. Suburban shopping malls, anchored by Bloomingdales, Macy's, Saks, or Strawbridge & Clothier, ring Center City, while soignee community shopping districts attract customers from across the metropolitan area. Yet the city still maintains a vibrant, broad-based downtown retail industry.

Thirteen percent of the buying power of the United States lives within a 100-mile radius of Philadelphia. The improving fortunes of the economy in the Northeast have given this concentrated consumer mass a more powerful voice, and have contributed to a flurry of store openings in Center City. Over the last decade Ralph Lauren has debuted at the Bellevue, and Tiffany & Co. have unveiled a branch store on Walnut Street. Near Rittenhouse Square, Ann Taylor, Burberry, Laura Ashley, and Borders Bookstore have moved in, keeping company with the venerable Nan Duskin store at the Rittenhouse Hotel. The shops at Liberty Place on Chestnut Street include a Coach leather goods store, Godiva Chocolatier, and Joseph A. Bank Clothiers.

In addition to celebrated new arrivals, Philadelphia boasts the largest urban shopping mall in the country,

Gallery I & II. Located on Market Street next to the Convention Center and Reading Terminal Market (one of the oldest farmers' markets in the country), the Gallery complex offers upscale department stores as well as clothing boutiques, gift shops, drugstores, pet stores—all the staples of an enclosed mall, including two food courts. Access to Pennsylvania suburban commuter trains, city subways, and high-speed trains to New Jersey can be found on the lower level of the Gallery. Mellon Independence Center, across Eighth Street, offers additional boutiques and a Conran's home furnishings store.

A few blocks south of the Gallery on Sansom Street lies Jewelers' Row, an eclectic bazaar of wholesale and retail jewelry shops where all things bright, beautiful, and sometimes gaudy are bought and sold. Pine Street harbors Philadelphia's antiques district, where the trash and treasures of an earlier age are sold from townhouse storefronts. Although "steals" in early Americana are rare these days, Philadelphia's antiques dealers do stock a wide variety of fine eighteenth- and nineteenth-century furnishings, housewares, and decorative items, often at fair prices.

South Street, at the border of Center City and the

Rittenhouse Square provides a sophisticated setting for the elegant boutiques that have opened for the shopping pleasure of Philadelphia residents in recent years. Photo by David H. Wells

gentrified Queen Village neighborhood, has become Main Street to Philadelphia's avant garde. Storefront windows display the sublime to the surreal; fine art galleries and one-of-a-kind designer jewelry shops sit sandwiched between health food stores and purveyors of punk paraphernalia. On sunny weekend afternoons browsers here fall into an informal parade with well-groomed mothers and toddlers, spike-haired teens, and aging hippies all contributing to the tableau. At night the ambiance is more like a high-voltage street fair, with people spilling out of restaurants and clubs to join the always-in-progress party.

Keeping Pace With Progress

In spite of Greater Philadelphia's bustling regional economy and revived urban landscape, the city still faces a number of challenges. Growing businesses and city residents demand consistent, high-quality public services. Finding ways to fund and upgrade such services without overtaxing, and ultimately stunting, economic growth remains a problem. Like most older U.S. cities, Philadelphia faces infrastructure problems: potholed roadbeds, crumbling bridges, a well-worn subway system. Rebuilding the city's arteries will be costly and inconvenient. Perhaps most vexing, city leaders are still trying to come to grips with Philadelphia's trash disposal problem. Landfills across the northeast are filled to capacity, no

new sites have opened up, and proposed local incineration schemes have met with fierce resistance from residents. No easy solutions appear likely.

But these are the problems of an evolving, thriving urban area. Ten years ago much of Philadelphia's central business district was decayed and neglected. Seedy taverns and X-rated moviehouses lined the streets where glistening skyscrapers now stand. Worrying about potholes seemed frivolous in the face of layoffs and unemployment.

Today Philadelphia fairly beams with pride of place. Civic groups, local companies, and government agencies are working together to maintain the city's newfound momentum. If there's a greater awareness of Philadelphia's problems, it's because there's a greater will to find solutions. The twenty-first century holds great promise for America's hometown.

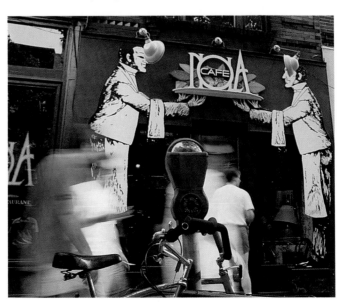

Above: John Christaldi of Albert Maranca Antiques, a Pine Street shop that specializes in European antiques from the eighteenth and nineteenth centuries, proudly poses with a selection of the store's fine wares. Photo by Rich Zila

Facing page: The Philadelphia Bourse opened in 1895 to house a grain and stock exchange. Now a National Historic Landmark, the handsome sandstone building has been restored to become home to four levels of specialty shops and restaurants. Photo by David H. Wells

Left: A bohemian atmosphere prevails in the South Street district with its eclectic mix of avant-garde shops, galleries, and trendy eateries. Photo by Rich Zila

The lights of the Benjamin Franklin Bridge dance across the Delaware River like strobing bulbs on a giant marquee. The first suspension bridge in the world to be accented with computer-controlled spotlights, the Ben Franklin connects bustling Center City Philadelphia with its New Jersey neighbors. The illuminated arch welcomes shipping traffic to the largest freshwater port in the country, and it presides over one of the most extensive waterfront redevelopment projects in the United States.

Since the founding of Philadelphia the wide, deep Delaware River has been the lifeblood of regional commerce. Trading ties between Delaware Valley merchants and foreign commodities dealers have been cemented at its docks. River currents powered Greater Philadelphia's rise as an East Coast manufacturing center. And in turn this industrial and trade bounty spurred development of road and rail lines leading from Philadelphia to all points north, south, and west.

The Delaware River still supports Greater Philadelphia commerce and industry. More than 3,000 ships and 70 million tons of cargo pass through the Ports of Philadelphia each year. Industrial giants like Rohm and Haas Company, Scott Paper, and ICI Americas rely on river water for

The towering Benjamin Franklin Bridge, which spans the mighty Delaware River, welcomes ships of all shapes and sizes to the largest freshwater port in the country. Photo by Rich Zila

Gateway to America

manufacturing processes and shipping. Smokestacks, crude oil tanks, and coal storage bins dot the waterfront from Trenton to the Delaware Bay, evidence of Greater Philadelphia's continued industrial strength.

But like every other facet of this thriving metropolitan area, the 20-mile riverfront has begun to change to reflect the diversified local economy. By the turn of the century more than one billion dollars will have been invested in recreation, residential, retail, and office properties along the river in Philadelphia and Camden, New Jersey. The Delaware River, which inspired not a few early American traders and industrialists to seek their fortunes, has become muse to the many.

The Central Waterfront

The Great Plaza of Penn's Landing extends from Market to South streets along the Delaware River in Philadelphia. Unveiled in 1976, this sculpted waterfront park and outdoor amphitheater serves as front porch to the city's historic Society Hill and Independence Mall neighborhoods. For visitors the park is a welcoming entry to the city; for natives it's a place to stop and sit, socialize, and watch the passing flotilla of ships and pleasure boats. Cruise ships dock at Penn's Landing, as do occasional U.S. Navy vessels. Several times a year thousands of people flock to this 37-acre common to attend concerts, ethnic festivals, and cultural events.

City planners and real estate mavens have long recognized the aesthetic appeal of the Delaware River waterfront. As early as 1965 plans for development of the central riverfront area included the construction of residential and multiuse buildings, plus relocation of docks and port-related facilities to areas north and south of Center City. A major imports distribution facility was moved from Society Hill to South Philadelphia, freeing both the land and nearby piers for other uses. State-funded landfill projects in the early 1970s shored up the waterfront and made development along Penn's Landing possible.

In spite of these early moves, realizing the potential of riverfront development in Philadelphia has been a slow, painstaking process. Only in recent years has the city found the economic strength and civic clout needed to bring such a massive, multifaceted project to the bricks-and-mortar phase. "Philadelphia has been a little slower than some cities in getting its act together on the waterfront," says Dick Huffman, a partner of Wallace, Roberts and Todd, a Philadelphia architecture and planning firm involved in numerous waterfront redevelopment efforts, including projects in Baltimore, New Orleans, and Norfolk. "But false starts aside, we've got some exciting things happening along the river now. At least half a dozen major projects are being implemented, and a few others are in the works."

As a consultant on several phases of Greater Philadelphia's riverfront revival, Huffman believes the evolving landscape will become a major regional at-

traction. "The port is consolidating, and that changes the nature of the central waterfront," he explains. "The river is cleaner, and more attractive for recreation. Tourists are drawn to the riverfront today, and as development continues that area will make a strong contribution to the local economy. Penn's Landing will be the center of a major entertainment center, drawing both area residents and tourists into the city."

The Central Waterfront stretches south from Spring Garden Street, just north of Center City, to Washington Avenue. Five blocks inland from the heart of this corridor lies Independence Mall and the city's historic district. By 1992 visitors to

Redevelopment along the banks of the Delaware River has created new recreation areas for the city's residents. A kite-flying expedition is an occasion for smiles at Penn's Treaty Park. Photo by Linda Zila

Independence Hall will be able to walk east from the park, stop to admire various landmarks and examples of early American architecture along the way, and stroll on to the river, where—against a majestic backdrop—music, films, shopping, hotels, and fine dining await them.

Plans for the Central Waterfront include a $300-million development at Washington and Delaware avenues that will include retail, office, residential, and hotel facilities on a 12-acre pier site. The project is a joint venture between the Sheetmetal Workers Union Local 19, which maintains its headquarters on the waterfront, and the Allentown-based Hampton Real Estate Group. Dubbed Liberty Landing, the development will feature townhouses, a 280-slip marina, and a yacht club. Moving north along the water, Philadelphia developer Asbell & Associates is building Portside, a luxury condominium, on piers 30 through 36. Docked at Pier 28, the 110-room Regalleon, a one-time oceangoing ship turned floating hotel, will serve tourists seeking a little nautical hospitality. Above the Regalleon the Penn's Landing development begins with the 15,000-square-foot Chart House restaurant. Construction on a $800-million mixed-use retail, entertainment, and convention hotel

Right: Recent environmental efforts have resulted in a cleaner Delaware River, which continues to be enjoyed by residents and visitors alike. Photo by Rich Zila

Facing page: Colorful tugboats and majestic cruise ships ply the waters of the Delaware River. Photo by George Adams Jones

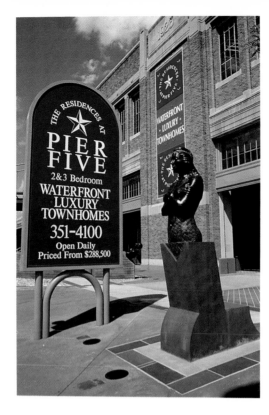

The Residence at Pier Five is a new 273-unit apartment and condominium complex that offers panoramic views of the Delaware River. Photo by Robert J. Salgado

complex surrounding the Great Plaza has begun under the auspices of The Welcome Partnership.

On piers 3 and 5 north, water-loving tenants and property owners have already staked their claim on a 273-unit apartment and condo complex that includes a marina and restaurants. Above that development the Comfort Inn at Penn's Landing has been serving up river views to budget-minded tourists since 1988. The Philadelphia Marine Trade Center, built over piers 12 to 24, includes a marine trade center, boat service and storage facilities, restaurants, and a marina. Hotels and parking garages are expected to rise up on property near the center.

Cooperation between public agencies and private

developers involved in Philadelphia's riverfront renaissance has helped ensure that ambitious new projects complement one another, and that the waterfront emerges as an integrated business and entertainment center. Riverwalk, a two-mile promenade at the water's edge, will span the complex, connecting individual attractions and framing the mise-en-scene.

Camden

Directly across from Penn's Landing in Camden, New Jersey, a $500-million waterfront redevelopment project has become the cornerstone of Camden's revitalization. The Cooper's Ferry Development will unfold along 90 acres of waterfront from the Ben Franklin Bridge to the South Jersey Port Corporation facilities at Beckett Street. The total project is expected to take 10 years to complete.

Phase One, which includes the $42-million New Jersey State Aquarium—an aquatic exhibition center expected to draw one million visitors a year—will be opened by 1991. The $10-million Ulysses S. Wiggins Waterfront Park, a green oasis along the edge of the city's industrial belt, opened to the public in 1985. Planned for construction nearby is a 300-room hotel and convention center, a 250-boat marina, and an 80,000-square-foot festival market. Luxury apartments have been planned for Cooper's Ferry, as well as more than one million square feet of office space. An International Trade Center, designed to centralize govern-

The Benjamin Franklin Bridge provides a striking backdrop for the boats moored at the Pier 12 marina. Photo by Linda Zila

ment and private offices engaged in maritime businesses, will be located on the Camden waterfront.

Corporate support for Camden's revitalization, along with a good measure of state and federal aid, has made the Cooper's Ferry project possible. Campbell Soup Co. and RCA (now owned by General Electric) have long-standing ties to the community. A stained-glass rendering of Nipper, the dog featured in RCA's "His Master's Voice" logo, graces the tower of one of RCA's original plants located just off the river in downtown Camden. Campbell Soup was founded in Camden, and has committed to anchoring a new office tower at the Cooper's Ferry site. Along with the International Trade Center and the New Jersey State Aquarium, the new Campbell offices will bring year-round pedestrian traffic to Cooper's Ferry. That infusion of shoppers, workers, and visitors to the

once-deserted Camden waterfront is expected to boost the city's fortunes and showcase new investment in the area. Negotiations are under way to build a sports and entertainment arena at Cooper's Ferry, further enhancing Camden's proud new profile.

The Camden waterfront facilities will be linked to Penn's Landing in Philadelphia by a ferry, which is expected to begin operation in 1991. Within minutes, and with minimum hassle, visitors to Philadelphia's historic district will be able to peruse Cooper's Ferry shops and tour the New Jersey State Aquarium. South Jersey residents can park in Camden, dine in Philadelphia, and go home without braving city traffic. More important, the ferry link will turn the Delaware River into a bond, rather than a boundary, between two mutually dependent activity centers. "The waterfront really belongs to the region, and not to any one juris-

Ulysses S. Wiggins Waterfront Park in Camden offers a spectacular view of the Philadelphia skyline across the Delaware River. Photo by Linda Zila

Above: These youngsters enjoy the redeveloped Camden waterfront. Photo by Rich Zila

Left: Although now owned by General Electric and occupied by its Camden Aerospace Division, this tower still proudly displays the stained-glass RCA logo of Nipper the dog. Photo by Mary Ann Brockman

Facing page: The stately Benjamin Franklin Bridge is currently the only link connecting Philadelphia and Camden, but ferry service between the two ports is scheduled to begin in 1991. Photo by Robert J. Salgado

The Packer Avenue Terminal is one of the modern bulk and cargo facilities operated by the Ports of Philadelphia. Photo by George Adams Jones

diction," says Dick Huffman. "With the ferry in place, Penn's Landing and Cooper's Ferry will mature into one unified development."

The Ports of Philadelphia

From the time William Penn allocated lots to First Purchasers, frontage along the Delaware River in Philadelphia has been intensely coveted real estate. Early settlers crowded their businesses and homes within sight of the docks, hoping the brisk, growing commerce of the port would fuel their personal economies.

Greater Philadelphia's port business is less visible from Center City these days, but it's no less viable. The Ports of Philadelphia—including terminals in Southern New Jersey, Wilmington, and Philadelphia—boast some of the most modern bulk and general cargo facilities in the country. An ongoing multimillion-dollar site improvement program has ensured that Greater Philadelphia will remain competitive with other East Coast shipping centers into the next century.

Located at the center of the Northeast megalopolis that stretches from Boston to Norfolk, the Ports of Philadelphia give shippers one-day overland access to 26 percent of the U.S. population. Close to 90 percent of general cargo arriving at the port is carried to inland

destinations by truck. North-south Interstate 95, east-west Interstate 76, and the Pennsylvania and New Jersey turnpikes are all within 10 minutes of the ports, giving quick access to inland-bound cargo. Delaware River port terminals also have on-site Conrail ramps and access to the CSX rail system. An intermodal rail facility, planned for the Greenwich Rail Yard in South Philadelphia, will allow direct transfer of ocean-borne cargo to and from western destinations. Warehousing and open storage space is available to accomodate a wide range of goods. The ports host more than 32 million cubic feet of temperature-controlled storage facilities.

Enhancing the efficiency of the ports without unduly increasing costs to port users has been a primary objective of port agencies. In 1989 the Ports of Philadelphia Maritime Exchange, a nonprofit organization representing port-related businesses, installed a computerized cargo tracking service linking shippers, Delaware River terminals, and the U.S. Customs Service. Called Transport Release Automated Cargo Status, or TRACS, the system eliminates much of the paperwork and legwork involved in monitoring the progress of goods moving through the port and through customs. Port officials say TRACS offers state-of-the-art automation to port users. And, since logging on requires nothing more complicated than a

Left: The Ports of Philadelphia provide a vital link in the nation's vast distribution network. Photo by Rich Zila

Below: A deep freeze of 20 degrees below zero maintains frozen cargo at the Philadelphia Distribution Center while it is being routed through the Ports of Philadelphia. Photo by Rich Zila

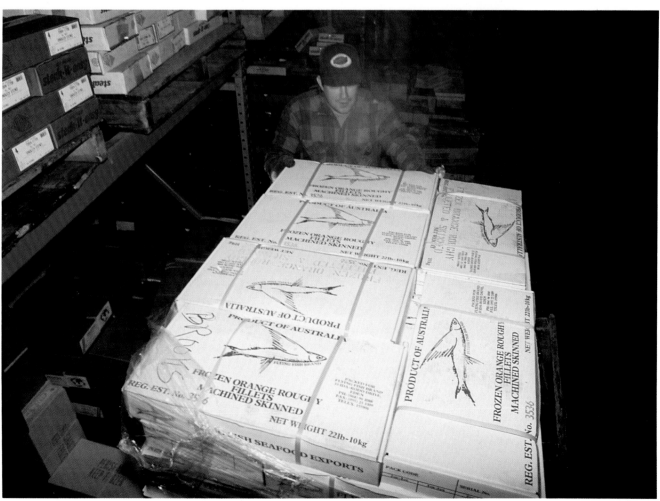

personal computer and a modem, small firms can afford to share in TRACS' advantages along with their more well-heeled peers.

International Breadbasket

Ships arrive and depart from the Greater Philadelphia docks laden with raw materials, pricey consumer goods, industrial products, and delicate foodstuffs. The ports are the second largest handlers of forest products in the country, and the complex serves the second largest oil-refining region in the U.S. Coal, iron ore, scrap metal, and automobiles move through the ports, as do meats, fruits, and vegetables.

Most of the Chilean fruit entering the United States arrives through the Ports of Philadelphia. Because fresh fruits and vegetables spoil rapidly, Greater Philadelphia's close proximity to major population centers makes the ports an ideal transfer point for these products. The Tioga Fruit Terminal and Tioga II in North Philadelphia handle 50 percent of the Chilean produce traffic on the Delaware River. The Port of Wilmington receives frozen orange juice from Brazil and seasonal fruits and vegetables from Morocco and New Zealand, and is the largest U.S. import center for Central and South American bananas. Other Delaware Valley terminals receive meats from Argentina, Australia, and New Zealand. The Ports of Philadelphia are the largest American import center for cocoa products from Africa and South and Central America. Nearly 400,000 tons of cocoa beans were off-loaded in Greater Philadelphia in 1988.

Serving the Ports of Philadelphia, as well as local food retailers and consumers, is the Philadelphia Food Distribution Center. Originally located in the Society Hill neighborhood of Center City, the Food Distribution Center was moved in 1959 to a 380-acre site at the eastern edge of South Philadelphia. Considered the prototype of the modern, integrated wholesale food market, the FDC provides a centralized location for companies engaged in the wholesale manufacture, marketing, distribution, and warehousing of food, beverages, and agricultural and horticultural products. It employs 5,000 people. The FDC's efficient operation and easy access to the port, railways, and major Philadelphia thoroughfares guarantee Delaware Valley consumers a continuous supply of fresh, relatively inexpensive food products.

Cars, Coal, Crude, and Paper

The Ports of Philadelphia provide many Americans with edible luxuries: year-round grapes and bananas, off-season melons and berries, exotic kiwis and mangoes. But the complex also serves as a conduit for many other less glamorous necessities. The ports accept imports of more paper products each year than any other Atlantic shipping center. In 1988 the region handled 719,000 tons of paper. A proposed $11-mil-

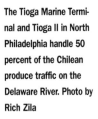

The Tioga Marine Terminal and Tioga II in North Philadelphia handle 50 percent of the Chilean produce traffic on the Delaware River. Photo by Rich Zila

lion paper warehouse will increase the ports' capacity for the future. The South Jersey Port Corporation terminals in Camden are the country's top receivers of imported plywood. Lumber from Europe arrives at several Delaware River terminals. And exportable forest products, including wood and finished lumber, leave the Ports of Philadelphia bound for construction projects in Europe and the Far East. As in Philadelphia's industrial heyday, coal and steel continue to be commodities important to the ports.

The Port of Wilmington is America's biggest point of export for automobiles, with some 60,000 American-made cars shipped to the Middle East each year. Wilmington also receives more Volkswagens headed for U.S. markets than any other port. The Pasha Auto Terminal in Philadelphia handles a broad range of import and export motor vehicles.

Regrouping for the Future

The Ports of Philadelphia have an extended family of committed stakeholders, overseers, and governing agencies. The World Trade Division of the Delaware River Port Authority markets the ports to foreign and domestic shippers, while the Philadelphia Regional Port Authority, the South Jersey Port Corporation, and the Port of Wilmington nurture traffic and facilities in their own backyards. The Philadelphia Industrial Development Corporation monitors the use and development of waterfront property. Through various public and private agreements and contracts, the shipping terminals and piers of the Delaware River are tied to the municipalities and states where individual facilities are located.

Although port-related agencies readily cooperate in matters concerning promotion and development of the ports, the labyrinth of bureaucracy surrounding the complex has occasionally interfered with the efficient management of this resource. Plans are currently under way to remedy that situation by creating one regional authority with responsibility for port marketing and management. In addition, a trust fund has been proposed to maintain the infrastructure of the ports. "These initiatives are designed to enhance Philadelphia's competitive position as an international port," says William B. McLaughlin III, spokesman for the Philadelphia Regional Port Authority. "Right now we're a strong niche port, but not really unified. Steps are being taken to change that."

Robert Damento, Jr., and crew take a break from the day's work at the Brooks Provisions facility at the Ports of Philadelphia. Photo by Rich Zila

he grand concourse of Amtrak's 30th Street Station in Philadelphia vaults nearly 100 feet from the building's marble floors. Ten 18-foot bronze and glass chandeliers hang from the polychrome ceiling, casting a soft light on the travertine walls. At the east end of the great hall stands an imposing travelers' icon: a muscular, cast-bronze angel lifting a fallen soldier to his rest. The towering statue was commissioned as a memorial to the Pennsylvania Railroad workers who died in World War II.

The station was conceived and built to be a national showplace for the Pennsylvania Railroad. Constructed during the line's heyday, the Neoclassical structure stands 637 feet wide, 327 feet deep, and 116 feet high. Its limestone facade and columned porticos grace the west bank of the Schuylkill River directly across from Center City. Begun in 1929 and completed in 1934, the station is at once a monument to the grand promise of the railroads and a memorial to an ironbound, industrial-age America. Philadelphia reigned as a smokestack capital of commerce during those years, and 30th Street Station was its seat of power.

Greater Philadelphia no longer lives by the roar of well-stoked factory furnaces, but the region's economic fortunes are still linked to transporta-

In 1973 the Regional Rail Reorganization Act created Conrail from the assets of six bankrupt railroads in order to preserve vital rail freight service on the East Coast. Photo by Rich Zila

Crossroads
of
Commerce

tion. The 30th Street Station now serves as operations headquarters for the National Railroad Passenger Corporation, commonly known as Amtrak, and some 3.5 million people pass through its doors every year. It is the second busiest station in the Amtrak system, with more than 65 trains pulling through every day.

A separate, 272-mile commuter rail network connects the station with terminals in Philadelphia, Wilmington, Trenton, and all major suburbs within a 50-mile radius of Center City. A high-speed line links the station with Philadelphia International Airport, where more than 1,000 flights arrive and depart every day. Highway traffic in the metropolitan area flows along several major east-west and north-south arteries, including the Pennsylvania and New Jersey Turnpikes. More than 100 trucking lines serve businesses in the Greater Philadelphia area.

Combined with the Ports of Philadelphia, this extensive air and ground transportation system sustains the city's current manufacturing base and is the lifeblood of the region's burgeoning service economy. Sales and distribution offices here can quickly tap into a large, lucrative marketing area. More than 20 per-

cent of the U.S. population—and 25 percent of the country's disposable income—resides within a 300-mile radius of Philadelphia. New York, Baltimore, and Washington are all within three hours' drive of Center City.

Greater Philadelphia's central location on the Northeast Corridor and easy access to transporation lines have drawn new businesses to the area. The combined economic clout of start-up companies, new regional operations, and expanding local firms has spurred dramatic growth in several suburban counties. Attracted by job opportunities, a strong cadre of professional, technical, and managerial workers has relocated to the area, bolstering the already broad-based labor force of Greater Philadelphia. With its vast public transportation network, access to urban and suburban work sites, and varied housing options, the Philadelphia metropolitan area appeals to many two-career couples who need the advantages of a large, diverse job market.

But transportation is more than just a resource in Greater Philadelphia. It remains one of the region's primary industries. Over the last 25 years, as economic

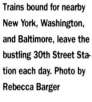

Trains bound for nearby New York, Washington, and Baltimore, leave the bustling 30th Street Station each day. Photo by Rebecca Barger

upheavals have changed the complexion of transportation in the Northeast Corridor, Greater Philadelphia continues to draw strength from the confluence of its crossroads.

The Iron Phoenix

The Pennsylvania and Reading railroads shaped Philadelphia's early industrial profile and ultimately gave the city much of its present-day character. The railroads linked iron-age manufacturers and shippers with the coal mines, iron ore, and cornfields north, south, and west of the city. Ornate Pullman cars carried affluent business barons and their families from the city to suburban mansions along the Main Line. Interstate travelers pursuing business or pleasure pulled in and out of 30th Street Station, and middle-class commuters rode the Reading from Germantown and Jenkintown to the neo-Venetian Reading Terminal on Market Street. During World War II easy access to interstate rail transportation helped Philadelphia win about one billion dollars in defense contracts.

Such glory days for the railroads ended rather abruptly after the war. Completion of the U.S. interstate highway system in 1966 hastened the decline.

Above: Philadelphia commuters are served by a system of subways, els, buses, and streetcars run by the Southeastern Pennsylvania Transit Authority (SEPTA). Photo by Rebecca Barger

Left: Arriving passengers at Philadelphia International Airport can get to any Center City rail terminal aboard convenient and speedy SEPTA trains. Photo by Rich Zila

Headquartered in Philadelphia, Conrail employs some 12,000 people in the tri-state region of Pennsylvania, New Jersey, and Delaware. Photo by Rich Zila

From 1950 to 1970 the railroads' share of total U.S. freight shipments dropped from 56 percent to less than 40 percent. Rail passenger service, the primary mode of transportation prior to World War II, dropped to less than 4 percent of intercity travel by 1958. In Greater Philadelphia, where the economy already had been flattened by the quieting of defense plants, the not-so-gradual demise of the railroads was viewed with considerable gloom.

Industrial migration to the Sunbelt states began shortly after the war and accelerated with the rising costs of labor and fuel in the Northeast. Eventually this erosion of freight customers sounded the last call for the established railroads. In an eleventh-hour effort

to preserve East Coast rail service, the 122-year-old Pennsylvania Railroad merged with the New York-based Central line in 1968. The resulting carrier, Penn Central, went bankrupt two and a half years later. The long-troubled Reading Railroad filed its own bankruptcy petition in 1971, as did several smaller regional lines. Court-appointed trustees of the bankrupt railroads determined that there was no way the trains could operate profitably; costs were too high for the amount of freight carried. They recommended liquidation.

In spite of the railroads' unprofitable balance sheets, much of the U.S. at that time still depended on

Forging agreements with other railroads across the country, Conrail has instituted door-to-door shipping and full-service distribution networks for many of the nation's leading industries. Photo by Rich Zila

rail service. In 1972 it was estimated that a Northeast rail shutdown would threaten half the manufacturing plants in the U.S., along with hundreds of thousands of jobs. To prevent economic chaos, the U.S. government stepped in with a massive reorganization effort designed to maintain Northeast rail service and nurse a pared-down system back to health. The Consolidated Rail Corporation—Conrail—was the result of that government intervention.

Headquartered in Philadelphia, Conrail now employs some 12,000 people in the tri-state Pennsylvania, New Jersey, and Delaware area. Created by the Regional Rail Reorganization Act of 1973, Conrail was melded together from the assets of six bankrupt railroads. For several years the amalgamated line fared little better than its predecessors. The government invested $3.2 billion in Conrail between 1976 and 1981, and in 1981 the Reagan administration recommended that the line be broken up and sold off.

Stanley Crane, a former Southern Railway executive and Conrail's chief executive officer from 1981 to 1988, notes that Conrail was always "a prime target" of Reagan budget slashers. A piecemeal liquidation of the line would have ended Philadelphia's reign as a Northeast rail hub, and would have damaged the region's chances for future economic growth. Crane and several local legislators lobbied hard for the survival of Conrail. At the same time Conrail executives cut costs, sold off unprofitable lines, and accepted labor concessions. By 1984 the once-sinking railroad posted earnings of nearly $500 million. In spite of subsequent

Facing page: Passenger rail service still provides an important transportation link for many Philadelphia residents, as illustrated by this Amtrak train rolling by the Merion Station on the Main Line. Photo by Rich Zila

Below: CSL Intermodal's nationwide shipping network provides reliable and competitive trucking service in markets across the United States and Canada. Philadelphia is just one of many CSL locations, making the city a vital link in this coast-to-coast distribution network. Photo by Rich Zila

government efforts to sell Conrail whole to a competitor, the railroad became a nonsubsidized public company in 1987 after raising more than $1.6 billion at a public stock offering.

Today Conrail is a viable, thriving contributor to the Greater Philadelphia economy. The railroad is a leader in intermodal transportation—a system that allows truck trailers and marine shipping containers to be loaded directly onto rail flatcars. Forging agreements with other railroads, Conrail has instituted door-to-door shipping service from the Northeast to West Coast cities. Full-service distribution networks geared to specific industries like paper, steel, and lumber are now part of the Conrail system, making the line more valuable to shippers. Ongoing customer service improvements and innovations have given the railroad a more competitive standing against other forms of transportation.

In 1989 Conrail invested some $680 million in capital improvements, including new equipment, terminal expansions, track upgrades, and better communications systems. The company's net income for that year topped $148 million—a great leap from its days on the public dole.

According to railroad chairman, president, and chief executive James A. Hagen, Conrail's future lies in diversification, and in responding quickly to the demands of a global marketplace. "We are a railroad, but our mind-set needs to be that of a transportation company that reaches beyond the rails," he states. "The world becomes a bit smaller, and our potential a bit larger, when we think like that."

Riding the Rails

While railroads were fighting for survival during the 1960s, many carriers allowed passenger service operations to fall into disrepair. Airplanes and highway travel had rendered many passenger connections obsolete, and the burden of running near-empty trains to unpopular destinations proved costly to the struggling railroads.

Rail service continued to be important to certain segments of the population: those who didn't own cars and couldn't afford to fly, the elderly, rural families, and people along the high-density Northeast Corridor where train travel was often more efficient than flying or driving. In an effort to keep passenger train service available to those who needed it, the U.S.

government stepped in. In 1970 Congress passed the Rail Passenger Service Act, which created Amtrak. Although Amtrak is a private corporation, incorporated in the District of Columbia, most of its stock is held by the U.S. Department of Transportation.

The Rail Passenger Service Act allowed railroads to transfer their passenger operations to Amtrak, and most jumped at the opportunity. In the early years Amtrak service was inconsistent at best, but the assurance of continued passenger traffic on the East Coast was a moral victory for Philadelphia. By 1976 Congress gave Amtrak authority to acquire railroad stations, track, and facilities from the bankrupt Penn Central, including much of the right-of-way between Boston and Washington and between Harrisburg and Philadelphia. As the subsidized railway began a $2.5-billion Northeast Corridor Improvement Project, Philadelphia regained much of its historic stature as the bustling hub of intercity passenger traffic on the most heavily traveled train line in the nation.

Today 30th Street Station is one of Amtrak's premier property holdings. "It's the most significant railroad station on the Northeast Corridor and the second busiest in the Amtrak system," says Donald Pross, Amtrak's director of real estate projects and head of the 30th Street Station renovations program. Pross recently supervised the $75-million rehab of the historic station, which included refurbishing the main concourse, restoring the building's original arcade, installing new electrical, air conditioning, and heating systems, renovating 247,283 square feet of office space in the building's two towers, and installing a new baggage retrieval system. Another $13.5 million was spent on improvements to suburban train platforms and on carving a new underground passageway to connect the station with an adjacent subway terminal. Visitors to 30th Street are likely to be drawn to the station's upgraded, 60,000-square-foot retail area featuring products and crafts indigenous to the Delaware Valley. For modern-day Philadelphians 30th Street Station is much more than a treasured relic from the past. It's also a symbol of the city's rebirth and a vibrant link to the future of the metropolitan area. Improved train service on the Northeast Corridor (including a recently-inaugurated Amtrak line from 30th Street to Atlantic City) has strengthened Philadelphia's economic position and augmented the city's slate of amenities.

Public transporation within the Greater Philadelphia area is handled by the Southeastern Pennsylvania Transportation Authority (SEPTA) and the Port
Authority Transit Company (PATCO). The
commuter network covered by these regional utilities
reaches from Trenton to Wilmington, and from
Southern New Jersey to the western Philadelphia suburbs. SEPTA's regional rail lines (formerly operated by
Conrail and its predecessors), city subways, trolleys,
and buses cover a service area of 2,200 square miles.
The transit authority employs 9,700 people and provides some 250 million commuter rides each year.
More than 10 million riders annually board the
PATCO high-speed trains from suburban New Jersey
to Camden and Philadelphia. An estimated four out of
five commuters to Center City use public transportation.

Taking Wing

Philadelphia International Airport, located on the
southeastern edge of the city limits, plays a critical role
in the economic growth and development of the

Right: USAir has designated Philadelphia as its latest hub city, with direct flights to many destinations and easy connections to other outlying areas. Photo by Rich Zila

Above: Philadelphia International's Cargo City moved some 233,000 tons of mail and cargo in 1988, and its services are expanding to meet the growing demand for shipping services in the 1990s. Photo by Rich Zila

Delaware Valley region. Nearly 16 million passengers passed through the airport's gates in 1989, and its runways accomodated nearly 420,000 landings and take-offs. Passenger totals for the airport are expected to exceed 50 million by 2010.

All major domestic and several foreign-based airlines serve Philadelphia International, offering flights to 270 cities a day. Direct flights to Paris, London, and Frankfurt are among the airport's international connections. USAir recently boosted its investment in Philadelphia with a full slate of direct flights to many large and small U.S. cities, plus easy connections to most others. The airline designated Philadelphia as its latest hub city and installed a local flight crew base of 400 pilots and 500 flight attendants.

A $695-million capital improvement program now under way should leave Philadelphia International prepared for its bustling, bright future. Runway improvements and expansion, renovation of existing terminal facilities, and creation of new terminals will be completed by 1991. A new 2,800-car, five-level

parking garage should accomodate increased traffic at the airport, and a planned 400-room hotel adjacent to the terminals will provide convenient lodging for visitors.

One reliable—if somewhat unconventional—barometer of business activity in the Delaware Valley is the amount of mail and cargo flowing in and out of the area. Philadelphia International's Cargo City freight center processed a record 233,000 tons of mail and cargo in 1988, and projections call for continued growth through the 1990s. Recent airport improvements include a $3-million, five-acre extension of Cargo City's aircraft access area to accomodate increased freight movement.

Prosperity in the Delaware Valley has triggered the expansion of many of the region's transportation facilities, including the airport. In 1990 United Parcel Service opened its East Coast package distribution hub on a 212-acre site at Philadelphia International. UPS' 630,000-square-foot air-delivery center is expected to employ 4,700 full- and part-time workers by 1993, with an annual payroll of $21 million. At the west end of the airport's Cargo City complex, the United States Postal Service recently leased a 31-acre site for its own $40-million airmail processing facility.

Growth Corridors

The intricate, sophisticated, and evolving transportation systems of Greater Philadelphia continue to attract new businesses to the area. IKEA, Inc., a Swedish furniture importer, established its first U.S. retail outlet in suburban Philadelphia and located its East Coast distribution center within the city. With assistance from the Philadelphia Industrial Development Corporation (PIDC), the company was able to find a suitable "free-trade zone" location for its warehouse, with access to the port and major highways. Other companies which moved to the area to take advantage of its location and transportation network include a British chemical company, a Swiss biotech enterprise, pharmaceutical companies, and several distributors. These recent arrivals join the ranks of existing Delaware Valley firms that have found life in the region to be satisfying and profitable.

Although economic development and prosperity has been widely shared by counties and towns throughout Greater Philadelphia, a few communities outshine their neighbors. Areas of Southern New Jersey and Philadelphia's western suburbs have become nationally recognized growth corridors. Superior location and transportation access attracted the original pioneers to these once-exurban locales, but now the synergy of like-minded companies, residents, and community leaders has turned these former city dormitories into independent economic hubs.

High-Tech Highway

In the eighteenth century the King of Prussia Inn—named for Frederick I—offered hospitality to George Washington and his revolutionary soldiers as well as to any Tory dissenters who happened by. Situated just a few miles from Valley Forge, the Inn was a refuge for Revolutionary War partisans moving in and out of the battle zone. A fireplace large enough to cook an ox over its coals dominated the kitchen, insuring sustenance for any number of guests. Lafayette joined the Masonic order here, and the Mount Joy Society for the Recovery of Stolen Horses and Detection of Thieves met in an upstairs room.

Now maintained by the King of Prussia Historical Society, the old King of Prussia Inn still stands as one of the few reminders of this land's rich history. King of Prussia, the settlement named for the Inn, is today a thoroughly modern metroplex and the capital of Greater Philadelphia's high-tech industry. The town lies at the heart of the Delaware Valley's dynamic Route 202 corridor, home of more than 850 companies. Only Boston and California's Silicon Valley rival Greater Philadelphia's Route 202 in the number and variety of technology-intensive businesses in residence. Manufacturing of computers and computer-related products, service industries, and information processing firms in the area employ approximately 110,000 people.

Located near historic Valley Forge, the King of Prussia region has become the capital of Philadelphia's high-tech industry. Photo by Mary Ann Brockman

Situated at the intersection of Route 202 and Interstate 76—15 miles west of Center City Philadelphia—the King of Prussia-Valley Forge area has been dubbed a "superburbia" by regional planners. Well-manicured office campuses here have spawned the development of newer and bigger corporate parks, sprawling out over onetime farmland. Between business centers, a patchwork quilt of single-family homes, condo developments, and apartment complexes has sprung up. And to serve the families and businesses, shopping malls, hotels, and professional office strips have proliferated. The Court and The Plaza at King of Prussia is one of the largest enclosed shopping centers in the country.

Since the 1970s King of Prussia has been the growth engine of Montgomery County, one of the richest counties in Pennsylvania in terms of both growth and per-capita income. Development has radiated out from King of Prussia and Route 202 over the last decade, reaching the Fort Washington and Con-

shohocken areas and penetrating into pockets of
Delaware and Chester counties. More than 185,000
people commute into Montgomery County every day
for work, while only 85,000 are employed outside the
county.

Unisys Corp., Ford Electronics Division, Sterling
Drug, and Merck, Sharp and Dohme are all headquartered in Montgomery County. Prudential Insurance
Co. and General Electric Aerospace Division are the
county's two largest employers, each with more than
7,000 workers stationed onsite.

Southern New Jersey

Thirty-five years ago returning World War II veterans
from Camden and Philadelphia began laying claim to
a bit of the American dream in what was then known
as Delaware Township, New Jersey. There, amidst the
cornfields and silos, these suburban pioneers bought
new three- and four-bedroom homes in neatly laid-out
tract developments. They commuted to jobs in Philadelphia, raised families, and watched their gardens grow.

In time restaurants, supermarkets, and retail shops
sprung up at the behest of the burgeoning local population. Commercial enterprises filled in the open
spaces between well-groomed subdivisions and established Camden County towns like Haddonfield,
Collingswood, and Haddon Heights. In 1961 the
Rouse Company built the first covered shopping center on the East Coast in Delaware Township and
dubbed it Cherry Hill Mall. Sheltered shopping became an instant sensation—Philadelphia tour bus

drivers included the new mall on their itineraries—
and Delaware Township gained a new identity. Soon
after the mall opened, township officials voted to
change the name of their suburban enclave to Cherry
Hill.

Unabashed enthusiasm for business, and a healthy
respect for good commercial ideas, continues to be a
hallmark of Cherry Hill—and of all Southern New
Jersey, for that matter. Shortly after the concrete settled around the Cherry Hill Mall, business towers and
office parks began to appear at formerly vacant sites
around the Camden County township. The luxury of
living and working in the same well-mannered suburban setting was enormously appealing to the local
population. Within a few years this former bedroom
community became the corporate domicile of RCA
(now GE) Defense Systems, Subaru of America, and
several other companies.

Now a mature community, Cherry Hill continues
to serve as the nerve center of South Jersey; vacated
homes and office space in the township are snapped
up quickly. But today the most rapid growth in the
area is taking place outside the borders of Cherry Hill,
along Route 73 in the neighboring Burlington County
towns of Marlton, Mount Laurel, and Moorestown. In
1988 Burlington County added 840 new businesses to
its commercial-industrial roster and more than 7,000
new jobs. Easy access to rail lines, the New Jersey
Turnpike, and the Newark and Philadelphia airports
has made the county a prime location for warehousing
and distribution operations.

Burlington Coat Factory, an off-
price clothing retailer headquartered
in Burlington County, recently built
a 500,000-square-foot distribution
center in the area. CVS Pharmacy
added its own 500,000-square-foot
facility to the landscape, and the
U.S. General Services Administration (GSA) has broken ground on a
supply depot of a million-plus square
feet at the northern end of the
county. Royal China & Porcelain
Co., Inc., the exclusive North
American distributors of Royal
Worcester and Spode china,
recently established its distribution
center in Moorestown.

King of Prussia is strategically situated at the
heart of the Delaware Valley's Route 202 corridor.
Home to more than 850
companies, many of the
businesses located along
this vibrant corridor are
involved in technology-
intensive fields. Photo by
Rich Zila

Available land and a good supply of first-class office space have made Burlington County attractive to companies seeking regional office quarters or space for claims processing facilities, computer services divisions, and research operations. General Electric Co., Pepsico, Inc., TTI, Decision Data Services, John Hancock, Burger King, and several regional banks, legal offices, and accounting firms have a presence in the county.

According to Pete Corcoran, an officer of Businesses Committed to Burlington County (BC2), a local trade and promotion group, growth is expected to continue. "We've seen an escalating demand for upscale, innovative office space and a corresponding need for a complement of onsite services like restaurants, conference centers, child care centers, banks, and health clubs," he states. "Burlington County already ranks as one of the most active markets in the Delaware Valley, second only to King of Prussia-Route 202. Things don't seem to be slowing down."

Back to the City

In Greater Philadelphia, as with all major U.S. metropolitan areas, the initial flight to the suburbs came at the expense of the city. That's no longer the case in Philadelphia. Although some businesses are still opting out of the city for the suburban life, others are moving in. Working in conjunction with city, state, and federal government agencies, the Philadelphia Industrial Development Corporation (PIDC) has been able to offer attractive financial packages, location assistance, and expedited permits and approvals for companies settling within the city limits.

Special "enterprise zones" have been set aside for labor-intensive, industrial activity with attractive fi-

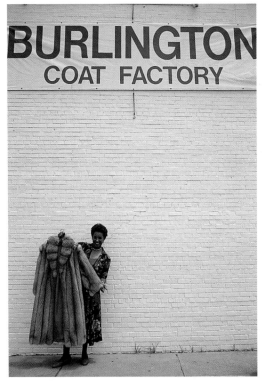

nancial incentives for firms locating in these areas. A special real estate tax abatement program encourages reinvestment in deteriorating commercial and industrial properties in the city, and a separate capital loan fund has been earmarked for the city's apparel industry.

Once a thriving textiles center, Greater Philadelphia still retains the biggest U.S. garment manufacturing district outside of New York. The Albert Nipon division of Leslie Fay, J.G. Hook, Jones of New York, Pincus Brothers-Maxwell, and H. Freeman & Sons all have manufacturing operations in the city. Mothers Work, an upscale manufacturer and retailer of maternity clothes, is headquartered in Philadelphia.

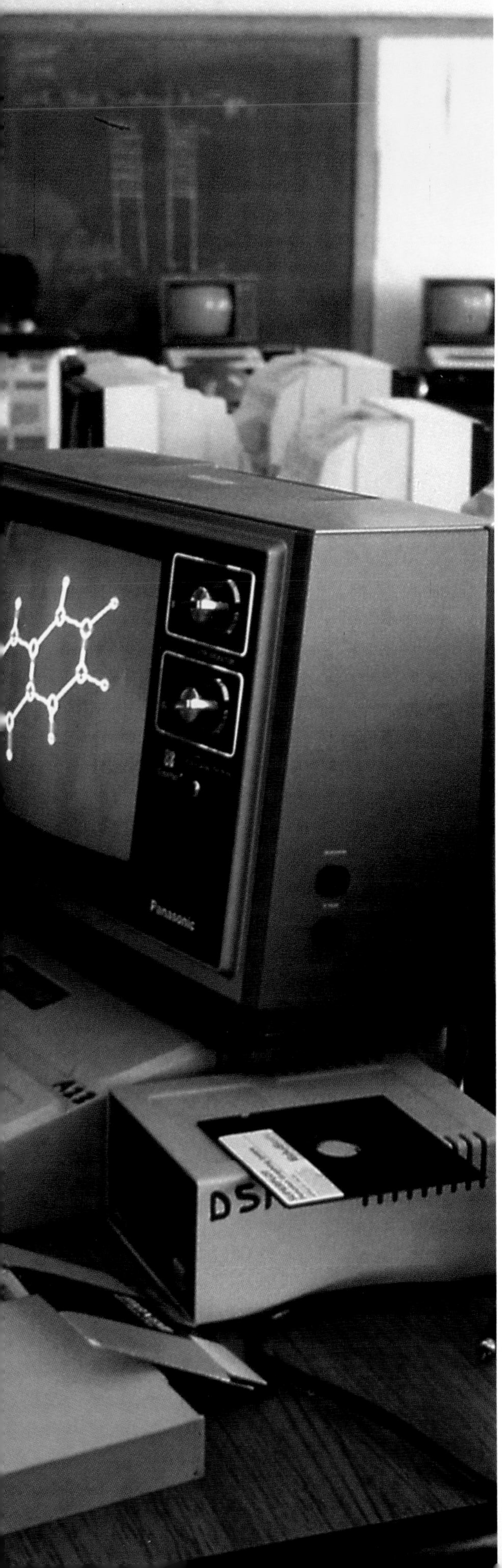

Raising Standards

The computer revolution began in Philadelphia. In 1943 two University of Pennsylvania scientists, J. Presper Eckert and John W. Mauchly, received U.S. Army funding to create an electronic computing machine that could quickly calculate artillery firing ranges. Over the next three years the pair built ENIAC—Electronic Numerical Integrator and Computer—a 30-ton technological leviathan, filled with 18,000 vacuum tubes, that took up 15,000 square feet of space in the university's Moore School of Engineering. After a year of testing ENIAC, the world's first digital electronic computer, was delivered to Aberdeen Proving Grounds in Maryland in 1947.

Eckert and Mauchly eventually left Penn to form the Eckert-Mauchly Computer Corporation. That fledgling company built UNIVAC (Universal Automatic Computer), the world's first commercially produced computer. UNIVAC I made its debut in 1951 when it was sold to the Bureau of the Census. While the UNIVAC project was under way, Eckert-Mauchly bowed to corporate suitor Sperry Rand. The scientists' partnership formed the basis for the company's Sperry Univac division, a direct predecessor to today's Unisys Corp., the international computer giant headquartered in the Philadelphia suburb of Blue Bell.

Now, nearly 50 years after Eckert and Mauchly worked their magic, the still-evolving computer

The Philadelphia High School of Science helps to prepare the future leaders of Philadelphia's ever-growing high technology industry. Photo by George Adams Jones

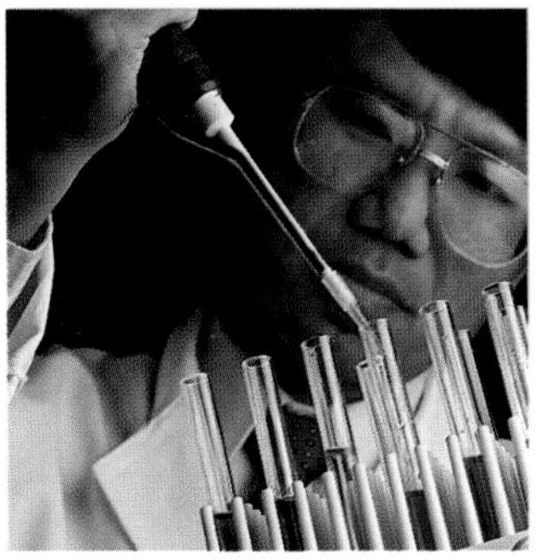

industry has infiltrated every aspect of the global marketplace and has revamped the economic profile of Greater Philadelphia.

From Laboratory to Life

Philadelphia colleges and universities have spawned many profitable and—as in the case of ENIAC—some historic ventures. The symbiotic relationship between academic and corporate research has benefited the area economy, nurturing start-up companies and bolstering established industries while increasing the pool of skilled, versatile technicians and managers for both public- and private-sector jobs. Greater Philadelphia boasts more scientists and engineers per capita than New York, Boston, Chicago, or Los Angeles.

More than 89 degree-granting institutions lie within easy commuting distance of Philadelphia, giving the area the highest concentration of colleges and universities in the country. Twenty-five institutions are located within the city itself. Six area schools offer advanced degrees in engineering, and 10 bestow graduate degrees in biological sciences. The city's six medical schools and two dental schools have graduated 20 percent of the doctors in the U.S. Local business colleges, including the world-famous Wharton School of the University of Pennsylvania, parent small businesses and provide research and consulting services for established companies. In addition, some 600 research laboratories serve the region's high-tech, health-care, manufacturing, and financial industries.

The University City Science Center in West Philadelphia stands as testament to the powerful synergy of business and education in the Delaware Valley. Located within the University of Pennsylvania-Drexel University campus complex, the UCSC is jointly owned by 28 universities and medical institutions. The Science Center, founded in 1963, was the first urban research park in the country. Sited on 19 acres along both sides of Market Street, the 12-building complex provides office and laboratory space for some 105 organizations, ranging from nonprofit trade groups to start-up companies to specialized divisions of large corporations.

During its history more than 120 companies have gotten started at the research park. Thirty-five graduated to expanded locations in Greater Philadelphia, where it is estimated that they now provide nearly 2,000 jobs. The Science Center's technology transfer

program promotes high-tech entrepreneurship by helping scientists turn innovative ideas into marketable products. The Entrepreneurial Management Resources (EMR) division recruits executives and specialists for small and medium-sized firms. And the Application Development Center (ADC) aids entrepreneurs in the creation and commercialization of new software products.

Ecological issues also are scrutinized at the Science Center. Energy management techniques for businesses are being explored, and under a U.S. Environmental Protection Agency grant, the center is working to create a national prototype program for minimizing hazardous wastes in industry.

Biosciences Research and Development occupies a very visible role at the Science Center. Here staff scientists conduct both basic and disease-related biological research under private contracts and federal grants. The Institute for Metabolic Research—part of the Biosciences division—works to develop new tools for the diagnosis and treatment of diabetes and other metabolic disorders. Other bio labs conduct tissue research, investigate the origins of genetic disease, and examine plant growth under various gravity conditions. The Monell Chemical Senses Center, a nonprofit organization that conducts research exclusively in the area of taste and smell, is a favorite resource for science and life-style journalists. Monell scientists recently documented several functions of human pheromones—chemicals in perspiration that trigger a physiological sexual response in members of the opposite sex. For Philadelphians, Monell's trademark bronze half-face sculpture outside the Science Center lab has become a local landmark.

The Ben Franklin Technology Center of Southeastern Pennsylvania, a Science Center affiliate created in 1983 with funds from the state's Ben Franklin Partnership Challenge Grant Program, has awarded $15.6 million in grants for more than 300 cooperative research projects linking universities and industry. Phil Singerman, executive vice president of the Technology Center, notes that the affiliate's aim is to promote growth throughout the Southeastern Pennsylvania area by forging profitable links between researchers and private industry. "The long-range goals are to make the region more competitive in technology-based companies," he explains. "To do that, you have to improve the capacity of the research institutions,

and you have to have the funds and capital investment in place to support small companies, train personnel, and build an environment that is supportive
and encourages entrepreneurs to create their companies here rather than go elsewhere."

Foundations for Innovation

Philadelphia's commitment to higher education pre-
dates the founding of the United States. In 1740 Benjamin Franklin served as the guiding force behind the
creation of a school "for the instruction of Poor Children Gratis." The Charitable School building went up
at Fourth and Arch streets, and by 1749 its mission
had been elevated to educating Philadelphians in the
advanced arts and sciences. Dubbed the Publick
Academy in the City of Philadelphia, the school
eventually blossomed into the University of Pennsylvania, the nation's first university, and the first nonsectarian institution of higher learning in the colonies.

Unlike most colleges of the day, Franklin's school
integrated classical studies like Greek and Latin with
the pursuit of practical knowledge. Physics, chemistry,

mathematics, economics, and modern languages were
all part of the program established at Penn in 1756,
considered the nations first modern liberal-arts curriculum. The university's past embraces many of the
acclaimed figures and notable events of early American history. Nine signers of the Declaration of Independence were either degree recipients, trustees, or
teachers from Penn, and the first public reading of the
Declaration occurred on the campus on July 8, 1776.

The University of Pennsylvania boasts an exhaus-
tive and diverse list of academic "firsts." The first university law professorship was established there in 1790;
the first collegiate school of business, the Wharton
School of Finance and Commerce, was established in
1881; the world's first chair in psychology was established in 1888; and the first black woman to receive a
Ph.D. from a university, Sadie Tanner Mosell Alexander, graduated from Penn's law school in 1921. The
University Museum and archaeology department carried out the first full-scale American archaeological
expedition in the Near East in 1888. Working with
the British Museum from 1922 to 1934, Penn archae-

**This dramatic sculpture in
front of the Physical Education Center is a favorite
meeting place for Drexel
University students.
Photo by David H. Wells**

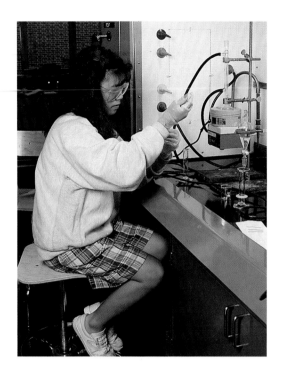

ologists uncovered the ancient City of Ur.

Today the rich history of the University of Pennsylvania continues on the school's 260-acre West Philadelphia campus—home to Franklin's legacy since 1872. Stately Gothic buildings and ivy-covered Victorian halls share the grounds with sleek modern laboratories and classroom buildings. Some 23,000 students attend classes at the university's four undergraduate schools and 12 graduate and professional schools. The student to faculty ratio is 10 to 1. Faculty members include Nobel laureates, Pulitzer Prize winners, and MacArthur, Guggenheim, and Fulbright fellows.

Located adjacent to the University of Pennsylvania in West Philadelphia is the 38-acre Drexel University campus. Founded in 1891 by Philadelphia financier Anthony J. Drexel, it is the second largest private institution of higher learning in the Greater Philadelphia area, with an enrollment of more than 12,000 students. Renowned for its science, engineering, and information sciences programs, Drexel was the first school in the country to require all undergraduates to have personal access to a computer.

Since 1919 Drexel has been a pioneer in cooperative education. With few exceptions Drexel undergraduates must work at public- or private-sector jobs for six months out of every school year. The remaining six months are spent in the classroom. More than 2,800 companies, government agencies, and other institutions participate in the co-op program, accepting as

many as 4,000 students a year as intern-employees. Students seek out the Drexel co-op program for its on-the-job training benefits and access to potential full-time employers.

North of Center City Philadelphia, the 93-acre main campus of Temple University flanks both sides of Broad Street. One of the largest urban public universities in America, Temple has played muse to thousands of Philadelphians, and in turn has been honored by the achievements of many distinguished alumni and professors. David Bradley, prize-winning novelist, is a Temple graduate, as is Dan Swern, the inventor of vinyl.

Perhaps the most famous Temple alum—and the one who's made Temple most famous—is comedian Bill Cosby. Cosby grew up in the North Philadelphia neighborhood that surrounds Temple and attended the university in the early 1960s. Now a benefactor of the school and a member of its board of directors, Cosby created and starred in Temple's first image campaign, a series highlighting the school's best and brightest teachers and students. The campaign slogan, "They could have gone anywhere . . . they chose Temple," has been a hit with local radio and TV audiences, many of whom have ties to the university. Regular viewers of "The Cosby Show" may recall spying Temple paraphernalia on the sitcom set.

Temple was founded in 1884 by orator-preacher Russell H. Conwell, author of the famous "Acres of Diamonds" speech—an uplifting paean to the powers

Left: University of Pennsylvania student Victoria Lee conducts an experiment at the school's organic chemistry laboratory. Photo by Rich Zila

The Computer Learning Center at the University City Science Center in West Philadelphia has been training individuals in the computer industry for more than 30 years with state-of-the-art equipment and a dedicated staff. Photo by Rich Zila

Right: Dr. Alfred Fink explores the fascinating world of psychology at Temple University. Photo by Rich Zila

Below: Higher education for Philadelphia's Catholic community is well-represented with La Salle University. Run by the Christian Brothers, La Salle features a 100-acre campus on the edge of the city's Germantown district. Photo by Rich Zila

of God and money. Conwell came to Philadelphia in 1880 to rescue the struggling Grace Baptist Church in North Philadelphia. Within a few years Conwell had transformed the church into a thriving Baptist Temple seating 3,000. At night he began teaching college subjects in the Temple basement to working-class citizens in the community. The "Temple" university curriculum and enrollment continued to expand until 1888, when it was chartered as a full-fledged institution of higher education. Conwell supported the school with earnings from his lectures, a sum estimated at $7 million over his lifetime. In 1965 Temple became part of the Pennsylvania Commonwealth System of Higher Education.

Like its Ivy League counterpart, the University of Pennsylvania, Temple claims a number of academic firsts. In 1933 Dr. Herman Nunberg of Temple became the first person appointed professor of psychoanalysis in the U.S. Temple launched the country's first bachelor's degree program in radio in 1946. Temple Law School was among the first to graduate women, and its Dental School (formerly the Philadelphia Dental College) is the oldest in the world. In addition, the school maintains several outreach programs to serve the community that surrounds the campus.

Catholic higher education has a strong tradition in the Greater Philadelphia area, where more than 35 percent of the local population embraces that faith. LaSalle University, located on 82 acres in Northwest Philadelphia, was founded in 1863 by Bishop James Wood, the fifth Bishop of Philadelphia, and Brother Teliow, a Christian Brother. The coeducational school continues to be run under the auspices of the Brothers of the Christian Schools, and its president, Brother F. Patrick Ellis, is well-known among Philadelphia civic leaders. The manicured campus of St. Joseph's University, Philadelphia's Jesuit university, borders both sides of City Line Avenue, spanning the boundary between Philadelphia and the Main Line suburb of Bala Cynwyd. Founded in 1851, St. Joseph's is known for its innovative, specialized curriculum, including an MBA program in Food Marketing, a BS in Health Administration, and a Women in Management & Information Systems program.

Basketball fans need no introduction to Villanova University—the school's Wildcats, under Coach Rollie Massimino, consistently turn in breathtaking performances. Among locals, however, Villanova is equally well-known for its broad-based academic curriculum and graduate programs in law and other disciplines. Villanova's lush, 240-acre suburban campus occupies the former estate of John Rudolph, a Philadelphia merchant and Revolutionary War officer. The university was founded in 1842 by members of the Order of St. Augustine.

Greater Philadelphia's Quaker heritage lives on at three small, academically distinguished colleges located in the city's genteel western suburbs. Haverford College in Haverford was the first U.S. college founded by the Religious Society of Friends. Established in 1837, Haverford officially admitted only men until 1977. Today women make up around 42 percent of the school's 1,200 students.

Haverford maintains close ties with nearby Bryn Mawr College. Students can cross-register at the two schools, take classes or pursue majors from either curriculum, and live on either campus. Bryn Mawr was founded in 1885 with the then-radical notion of offering women educational opportunities equal to those offered men. Technically, it remains a women's college, but through cross-registrations with Haverford,

Founded in 1883 by the Religious Society of Friends, Haverford College is a small, academically distinguished institution located in Philadelphia's western suburbs. Photo by Mary Ann Brockman

the 1,700-student Bryn Mawr is in fact coeducational. In addition, the graduate schools of Social Work and Social Research and Arts and Sciences at Bryn Mawr graduate both men and women. Bryn Mawr claims a place among the top 10 institutions in the country for National Science Foundation Fellowships, and the percentage of undergraduates completing the physics major at Bryn Mawr is 40 times the national average for women. A 1989 study ranked Bryn Mawr first in the country for undergraduates who go on to earn doctoral degrees in social sciences, humanities, and languages.

Both Haverford and Bryn Mawr maintain cooperative exchange programs with the University of Pennsylvania, as well as with Greater Philadelphia's third Quaker-born institution, Swarthmore College in Swarthmore. Founded in 1864 by the Society of Friends, Swarthmore's 300-acre Brandywine Valley campus is today a registered arboretum where 1,300 students pursue degrees in 19 majors. Swarthmore Alumni include Nobel Prize winners David Baltimore and Howard Temin, Pulitzer Prize-winning author James Michener, and Massachusetts Governor Michael Dukakis. The Friends Historical Library at Swarthmore holds more than 38,000 books and pamphlets relating to the Religious Society of Friends. Together with the Quaker Collection at Haverford's Magill Library, these holdings represent the largest repository of Quaker documents in the world.

Widener University made its debut in 1821 as a select boy's school in Wilmington, Delaware. Although founded by Quaker John Bullock, the school quickly evolved away from its pacifist philosophical and religious heritage: As the Civil War approached, the school added military instruction to the curriculum and in 1859 became Delaware Military Academy. At the beginning of the war the academy moved to Pennsylvania, where Union sympathies ran higher. By 1892 the school, rechristened the Pennsylvania Military College, had established itself on the current Widener campus in Chester, Pennsylvania.

Widener remained a military college until 1972 when, in deference to the tenor of the times, the Corps of Cadets was disbanded and the school name changed to Widener University, honoring a philanthropic Philadelphia family. The school still maintains strong ties to Delaware, with a thriving campus in Wilmington. Widener's School of Hotel and Restaurant Management, headquartered in Delaware, gets good marks from the hospitality industry for the high

caliber of its graduates. The only university in the country that maintains law schools in different states, Widener prepares students for the bar both in Delaware and on its new Harrisburg campus in Pennsylvania. Cecil B. DeMille was one of Widener's more famous alumni; the legendary movie mogul scratched his name into the wooden beams inside the dome at the top of the campus' Old Main building.

Greater Philadelphia's New Jersey suburbs are served by several small colleges as well as one major urban campus, Rutgers University-Camden. Although Rutgers Camden is now a satellite campus of the State University of New Jersey, it originated as an independent college. In 1926 Collingswood, New Jersey, mayor Arthur E. Armitage, Sr., mobilized a group of citizens interested in establishing a local law school. The South Jersey Law School expanded within a year to include the College of South Jersey, both of which were absorbed by the New Brunswick-based Rutgers in 1950.

Today Rutgers Camden offers a full slate of undergraduate programs as well as seven graduate majors, including advanced degrees in education, public policy, and social work. The Rutgers School of Law enrolls 725 full- and part-time students annually, and the recently opened School of Business has become a popular resource for cross-studying MBA candidates who want to combine management savvy with other professional skills. In recent years Rutgers' 35-acre campus has been the focus of a near-$70-million capital expansion and improvement program. The university's dynamic growth has spurred much of the ongoing urban renewal effort in downtown Camden.

In addition to its bounty of traditional colleges and universities, Greater Philadelphia also claims a lively collection of specialized schools offering degrees in the performing arts, music, visual arts, and various crafts. The country's oldest art school, The School of the Pennsylvania Academy of the Fine Arts, offers a classical curriculum in painting, sculpting, and printmaking. Founded in 1805 by Rembrandt Peale (son of painter Charles Willson Peale) and sculptor William Rush, the school counts Cecilia Beaux, Mary Cassatt, and A. Milne Calder among its alumni. Its twentieth-century notables include architect Louis I. Kahn and filmmaker David Lynch. Today more than 800 students a year attend classes or work toward degrees at the school's historic studios at Broad and Cherry streets, two blocks from Philadelphia City Hall.

The University of the Arts, also in Center City Philadelphia, offers undergraduate, graduate, and fine arts degrees in majors ranging from industrial design to animation to dance and theater arts. The university's Master of Fine Arts in Book Arts/Printmaking is unique, focusing on the nearly lost art of limited edition bookmaking.

Midday strollers in Rittenhouse Square are often treated to impromptu serenades courtesy of the students of the Curtis Institute of Music, which occupies the former George W. Childs Drexel mansion at the

The only tuition-free music conservatory in the country, the Curtis Institute of Music on Rittenhouse Square accepts students solely on their talents and merit. Photo by Rich Zila

Philadelphia College of Textiles and Science student Darcy Heppenstall loads a hand flat machine at the school's knitting lab. Photo by Rich Zila

corner of Locust Street and Rittenhouse Square in Center City. Voice and music students at the exclusive conservatory occasionally practice their repertoires near the open windows of the school, providing a treat for anyone walking by. Founded by Mary Louise Curtis Bok in 1924, Curtis is the only tuition-free music conservatory in the Western world, accepting on merit alone a limited number of students each year.

Although some of the gifted musicians studying at Curtis are as young as 11 years old, many more are college-aged students working on bachelor's or master's degrees in music. Curtis alumni include Leonard Bernstein, Gian Carlo Menotti, Peter Serkin, Leonard Rose, and Anna Moffo.

At least one of Greater Philadelphia's specialty schools evolved from concern for business as well as craft. The Philadelphia College of Textiles and Science traces its ancestry to the booming industrial era of the late 1800s. A group of area textile manufacturers, lamenting the quality gap between European and American fabrics, established a school to train local textile mill workers and managers. Founded in 1884, the Philadelphia Textile School remained true to its mission, surviving the Depression, wars, and even the decline of the local textile industry. Eventually it earned the right to confer baccalaureate degrees, and as programs in the arts, sciences, and business management were added, the onetime trade school evolved into a full-fledged college. Today 3,500 full- and part-time students attend classes at Textile's 86-acre campus in Philadelphia's East Falls neighborhood, as well as at satellite campuses in Bucks and Montgomery counties. The curriculum maintains a textile industry focus, with majors in textile design, textile technology, fashion merchandising, and chemistry degrees with polymer/textile options.

Outside the fashion and textile industry, the college is probably best known for its role in developing fabric-based biomedical devices. The knitted arterial graft introduced by heart surgeon Dr. Michael DeBakey in Houston was developed by Professor Tom Edman, a knitting specialist at Textile. Various fabric and textile surgical implants, like the woven tendon graft, artificial ligaments and tendons, and other surgical aids, have been born in the Textile college laboratories.

Wellness and Everyday Miracles

Medical research and the health-care industry have had a profound impact on Greater Philadelphia educational institutions—funneling research dollars into university labs, supporting college programs in a broad variety of disciplines, and providing employment for hundreds of graduates of local universities and medical schools. Health care's role as an economic and intellectual catalyst has remained consistent, even in the face of major changes in the industry itself.

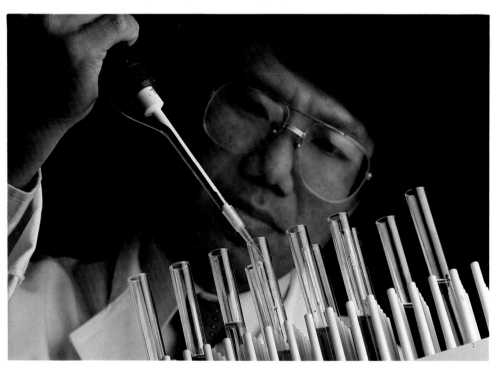

The 1980s were a time of upheaval and strain for Greater Philadelphia's wellness businesses. Rising production costs drove some local pharmaceutical houses to move manufacturing operations offshore, resulting in the loss of thousands of jobs. Government-dictated Diagnostic Regulatory Guidelines (DRGs) for Medicare and Medicaid payments—and the private health insurance industry's subsequent embrace of suggested-pricing tactics—forced many hospitals and clinics to change their practices. Straight business concerns and market assessments soon claimed equal weight with pure medical issues in determining hospital policies.

Medical research and the health-care industry have had a profound impact on Philadelphia's educational institutions. Photo by Bruce Stromberg

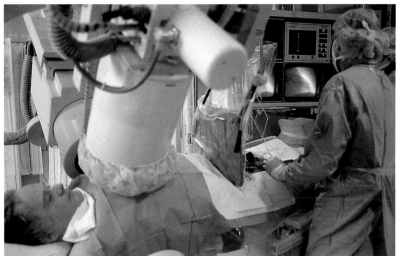

Medical centers quickly learned to play to their own strengths, to avoid redundant facilities where possible, to forge beneficial associations with other hospitals and clinics, and to aggressively market their wares to the public. The resulting plethora of ads, and shifts in long-standing industry practice, may have been unsettling to consumers, but most of the Greater Philadelphia health-care complexes that survived the decade of change are stronger as a result.

Modern American medicine was born in Philadelphia. Here, again, the city boasts an impressive array of "firsts": the first hospital in the colonies was established in Philadelphia, as well as the first medical school, nursing school, pharmacy school, and dental

Above: Nearly 10 percent of Philadelphia's skilled work force finds employment in the challenging world of health care. Photo by Bruce Stromberg

Right: Pennsylvania Hospital was established 25 years prior to the American Revolution. Its Pine Building, which was designed by Samuel Rhoads, is acknowledged as one of the finest examples of Colonial and Federal period architecture. It has been in continuous use since 1755. Photo by Robert J. Salgado

school. The Greater Philadelphia health-care complex today provides a fitting legacy to those early achievements. Ten percent of the area labor force works in the health-care industry. Twenty-nine pharmaceutical companies and 77 manufacturers of medical instruments and supplies are located in the Delaware Valley. Sixty of the area's research labs conduct biomedical research.

Greater Philadelphia's six medical schools, two dental schools, two pharmacy schools, nursing schools, and more than 100 hospitals continue to uphold the city's reputation as a center for medical innovation and pioneering research. Some of Philadelphia's most prestigious, forward-thinking health-care institutions are direct descendants of the city's early hospitals and medical schools.

Pennsylvania Hospital, founded in 1751 by Benjamin Franklin, Dr. Thomas Bond, and a group of civic-minded Philadelphians, claims the distinction of being America's first hospital. The hospital's Pine Building, located on Eighth Street in Center City between Eighth and Ninth streets, was designed by Samuel Rhoads, a member of the hospital's first Board of Managers, and has been in continual use since it was completed in 1757. Although the building was expanded—first in 1797 and again in 1804—visitors to the graceful Colonial and Federal complex can still view Benjamin Franklin's inscription on the cornerstone of the original building. His dedication reads:

In the Year of Christ
1755
George the Second Happily Reigning
(For he sought the Happiness of his People)
Philadelphia flourishing
(For its inhabitants were public spirited)
This Building,
By the Bounty of the Government,
And of many private Persons,
Was piously founded,
For the Relief of the Sick and Miserable.
May the God of Mercies
Bless the Undertaking!

Although Pennsylvania Hospital traces its roots to the Founding Fathers, its present-day reputation rests on the hospital's state-of-the-art facilities and medical procedures. The Eichler Laser Center of Pennsylvania Hospital has been a trailblazer in the use of various types of lasers for surgery, as well as a resource center for doctors who wish to learn about laser-based surgical techniques. The hospital's orthopedic surgery department currently is involved in more than 50 research projects relating to joint replacements and revisions. Nearly 1,000 joint replacements are performed each year at the hospital's Rothman Institute, using such advanced techniques as antibiotic cement, non-cemented artificial joints, and frozen bone grafts.

Thousands of residents of Greater Philadelphia owe their start in life to Pennsylvania Hospital. With more than 4,000 babies born there each year, the hospital is the largest birth facility in the Delaware Valley. The hospital obstetrics department specializes in high-risk pregnancies, and its infertility services are extensive. Pennsylvania Hospital maintains the national registry for PUBS, a procedure used to test a baby's blood in utero in order to diagnose potential health risks to the unborn child.

Benjamin Rush, the "Father of American Psychiatry" served as an attending physician at Pennsylvania Hospital from 1783 to 1813. As he began treating the mentally ill of old Philadelphia—a group that included his son and the spouses and siblings of several prominent citizens—Pennsylvania Hospital's reputation for psychiatric healing grew. Today the Institute of Pennsylvania Hospital, a 234-bed psychiatric facility in West Philadelphia, continues the tradition, offering inpatient care to mentally ill adults and adolescents as well as substance abuse programs and treatment programs for anxiety, dissociative disorders, eating disorders, and geriatric mental health problems. The institute's research umbrella includes the Dave Garroway Laboratory for the Study of Depression.

It's hard to read a newspaper or magazine article on medical trends or health topics without coming across a quote from someone at the University of Pennsylvania School of Medicine, or the Hospital of the University of Pennsylvania. The country's first medical school and hospital complex continues to be at the forefront of health-care research and discovery. The 1980s' much-touted "fountain of youth" drug, Retin-A, was developed at the Penn medical center by Dr. Albert Klingman, professor emeritus of dermatology. The Obesity Clinic, run by Dr. Albert Stunkard and Ph.D.'s Thomas Wadden and Kelly Brownell, has been responsible for numerous breakthrough studies on human metabolism and weight control, and Penn's

Center for Human Appearance, headed by renowned plastic surgeon Dr. Linton Whitaker, is one of the first multidisciplinary clinics for cosmetic procedures in the U.S. Penn's in vitro fertilization program, under the auspices of obstetrics professor Dr. Luigi Mastroianni, ranks as one of the oldest and most successful in the world.

The University of Pennsylvania medical school was founded in 1765 by Dr. John Morgan. His mission was to establish a medical school in the colonies, thereby enabling the education of new doctors and providing a resource for foreign-trained physicians wanting to improve their craft. The Hospital of the University of Pennsylvania—the first university-owned teaching hospital in the country—came along more than a century later in 1874. During its illustrious history, Penn medical school graduates and affiliated physicians were responsible for the first use of ether as an anesthetic, established the first university institute devoted to anatomy and advanced biological research, and in 1952 performed the first televised surgical procedure.

The Penn medical center in West Philadelphia today treats some 300,000 outpatients and 28,000 inpatients each year, not including the 3,250 babies born at HUP. Six hundred and fifty medical students and more than 500 residents work and study under the direction of the center's 750 faculty and staff physicians.

The Graduate Hospital, on 19th and South streets in Philadelphia, was once owned by the University of Pennsylvania and remains an independent teaching affiliate of the university. Since its rebirth as an independent health center in 1977, Graduate has been one of the more dynamic medical institutions in the Delaware Valley, conducting community outreach programs and educational seminars and linking together several complementary suburban hospitals into the Graduate Health System.

The Graduate Hospital Center for Preventive Medicine stresses wellness through weight control, physical fitness, stress management and special treatment for osteoporosis, prevention and rehabilitation of back injuries, and cholesterol monitoring and control.

Founded in 1824, Jefferson Medical College is the nation's largest private medical school.
Photo by George Adams Jones

The hospital's Eating Disorders Service, which offers inpatient and outpatient treatment for anorexia nervosa and bulimia, is headed by Dr. Michael Pertschuk, a nationally recognized expert in the field. In 1990 a new Diagnostic Building opened across from the main Hospital, housing Graduate's state-of-the-art Imaging Center.

Thomas Jefferson University Hospital, located on South 11th Street in Center City, is the teaching hospital of Jefferson Medical College, the largest private medical school in the country. Jefferson has more than 8,700 living alumni, including doctors who founded 10 other medical schools in the U.S. Founded in 1824, Jefferson Medical College is one of four divisions of Thomas Jefferson University, a school that offers degrees in medicine and nursing as well as bachelor's and master's degrees in several allied health fields.

Jefferson University and Hospital maintain a high-profile position in medical research and unique therapies. The Cardeza Foundation at Jefferson is world-renowned for its work detecting and identifying blood disorders such as hemophilia, sickle cell disease, leukemia, and lymphoma. Foundation scientists, working under a $496,000 grant from the National Heart, Lung and Blood Institute, are investigating the potential benefit of the hormone erythropoietin in treating AIDS patients with anemia. The Hand Center at Jefferson developed the world's first artificial tendon, and is nationally acclaimed for its success in reattaching severed hands and digits. Jefferson doctors were pioneers in chorion villus sampling (a prenatal test) and the hospital has the only heart-lung bypass machine for newborns in the Delaware Valley. It is one of the few hospitals in the U.S. that offers radioactive implants for breast cancer patients.

Hahnemann University Hospital in Philadelphia got its start in 1848 as the Homeopathic Medical College of Pennsylvania, an institution devoted to the medical teachings of Samuel Hahnemann, a German medical reformer who believed that small doses of gentle natural remedies were superior to the "heroic"

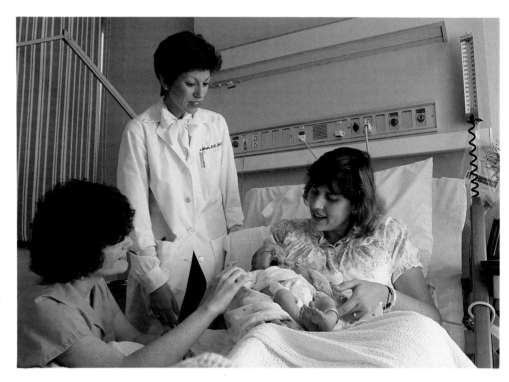

practices of the time—bleeding, leeching, and purging. Despite that early countercultural heritage, Hahnemann Hospital entered the mainstream of medical practice in 1928, and in 1948 Hahnemann surgeon Dr. Charles Bailey made the cover of *Time* magazine after performing the world's first successful heart valve repair.

Today Hahnemann ranks as one of the premier critical-care hospitals in the Northeast. The hospital's Trauma Center, the first Level I Regional Resource Trauma Center in the Delaware Valley, is served by its own MedEvac air ambulance service, which brings in patients from across eastern Pennsylvania. The Division of Nephrology and Hypertension boasts one of the largest outpatient dialysis units in the state, and the acclaimed Renal Transplant Unit performed the Delaware Valley's first kidney transplant in 1963. The hospital's Institute for Cancer and Blood Diseases has received more than $10 million in National Cancer Institute grants for research on the effects of interferon on cancer cells.

Temple University Hospital and Medical School took the limelight in 1990 when a veteran *Philadelphia Inquirer* reporter and heart patient printed a detailed account of his heart transplant surgery at the medical center. Temple doctors performed the first heart transplant operation in the Delaware Valley in 1984, and today Temple remains Greater Philadelphia's primary

Among the many health care advances achieved at Thomas Jefferson University Hospital, medical breakthroughs have included chorion villus sampling (a prenatal test) and the only heart-lung machine for newborns in the Delaware Valley. Photo by Bruce Stromberg/Thomas Jefferson University Hospital

The Trauma Center at Hahnemann University Hospital is served by its own MedEvac air ambulance service, which can provide emergency transportation for patients all across eastern Pennsylvania. Photo by Rich Zila

resource for this life-renewing procedure. Temple's other claims to fame include its oncology research program, which conducts clinical trials on new cancer treatments under the auspices of the Southwest Oncology Group. During its nearly 100 years of operation, Temple Hospital and School of Medicine has earned several mentions in medical history texts: Temple's Dr. Wayne Babcock introduced spinal anesthesia to the U.S., Dr. O. Spurgeon English is recognized as the founder of psychosomatic medicine, and Dr. Temple Fay first used hypothermia—the lowering of a patient's body temperature—during special surgical procedures. Temple School of Medicine also has the distinction of being the first American medical college to accept and graduate a blind student, Dr. David Hartman, who was awarded a degree in 1976.

Founded by Russell Conwell in 1891, Temple University Hospital has grown along with its academic affiliate. In 1986 the hospital unveiled a new $129-million, 504-bed facility on North Broad Street, funded by state, city, and private contributions. The new hospital's Emergency Department offers a walk-in psychiatric crisis center, as well as separate treatment areas for specific types of injuries.

Philadelphia's egalitarian Quaker sensibilities first bolstered the creation of the Medical College of Pennsylvania. Founded in 1850 as the Female Medical College of Pennsylvania, it was established by Quaker civic leaders and philanthropists to give women equal access to the medical fraternity. Graduates of the country's first medical school for women had a tough time finding hospitals that would allow admissions

from women doctors, and so, in 1861, Women's Hospital was born under the auspices of an all-woman governing board.

Men have been admitted to the college in Philadelphia's East Falls neighborhood since 1969, one year before the institution changed its name to The Medical College of Pennsylvania. However, the medical complex claims a number of professional firsts for women and for medicine in general. Professor Catharine Macfarlane, an 1898 MCP graduate, in 1938 initiated a 10-year cancer detection study that proved the value of regular pelvic exams in the detection of uterine cancer. She was the first doctor in the city to use radium in the treatment of cervical cancer. Dr. Katherine Boucot Sturgis, another graduate, was a pioneer in the detection of lung cancer through x-rays and first sounded the alarm against asbestos spray fireproofing in buildings. She was named president of the Philadelphia County Medical Society in 1968, the first woman to hold the chair.

The MCP complex today houses the first four-year medical school program on geriatrics and gerontology in the world. The school's work on aging and age-related disorders has won accolades from the medical community and extensive research funding from the National Institute on Aging.

Philadelphia College of Osteopathic Medicine, located on City Line Avenue, is the largest of 15 osteopathic medical colleges in the U.S. Osteopathic medicine emphasizes the interrelationship of all body systems in maintaining health and treating disease. In addition to the standard medical curriculum, osteopathic medical students learn special manipulative therapies and diagnosis techniques. Osteopathic Hospital, which opened in 1968, is a 200-bed acute care facility adjacent to the college. Students at Osteopathic have the option of pursuing a combined DO/MBA degree in a five-year program operated in conjunction with St. Joseph's University.

Healing the Future

Some of the most heartrending—as well as the most joyful—milestones in Philadelphia medical history have issued from the city's hospitals for children. Pediatric medicine has a noble history in Philadelphia, beginning with the founding of the Children's Hospital of Philadelphia in 1855 in a small house in Center City. Today Children's Hospital occupies a 284-bed facility adjacent to the University of Pennsylvania. Its doctors treat some 150,000 outpatients and 13,000 hospitalized children, from infants to teenagers, each year. The hospital boasts one of the largest pediatric oncology centers in the country, with a dedicated bone transplant unit, a sickle cell center, and specialized diagnostic center that assists community physicians in diagnosing complex illnesses. Children's

Hospital surgeons have successfully performed intricate cardiovascular operations on children with rare or complicated heart defects.

The Joseph Stokes, Jr., Research Institute of the Children's Hospital conducts one of the largest pediatric research programs in the country. Institute scientists invented the Isolette closed incubator for newborn infants, and developed vaccines for rubella, mumps, and influenza.

St. Christopher's Hospital for Children in Philadelphia offers one of the top-ranked pediatric liver transplant programs in the country. In 1986 the hospital became the first in the Delaware Valley to perform a liver transplant on a child. Since then 36 children from all over the U.S. have undergone this lifesaving operation at St. Christopher's. The Pediatric Transplant Institute at St. Christopher's also offers the only heart, heart-lung, and kidney transplant program in the Greater Philadelphia area. The hospital's burn treatment center is the only such facility available between Boston and Washington on the East Coast. In 1989, 115-year-old St. Christopher's moved to a new, 183-bed facility in Northeast Philadelphia.

Children's Hospital of Philadelphia treats 150,000 outpatients and 13,000 hospitalized children each year. Photo by Rich Zila

The gang's all there. Etched in the sidewalk along South Broad Street, the names of Philadelphia's musical icons are enshrined so that present and future generations may pause and pay homage. This two-block-long Walk of Fame—a series of bronze plaques dotting the walkway in front of the Academy of Music—gives testament to the region's rich cultural legacy and to the eclectic musical tastes of Greater Philadelphians.

Strollers will find the names of Philadelphia's classical music legends, like Leopold Stokowski and Marian Anderson, sharing the pavement with the monikers of pop singer Frankie Avalon, jazz great Dizzy Gillespie, and eternal rock-'n-roller Dick Clark. So far, more than 30 Hall of Fame award winners have been immortalized along the walk.

The Walk of Fame and the Hall of Fame Awards were created in 1987 by the Philadelphia Music Foundation, a nonprofit education and resource center for aspiring Delaware Valley musicians. The awards honor nationally known music industry talents from all genres who have strong ties to Philadelphia. Celebrating both individual achievement and the collective artistic heritage of Greater Philadelphia, the awards have become a source of pride for fans as well as recipients.

A pivotol feature of Philadelphia's cultural and artistic community, the stately Academy of Music hosts, among others, performances by the Pennsylvania Ballet, the Opera Company of Philadelphia, and the Philadelphia Orchestra. Photo by George Adams Jones

From Mummers to Muti

Above: A climate of cultural awareness and a rich artistic heritage make Philadelphia a hospitable environment for working artists. Photo by George Adams Jones

Greater Philadelphians take their local heroes to heart—and artists here do achieve hero status. The man on the street in Center City is as likely to sing the praises of the internationally acclaimed Philadelphia Orchestra as he is a neighborhood string band or a college football team.

The urge to create, and an appreciation for talent of all kinds, is deeply rooted in the Philadelphia psyche. Benjamin Franklin and his friends performed chamber music for colonial audiences, who already were seasoned opera and theatergoers. A century later Philadelphia's National Opera Company presented the American premiers of *I Pagliacci* and *Cavalleria Rusticana*. The Barrymores—Lionel, Ethel, and John—were born in Philadelphia and laid claim to the stages of the world. And the visual arts would certainly be poorer without the contributions of Philadelphians like Thomas Eakins, Mary Cassatt, and Charles Willson Peale, as well as three generations of Calders and three generations of Wyeths.

Today it's hard to turn a corner in Philadelphia without running into a marquee boasting a popular play, a poster for a concert by an acclaimed musician, or a work of art by a famous sculptor. According to the Mayor's Cultural Advisory Council, the economic impact of working artists, cultural organizations, and arts-related businesses on the city tops $1 billion a year. That doesn't include periodic cash infusions from film crews who capitalize on the Delaware Valley's rich palette of movie locations, choosing sites that range from gritty urban alleys to bucolic woodlands to rarified estates. The hardworking, hard-dreaming soul of Philadelphia figured prominently in the *Rocky* movies; native son Brian DePalma immortalized Fairmount Park and 30th Street Station in his thriller *Blow-Out*, and the region's Amish tradition was showcased in *Witness*.

Greater Philadelphia natives consider access to great performances and exhibits to be part of their birthright. Here, art incites passions usually reserved for sporting events and political issues. Sometimes artistic controversy *becomes* a political issue. During the filming of the movie *Rocky V*, a bronze statue of the mythical Philadelphia-born boxing hero Rocky Balboa got a temporary berth on the steps of the Philadelphia Museum of Art. The prop attracted a

Right: With faces set in intense concentration, their bodies moving in graceful rhythym, ballet students at the Philadelphia High School of the Performing Arts practice their barre. Photo by George Adams Jones

Under the musical direction of Riccardo Muti, the renowned Philadelphia Orchestra presents its winter season at the Academy of Music. Photo by Ed Wheeler/Philadelphia Orchestra

broad popular constituency of devotees, as well as detractors who insisted that the statue simply wasn't art. Eventually, Rocky was returned to his permanent perch outside the Spectrum sports arena, but for months public debate over the merits of the statue raged on. The bronze boxer even became the subject of several City Council resolutions!

The 1990s are likely to be watershed years for the Greater Philadelphia cultural community. Many of the city's established institutions began the decade in a state of flux. Soaring production costs and declining government support of the arts have sent many performing groups scrambling for a limited pool of private funds. Outside the melee, art patrons and administrators have begun to reevaluate the wisdom of business as usual in an era of tight money. Boards of directors of

Philadelphia art institutions have become more assertive, in some cases questioning their organizations' traditional artistic direction and focus.

Both the Pennsylvania Ballet and the Opera Company of Philadelphia launched searches for new artistic directors in 1990. At the same time, the Philadelphia Orchestra's beloved conductor Riccardo Muti announced that he would end his reign in 1992. Speculating on successors for these posts quickly became lively cocktail-party sport, with no shortage of candidates in the wings. Popular support for the arts continues, undaunted by the specter of change. In fact, attendance figures are holding steady, and audiences seem excited by the possibilities. In Greater Philadelphia there's always the chance that turmoil might be followed by the birth of something truly grand.

Stokowski, Ormandy, Muti—and All That Brass

The Philadelphia Orchestra celebrated its 90th birthday on November 16, 1990, marking nearly a century of musical innovation, technical virtuosity, and worldwide acclaim. Known among music lovers for its distinctive "Philadelphia Sound," the orchestra's style can be identified by a certain sheen to the strings and the dramatic spark of its powerful brass section. The orchestra attracts some of the finest performers in classical music, both as orchestra members and as guest soloists and conductors. Superstar soloists who have recently appeared with the orchestra include Emanuel Ax, Yo-Yo Ma, Itzhak Perlman, Nadja Salerno-Sonnenberg, and Frederica von Stade.

The orchestra got its start under the baton of Fritz Scheel, a veteran conductor of European orchestras and a confrere of such legends as Brahms, von Bulow, and Tchaikovsky. The first Philadelphia concerts conducted by Scheel were given as benefits for families of soldiers killed in the Spanish-American War. Dubbed the "Philippine Concerts," these perfomances were so successful that they led to the birth of a permanent orchestra for the city in the fall of 1900.

The Philadelphia Orchestra quickly established a reputation for excellence. During its early years composer Richard Strauss served as a guest conductor, conducting his own Death and Transfiguration, and a 19-year-old Arthur Rubinstein made his U.S. debut as a piano soloist. But it was in 1912, with the tapping of a new, 30-year-old fledgling conductor, that the Philadelphia Orchestra laid claim to history. Leopold Stokowski, a former church organist and three-year veteran conductor of the Cincinnati Symphony, arrived in Philadelphia determined to build the greatest orchestra of the day, and to fuel that orchestra with demanding, challenging projects.

Over a period of several years, the flamboyant and sometimes temperamental Stokowski replaced weak orchestra members with stronger players. In 1916, satisfied with the ensemble, he arranged a breath-stopping showcase event. The Philadelphia Orchestra's awe-inspiring performance of Mahler's Symphony No. 8—known as the "Symphony of a Thousand" because it takes so many singers and musicians to perform the piece—gave the orchestra international stature. It was the U.S. debut of Mahler's Eighth, with the orchestra playing to packed houses both in Philadelphia and New York.

The orchestra's fame spread quickly when, the following year, Stokowski and crew crossed the Delaware River to the RCA Victor recording studios in Camden, New Jersey, becoming one of the first American orchestras to record under under its own name. To this day the Philadelphia Orchestra remains among the most oft-recorded symphony orchestras in the world, with 200 records to its credit.

Stokowski gave the orchestra a reputation for innovation and experimentation which was not always appreciated by conservative Philadelphia concert patrons. Some concerts met with outright booing from the audience. One of the conductor's more successful—and enduring—experiments was his 1939 collaboration with Walt Disney on the cartoon classic Fantasia, which uses Stravinsky's Rite of Spring to inspire its animation. (The Philadelphia Orchestra had premiered Rite of Spring in the U.S. in 1922.) The cartoon, which seamlessly welds animation to a classical music score, used a multitrack sound system that was a precursor to modern stereo.

By the time Fantasia was released, however, Stokowski's involvement with the Philadelphia Orchestra was already on the wane. Picking up the baton after him was the considerably more mild-mannered Eugene Ormandy, who during his 44-year tenure became known as the auteur of "The Philadelphia Sound." During Ormandy's reign the orchestra premiered numerous works, including Shostakovich's First Cello Concerto, Bartok's Third Piano Concerto, and Virgil Thomson's Louisiana Story. Sergei Rachmaninoff was one of the orchestra's biggest fans, and during that period served as an occasional guest conductor in Philadelphia. His First Symphony and Symphonic Dances were premiered by the orchestra; several scores, with his handwritten corrections, are part of the orchestra's library.

In 1980 Eugene Ormandy retired as music director of the Philadelphia Orchestra, relinquishing the title to Riccardo Muti, then the orchestra's principal guest conductor. The young Italian maestro quickly took advantage of the orchestra's versatility to program music from all periods, much of it previously unheard in Philadelphia. Muti actively sought music by contemporary composers, particularly new American works. Several pieces have been commissioned by the orchestra and premiered before Greater Philadelphia audiences. With its flair for drama and contrast, the

Designed by architect Napoleon Lebrun and completed in 1856, the magnificent Academy of Music, which is home to the Philadelphia Orchestra, is now a National Historic Landmark. Photo by George Adams Jones

orchestra has been able to touch a broader audience under Muti than perhaps at any time in its history. Orchestra tours across America and Europe regularly are greeted by sold-out houses and rave reviews.

In 1992 the Philadelphia Orchestra will begin a new phase in its development as Wolfgang Sawallisch, the 67-year-old conductor of the Bavarian State Opera Orchestra, succeeds Muti as music director. Acclaimed by musicians for his artistic vision, Sawallisch was offered the post after an intensive five-month search. The German maestro (and occasional Philadelphia guest conductor) has been a longtime fan of the orchestra, often praising its sound and style. Classical music fans expect the mutual admiration between Sawallisch and orchestra musicians to produce many memorable seasons.

During the summer months Greater Philadelphians, taking their appetite for classical music alfresco, attend the Philadelphia Orchestra's outdoor concerts at the Mann Music Center in Fairmount Park. The center offers overhead shelter for the musicians and a limited-seating audience. A far larger number of people attend the concerts for free, carrying picnic baskets to the site and sitting on the sloping lawn surrounding the open-sided building. The concerts are supported by the City of Philadelphia and by patron donations; a seat on the lawn can be had for the price of a coupon published in area newspapers and a self-addressed, stamped envelope.

Since its inception the Philadelphia Orchestra has made its regular-season home at the Academy of Music, a National Historic Landmark designed by

Napoleon LeBrun and Gustav Runge. Inspired by the interior of LaScala in Milan, the then acoustically near-perfect academy was unveiled in January 1857. The site of operas, chorales, concerts, ballets, and numerous other events, the academy is part of the fabric of Philadelphia life. It is also a terribly overworked building.

Responding to the city's need for an additional performing-arts facility, the Philadelphia Orchestra has announced plans to build a new Orchestra Hall one block south of the Academy on Broad Street. Renowned local architect Robert Venturi has designed the planned 2,800-seat concert hall to be strikingly modern, yet in harmony with classical buildings nearby. Unlike the academy, which was originally designed as an opera house, the interior of Philadelphia Orchestra Hall will be visually and acoustically tuned to concert performances. Groundbreaking for the $110-million structure is scheduled for mid-1991.

The Philadelphia Orchestra isn't the only purveyor of symphonic sounds in the Delaware Valley. Far from it. The Philadelphia All-Star Forum, a 53-year-old nonprofit organization, sponsors some 30 musicals, ballets, and theatrical performances a year, including the often-sold-out Great Performers Series at the Academy of Music. Under the auspices of the All-Star Forum, Greater Philadelphians have enjoyed London's Philharmonic Orchestra, the Boston Symphony, and the New York Symphony, as well as solo artists like Andre Watts, Beverly Sills, Rudolf Nureyev, Emanuel Ax, James Galway, and Kiri Te Kanawa.

Moe Septee, a legendary showman, music impressario and director of the All-Star Forum since 1967, has likened his role in Philadelphia to that of middleman between artist and public, never pandering or bowing to either side. His open-minded, fresh approach to music is perhaps best illustrated by his special programming for the Philly Pops. Conducted by Peter Nero, this tightly run, highly skilled symphonic pops organization made its debut in 1979. Sponsored by the All-Star Forum, the Pops is known for its license with classical music—performing jazzed-up renditions of Beethoven next to fully orchestrated pop music and show tunes—and for Septee's innovative productions. One of the group's most fondly recalled performances featured Philadelphia Phillies relief pitcher Tug McGraw, decked out in black tie for his Academy of Music debut, dramatically narrating "Casey at the Bat" against the orchestra's musical backdrop. At a Fourth of July Pops concert held outside the Philadelphia Museum of Art, tens of thousands of people turned out to hear basketball wizard Julius "Dr. J." Erving reading excerpts from the Declaration of Independence. Other Septee-Pops experiments include signing break dancers to appear with the orchestra. One outdoor extravaganza, a Fourth of July Philly Pops/International Fireworks Festival in Philadelphia, drew more than one million people.

Newer to the Greater Philadelphia cultural community is the Opera Company of Philadelphia, founded in 1975. Dedicated to the production and promotion of grand opera, the company mounts several productions each year, including traditional favorites, avant-garde works, and specially commissioned operas. In 1977 the Opera Company premiered Gian Carlo Menotti's *The Hero* at the Academy of Music—a work commissioned by the company. In 1989 Menotti returned to Philadelphia to direct the company's production of his *The Saint of Bleeker Street*. Other premieres have included Joseph Barber's *Rumplestiltskin*, an opera for children. Jessye Norman has appeared with the OCP, and Cheryl Studer made her Philadelphia debut in the company's production of *Lucia di Lammermoor*.

Although the Opera Company's professional productions have won fans and critical acclaim throughout the Delaware Valley and beyond, it is the Opera Company of Philadelphia/Luciano Pavarotti International Voice Competition that has given OCP an international audience. Since 1980 OCP officials have joined the great tenor in launching three separate worldwide searches for new operatic talent. More than 2,500 young singers from five continents have participated in preliminary auditions, with the local winners of each search being flown to Philadelphia for the competition finals. After competing at the Academy of Music, contest winners join Pavarotti in one or more full-scale operatic performances. In 1982 the competition's crowning event turned into a record-shattering PBS broadcast titled "Pavarotti in Philadelphia: La Boheme," which attracted 22 million viewers. The Opera Company won an Emmy for that produc-

tion, one of the group's five national, prime-time Emmys. To date the OCP is second only to New York's Metropolitan Opera in the number of opera telecasts to its credit.

Dick Clark, Patti LaBelle—and All That Jazz

Highbrow classical music commands a broad audience in Philadelphia, but certainly not at the expense of toe-tapping, hip-shaking popular fare. The week-long Mellon Jazz Festival brings jazz legends like Miles Davis, Chick Corea, Cleo Laine, and Jimmy Heath to town for special performances every summer along with newly discovered talents and local lights. In addition to staged concerts all over town, the festival also offers numerous "freebie" events featuring local combos, school ensembles, and name performers.

At Penn's Landing the Philadelphia riverfront takes on a Cajun-Creole flavor each Memorial Day weekend as the three-day Jambalaya Jam food-and-music festival attracts thousands of zydeco, Dixieland, and gumbo-rock fans. Dr. John, Irma Thomas, the Neville Brothers, Beausoleil, and Pete Fountain are among those who have taken the stage here, giving Philadelphians a reason to stay home for the holiday. Another Penn's Landing weekend music fete with a solid constituency is the late-July Riverblues Festival, where crowds stomp and sway to the sounds of B.B. King, John Mayall, and the Fabulous Thunderbirds.

The national contemporary music scene owes a lot to Philadelphia. "American Bandstand" got its start in the city in 1952 when a local TV station invited teens into its West Philadelphia studio to dance to popular songs on camera. By 1956, 27-year old Dick Clark had been tapped to host the show. He added rock 'n roll tunes to the format and the show went national in 1957. "American Bandstand" left the city in the 1960s, but a number of hometown crooners made their national debut on the show's afternoon time slot. "Bandstand" guests Fabian, Frankie Avalon, Bobby Rydell, and Chubby Checker all are natives.

A Philadelphia band, Bill Haley and the Comets, gave early rock 'n roll its anthem when they recorded "Rock Around the Clock" in 1955. Local rhythm-and-blues songwriters Kenny Gamble and Leon Huff gave a different "Philadelphia Sound" to the music of the 1970s, writing songs for Harold Melvin and the Blue Notes, the O'Jays, and Hall and Oates. Today the "Sound of Philadelphia," an exuberant blend of disco,

pop, and R & B, continues in the music of well-known local artists like Patti LaBelle, Teddy Pendergrass, and the Stylistics.

In 1989 the Philadelphia Music Foundation sponsored an album that showcased the city's favorite native and adopted rock artists. Titled "Philadelphia Freedom—Together," the fundraiser-recording features more than a dozen musicians trading licks on a remake of Elton John's "Philadelphia Freedom," plus solo numbers by the Hooters, Patti Labelle, Sister Sledge, Robert Hazard, and others. Of course, a true roundup of Philadelphia-inspired songs would have included a number of pop-rock classics: "South Street" by the Orlons, "Lightning Strikes" by Lou Christy, the Dovells' "Bristol Stomp," and hometown girl Dee Dee Sharp's dance hit "Mashed Potato Time." Smokey Joe's—the place where the Mashed Potato began—is still hoppin' in West Philly.

Contemporary rock artists find huge, welcoming audiences in Philadelphia, and there's always somebody big turning up at the Spectrum, the Tower Theatre, Veterans Stadium, and other smaller auditoriums and clubs around town. Hosting the famine-relief "We Are The World" benefit concert cemented the city's reputation as a rock 'n roll mecca. Since then David Bowie, the Rolling Stones, and other performers have launched national tours in the City of Brotherly Love.

On Their Toes

The Pennsylvania Ballet was founded in 1963 by Barbara Weisberger, with help and artistic support from the late George Balanchine. Although the company has had a series of artistic directors in its history, it has built a reputation for versatility and excellence unmatched by most regional dance groups. More than 45 ballets have been added to the group's repertoire since 1983, and of those, 20 are original works. The company's 38 dancers glide through *Swan Lake*, as effortlessly as they perform John Cranko's athletically choreographed *Romeo and Juliet*. Unusual contemporary works, like Balanchine's *Love Songs* and Christopher

Above: Pennsylvania Ballet soloists perform a scene from John Cranko's interpretation of the ever-popular *Romeo and Juliet*. Photo by Rich Zila

Host to many touring dance companies, Philadelphia presented the Kirov Ballet at the Mann Music Center in Fairmount Park. Photo by Rebecca Barger

d'Amboise's specially commissioned *Franklin Court*, balance against the group's more traditional performances. The Pennsylvania Ballet has performed at the Kennedy Center in Washington, D.C., and at the Spoleto Festival in Charleston; the company also has been featured on PBS "Dance in America" programs.

The Philadelphia Dance Company (Philadanco), a modern dance troupe performing at the Annenberg Center, is one of the most distinguished black dance companies in the country. Founded in 1970 by artistic director Joan Myers Brown, Philadanco serves as both school and professional forum for African-American dancers and choreographers. In 1990 the company celebrated its 20th anniversary with a triumphant New York debut of "Rosa," a dance tribute to civil-rights pioneer Rosa Parks.

Each year Greater Philadelphia dance enthusiasts

The historic Schubert Theater is newly renovated and offers a seating capacity for 1,668 avid theatergoers. Photo by Rich Zila

welcome a smorgasbord of ethnic, modern, and international dance touring companies. The Dance Celebration series has hosted Momix, Ballet Hispanico, Lar Lubovitch Dance, and numerous other companies. In addition, the Carlisle Project, a unique choreographer's workshop in Carlisle, Pennsylvania, presents showcase performances of new ballets at Philadelphia's Painted Bride Art Center each summer. Founded in 1985 by Pennsylvania Ballet mentor Barbara Weisberger, the Carlisle Project has become a nationally recognized proving ground for young dance artists as well as an important link between dance education and the high-pressure world of professional dance companies.

On the Boards

Professional theater is alive and thriving in Greater Philadelphia. From touring companies of Broadway shows to established regional houses and avante-garde local troupes, Philadelphia audiences can find a ticket to laugh, cry, or ponder fate within easy reach, all year-round. Theater outreach programs, professional schools, and play workshops serve to broaden the local audience for drama and nurture local talent. As a result some of the most innovative theatrical experiments in the country happen on the Philadelphia stage, and area companies command a loyal, involved audience.

Philadelphia boasts the oldest live theater still in use in America. Opened in February 1809, the Walnut Street Theatre is a National Historic Landmark, site of the acting debuts of the great Philadelphia actor Edwin Forrest and, a few years later, an actress named Louisa Lane—soon to be known as Mrs. John Drew, grandmother to the famed Barrymore clan. For many years the theater was partly owned and operated by Edwin Booth, actor and brother of John Wilkes Booth. Edwin bought into the Walnut because he could no longer find work as an actor after his brother assassinated President Lincoln.

During its many-storied history the Walnut has served as an equestrian show arena, a proving ground for original works and pre-Broadway tryouts, and a harbor for touring shows and celebrity acts. *A Streetcar Named Desire, Look Homeward Angel*, and *Porgy and Bess* previewed at the Walnut, as did the contemporary comic-stunt duo Penn and Teller. Strange-but-true legends surrounding the denizens of the Walnut abound. One stagehand, John "Pop" Reed, worked at the theater for 50 years. Upon his death he willed his head to the Walnut to be used as Yorick's skull in *Hamlet*. It's said that Reed's skull was used at least once, in a 1875 production of the play.

Today the Walnut operates as a not-for-profit regional theater, offering major Mainstage and more intimate Studio productions of new and traditional works each year. In addition, the Walnut runs a Theatre School with more than 1,000 students, an Apprentice Program for aspiring theater professionals, and an Outreach Program that brings Shakespeare and American literary drama to area public schools. The theater building remains a living historical monument: the original fly-loft and its equipment are still in use,

and eighteenth-century wooden wheels, axles, and drums for moving scenery are still in place.

A former occupant of the Walnut Street Theatre, the Philadelphia Drama Guild was established in 1956 as an amateur stock company. Today it serves as Greater Philadelphia's resident professional theater, producing provocative original works and mounting new productions of established plays at the Zellerback Theatre in West Philadelphia. The guild's Playwrights of Philadelphia (POP) Festival annually produces new works by talented local writers, some of which ultimately become part of the guild's main stage offerings.

Greater Philadelphia's newest theater is scheduled to open in 1993 on South Broad and Spruce streets, across from the new Philadelphia Orchestra Hall. The state-of-the-art, 300-seat facility will give a new, expanded home to The Wilma Theater, a professional, avant-garde theater group that was founded in 1973 specifically to encourage productions of original material and to develop local artists. Led by artists-in-residence Blanka and Jiri Zizka, the Wilma has consistently won accolades for its provocative offerings. A 1986 production of Pavel Kohout's adaptation of George Orwell's *1984* resulted in the Wilma's making its Washington, D.C., debut at the Kennedy Center and landing an off-Broadway showing at the Joyce

Theater's American Theater Exchange Festival. In 1990 WNET in New York aired The Wilma Theater's production of Vaclav Havel's *Largo Desolato*.

Greater Philadelphians often get to sneak a peak at popular Broadway shows weeks before the curtain opens in New York. The Forrest Theater—a baroque, 1,800-seat playhouse on Walnut Street—has previewed numerous bound-for-Broadway shows over the years, including the Tony Award-winning *Cat On a Hot Tin Roof* with Kathleen Turner and Charles Durning. Other recent Philadelphia tryouts have included the long-running *Dream Girls* and the Duke Ellington revue *Sophisticated Ladies*.

Built at a cost of $2 million, the Forrest Theater opened in 1928 and was named for actor Edwin Forrest, who died in 1872. The theater, now run by the Schubert Organization, continues to thrive on previews and touring company productions of major Broadway shows. *Cats, Les Miserables,* and *A Chorus Line* all made their Philadelphia debuts at the Forrest.

Artistic expression doesn't always fit into neat categories, particularly in a city that embraces the oddly wonderful even as it clings to the familiar. The Painted Bride Art Center, located in a renovated industrial building just north of Center City, gives shelter to many hard-to-place and hard-to-resist

The Mummers have been a beloved Philadelphia tradition since 1876. Each New Year's Day brigades of comics, string bands, and fancies in elaborately feathered, sequined, and bejeweled costumes have paraded before enchanted crowds. Photo by George Adams Jones

performing and visual artists. The Painted Bride has hosted "A Tribute To Billie Holiday" as part of Black History Month, as well as one-woman shows by Karen Finley, a performance artist whose act often includes covering her nude body with food while reciting stream-of-consciousness monologues on contemporary issues. In its staggering agenda of 160-plus events a year, the Painted Bride offers performances by modern dance troupes, a variety of musicians, plays, poetry readings, and gallery exhibits.

Of course, some of Philadelphia's most famous performing artists come out en masse only once a year and consider Broad Street to be their theater. The Mummers' string band, fancy, and comic brigades strut up Broad Street every New Year's Day—in makeup,

Constructed of Cor-ten steel, Claes Oldenburg's *Clothespin* across from City Hall is one of Philadelphia's most famous landmarks. Photo by George Adams Jones

sequins, and feathers—to the delight of thousands who line the parade route. Mummery dates back to fifteenth-century England, where during Christmas week village youths would don costumes and go about the countryside pantomiming short plays. The Philadelphia tradition began with neighborhood groups who roamed the streets of South Philadelphia and Kensington in disguise on New Year's Eve, paying calls on friends and tavern owners. On January 1, 1876, the first official Philadelphia Mummers' Parade took place with neighborhood groups marching separately to Independence Hall. The current combined parade on Broad Street began in 1901. After New Year's, most Mummers manage to stay out of the spotlight until the next parade, but their antics and costumes can be perused year-round at the Mummers Museum in South Philadelphia.

The Parkway and Beyond: The Visual Arts

Drive across the Ben Franklin Bridge into Philadelphia and you'll spot it: Isamu Noguchi's 30-ton, 96-foot *Bolt of Lightning,* a $500,000 steel sculpture that pays homage to the man who discovered electricity. Located on a raised plaza at the foot of the bridge, the sculpture was Noguchi's last major work before he died, and yet another artistic landmark for Philadelphia.

Dubbed "The Florence of America" by Frank Lloyd Wright, Philadelphia offers more public art than any other city in America. Center City alone boasts more than 40 major outdoor sculptures, including Claes Oldenburg's giant *Clothespin* at Centre Square and Robert Indiana's painted aluminum *Love* at 15th Street and John F. Kennedy Boulevard. More traditional works, like Alexander Milne Calder's statue of William Penn atop City Hall tower and Alexander Stirling Calder's intricately carved Swann Fountain at Logan Circle, share the landscape with abstract or controversial pieces like Timothy Duffield's nude representation, *The Family.* Another 200 sculptures dot the landcape of Fairmount Park.

Philadelphia has a long history of supporting the visual arts. The Fairmount Park Art Association, the country's first private, nonprofit corporation, has since 1872 commissioned and placed public sculpture throughout the city, including works by Frederic Remington, Jacques Lipchitz, and Louise Nevelson. In

Above: The delightful
Playing Angels sculpture
helps make Fairmount
Park a kind of alfresco
museum. Photo by
George Adams Jones

Left: Frederick Reming-
ton's *Cowboy* is a
favorite Philadelphia
sculpture. Photo by
George Adams Jones

1959 the Philadelphia Redevelopment Authority passed a landmark resolution stating that anyone redeveloping city-owned property had to set aside one percent of the total construction budget for fine art. A few months later the city passed an ordinance requiring that new municipal buildings also set aside space and one percent of construction costs for art. The result has been more than 400 new artworks added to the cityscape in recent decades. Some pieces are representational, many are abstract, and a few are functional; all contribute to a sense of the city as an open-air gallery.

The city's most beautiful boulevard, Benjamin Franklin Parkway, is considered by many to be a work of city-planning-as-art. Modeled on the Champs Elysee in Paris, the tree-lined parkway diagonally slices across the northwest quadrant of the city, connecting City Hall to the lush greenery of Fairmount Park.

Stately public buildings, like Horace Trumbauer's Free Library of Philadelphia, line the street, while at the foot of the parkway, facing City Hall, is perhaps Trumbauer's most impressive building: the Greco-Roman inspired Philadelphia Museum of Art. Architects Charles C. Zantzinger and Charles L. Barie collaborated with Trumbauer on the museum.

The museum building rises majestically from a hill overlooking the City of Philadelphia on the east and the Schuylkill River and Fairmount Park on the west. Its 10 acres contain more than 200 galleries, making art browsing here a feat of athletic endurance. However, the museum's collections make all that footwork worth the effort.

Founded in 1876, the museum harbors one of the country's finest collections of nineteenth- and twentieth-century paintings. Fully appointed period rooms—including one from sixteenth-century Lon-

don, a fourteenth-century German renaissance room, and a fifteenth-century Italian room—give visitors a historic context for some of the decorative and fine arts on display. On the second floor of the museum's South Wing, major architectural units of the Middle Ages are housed: an eleventh-century Romanesque cloister from the Pyrenees, the portal of a twelfth-century French abbey, and a fourteenth-century French Gothic chapel. The museum's seven-gallery Oriental Wing includes architectural, decorative, and fine art holdings from the Near and Far East—a collection for which the institution is justifiably renowned. Among the artifacts are a Hindu stone temple from India dating to the sixteenth century and delicate Chinese porcelain and crystal pieces. American decorative arts, including Pennsylvania German and Shaker furniture, are well represented. In addition, the museum's cache includes a solid collection of modern art and sculpture, including the world's greatest collection of works by Marcel Duchamp.

Operating under the auspices of the Museum of Art, the Rodin Museum in Philadelphia houses the largest collection of the sculptor's works outside of

Paris. Located on the Benjamin Franklin Parkway, the museum entrance is guarded by Rodin's *The Gates of Hell,* while the sculptor's famous *The Thinker* presides by the entrance. Both the museum, which opened in 1929, and its 124-sculpture collection were bequeathed to the public by Philadelphia movie theater magnate and philanthropist Jules E. Mastbaum.

Although it has been eclipsed in size by the Museum of Art, the Museum of the Pennsylvania Academy of the Fine Arts, at Broad and Cherry streets in Center City, remains one of the city's great assets. Founded in 1805, it is the country's oldest art museum and one of the finest repositories of American art in the world. Contemporary works by students of the academy hang beside paintings by Mary Cassatt, Ce-

cilia Beaux, Thomas Sully, and Winslow Homer. The building that houses the academy and museum—the institution's third home—is considered the city's finest example of High Victorian Gothic architecture. It features two colors of sandstone, gold-backed enamel tiles, two colors of brick, and carved relief panels, all layered into an ornate, imposing facade. Designed by Philadelphia architects Frank Furness and George Hewitt, the structure opened in 1876 and cost $400,000.

Just outside Philadelphia, in Montgomery County, lies the Barnes Foundation, one of the world's quirkier museums and home to a magnificent collection of more than 1,000 Impressionist paintings, including 175 Renoirs, more than 60 paintings each by

Facing page top: Art lovers browse through the Philadelphia Museum of Art, the third-largest art museum in the country. The museum is noted for its Oriental collection as well as a permanent display of arms and armor, which is the most extensive of its kind in the world. Photo by George Adams Jones

Left: Located on the Benjamin Franklin Parkway, the Rodin Museum houses a priceless collection of the sculptor's originals and casts. "The Thinker" presides over the museum's arcade. Photo by George Adams Jones

Facing page bottom: An imposing figure of Diana overlooks the staircase at the Philadelphia Museum of Art. Photo by George Adams Jones

Wood sculptor Tom Paris
demonstrates his tech-
nique at the Rittenhouse
Square Fine Arts Annual.
Photo by Rich Zila

Cézanne and Matisse, and works by many other artists. The museum is the former domain of Dr. Albert C. Barnes, curmudgeon, art lover, and creator of an eye-disinfectant fortune. Outraged when, in 1923, art critics and the general public responded badly to a showing of his modern art collection, Barnes conspired to hide the works from ignorant viewers. His will stipulated that after his death the collection be shown only to students, by appointment, and that the works not be catalogued nor transported or hung in any manner other than in the way he left them. A 1961 court order opened the museum to the general public, but visitors often still find the place as unwelcoming as Barnes intended—take it or leave it. In 1990 Richard H. Glanton, a Philadelphia lawyer, took office as president of the foundation and vowed to take a broader view of the Barnes' mission. Observers consider it a good sign that a possible PBS documentary on the doctor and his collection is under review.

The Greater Philadelphia art community isn't confined to the city's large, established museums. More than 100 smaller galleries and art museums serve the artists and art lovers of the Delaware Valley area. Sometimes fine art exhibits just *happen*. In 1990 the Philadelphia Museum of Art hosted a juried exhibition of local artists' works in conjunction with Philadelphia Art Now, a three-year, $1.1-million program designed to focus public attention on local artists. More than 2,000 area artists submitted pieces for consideration; 129 were selected. But those who didn't make it, didn't despair. Four hundred of the also-ran painters, sculptors, printmakers, and photographers staged their own showcase—a modern day *salon des refuses*—at the 103rd Engineers Armory. The four-day affair attracted hundreds of browsers and art patrons and set the stage for future outside-the-establishment exhibits.

The beautiful vistas of Fairmount Park provide continuing inspiration for area artists. Photo by George Adams Jones

Philadelphia sports fans don't pull punches. Kiteman, a promotional hang glider pilot, learned that the hard way. In his debut with the Philadelphia Phillies, Kiteman swooped into Veterans Stadium to throw out the first pitch of the season. Unfortunately, he misjudged the distance to the pitcher's mound and crashed in a heep at the foot of the bleachers. Bruised, but not seriously hurt, Kiteman got up, dusted off, and showed himself to the fans—whereupon he was resoundingly booed. "Talk about your tough crowds," he muttered as he limped off the field.

Kiteman isn't the only performer to have felt the wrath of the Greater Philadelphia audience. Old-time football fans swear that at one disappointing Eagles home game, Santa Claus himself got booed at halftime. And woe to hometown athletes who perform below their perceived potential! Fans, including local sportswriters, aren't likely to let it slide. Legendary Phillies hitter Mike Schmidt once noted that only in Philadelphia can you have both "the thrill of victory and the pain of reading about it the next morning."

Whether the crowd is booing or cheering, local athletes know the stands will be filled with loyal followers. Greater Philadelphians take the old adage about working hard and playing hard a step further: They work hard at playing. And they have lots of opportunities to take their leisure time seriously.

History comes alive for this young visitor at Philadelphia's Independence National Historic Park, just one of the city's many recreational and cultural spots. Often called America's most historic square mile, Independence Park features carefully restored buildings that recall specific moments in the birth of our nation. Photo by Rich Zila

Running
Free

Four professional sports teams keep the bleachers jumping at local arenas, and dozens of high-caliber college athletic teams round out the seasonal calendar.

Of course, spectator sports aren't the only games in town. Philadelphians who get tired of sitting on the sidelines can practice their backhand at hundreds of public and private tennis courts in the area. Golfers love to pay homage to Delaware Valley links. The region has hosted the U.S. Open six times since the tournament's inception, most recently at the highly rated Merion Golf Club in Ardmore. In addition, the City of Philadelphia operates five public golf courses with very reasonable fees. Venues for cycling, rowing, boating, jogging, and hiking—in this region of rivers, woods, hills, and valleys—are almost unlimited.

Those who seek more urbane leisure pursuits will not be disappointed here. The town that once reveled only in its own patrician stodginess has long since kicked up its heels. Fine restaurants, clubs, and entertainment centers beckon from every quarter. And when "getting away from it all" becomes the order of the day, the Atlantic seashore is less than 90 minutes to the east, the Pocono mountains lie two hours northwest, and New York, Baltimore, and Washington are all a quick train ride away.

Play Ball!

Even before the Civil War, they were playing baseball in Philadelphia. Neighborhood clubs like the Athletics, the Keystones, and the Mercantiles faced each other at makeshift diamonds on the edge of town. When the first professional baseball team, the Cincinnati Red Stockings, played an exhibition game in the city in 1869, 15,000 people turned out. The popularity of the sport grew to its height in the 1930s when Philadelphia supported two major league ball clubs and 22 minor league teams. The now-fabled Philadelphia Athletics (predecessors to the modern-day Oakland A's) claimed two American League pennants and two World Series titles during the early years of the Depression.

When the National Baseball League launched its first season in 1876, Philadelphia was part of the lineup. Unfortunately, the city's team—an early incarnation of the Athletics—lasted only one season. They were booted out of the league for refusing to make a final trip west for an end-of-season game. A few years later city investors got a shot at a second National

Whether it be a game of football or ice hockey, Philadelphia sports fans crowd the stands to support the home team. Their spirit is legendary. Photo by A. Gurmankin/ Unicorn Stock Photos

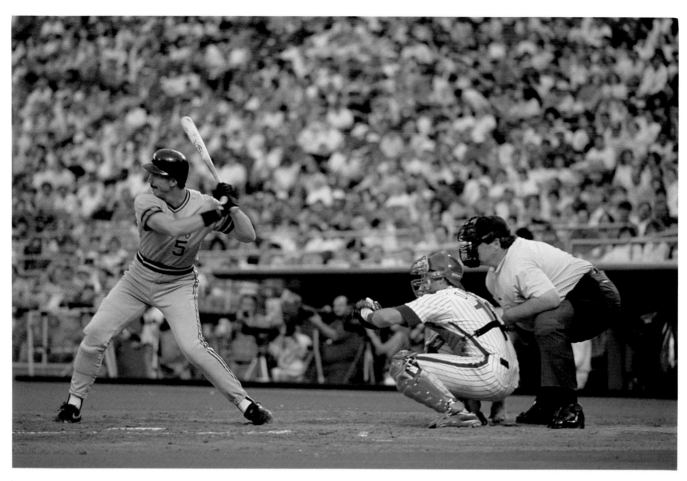

A batter faces the opposing pitcher before a packed Veterans Stadium as the Phillies compete in the Eastern Division of the National League. Photo by Rebecca Barger

League franchise and grabbed it. The Philadelphia Phillies came to bat in 1883 and have been slugging away ever since.

The Phillies have never been consistent performers, but over the decades they've given fans enough title wins and come-from-behind victories to ensure a loyal following. The team's first World Championship, won in 1980, was so fraught with near-misses and nick-of-time plays that sportscasters dubbed the team "the heart-attack kids." Annual attendance at Phillies games regularly tops one million, rising to two million in winning seasons. Even when the team is down, individual Phillies players have given fans their money's worth. The Phillies lifetime roster reads like a who's who of baseball: Grover Cleveland Alexander, Richie Ashburn, Steve Carlton, and Mike Schmidt have all left their marks on the record books.

The Philadelphia Phillies' home field is Veterans Stadium, located at the foot of South Broad Street. Opened in 1971, the 56,000-seat open-air stadium cost $52 million to build and was once the largest baseball stadium in the National League.

The Phillies share Veterans Stadium with the

Philadelphia Eagles football team, founded in 1933. The Eagles got a slow start in Philadelphia, but their performance picked up after World War II when the NFL team took the 1947 Eastern Conference Championship. The Birds followed that victory by claiming the league championship in 1948 and 1949.

Some fans and historians contend that the Eagles have 10-year "cycles," with a few good seasons followed by years of subsistence playing. If so, the 1990s may witness some spectacular football in Philadelphia. Former Eagles coach Buddy Ryan, a tough-talking pro-football and Super Bowl veteran, rebuilt the team when he came to town in 1986, and since then the team's record has gradually improved.. The Eagles won the Eastern Division title in 1988 and made it to the playoffs in 1988 and 1989. The outlook for a Super Bowl berth seems promising.

The Philadelphia '76ers are relative newcomers to the Greater Philadelphia area. The basketball team came to town in 1963, fast on the heels of the departing Philadelphia Warriors—a team founded in 1946 and transferred to San Francisco in 1962. The Sixers (formerly the Syracuse Nats) claimed the NBA's

Above: The 56,000-seat Veterans Stadium opened in 1971 and is home to the Philadelphia Phillies and the Philadelphia Eagles. Photo by Rich Zila

Left: The Philadelphia Eagles defensive line is shown here battling against the New York Giants. Photo by Ed Mahan/Philadelphia Eagles

Rowing on the Schuylkill River is a perennially popular sport for both athletes and spectators. As the graceful sculls skim the water during one of Philadelphia's many annual regattas, afficionados can get a great view of the action from Fairmount Park. Photos by David H. Wells

and Hockey Hall of Fame member Ed Snider introduced Greater Philadelphians to professional hockey by securing a NHL franchise in 1967. The team subsequently made it to the play-offs 20 times in its first 22 years on the ice. The Flyers brought home the Stanley Cup in 1974 and again in 1975, and two of its star players at the time, center Bobby Clarke and goalie Bernie Parent, are now members of the Hockey Hall of Fame. The Flyers share the Spectrum arena with the Sixers.

Notable athletic events in Greater Philadelphia aren't limited to professional team sports, however. Rowing on the Schuylkill River has been a popular sport in Philadelphia for centuries, and was glorified in the late-nineteenth-century paintings of Thomas Eakins. Olympic-caliber rowers, including the late John B. Kelly, Jr. (Philadelphia city councilman and brother of Princess Grace), have trained on the Schuylkill. Boathouse Row, a collection of Victorian boating clubhouses, lines the banks of the Schuylkill in Fairmount Park. The clubs continue to groom amateur athletes, and provide the city with one of its more striking nocturnal landmarks. Architectural lighting was installed on the boathouses for the 1976 Bicentennial, and every evening the glittering outlines of the great buildings reflect on the water.

In 1985 Philadelphia became a rallying point for professional bicyclers from all over the world. The annual CoreStates U.S. Pro Cycling Championship, held each June, is one of the four top cycling events in the world. It's also the richest one-day contest, with prizes totaling $110,000. Participants run a 156-mile course, which includes 10 trips up the dreaded Manayunk Wall, a 250-foot vertical climb through the heart of one of Philadelphia's revitalized industrial neighborhoods.

Eastern Division title in 1966—with a little help from star Wilt Chamberlain—and went on to win the NBA title in 1967. Julius "Dr. J." Erving joined the Sixers in 1976, and was part of the team that claimed the NBA championship in 1983. (Now retired, Erving has become a prominent member of the Greater Philadelphia business community.)

The Sixers' home court is now at the Philadelphia Spectrum, a 17,000-seat sports and entertainment arena opened in 1967. However, team owner Harold Katz has been discussing the possibility of moving the team to a new sports complex in Camden, New Jersey, or possibly to a new arena in Philadelphia.

The Philadelphia Flyers hockey team is the youngest—and arguably the most successful—pro sports organization in the city. Current team owner

Above: Nature lovers can
get away from it all at
Fairmount Dam, located
just minutes from the
heart of Center City.
Photo by Rich Zila

Naturally Philadelphia

Greater Philadelphia sits at the center of the most active, densely populated region of the United States. Yet few other metropolitan areas offer its citizens access to so many seductive, bucolic retreats. Within a short drive—or in some cases, walking distance—from home or work, local nature lovers can delight in pristine forests, wooded creeks, manicured park lawns, and well-tended horticultural exhibits. Minutes from Center City lie nature preserves that seem so isolated and remote that it's hard to believe civilization thrives over the next ridge.

Much of Greater Philadelphia's green space originally was set aside to protect Delaware Valley watersheds and ensure a steady supply of fresh water for area homes and businesses. Practical concerns notwithstanding, these open refuges from urban life contribute mightily to the city's quality of life and the metropolitan area's reputation for being "liveable."

Fairmount Park, the jewel of Greater Philadelphia's public recreation amenities, was founded in 1855 with the city's annexation of the Lemon Hill area just north of the Fairmount Water Works on the Schuylkill River. As the city grew, additional acreage was added to the park, and today the Fairmount Park System encompasses 8,900 acres of wilderness, formal gardens, playgrounds, former estates, sculpture gardens, and historic and special-purpose buildings. It is one of the largest urban park systems in the world; more than 10 percent of Philadelphia's land mass falls within its borders.

Hikers and foliage fanatics favor the natural forests of Fairmount Park's creek valleys and ravines. A wide variety of hardwood trees—oak, beech, red and sugar

Above: Cyclists from around the world compete in the Core States U.S. Pro-Cycling Championship, the only Grand Prix event held outside Europe. Photo by George Adams Jones

Facing page below: Joggers and bicyclists are but a few of the many athletes who find room to enjoy their sports in Philadelphia's many parks. Photo by George Adams Jones

Founded in 1874, the Philadelphia Zoo is home to more than 1,800 exotic animals in a nineteenth-century Victorian garden setting. Photo by Linda Zila

maples, hemlock, and black birch—populate those areas. Joggers and picnickers seem drawn to the open, rolling lawns that line both banks of the Schuylkill River. And the broad, elevated Belmont Plateau is a preferred gathering sight for concerts and celebrations or, on quiet days, for enjoying one of the most striking views of the Philadelphia skyline.

Rowing, biking, horseback riding, golf, and tennis facilities are all available and open to the public within the park. In addition, weekend athletes will find baseball diamonds, a rugby field, soccer fields, a bowling green, swimming pools, bocce courts, and an

archery range. More genteel pursuits might include a visit to the classically designed Memorial Hall—the only major structure remaining from Philadelphia's 1876 Centennial Exhibition—or a tour of any of the handful of eighteenth-century mansions now located within the park. The Fairmount Water Works, situated on the east bank of the Schuylkill River just above the Art Museum, is a National Historic, Civic, and Mechanical Landmark. Designed by Frederick Graff in 1812, this composite Federal and Greco-Roman Revival structure provided drinking water for the city for most of the nineteenth century.

Fairmount Park also harbors the 42-acre Philadelphia Zoo—the first zoo in America and one of the most visited. Nearly 1.5 million people tour the zoological gardens each year. Sited on the west bank of the Schuylkill River, the zoo houses more than 1,800 birds, mammals, reptiles, and amphibians from around the globe. Many of the animals inhabit artfully created exhibits that mimic their natural habitat. The polar bear exhibit in Bear Country is one of the zoo's most popular attractions; guests can peer into the bears' 200,000-gallon swimming tank through an eight-foot viewing window. The zoo maintains educational programs both on the zoo grounds and through "Zoo on Wheels" traveling shows. In addition, zoo personnel are constantly engaged in research aimed at wildlife conservation and ensuring optimum care for zoo animals.

Outside Fairmount Park, formal gardens, nature centers, and arboreta can be found tucked away in various corners of the Greater Philadelphia area. Morris Arboretum of the University of Pennsylvania lies at the far northwest corner of the city—166 acres of woodlands and gardens, including an English garden, a Japanese garden, and a formal rose garden. Bequeathed to the University of Pennsylvania in 1932 by John and Lydia Morris (siblings who established the preserve some 45 years earlier), Morris Arboretum features more than 3,500 specimen plantings, including an expansive 100-year-old Asian katsura tree that some experts consider the pride of the collection. In the industrialized southwest corner of Philadelphia, nature lovers can visit Bartram's Garden, the oldest surviving botanic garden in the U.S. This 44-acre tract near the Schuylkill River was first planted in 1728 by self-taught botanist John Bartram. His farmhouse, a National Historic Landmark, still stands on the property.

Outside Philadelphia, in adjacent Delaware County, Tyler Arboretum offers 700 acres of formal and informal gardens, hiking trails, and nineteenth-century historic buildings. Tyler Arboretum is famous among nature lovers both for its extensive rhododendron collection and a resident 120-year-old giant sequoia tree. Birdwatchers flock to the area for glimpses of great horned and eastern screech owls, hummingbirds, and assorted other feathered friends. In nearby Chester County, the internationally acclaimed Longwood Gardens features 350 acres of landscaped gardens, illuminated fountains, and ponds. Established by Pierre-Samuel DuPont, the elaborate gardens were once part of his 1,000-acre country estate. Longwood Gardens is open year-round, and includes more than three acres of indoor exhibits.

Most Greater Philadelphia public gardens and nature centers are three-season affairs. Although many facilities are open year-round, few people venture out in the dead of the mid-Atlantic winter. But those starved for the sight of a colorful bud, a shiny green leaf, or a sweet-smelling bouquet can bide their time until early March, when the Philadelphia Flower Show bursts through the winter doldrums. Considered by many horticulturalists to be the finest flower show in the world, Philadelphia's winter bloomfest is in fact America's largest and oldest indoor garden event. Held each year at the Philadelphia Civic Center, the Flower Show covers a six-acre expanse with more than 1,500 professional and amateur exhibits. Self-contained, 2,000-square-foot landscapes vie for attention with single, perfect potted orchids and rare, aged bonsai trees. At the 1990 show, built around the theme "Purely for Pleasure," the title exhibit featured some 800 rose plants, a thousand perennials, a 50-foot pond, flowering trees, statues, and a tiered fountain. Proceeds from the Flower Show, sponsored annually by the Pennsylvania Horticultural Society since 1829, help support Philadelphia Green, PHS's community outreach program and one of the largest public "greening" efforts in the U.S.

Mind Games

Benjamin Franklin, statesman, scientist, and entrepreneur, would have approved. Philadelphia's Franklin Institute Science Museum—founded in 1824 as the country's prototype "hands-on" learning museum—recently opened a new Futures Center devoted to science and technology in the twenty-first century. Unveiled in 1990, the $72-million, 90,000-square-foot addition features state-of-the-art exhibits and an interactive, computerized information system that allows visitors to design their own customized tour of the facility. Permanent exhibits focus on computers, robotics, energy, health, conservation, new materials, technology, and careers of the future. Given a preview of the possibilities, visitors can actually vote on the kind of future they'd like to see in the Musser Choices Forum. The center's four-story Omniverse Theater, with its 79-foot-wide screen, literally surrounds view-

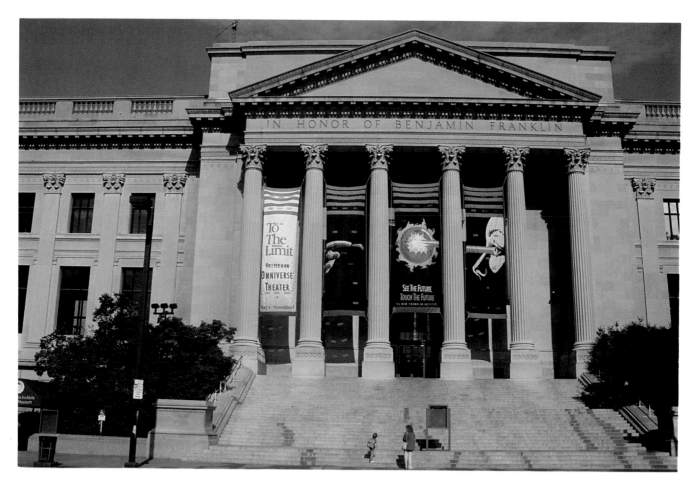

Above: The Franklin Institute was established in 1894 as an educational institution dedicated to the spirit of Benjamin Franklin. The Science Museum was established in 1934 and was soon joined by the Fels Planetarium, the Benjamin Franklin National Memorial, and an extensive collection of Franklin artifacts. The facilities were again expanded in 1990 to include a Futures Center and Omniverse Theater. Through commitment to science, past and future, the Franklin Institute keeps Benjamin Franklin's spirit of discovery alive and thriving in Philadelphia. Photo by Rebecca Barger

ers with action. It is the largest theater of its kind in North America. One of the Omniverse's feature presentations is *Philadelphia Anthem*, a 70mm, seven-minute tribute to Greater Philadelphia's quaint streets, bustling traffic, rural vistas, and powdery beaches.

In addition to the Futures Center, the Franklin Institute continues to offer all the do-it-yourself exhibits that have made the museum one of Greater Philadelphia's most popular attractions. A walk-through human heart (36 times life size) is particularly popular with children, as is the 101-foot-long steam locomotive that gives brief rides across the museum floor. Fels Planetarium, located within the museum, is the largest public observatory in the country.

One block away from Franklin Institute on the Benjamin Franklin Parkway sits the Academy of Natural Sciences and the Academy Museum. Founded in 1812, the academy is well regarded for its basic and practical research in aquatic environmental sciences, and in systematics and evolutionary biology. The Academy Library, with its collection of 200,000 books,

250,000 manuscripts, maps, and periodicals, serves a worldwide scientific community. However, most Philadelphians know the academy through its Natural History Museum, the country's oldest natural sciences museum and a popular field trip destination for area schools. The museum's collection of minerals and preserved animals, birds, and insects is impressive, but older displays are often upstaged by "Discovering Dinosaurs," the academy's newest major permanent exhibit. This panorama of prehistoric life includes hands-on exhibits and computer videos, plus reconstructed skeletons of *Tyrannosaurus rex* and other dinosaurs.

In addition to its internationally acclaimed art and science institutions, Greater Philadelphia also offers dozens of smaller ethnic, cultural, and special-interest museums. Near Independence Mall the museum and library at the Balch Institute for Ethnic Studies sheds light on the history of immigration and ethnic cultures in the U.S. A few blocks away the Afro-American Historical and Cultural Museum, opened in 1976, was the first museum in the country built specifically to showcase African-American cultural artifacts, crafts,

Top: Comedian Doug White entertains his audience at the Comedy Factory Outlet on Bank Street. Photo by Rich Zila

Left: The opening of the Zanzibar Blue Restaurant and Jazz Cafe was the realization of a longtime dream for owners Robert and Benjamin Bynum. Their club was designed to bridge the gap between perennial fans and those to whom jazz is a new experience. Shown here with their staff, Robert and Benjamin are in the rear, second and third from left, respectively. Photo by Rich Zila

and history. Also opened in 1976, the National Museum of Jewish History on North Fifth Street focuses on Jewish participation in the growth and development of the U.S. Swedes settled in the Philadelphia area before William Penn, and their history here is traced at the American-Swedish Historical Museum on Pattison Street. At Penn's Landing the Port of History Museum offers an ever-changing array of maritime exhibits, and at the University Museum in West Philadelphia, armchair archaeologists can view treasures of the ages unearthed by University of Pennsylvania scholars. Some of the artifacts on display include Sumerian cuneiform clay tablets, ancient Oriental artworks, and objects from the royal cemetery at Ur dating from circa 2600 B.C.

Delicious Diversions

A night on the town in Philadelphia might include a concert or a play opening, a trip to the ballet, or a stop at one of the area's many brash, lively comedy clubs. But regardless of the evening's final agenda, a respite at one of the city's new eclectic bistros or dinner at an old favorite eatery is de rigueur. The restaurant renaissance that in the mid-1970s jolted local palates out of their meat-and-potatoes complacency is still in full swing. Dozens of restaurants open in the city every year, and while many don't make it, the pace of new arrivals hasn't slowed down. Philadelphia has become a restaurant town, and checking out the latest in cafe chic is one of the most popular local pastimes.

Benefiting from this eatery explosion has been a

Right: One of Philadelphia's most famous foods is the cheesesteak, a hearty sandwich of thinly sliced steak, melted cheese, and cooked onions. A waitress at the Society Hill Hotel proudly shows off that establishment's award-winning version of this tasty treat. Photo by Rich Zila

Facing page: Children of all ages can enjoy the natural beauty of Penn's Treaty Park along the Delaware River. Photo by Linda Zila

myriad of long-established ethnic and neighborhood restaurants in Greater Philadelphia. Once natives got in the habit of dining out, they rediscovered the many culinary gems tucked away in various corners of the city. In the Italian enclave of South Philadelphia, informal restaurants serve up pizza, pasta, and red gravy according to recipes that have been in the family for generations. North of Center City in Chinatown, Szechuan, Cantonese, and Mandarin specialty restaurants nestle beside Peking duck and dim sum houses, macrobiotic Chinese restaurants, *nouvelle Chinoise* emporiums, and a sprinkling of Thai, Vietnamese, and other Asian-specialty bistros.

Virtually every ethnic, regional, and traditional cuisine imaginable—from Ethiopian to French *a la Cordon Bleu*—can be found in the Delaware Valley area. In March 1984 the City of Philadelphia launched an annual celebration of the region's gastronomic diversity, bringing national attention to local products and Philadelphia restaurants. Dubbed "The Book and the Cook," this four-day food fest pairs bestselling cookbook authors with local restauranteurs. The result is a mouth-watering array of breakfast, lunch, tea, and dinner menus designed by the authors and prepared by local chefs and caterers. Foodies from all over the U.S. make reservations weeks in advance for these usually-sold-out meals, paying between $15 and $100 for the privilege of dining in the company

Many opportunities for outdoor recreation can be experienced in the areas surrounding Philadelphia. Canoeists find a tranquil setting in Wharton State Forest, which encompasses 109,298 acres of pristine wilderness in New Jersey's Pine Barrens. Photo by Mary Ann Brockman

of culinary celebrities. Along with the dining events, The Book and The Cook Fair offers food-lovers a two-day festival of related exhibits, demonstrations, and opportunities to hobnob with cookbook authors.

Day Trips and Weekend Jaunts

Greater Philadelphians can duck out of town more quickly and easily than folks residing in most other metro areas. The glittering lights of Manhattan and the mysteries of the Smithsonian Institution in Washington, D.C., are mere day trips via Amtrak's northeast corridor service. Turnpikes lead to the mountains and the sea, and to a broad range of scenic points in between.

Less than 90 minutes from Center City, Atlantic City lures high rollers and slot grinders alike to its gaming towers by the sea. More than a dozen casino hotels line the Boardwalk and bay front in this boom-

ing resort town. At night casino nightclubs bring glitzy reviews and big-name entertainers to the shore. And during the daylight hours gambling-weary visitors can stroll the Boardwalk, shop at Pier One, or just head out to the sand to get a little sun. Elsewhere along the South Jersey shore—in towns like Wildwood, Avalon, and Ocean City—Greater Philadelphians boost the summer population into the thousands, migrating to the sea year after year, generation after generation.

Northwest of Philadelphia the Pocono Mountains offer skiing, hiking, fishing, and scenic, rural vistas just two hours from the city. Cool in the summer and snowy-cold in winter, the Poconos are a favorite second-home location for many Delaware Valley families, and a reasonable weekend getaway site for others. Large conference resorts—and more than a few "honeymoon hotels"—scattered around the Poconos have

A gazebo evokes the romance of an earlier era in the soft glow of sunset on the Schuylkill River. Photo by Rich Zila

introduced many out-of-staters to the peaks and valleys of this upland plateau. The Delaware Water Gap, the "Gateway to the Poconos," rises up 700 feet on both sides of the Delaware River—geological evidence of more than 400 years of erosion.

Pennsylvania's Amish country, near Lancaster, is a favorite haunt for antique and farm market lovers and students of cultural diversity. The Pennsylvania Dutch (who are actually of German descent) continue to farm this rich land and provide much of its character. Amish families, who by religious conviction eschew modern conveniences, till the land with the help of farm animals and ride to town in horse-drawn buggies. Travelers can sample the bounty of the Amish farm table at several family-style restaurants in the Lancaster County area. Occasionally, farmsteads will display signs offering quilts or fresh produce or eggs—a sure sign that brief visits are welcome.

Philadelphians often liken their childhood experiences to growing up in a small town. And while the analogy might sound odd to outsiders—since Greater Philadelphia is the fifth largest metropolitan area in the U.S.—it rings true to anyone who has spent any time in the area. That's because Philadelphia is not so much a city as it is a collection of neighborhoods.

Natives grow up in storybook-village small towns, or on tree-lined suburban streets, or in densely populated row house neighborhoods—often just a few blocks or doors away from grandparents, aunts, uncles, and lifelong family friends. Roots bind Greater Philadelphians to their hometown; the transient rate for natives is extremely low, and it isn't unusual for young couples in the Delaware Valley to look for homes in their "old neighborhoods." Since nearly everybody stays in town—or comes back to settle down—people are constantly running into old friends, former classmates, and relatives on the streets.

Immigration and domestic migration patterns over Greater Philadelphia's history have created an ethnically and architecturally diverse coalition of more than 100 communities within the metropolitan area. There are row house neighborhoods with shot-and-a-beer taverns on every corner, old-world

From the stately homes of the Main Line to the colorful atmosphere of Chinatown, the vital spirit of Philadelphia's many neighborhoods creates a special environment in which to live, work, and play. Photo by George Adams Jones

A City
of
Neighborhoods

enclaves where residents speak English as a second language, renovated historic districts, and wooded suburban towns. Transferees usually feel right at home in Greater Philadelphia—there's always at least one neighborhood in the city that suits their tastes.

Center City

Downtown Philadelphia is a thriving residential neighborhood, with gracious townhouses and chic high-rises sited in and around the city's corporate towers and historic shrines. William Penn himself laid out the Center City area from the Delaware to Schuylkill rivers and from South Street to Vine. Current residents can thank the city founder—and Philadelphia's general aversion to change—for their neighborhood's lush green spaces and much of its orderly, human-scaled development. Many of the residences occupied by Center City dwellers today date back to the eighteenth and nineteenth centuries. Modern townhouses were built to complement, but not mimic, neighboring historic structures. High-rise apartments, such as the I.M. Pei-designed Society Hill Towers, often occupy sites made vacant by industry or neighborhood reclamation efforts.

Center City itself can be broken down into a number of separate neighborhoods. Old City, north of Market Street near the Delaware River, was once home to craftspeople and dockworkers as well as the site of riverfront warehouses. Wholesale merchants still occupy many storefronts in the area, while some former warehouses and factories have been turned into loft apartments tenanted by artists and young professionals. Attracted by wide spaces and reasonable rents, several art galleries recently have opened their doors in Old City, which has led some to dub the district "SoHo by the Delaware." Elfreth's Alley, believed to be the oldest continuously occupied residential street in America, is located in Old City. Small, two-story houses dating to 1725 line the block-long cobblestone way.

South of Market Street, Society Hill encompasses Independence Mall and much of the city's historic district. Colonial Philadelphia's wealthy merchant class settled this community; post-World War II restoration efforts restored its genteel ambiance. Low, gable-roofed Colonial homes from the early eighteenth century, still in use as private residences, can be found in Society Hill. The Washington Square West neighborhood features three- and four-story Colonial and Victorian townhouses and apartment buildings. Portico Row, architect Thomas U. Walter's development of 16 row houses with Ionic-columned front porches, was built in 1831-33. Located on Spruce Street between Ninth and Tenth streets, the now-historic Row adds a touch of Greek Revival elegance to the city's basic row house design. Washington Square West residents share their neighborhood with the antique alley on Pine Street and a number of taverns and after-hours clubs.

Left: Delightful window boxes and fine architectural details enhance the neighborhood charm of Delancy Street in Center City. Photo by Linda Zila

Facing page: More than 100 different communities within the metropolitan region comprise the rich and diverse city that is Philadelphia. Photo by Rich Zila

An oasis of blooming flowers and cool shade, this Center City park creates an ideal place in which to peruse the Sunday edition of the *Philadelphia Inquirer*. Photo by Rich Zila

Above: Elegant townhouses line picturesque Spruce Street in the heart of Philadelphia. Photo by Mary Ann Brockman

Right: Settled by Philadelphia's wealthy merchant class during the city's colonial period, affluent Society Hill still offers an atmosphere of gracious living. Photo by David H. Wells

West of Broad Street, the area bordering Philadelphia's fabled Rittenhouse Square boasts elegant Victorian and early-twentieth-century brick townhouses and brownstones. Named in honor of David Rittenhouse, astronomer and first director of the U.S. Mint, Rittenhouse Square was once Philadelphia's most prestigious address. Some of that early glory has faded as pricey apartment towers have replaced private mansions on the square, but an address in this neighborhood still carries clout. South of Rittenhouse Square, small cobblestoned streets cut between city blocks have the feel of country village paths. The grandest of all these narrow lanes is Delancey Street, a gallery of large, beautifully crafted homes, some dating to 1854.

South Philadelphia

People who've never been to Philadelphia feel like they know South Philly. This colorful, charming, largely Italian neighborhood makes the nightly network news during most presidential election years. Politicians come to the lively open-air market on Ninth Street to grip hands, grin for the cameras, and get a sense of how they're doing with working-class men and women. Here first-, second-, and third-generation Americans sell produce and fresh meats as well as imported cheeses, homemade pastas, sauces, and seasonings. Strolling through the market, shoppers can find live chickens and fresh rabbit for sale, as well as salad greens and extra virgin oils. Occasional voices conversing in Italian—or on some blocks, in Vietnamese—give visitors a sense of having dropped into a foreign country.

Off Ninth Street, South Philadelphia is one of the most stable, closely knit neighborhoods in the city. One woman, who now lives in the South Philly row house that once belonged to her parents, remembers her childhood there as one ongoing family gathering. "If I fell and skinned my knee, my mother knew about it before I got home," she recalls. "That's why I came back here. I like that sense of community, of people caring." Although newcomers have been welcomed to the neighborhood, South Philadelphia still feels like a family affair, with old-timers pulling out lawn chairs on warm summer nights to sit and chat with neighbors in front of their well-scrubbed front steps. The sounds of Verdi and Puccini might float through an open row house window or from a passing car.

Above: Boasting a large Italian population, South Philadelphia is one of the most stable and closely-knit communities in the city. Here, a Sunday procession marches along the neighborhood's colorful Ninth Street. Photo by George Adams Jones

Left: Authentic ethnic flavor and farm-fresh produce make the Ninth Street Market in South Philadelphia a favorite place to shop. Photo by Rich Zila

Philadelphia's wealth of neighborhoods provide a safe and comfortable atmosphere in which to raise a family. Photo by Rebecca Barger

Greater Philadelphians from outside the neighborhood trek to South Philadelphia to patronize the Ninth Street Market or, more often, to stop into one of the dozens of family-run, red-checkered-tablecloth Italian restaurants in the area. The smells of garlic, cheese, and savory sauces that waft onto street corners in South Philly can be seductive, and most locals have their own favorite spot for white pizza, spaghetti with crab sauce, or lasagna.

South Philly celebrities include more than a few 1960s-era crooners: Bobby Rydell, Frankie Avalon, James Darren, and Fabian. Tenor Mario Lanza also was a local. Most people, however, remember South Philly as the home of Rocky Balboa of movie fame. Although parts of some *Rocky* movies were shot in the neighborhood, the gritty under-the-el shots in the first

film of the series were actually taken in another part of the city. There's no elevated subway in South Philadelphia.

Germantown, Mount Airy, and Chestnut Hill
In 1683 William Penn granted a 5,700-acre tract of land six miles northwest of Philadelphia to Francis Pastorius, a lawyer for several well-heeled German investors, and to 13 German Quaker families from the town of Krefeld. Within a few decades this early Philadelphia suburb—then known as the German Township—grew into a center for German culture in America. A religiously diverse community, the township included Mennonites, Dunkards, Lutherans, and other sects among its inhabitants, as well as Quakers. Local residents were skilled linen weavers and quickly

established textile manufacturing and retail operations in the area. By the late seventeenth century Germantown was a thriving industrial center boasting the first paper mill in the colonies and one of the first gristmills in the Philadelphia area. Germantown printers printed the first American edition of the Bible.

In 1854 the Germantown tract was incorporated into the City of Philadelphia as three distinctive neighborhoods: Germantown, Mount Airy, and Chestnut Hill. The largest and oldest of the three districts, Germantown today offers many reminders of its storied past. The Deshler-Morris House on Germantown Avenue was home to President George Washington and his family from 1793 to 1794, when Philadelphia served as capital of the U.S. One of the oldest houses in Philadelphia, Wyck, was home to nine generations of the same Germantown Quaker family from 1689 to 1973. In 1973 the house was taken over by the Wyck Charitable Trust to be run as a museum, complete with family manuscripts and period furnishings.

Massive stone colonial homes and ornate Victorian mansions testify to Germantown's late-eighteenth-century incarnation as a wealthy enclave of old Philadelphia families. Many of the early row houses that sheltered domestic workers and turn-of-the-century mill employees are still standing. Unfortunately, Germantown today also carries remnants of the area's slide into urban decay during the Depression and postwar periods. On some streets, blocks of neat row houses and large family homes stand adjacent to abandoned buildings and empty lots. Restoration of historic landmarks in Germantown, the renovation of

many private homes, and rejuvenation of the Chelten and Germantown Avenue business districts have all contributed to neighborhood improvement efforts.

Northwest of Germantown lies Mount Airy, a pastoral, ethnically diverse middle-class neighborhood that is home to several of Philadelphia's elected and appointed officials, as well as a polyglot of artists, teachers, professionals, and craftspeople. Local residents take pride in their community, which has a history of welcoming newcomers while maintaining a sense of quiet stability. During the 1950s and 1960s the citizens of Mount Airy encouraged integration, becoming a model for positive race relations in the U.S.

Named for the summer estate of Chief Justice William Allen, Mount Airy gained favor as a Philadelphia suburb after James Gowen built his own estate, Magnolia Villa, in the neighborhood in 1846. Gowen had purchased the Allen property and razed the Mount Airy mansion to construct his baronial digs. Magnolia Villa is now home to the Lutheran Theological Seminary. Other historic sites in Mount Airy include Cliveden, the eighteenth-century home of Benjamin Chew and site of the Revolutionary War's Battle of Germantown.

The Mount Airy neighborhood appeals to homebuyers who want suburban amenities—quiet, tree-lined streets, big backyards, and roomy houses—while still living inside the city of Philadelphia. Diverse architectural styles in Mount Airy include colonial farmhouses, three-story Victorian doubles and row

These proud Mount Airy homeowners pose in front of the stately residence in which they have lived for the past 35 years. Photo by Rich Zila

One of the oldest neighborhoods in Philadelphia, Germantown is an enclave of Colonial homes, Victorian mansions, and charming row houses. Photo by Rich Zila

houses, and 1950s-era "modern" homes. Behind these facades, houses may have been restored to near-historic accuracy, or gutted and transformed into contemporary showplaces. Although Mount Airy real estate prices have risen appreciably over the last decade, the neighborhood is still considered a bargain, given its location and high-quality housing stock.

Located at the northwest boundary of Philadelphia, Chestnut Hill retains the appearance of a self-sustaining, bucolic village. This affluent suburb-within-the-city has been home to mayors, senators, and numerous members of Greater Philadelphia's power elite. Strolling around the Hill's studied-Colonial shopping district—which features pricey antique stores, art galleries, and designer boutiques as well as basic drug and hardware stores—one gets the sense of being on a movie set. Chestnut Hill and its denizens look like something out of a mythical "Main Street, U.S.A." vignette—almost too well-scrubbed and well-bred to be real.

Although Chestnut Hill was settled as part of the original Germantown tract, the village gained its current rarified image through the attentions of Henry Howard Houston, an early partner of John D. Rockefeller in Standard Oil and a director of the Pennsylvania Railroad. In the late nineteenth century Houston bought up large parcels of land in Chestnut Hill, which he called Wissahickon Heights, just before the railroad (on whose board he sat) built a line through the area. Houston commissioned a summer resort, the Wissahickon Hotel (now Chestnut Hill Academy), to serve the community and was chief patron of a new Episcopal church, St. Martin-in-the-Fields. He also donated the grounds of the Philadelphia Cricket Club and the 1,000-acre Andorra Nature Preserve.

The industrialist built an estate for himself in Chestnut Hill, and ordered an estimated 100 other homes constructed on his properties in the area. Built primarily for sale, these early "spec" properties were mostly large, well-constructed, Queen Anne-style dwellings typified by the historic Houston-Sauveur House, which is still standing at Seminole Avenue and Hartwell Lane. Houston rented some of the homes at reasonable rates to the types of people he wanted to attract to his neighborhood—teachers, lawyers, civil servants, and other professionals. Houston's son-in-law, Dr. George Woodward, continued the practice of building Chestnut Hill's housing and population base

in an orderly, well-considered manner. Woodward built single-family homes as well as row houses and semidetached dwellings, some for sale and some for rent. Woodward family members still own numerous properties in the area, some of which are rented at below market rates.

Although Chestnut Hill property values are among the highest in the Greater Philadelphia area, both rental and sale prices vary widely. Average sale prices on the Hill hover around $250,000, although individual properties occasionally can be found for as little as $100,000 or as much as $1.3 million. For home prospectors in Chestnut Hill, pricing is only one obstacle to settling in. This stable, highly desirable community has a very low turnover rate, so finding an available property at all can be tough.

Germantown, Mount Airy, and Chestnut Hill are laid out along Germantown Avenue, originally an old Indian path. Commuter trains spurred residential

A mother, daughter, and cherished family pet enjoy a fine summer afternoon at their Chestnut Hill home. Photo by Linda Zila

growth in the area during the nineteenth century; the current Chestnut Hill East and West rail lines are a direct legacy of that period. SEPTA's number 23 trolley line, running along Germantown Avenue from Chestnut Hill to South Philadelphia, is believed to be the longest trolley line in the world. Area residents enjoy easy access to scenic Wissahickon Creek, and the lush, wooded Valley Green area of Fairmount Park. In addition, the 170-acre Morris Arboretum and Woodmere Art Museum, both in Chestnut Hill, serve as cultural retreats for these neighborhoods.

The Main Line

Once, it is said, an American debutante was presented to the Queen of England. As the young woman came up from her curtsy, the Queen asked, "My dear, where do you come from?" Without hesitation, the debutante answered, "The Main Line, Ma'am." For Philadelphians that apocryphal story embraces all the legend and lore of the city's fabled Main Line suburbs—a self-anointed preserve of wealth and good breeding.

Stretching from the western border of Philadelphia, through Montgomery County, and into parts of Delaware County, the mid-Atlantic's most prestigious bedroom communities follow the "main line" of the old Pennsylvania Railroad's best-known commuter run. In the 1870s railroad executives seized on the idea of promoting the Main Line area as a resort community, thereby ensuring a steady stream of passengers for what was originally a freight run from Philadelphia to Paoli. To give the area added cachet, established small towns were renamed after settlements in Wales—an homage to the area's original Welsh Quaker proprietors. Elm and Athensville became Narberth and Ardmore; other towns along the route included Radnor, Rosemont, and Villanova. The Bryn Mawr Hotel, now the imposing home of the Baldwin School for girls in Bryn Mawr, was to become the resort's centerpiece.

Unfortunately for the railroad, Philadelphians of affluence never really bought into the idea of vacationing just outside the city. They preferred to take their leisure at the beach in Atlantic City or at other established resorts on the east coast. After a few years, railroad chieftains revamped their original plan, and began touting the Main Line as an affluent suburban residential district. Executives built homes along the Main Line as an example, and they advised subordinates who valued their jobs to do the same. By 1880

Bright red trim and a well-manicured lawn adorn this cozy Wynnewood home. Photo by Rich Zila

the pastoral hillsides on both sides of the tracks were dotted with sumptuous Victorian estates, with occasional clusters of modest homes where servants and craftspeople lived.

Although the Main Line is now synonymous with old money in Greater Philadelphia, much of the original gentry there was comprised of the city's industrialists, bankers, lawyers, and other newly affluent professionals. Main Line social life—traditionally a strictly WASP affair, conducted against a backdrop of country clubs, horse shows, and coming-out parties—has been chronicled in film and fiction. The

real-life woman upon whom the heroine in *The Philadelphia Story* was based is Hope Montgomery Scott, mother of Robert Montgomery Scott—the current president of the Museum of Art and former special assistant to Walter Annenberg when Annenberg was Ambassador to the Court of St. James'. The Scott family presides over Ardrossan Farm, 1,000 acres between Wayne and Villanova which comprise the grandest of all the Main Line estates.

Today the gilded, turn-of-the-century opulence of the old Main Line lives on at places like Ardrossan Farm, and at numerous other estates in the area. But

for the most part the Main Line towns of Merion, Haverford, Gladwynne, Ardmore, Bryn Mawr, and Devon have ceased to be the exclusive provinces of the ultra-rich and pedigreed. Demand for less pricey housing by would-be residents—often the scions of mansion-dwellers—as well as prohibitive maintenence costs for many grand residences, has prompted the breakup of many old estates. Grounds have been subdivided into tony middle-class enclaves, and some former mansions have been turned into condominiums. Between the subdivisions and manicured estate lawns, cramped business and shopping districts give this once-bucolic area a decidedly modern suburban feel. Of course, a "modest" home in Bryn Mawr or Gladwynne is still likely to cost twice as much as the same house in another Philadelphia suburb. Nor has the Main Line area lost its attraction for the newly wealthy. Currently some of the hottest residential properties in the Greater Philadelphia area are new, $1-million-plus tract houses going up on one-to-four-acre lots in Lower Merion Township.

South Jersey

The sprawling suburbs of southern New Jersey were born of the postwar migration of young families from the then-crowded inner cities of Camden and Philadelphia. Settling on former farmland in Camden, Burlington and Gloucester counties, these 1950s-era pioneers bought tract houses sporting state-of-the-art kitchens and baths, landscaped their yards, and made contributions to the ongoing baby boom. During subsequent growth periods in the Delaware Valley, these early settlers have been joined by transferees to the area, and eventually by their own adult children and grandchildren. New housing developments—ranging from middle-class starter homes to pricey executive enclaves—have accomodated every surge in demand for the South Jersey life-style.

Above: Turn-of-the-century affluence still pervades many of Philadelphia's Main Line neighborhoods. Photo by George Adams Jones

Left: Philadelphia's numerous community sports programs help to instill a healthy sense of competition and team spirit among the area's youths. Photo by Rebecca Barger

Elbon's Farm in Mount Laurel, New Jersey, is part of the region's bucolic landscape. Photo by Linda Zila

Natives of towns like Cherry Hill, Mount Laurel, and Voorhees identify their "old neighborhoods" not so much by street names as by subdivision monikers: Barclay Farms, Ramblewood, Fox Hollow. Split-level-home-dwelling kids from Kingston Estates still meet up with teens from Knollwood colonials at Cherry Hill West High School. After-school socializing is more likely to take place at the Cherry Hill, Moorestown, or Echelon malls than at any corner malt shop. Mall culture flourishes throughout the tri-county South Jersey area; "Main Street" here is, literally, a shopping and

apartment complex in Voorhees.

Broad tract developments, with their promise of safe streets and easy living, cover much of Greater Philadelphia's New Jersey suburbs, and contribute greatly to the area's image. But South Jersey offers much more than malls and subdivisions. Nestled along Delaware River tributaries, and between major state highways, lie several of Greater Philadelphia's most charming and historic towns and villages. Some patrician communities date back almost to the founding of Philadelphia; others are working-class boroughs where,

the day, including Dolly Payne Todd—the future Dolly Madison—who is said to have danced away many evenings in the upstairs ballroom. During the Revolutionary War the New Jersey Assembly convened at the inn.

Haddonfield was named for Elizabeth Haddon, the daughter of an English Quaker who owned property in the area. Elizabeth was sent to the New World at the age of 18 to look after her father's interests; historians record that she served ably and was a woman of high spirits. Henry Wadsworth Longfellow immortalized her in *Tales of a Wayside Inn*, recounting the legend that she proposed to John Estaugh, a traveling Quaker missionary and attorney. Haddon and Estaugh were married and reigned as Haddonfield's first couple for many decades. They founded the Friends Meeting House of Haddonfield, the town's first place of worship, where Elizabeth served as clerk for more than 50 years. Haddon and Estaugh occasionally sold tracts of land in the town to other settlers and businesspeople, thus insuring a well-populated, thriving community.

Today Haddonfield retains much of its early

for the past 100 years, merchants have unfurled the flag for holidays and citizens have gathered in the park for fireworks on the Fourth of July.

Haddonfield is one of the oldest, and perhaps the best known, of South Jersey's bucolic small towns. Founded in 1701, the borough served as a trading post and transportation center for the region's farms for nearly two centuries. Haddonfield's Indian King Tavern, now a museum, figured prominently in Greater Philadelphia's social life during the late eighteenth century. The inn hosted many notable public figures of eighteenth- and nineteenth-century heritage. A strict historic preservation ordinance passed in 1972 prohibits razing of historic structures and limits renovations that might alter the character of designated buildings. Downtown Haddonfield, which runs for several blocks along Kings Highway, sports a combination of Colonial and Victorian facades. Residential streets are lined with Victorian-era homes as well as contemporary houses of traditional design. The town itself is small, covering only 2.9 square miles, but supports a population of some 12,000 people. In addition, Haddonfield's business district, with its gourmet food shops, fine arts and crafts galleries, and antique shops, attracts shoppers and browsers from surrounding South Jersey communities. The PATCO High-Speed Line's Haddonfield terminal is a busy transportation hub for daily commuters to Camden and Philadelphia.

About two miles south of Haddonfield along Haddon Avenue lies Collingswood, a late-Victorian-era town that has maintained both its historic charm and its solidly middle-class character. Although downtown Collingswood boasts a pricey boutique or two, the business district primarily exists to meet the needs of local residents. Accessible real estate prices and the borough's well-regarded schools have made Collingswood a popular nesting place for young families. Many current borough residents have long-standing ties to the community. Local attorney and Collingswood Mayor Michael Brennan, for example, is a 1963 graduate of Collingswood High School.

Collingswood celebrated its first centennial in 1988, though settlements in the area date back to the late seventeenth century. The borough was originally part of Newton Township, a farming community that grew up at the mouth of Newton Creek around 1682. The names of early settlers—particularly the Zane, Collings, and Knight families—are memorialized on buildings and street signs all over town. Revolutionary War-era homes still standing in Collingswood include the Thackara House on Eldridge Avenue and the Stokes-Lee house on Lees Avenue, both of which are currently maintained as private residences. The Collings-Knight Homestead at the corner of Collings Avenue and Browning Road, which was built around 1824, is currently owned and maintained by the borough of Collingswood. All three structures are on the New Jersey Register of Historic Places.

Today Collingswood covers nearly two square miles, stretching from Newton Creek to Cooper River. Located a mere 15 minutes from the Ben Franklin Bridge, Collingswood is an easy commute from Center City Philadelphia. The PATCO High Speed Line also stops in town. The borough's 15,000-plus residents enjoy direct access to scenic Cooper River Park. Knight Park, a 60-acre landscaped tract at the center of town, was donated to the borough in 1892 by the estate of Edward C. Knight. For the past 100 years the park has been a favorite site for picnicking, summer concerts, and sporting events.

Moorestown is the largest of the historic towns in Greater Philadelphia's New Jersey suburbs, covering 15 square miles of Burlington County. Settlement in the area is generally acknowledged to have happened around 1682, a few years after the first English Quakers landed on the east bank of the Delaware River. The town began to establish itself in earnest in 1700 when a Friends Meeting House was built on land now used as a burial ground by the Moorestown Monthly Meeting of the Religious Society of Friends. Two early communities—Rodmantown and Chestertown—had, by the late eighteenth century, combined to form Moorestown. The name honors one Thomas Moore, reputedly the town's first tavern keeper and real estate agent.

Modern Moorestown is often characterized as "quaint," with its many restored Colonial and Victorian structures and its historic, boutique-filled Main Street. In fact, the town is one of the more eclectic suburbs of Philadelphia. In addition to tree-lined Victorian neighborhoods with brick sidewalks, it also boasts a good variety of middle-class homes from the 1950s and 1960s, groomed townhouse developments, and enclaves of modern "executive" mansions with six- and seven-figure price tags. Perhaps even more notable are the things the town doesn't have. With a population of 15,000 spread over 15 square miles, Moorestown is one of the least densely developed communities in Greater Philadelphia. There are still farm sites within the town, as well as public woodlands, open fields, and parks.

Strawbridge Lake Park and Pompeston Creek Park are among Moorestown's recreational sites. In addition, the town offers paved bike paths and jogging trails, ice skating in winter, golf, indoor basketball and volleyball, tennis, and a variety of other sporting ac-

The largest of Greater Philadelphia's historic suburban towns, Moorestown, New Jersey, is a quaint community of restored Victorian and Colonial homes enhanced by tree-lined streets and public woodlands. Photo by Mary Ann Brockman

tivities. Perkins Center for the Arts, located on the four-acre Perkins Memorial site, hosts concerts, arts and crafts exhibits, and classes.

Although Moorestown is primarily a residential community, several manicured corporate campuses have been developed around the periphery of the town. Companies with offices in Moorestown include Chevron Chemical Co., Northern Telecom, Inc., Western Union, General Motors, and INA.

All Around the Town

Any overview of Greater Philadelphia neighborhoods is likely to draw protests. "What about Fishtown?" natives will ask. Or maybe their loyalties run to Over-

brook, or Manayunk, or Bristol, or Merchantville, or any of a hundred other communities in the Delaware Valley. It would take a separate book to chronicle the histories and current attributes of all the towns and neighborhoods in the area.

For outsiders, the quickest and surest way to get the scoop on "the real" Melrose Park, or Pennsauken, or other Greater Philadelphia domain is to ask a resident. Locals generally have no qualms about providing detailed portraits of their neighborhoods, warts and all. They'll complain about city services, point to potholes, offer a few anecdotes about the neighbors, and calmly explain why they wouldn't live anywhere else in the world.

Philadelphia''s dynamic
skyline reflects the city's
ever-changing economy.
Photo by George Adams
Jones

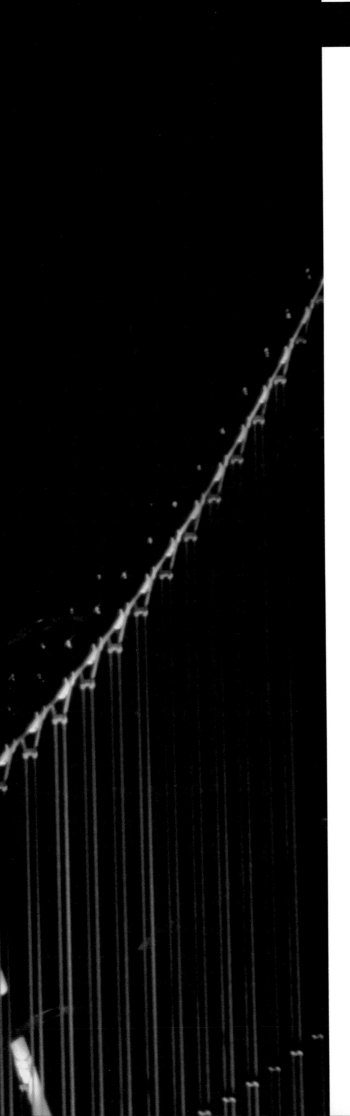

Energy and communication firms play an important role in Phildelphia's economy, providing power and information to the area's residents.

Networks

Harron Communications Corp.

At first glance, old-time vaudeville and cable television have nothing in common, except when it concerns Harron Communications. Perhaps if the curtain had not come down on the vaudeville era, Paul Harron, Sr., may never have founded Harron Communications, the Frazer-based owner of two network television stations and operator of the country's 45th-largest cable television system, serving more than 200,000 subscribers.

The company's roots stretch back to the days of vaudeville, when Paul Harron, Sr., sold advertising space on vaudeville curtains along the New York theater circuit. That was long before commercial television existed, let alone cable television.

As the vaudeville era began to wane, the senior Harron entered the broadcasting business by purchasing a New York City Spanish-speaking radio station. But it was not until 1950 that the entrepreneur gathered a group of friends to form WPFH (Channel 12), designed to be the first independent television station in Philadelphia. The effort faltered, so he sold the television and radio properties in 1958. A year later he formed Mid New York Broadcasting Co. with the purchase of WKTV (Channel 2) in Utica, New York.

At the time, the fledgling cable industry was not an attractive medium to the senior Harron. He was focused on the traditional broadcasting business.

But in 1964 Harron acquired Utica's cable franchise. "It was a defensive move against his TV business," explains Paul Harron, Jr., president of Harron. WKTV (Channel 2) in Utica, the NBC affiliate, is still part of Harron Communications today, and the Utica cable system has become Harron's largest single system, with more than 45,000 subscribers.

It was not until the mid-1970s that cable television became the company's focus. By then it had already acquired ABC-affiliate WMTW-TV (Channel 8) in Portland, Maine. When Paul Harron, Jr., took over the company's reins in 1976, the cable television industry was just entering an age of awareness, and the growth of the industry accelerated. Harron's growth accelerated, also, as Paul Harron, Jr., embarked upon an ambitious cable television expansion program, adding more than 30,000 subscribers.

Since then the company has continued to add franchises in New Jersey, sections of Chester and Delaware counties in Pennsylva-

nia, Michigan, New Hampshire, Massachusetts, and upstate New York. The expansion has been controlled by a consistent philosophy, designed to cluster systems in each market that Harron serves. According to Harron, "Our goal is to continue to have steady growth and maintain our independence."

METROBASE CABLE ADVERTISING, INC.

Recognizing the need for a professional advertising sales operation within the cable industry, as well as the potentially significant source of revenue cable advertising represented, Harron Communications launched Metrobase Cable Advertising in 1983.

By interconnecting six cable systems in Philadelphia's western suburbs, Metrobase was able to offer advertisers commercial time on cable satellite networks such as CNN, ESPN, MTV, among others. Cable television was a new medium, tailor-made for local retailers as well as regional accounts, which, not surprisingly, generated great interest in the local advertising community. Previously, if a cable system offered advertising and a local business was interested in more than what one system covered geographically, they were faced with dealing with multiple salespeople, which created confusion and frustration. Metrobase offered a convenient solution to the problem. Dealing with Metrobase meant advertisers could purchase time on more than one cable system, have one salesperson handle their account, and receive one invoice after the fact.

The next few years led to rapid expansion in the Philadelphia market, creating the need for additional sales offices in Allentown, Pennsylvania, and southern New Jersey. Philadelphia market coverage currently includes close to 30 systems reaching nearly 600,000 cable households. Building on the reputation created by the success of the Philadelphia operation, Metrobase answered requests for proposals from systems in other markets. This quickly led to the opening of an office in the Pittsburgh area in June 1988, followed by an office in upstate New York in January 1989. Today Metrobase represents 92 cable systems reaching more than one and a half million subscribers throughout the Philadelphia, Pittsburgh, New York, Massachusetts, and Detroit markets.

Metrobase operates a central office in each

of the regions from which all billing and traffic originates. Multiple satellite sales offices were set up to ensure affiliate systems adequate market coverage. The centralized billing and traffic provide Metrobase's clients with accurate, easily understood monthly invoices and affidavits of performance. This system also provides monthly sales activity and revenue distribution for affiliate systems.

According to Alan Eisenstein, general manager of Metrobase, "Our long range plan for Metrobase is to broaden our coverage in existing regions by signing additional affiliates within the market, as well as developing new regional operations by targeting clusters of small- to medium-size systems in undeveloped markets."

Cable advertising is now recognized by local, regional, and national advertisers as a highly effective new advertising medium, combining a desirable upscale audience with geographic selectivity, the dramatic appeal of color television, and low costs. Metrobase currently holds the distinction of being one of the largest and most successful turn-key cable interconnect operations in the Northeast. Much of this success is due to the untiring efforts of the Metrobase staff in introducing this new medium and educating the advertising community on how to use it most effectively.

Paul F. Harron president of Harron Communications. Photo by Howard Gordon

KYW-TV

It is somehow appropriate that KYW-TV (Channel 3) is a Philadelphia TV station. The station and the city have so much in common—Philadelphia served as the first capital of the country, fostering the birth of the United States. And, many years later, KYW-TV made broadcasting history when it went on the air as Philadelphia's first television station, developing into an innovator of news, entertainment, and public affairs programming.

Channel 3's history goes back well beyond the general public's recollection of the beginnings of television. Originally known as W3XE, the station was an experiment set up by Philco Corporation in 1932. It broadcast into the homes of 100 employees, mostly company engineers, offering a rather limited fare of employee talent shows and travelogues. But the audience did not mind the programming, because this enabled the engineers to improve the technology and eventually become involved with the broadcast product itself. It was not long before W3XE began televising college football games, and, in 1940, it offered the first major coverage of a national political convention, when it broadcast 60 hours of the National Republican Convention nationwide through NBC.

The station attained commercial status in 1941, when the Federal Communications Commission licensed it under the call letters of WPTZ-TV, the first licensed commercial television station in Philadelphia and only the second in the country.

WPTZ-TV's programming switched to fast forward in the early 1950s, when television sets began popping up in more homes around the country and in Philadelphia. Channel 3 gave viewers their first television celebrity when it began broadcasting Ernie Kovacs' early NBC program, "It's Time for Ernie," in 1951. Children's programming moved ahead quickly, too, with shows such as "Chuckwagon Pete" and "Buckskin Billy."

Channel 3 became KYW-TV in 1965, renamed by its parent company Group W Television. Along with the new call letters came the first live syndicated program to originate in Philadelphia—"The Mike Douglas Show."

Along the way, the station has also strung together a series of news and public affairs innovations. It introduced the concept that allows reporters to deliver their own stories instead of having the station anchors read them. This concept is now commonplace all over the country. KYW-TV also introduced the first local version of an early morning newscast.

One of KYW-TV's most recent local firsts was its development of a close-captioned newscast for the hearing impaired. Now hearing-impaired viewers throughout the Delaware Valley, who have special decoders hooked up to their television sets, can "listen" to the 11 p.m. weeknight newscast.

Today, from its home on Independence Mall, KYW-TV continues to bring innovative entertainment, news, and public affairs programming to more than 3.6 million homes. Those Philco engineers of more than five decades ago would be proud of the results of their experiment.

KYW-TV is located in the heart of Philadelphia's historic Independence Mall, just a few steps from the revered Liberty Bell.

Philadelphia Suburban Water Company

The company known today as the Philadelphia Suburban Water Company started in the late 1800s when a group of enterprising professors from Swarthmore College and other citizens from the village of Swarthmore, Springfield Township, Delaware County, built a small water system to supply water to their homes. As the system grew it became the Springfield Water Company, incorporated on January 4, 1886.

In 1908 the Springfield Water Company and 31 other small independent water companies were merged into the Springfield Consolidated Water Company. This was the initial step that made possible today's unified modern water supply system, serving the suburbs north and west of Philadelphia. In 1925 the company was renamed the Philadelphia Suburban Water Company.

Today more than 500 employees of the Philadelphia Suburban Water Company provide quality water service to over 236,000 customers. The average daily usage for all customers in 1990 was 88.4 million gallons. During the summer months, however, customer usage often exceeds 110 million gallons per day.

The company's service territory and its customer base continues to increase in size as additional service area is acquired. The most recent acquisitions have been the Great Valley, Beversrede, and Pocopson water companies, which serve nine municipalities in Chester County.

Above: Utilizing ultra-modern laboratory equipment, chemical substances found in water are analyzed and monitored on a regular basis.

Below: Green Lane, the largest of the company's four impoundment reservoirs, has a capacity of 4.4 billion gallons.

The company's water sources include the Schuylkill River, five rural streams, 35 wells, and the Upper Merion Reservoir which is fed by ground water. All water is treated, as appropriate, either by sedimentation, filtration, or chlorination. The company has also augmented its supply through the development of service connections with neighboring water utilities. The total safe yield of water from all sources exceeds 117 million gallons per day.

Thirty-eight distribution reservoirs and standpipes are maintained with a total capacity of more than 131 million gallons. There are also 38 booster pumping stations strategically located to accommodate the varying elevations of the service area, which range from sea level to approximately 710 feet above sea level. In addition, the company owns and maintains more than 10,200 fire hydrants, providing its customers with round-the-clock fire protection.

Since 1971 Philadelphia Suburban Water Company has been the major business entity of Philadelphia Suburban Corporation (PSC). Since PSC's founding, its mission, as the parent company, has been to provide to its shareholders the investment stability provided by the Philadelphia Suburban Water Company, as well as the added opportunity for investment growth provided by the corporation's nonregulated businesses. These businesses provide technical and managerial services to water and waste-water utilities.

For more than a century Philadelphia Suburban Water Company has been building a foundation that will carry it through future generations. Today, as the company faces the ever-increasing challenges of managing a water utility business, it is well positioned for the future.

Its primary objective, however, remains unchanged: To provide for its customers a reliable water supply of the highest quality at the lowest possible cost.

EZ Communications

EZ Communications, Inc., is one of the largest privately owned radio broadcasting companies in the country, with 14 radio stations in 10 markets, more than five million listeners, and $70 million in gross revenues.

And the 23-year-old company is poised to grow even stronger. While limited to owning FM and AM stations to include 12 markets, EZ's goal has always been to move into the top 25 markets with as many stations as possible. The new decade will no doubt witness more expansion for EZ, which in 1990 posted increased revenues of 7 to 9 percent with broadcast cash flow up 30 percent.

EZ Communications was built by Art Kellar, an avid radio buff who learned the business from top to bottom. To follow the corporation's beginnings is to follow Kellar's own career, which began in radio broadcasting after his return from France during World War II. A dedicated listener of the Arthur Godfrey radio show, Kellar was inspired to make broadcasting his career. Kellar began

this career as a morning air personality at WRON-AM in Roncevert, West Virginia.

"I loved being a disc jockey," Kellar once said, "especially with all the girls calling requesting songs." His career on the air took him to six stations in four years, with Kellar returning to WRON in 1951. He continued his career in radio, assuming various positions as account executive, sales manager, and general manager.

In 1967 Kellar purchased WCRW-FM in Manassas, Virginia, for $125,000. It was, for those times, a risk. FM stations had been on the market since the late 1940s, but they were still not as profitable or as popular as their AM counterparts. Kellar remembers precisely what convinced him to make his first FM purchase.

"I can still picture the moment in my mind," he says. "I read this article in a magazine about the new medium of FM. The article so stimulated me that I knew that FM could and would be the dominant radio medium. No question in my mind about it. It took me three years, because of limited financial capabilities, to buy that first FM property.

It was just a bare license, no equipment, no programming, no tower site, nothing."

That simple station, later known as WEZR and then finally as WBMW, was sold 20 years later to Infinity Broadcasting for $13 million.

In 1986, EZ exploded in size with its purchase of Affiliated Broadcasting's radio properties for $65 million. The nine stations obtained under the deal nearly doubled the size of EZ Communications. "It was quite a bite, $65 million, but we felt we had the organization and the people capable of handling the deal," Kellar says. "We felt we were ready to tackle something larger."

Today Kellar is chairman and principal owner of the company, with corporate headquarters in Fairfax, Virginia. Alan Box is president, and Woody Allen is vice president/secretary treasurer. The company has approximately 100 stockholders, and around 350 full-time employees.

On January 20, 1989, EZ made its most recent radio acquisition when it bought the WIOQ-FM station in Philadelphia, known as

Art Kellar, chairman and principal owner.

Alan Box, company president.

too," he says. The EZ station formats range from country, adult contemporary (light rock), oldies, all news, to Top 40 and dance rock. "With this diversity in format, when one format loses its luster it has minimal effect on the company as a whole," says Allen.

And Allen explains that maintaining a strong, overall position is particularly important. "The radio market is extremely unstable at the moment," he says. "There are a lot of relatively large broadcasters who are finding that the debt service load they took on in the 1980s is beginning to haunt them. There are a great many stations for sale, both announced and unannounced. We do not have any for sale. We are in the buying mode."

And while EZ Communications will be cautious in making any new acquisitions —"We are not willing to be a price trendsetter," Allen says—the current recession is no reason for gloom and doom. "From what we've seen, radio thrives in recessions," says Allen. "Big advertisers decide not to pay the prices to get into newspapers and television, which are a much more expensive medium than radio, and tend to focus on radio advertising."

In addition to its radio stations, EZ Communications owns a cellular telephone franchise in eastern Ohio. The company has until the end of 1991 to build the system.

"Q-102" to all its listeners throughout the Delaware Valley. The format was changed from oldies to dance rock, and Allen says that the company is pleased with its audience and revenue numbers.

According to Allen, EZ now owns 10 FM stations and 4 AM stations. Based on FCC regulations, they are allowed to own 12 of

each, and Allen says they are working to "get the full complement of radio stations allowed."

In an increasingly competitive environment, Allen notes that one of EZ's strengths is its wide variety of formats. "We are not only geographically diverse, with stations all over the country, but our formats are diverse,

And as the company continues to grow, Kellar has this remark. "One of the things I'm most proud of is the team of professional people we've built, very capable, talented, energetic, dedicated people. People dedicated to broadcasting, to EZ, to success, and to being the very best there is."

Philadelphia Newspapers Inc.

Newspapers and those who publish, edit, and distribute them have certain responsibilities to their readers, advertisers, and the communities they serve. At Philadelphia Newspapers Inc., publisher of *The Philadelphia Inquirer* and the *Philadelphia Daily News*, respect for those responsibilities has been demonstrated for a number of years, through the investigative reports that seek to uncover injustices and the community programs geared toward encouraging people to reach for their goals.

This respect for responsibility is especially evident in the company's commitment to journalistic excellence. Any newspaper can give its readers the news and act as a watchdog for the community, without any special kind of journalistic ideals. But that is not how Philadelphia Newspapers, nor its parent company—Knight-Ridder Inc. based in Miami—believes it should operate.

PNI believes newspapers should adhere to the highest journalistic standards possible, and the executives and staff at *The Inquirer* and *Daily News* have never stopped looking for ways to improve the product that rolls off

the presses every day and appears on the doorsteps of homes throughout the Delaware Valley. These prize-winning newspapers have taken the time to learn about their readers and advertisers—who they are and what they need.

The Philadelphia Inquirer is the larger of the two papers, both in size and circulation. It is published in the traditional broadsheet format and is read by more than 500,000 city and suburban people on weekdays and one million on Sundays. As the "newspaper of record," numerous readers begin their days with a cup of coffee and the morning *Inquirer*. It is generally regarded as one of the best newspapers in the country.

The *Philadelphia Daily News* is published in tabloid format, featuring bold photography and lively writing. It is read by more than 235,000 people daily, mostly in the city, where it's primarily distributed through newsstands. Sports fans are especially loyal to the *Daily News*. City or suburbanite readers might pick up a copy in the morning on their way to

Left: The reporting, printing, and administrative functions for both newspapers are currently handled in this plant located in downtown Philadelphia.

Below: *Inquirer* and *Daily News* trucks await newspapers to make early morning deliveries.

Front page prototype of *The Philadelphia Inquirer* as it will appear when color capability is available.

Sports page prototype of the *Philadelphia Daily News* as it will look with color graphics.

work, and stop by for the afternoon edition on their way home. It is frequently pointed to as a model for other tabloid newspapers.

Together the two papers offer Philadelphia and its suburbs a complete package of news and information, representing a major force in one of the most competitive newspaper markets in the country. PNI operates in a unique environment, publishing two daily newspapers in a city surrounded by 12 other daily newspapers and 8 Sunday papers. Yet PNI has withstood that challenge and is in the process of a new development that will cement its leadership role in the Delaware Valley.

PNI announced plans in the fall of 1989 for a new state-of-the-art production and distribution facility in Upper Merion Township that will set new standards for newspaper printing and customer service in the Delaware Valley. The 670,000-square-foot facility should be fully operational by mid-1993, but readers will begin seeing the results of the new plant's efforts much sooner.

Readers of both newspapers can expect to see dramatic differences. For example, no newspaper in the area is currently capable of producing the caliber of high-quality color printing that will be contained in both newspapers. Color photos, graphics, and advertisements as well as black and white images will be bolder and sharper. Both newspapers expect to make liberal use of the color capabilities, especially on the front page of *The Inquirer* and on the sports page of the *Daily News*.

The facility will also enable PNI to make other improvements that directly affect customer service, which is one of PNI's primary goals. For example, the suburban location of the distribution plant will significantly reduce the delivery time to major distribution points in the Pennsylvania suburbs, while also allowing for improvement in delivery to the city and New Jersey. Because the new Goss Colorliner presses operate at higher speeds, the newspapers won't have to begin rolling off the presses until later. That means news deadlines can be adjusted, allowing the home delivery editions of *The Inquirer* to carry the latest news and final sports scores. Ultimately, all *Inquirer* subscribers will receive their newspapers no later than 6 a.m. on weekdays and 7 a.m. on Sundays.

And, finally, readers will appreciate that the ink will be less likely to rub off on their hands and clothing.

This new production and distribution facility is a major undertaking for Philadelphia Newspapers Inc., but it represents yet another step toward giving its readers and advertisers a product that truly reflects PNI's commitment to the Delaware Valley.

Philadelphia Electric Company

In 1987 the Philadelphia Electric Company faced a monumental task: How could this utility, with more than 1.45 million electric customers and 300,000 suburban gas customers in Southeastern Pennsylvania and Northeastern Maryland, regain the support and confidence of its customers and shareholders?

After all, the daily press on this public utility known as PE or PECO was a public relations nightmare. To the public's chagrin, the company had been asking continually for rate increases from the Pennsylvania Public Utilities Commission since 1968. In 1987 the Nuclear Regulatory Commission had ordered PE to shut down its Peach Bottom Atomic Power Station, due to operator inattentiveness and a variety of other plant and corporate management problems.

PE Chairman and Chief Executive Officer Joseph F. Paquette, Jr., acknowledges that it was an "embarrassing shutdown," and that it took "two long years to assess and correct Peach Bottom and corporate problems, and to convince the NRC to allow us to restart the plant."

And in its efforts to recover from the Peach Bottom crisis, PE took stock of its future. "In dealing with the problems of Peach Bottom and their root causes, we found an absolute and critical need for change in the way we do business. We found that our culture must change to reflect the new economic realities of the marketplace. That in the faces of change in our industry and continuing market pressures, our future will depend upon our ability to meet our customers' needs, to find new ways to control costs and to maintain competitive rates.

"We found, frankly, that we had no alternative—we had to become more efficient and cost conscious. We found that even with Peach Bottom back on line, we could never again return to business as usual."

By the time Paquette addressed nearly 300 PE officers in the fall of 1990, he was ready to unveil PE's strategy for the 1990s—a combined mission and vision agenda that placed a premium on the utility's customers, shareholders, the environment, the community, and conservation.

Photo by Rich Zila

"Our mission is very simple: to provide safe and reliable electric and gas services," says Paquette. He admits that the company's new vision, to become a premier regional energy service company, is at once simple but ambitious.

Towards achieving its vision, PE established seven fundamental values to guide it through the 1990s, a list of values that the public will no doubt be hearing about throughout the new decade.

At the top of the list is customer satisfaction, with PE pledging to strive to anticipate, understand, and meet its customers' changing needs and expectations so that PE remains their preferred supplier of energy. The list of values continues with emphasis on shareholders and employees values, followed by safety, integrity, environmental commitment, and community involvement.

During 1990 PE aggressively pursued its environmental agenda to protect, conserve, and enhance the natural resources of Southeastern Pennsylvania and Northeastern Maryland. During the year, 65-percent of the electricity produced by the company

was generated with nuclear fuel, which PE argues does not emit pollutants that contribute to environmental problems like global warming and acid rain. While coal produced 20-percent of the company's energy, the great majority of that was generated at plants equipped with state-of-the-art scrubbing equipment to clean their emissions. Oil produced just four-percent of the company's total generation, a source of pride for PE during the days of oil's high price tag and uncertain resources.

Also during the year, construction proceeded on schedule for a $12.5-million permanent fish passage facility that PE is building at the Conowingo Dam to help restore American Shad to the upper Susquehanna River. The facility, which is scheduled to open in the spring of 1991, will allow the collection and transport of up to 1.5 million American Shad and 10 million

River Herring to their upriver spawning grounds each year.

Concerning community involvement, PE continued this initiative through a wide range of services. In cooperation with the Pennsylvania Office of Voter Registration, PE undertook an extensive campaign to urge its customers and its employees to register to vote. "Register to Vote" messages were carried in bright white lights on the company's signature four-sided sign on top of its downtown Philadelphia headquarters, and distributed bill inserts and news releases in company publications. In addition, the company continued to provide financial contributions and in-kind services to a wide variety of community projects, from training volunteer firemen to conducting electric safety and anti-drug campaigns in area schools.

Through an advertising campaign—"The Power Is In Your Hands, Use It Wisely"—the company informed its residential, commercial, and industrial customers how to use energy more efficiently.

"Responsible utilities care about their customers," says Paquette. "It is quite clear that what is good for our customers is good for the company." Not only can customers save on their bills, he says, but the more they can conserve, the longer the company can delay the need to build or buy expensive additional electric capacity which will be necessary after the year 2000.

"Our mission for the future is to please our employees, shareholders, customers, regulators, and the communities in which we serve," says Paquette. "It is a lofty goal, but we have no doubt it is attainable. With constant attention to our values, we can, and I believe we will, achieve our vision—to become one of the nation's premier energy service companies."

Focus: Metropolitan Philadelphia's Business Magazine

*F*ocus, Metropolitan Philadelphia's Business News Magazine, was never intended to be the voice of the local business community. Yet today the publication is found in the offices of most every Philadelphia company.

In the late 1960s while working as the assistant director of purchasing at Curtis Publishing Company, *Focus* founder and president John W. Rorer started dabbling with the notion of a local weekly business publication. The magazine he envisioned would include listings of new businesses, real estate transactions, and other types of information that would interest local business people—the kind of information that interested Rorer.

"When I looked at the daily newspapers, there wasn't much local business news," recalls Rorer. So with little more than a desire to enter the business publishing world, on February 7, 1968, John Rorer published the first edition of *Focus* magazine from a one-room office at 1015 Chestnut Street, down the street from Curtis Publishing Co. He chose the nearby location so he could run over to *Focus'* office during his lunchtime and after work.

There really were not any publications available to use as a model because *Focus* was one of the very first regional business publications in the country. But Rorer had obviously hit the right chord with *Focus*, because his first 500 subscribers paid $10 each for a charter subscription to the completely unknown publication. The inaugural issue ran 16 pages and contained no advertising. The first advertisement did not appear until more than two years later, when Rorer sold a $90 advertisement in order to pay a month's rent.

Rorer was so dedicated to his moonlighting publishing project that he worked 100 hours per week, devoting his evenings and weekends to *Focus*. That dedication did not swerve, when a few months after the magazine's debut, Rorer received an attractive job offer from the Chilton Company, a publisher of numerous trade magazines, to become its director of purchasing. Even though the new position would move him farther away from

Founder and President John W. Rorer with *Focus* community affairs director Sandra P. Kenton.

Focus' office, he accepted the offer to make it easier to finance what was quickly becoming more than a hobby.

Focus' original staff consisted of Rorer, a former-Curtis-employee typist, who Rorer trained to be a typesetter, and a friend from Chilton Company who served as the voluntary editor. Rorer performed all the administrative and business functions, including advertising sales. Rorer had never sold anything in his life until he sold *Focus'* first ad. "I couldn't afford to hire an ad salesman," he says.

Rorer did not intend the fledgling publication's name to remain *Focus*. "It was supposed to be a temporary name," Rorer says. After a few months of publishing, he also had intended to change the format to a tabloid from the 8 ½-by-11-inch magazine size and name it *Philadelphia Business News*. But when Rorer incorporated the operation in 1969 as Business News Inc., it was already well known as *Focus*, so it made no sense to change it. The magazine remained 8 ½ by 11 inches.

Today Business News Inc. is still the publisher of *Focus*, which is still produced out of the same building where John Rorer first set up shop more than 20 years ago. It employs 22 full-time employees who produce the magazine and 18 annual special sections. Rorer pioneered the special section concept in Philadelphia, introducing the "Plant and Office Location Guide" in 1969.

This immediate hit was gradually followed by more special sections, including its January "Annual Review/Preview" issue, its "Corporate Close-Up," and the "Guide to Meeting Facilities & Services." On the average, *Focus* publishes close to 10,000 pages per year, including 2,500 pages of advertising. Its circulation now exceeds 22,000, and it is read by more than 75,000 decision makers in Philadelphia.

Most magazine publishers enter the business either through the editorial or sales side of the operation. Even though Rorer spent more than

a decade working for publishing companies, he did not have experience in either craft. Instead, he came up through the business side in the purchasing department of his former employer, Curtis Publishing Co., followed by his stint at Chilton Company. At Chilton, he ran three cafeterias and all the company's vending machines and eventually turned a money-losing operation into a profiting center.

As it turns out, his knowledge of the purchasing business served him well as a magazine publisher, because he was adept at keeping costs under control while producing

John W. Rorer "after hours" in his Early American-style office. Rorer sits next to a Ben Franklin miniature statue that was sculpted by former Chief Justice Warren E. Burger. Also of note in his office is a J.C. Clayhern painting of Independence Hall.

an excellent product—necessary skills for a publisher. "That's how I learned to run a business," he says.

And he learned that lesson well. Since the initial start-up, Rorer has never been forced to borrow money to fund the operation, a fact

that he calls an important ingredient of success. He believes in reinvesting the profits in the publication, while keeping rates attractive for advertisers. With this formula, Rorer believes he has saved well over one million dollars in interest.

He has also accomplished what few publishing companies can claim: Rorer has published a weekly business magazine uninterrupted for nearly 25 years. Rorer says "The Internal Revenue Service doesn't let you make a business out of a hobby, but I've made a hobby out of a business."

WFLN-FM

When the sweet strains of violins first began drifting over Philadelphia's radio airwaves more than 40 years ago, few listeners tuned to the new classical music station, which signed on in 1949 as WFLN-FM. At the time, classical music only appealed to a small, elite audience.

But the founders of WFLN—former Senator Joe Clark and philanthropist L.M.C.

Smith—were eager to share their love of classical music with a broader Philadelphia audience, so they persisted in offering listeners a pure format of great classical recordings.

Today more than 300,000 loyal listeners regularly tune into WFLN, Philadelphia's only full-time, 24-hour-a-day classical music station. In fact, its listeners are so devoted

Right: Richard Tedesco, vice president, general manager

Below: Thomas D. Moyer, vice president, director of engineering

Above: Denise McDevitt, general sales manager

Left: David Conant, operations manager

that some have been known to call the radio station to comment on individual commercials. In an industry where changes in radio call letters and formats are common, WFLN is one of the few stations that has had the same call letters and has broadcast the same format since its sign on.

From the beginning, WFLN experimented with broadcast methods and programming

design to appeal to a wider audience and make the music more enjoyable to the listener. In 1950 it experimented with a stereo format, collaborating with a Philadelphia AM-radio station to produce one of the first radio simulcasts.

Eight years later it was able to regularly simulcast programs on the FM and AM dials following the construction of WFLN-AM in 1958. Today, on occasion WFLN will do a stereo simulcast with local television stations.

For nearly 20 years WFLN-FM was renowned for its broadcast of the Philadelphia Orchestra concerts, which were syndicated to 82 stations across the country, plus over the Voice of America and Armed Forces Radio Network. Today it regularly broadcasts performances from the Academy of Music.

Since it was purchased by Marlin Broadcasting in 1988, which owns several other classical music radio stations, WFLN has introduced a number of innovative programs, designed to actively involve the listener. "At Your Request" takes requests from listeners, even over a fax machine. Listeners can awaken to a John Philip Sousa march at 7:15 a.m. weekday mornings and win a certificate for membership in the "Sousalarm" wake-up club.

Over the years, the station that now bills itself as Philadelphia's Voice of the Arts, has become an active participant in all aspects of Philadelphia's cultural community. Its activities span sponsorship of Awareness Day and free concerts to assisting the Philadelphia Orchestra's fund-raising efforts. Now that the appeal of classical music has broadened to a younger, more mobile audience, it gives WFLN an opportunity to introduce its listeners to the other cultural arts.

Philadelphia Business Journal

I t's rare when any single entity can have an impact on a major city's business community, but that's what the *Philadelphia Business Journal* has done. Since it was founded in 1982, the *Journal* has built a reputation among the business community as the publication to rely on for objective, hard-hitting news reporting and analysis—information that you just can't find anywhere else.

The *Philadelphia Business Journal* was established in March of 1982 on the heels of a major recession, which inadvertently fostered a new, keener interest in business among newspaper readers. The concept of a city business journal that offered a greater number of in-depth business stories and could go beyond

Founded in 1982, the Philadelphia Business Journal is quickly becoming the leading business authority of the Delaware Valley.

the news reported in the daily newspapers was still in its infancy.

As one of the first city business journals, the *Journal* helped set the standards for weekly business reporting, and has since emerged as one of the leading city business publications in the country.

The paper serves the entire eight-county region—Philadelphia, Delaware, Chester, Bucks, and Montgomery counties in Pennsylvania, and Camden, Burlington, and Gloucester counties in New Jersey.

Much of the *Journal*'s reputation as a unique information provider has been built upon its ongoing special sections and corporate listings. The *Journal*'s policy is that special sections are published with the same editorial standards as main news. Among the most popular features is the "Philadelphia Inc." annual report issued each May that gives information on the top 150 public companies in Philadelphia area.

Perhaps the most popular feature is its annual "Book of Lists," which provides in depth listings on the leading companies and executives in 60 business categories. The *Journal* also publishes numerous special sections, such as the "Small Business Resource Guide" and the "Philadelphia 100," featuring the fastest growing privately held companies in the region.

The publication is "news-driven," preferring to uncover stories in the making instead of simply reacting to what has happened in the business community in the previous week. The large editorial staff is schooled in enterprise reporting and believes in aggressively reporting the news, giving its thousands of readers a fresh, incisive product. It's not uncommon for a story that breaks on the front page of the *Philadelphia Business Journal* to scoop all other area news media.

When it's not reporting the news of the region, the paper is actively involved in the business community. The publication believes in recognizing business leadership, entrepreneurship, achievement, and growth. The *Journal* is a sponsor along with Ernst and Young of the annual Entrepreneur of the Year Awards, for example, as well as other leadership awards, seminars, and breakfast meetings throughout the year. It also supports the business community's civic efforts, and among these activities co-sponsors the annual Corporate Sports Battle to benefit the Big Brothers/Big Sisters of Philadelphia. Not unlike the companies it writes about, the *Journal* is also continuously seeking ways to improve its news product and the distribution of information to its subscribers. It is growing right along with the Philadelphia business community, continually adding more quality information and news to serve its readership. Its mission is to continue to meet the growing information needs of this burgeoning business community and truly be the Delaware Valley's business authority.

WTXF-TV Channel 29

When people talk about television programs and what they like to watch, they are used to thinking in terms of the three major networks, cable, public TV, and independent stations. But in Philadelphia, viewers have the unique opportunity to tune into a fourth major network on WTXF-TV Channel 29, Fox Broadcasting's fourth-largest affiliate TV station.

When Channel 29 first went on the air in 1965 with the call letters WIBF, it looked and felt like most so-called independent stations. It was known primarily for showing black-and-white reruns of old TV shows, but Channel 29 was destined to be more than just another independent TV station. When Taft Broadcasting purchased the station in 1969 and changed its call letters to WTAF, the station managers were already starting to tinker with the programming, seeking shows that would set it apart from the other independents and attract larger audiences. Within a few years, innovative programming would become a way of life at Channel 29.

In the early and mid-1970s, viewers started tuning into numerous first-run movies that appeared on Channel 29, such as *Jamaica Inn*, starring Jane Seymour, and, later, *The Key to Rebecca*. Probably one of its most significant programming changes took place in September 1979, when Hawkeye, Radar, Hot Lips, and the rest of the "M*A*S*H" gang reappeared in syndication on Channel 29. As one of the most popular TV shows ever to hit the airwaves, "M*A*S*H" represented the kind of blue-chip programming that Channel 29 believed its viewers wanted. Response to the telecasts was so encouraging that it enabled Channel 29 to continue building an audience for future novel programming.

The next major opportunity to present programming that its audience wanted came in 1983 when it began broadcasting the

(From left) Bill Elias, Lee McCarthy, Jill Chernekoff, and Carl Cherkin are the on-air principals of the groundbreaking 10 O'Clock News team.

Phillies' baseball games. Shortly thereafter, Channel 29 began offering some of the most original new syndicated programming available, such as "Lifestyles of the Rich and Famous" and "Star Search." By the mid-1980s Channel 29 was well on its way toward becoming a station known for its entertainment and sports. And as syndicated first-run programming improved, so did Channel 29's lineup of first-run shows.

Around the same time, in 1986, the TVX Broadcast Group purchased the station from Taft Broadcasting, and in February Channel 29 made one of its most innovative programming moves yet. That was when it launched the "10 O'Clock News," the first 10 p.m. news broadcast in Philadelphia since the 1960s. The half-hour show was a convenient alternative for viewers who wanted to watch the news, but did not want to stay up until 11 p.m. to see it. The unique broadcast was designed to give the news of the day, like a 6 p.m. news program, but without any glitz. As news director Roger LaMay describes it, the

broadcast was "time driven and information driven." Journalist Lee McCarthy, a former NBC network correspondent, led the broadcast as the news anchor, supported by several talented reporters and writers.

After launching the news show and watching it gradually attract a loyal audience, Channel 29 continued to move ahead in entertainment programming, striking its first affiliation deal with Fox Broadcasting in the fall of 1986 with the introduction of "The Late Show Starring Joan Rivers." Even though that show had a short run, it marked the beginning of Channel 29's affiliation with Fox. In the spring of 1987 that affiliation became official when Fox became the "fourth network," and numerous new first-run syndicated programs from Paramount Pictures began appearing at a rapid pace. There were, for example, "Friday the 13th" and "Star Trek: The Next Generation." Fox's "Night of Primetime" programming introduced the Sunday night hit shows, "Married with Children" and "21 Jump Street." Many more successful new shows have since entered the Channel 29 lineup, including Johnny Carson's first real late-night talk show threat—"The Arsenio Hall Show," another Paramount program.

On the news side, Channel 29 made history again in March 1990 when the area's first hour-long news broadcast made its debut. In addition to its news/information format, news director Roger LaMay added more business, entertainment, and medical reports and a special feature from *Consumer Reports* magazine.

In addition, Channel 29 has already been reaping the programming benefits from its newest affiliation with Paramount Pictures, which purchased a controlling interest in 1989.

With all that activity the station has still found time to support various community activities, culminating with an ambitious public service campaign, introduced in 1990, called "Sharing Together." That theme was carried throughout the year, and was highlighted when the station celebrated its 25th anniversary on the air in May 1990. And WTXF-TV Channel 29 plans to continue its commitment to quality news, entertainment, and sports programming for another 25 years.

Since the station began its affiliation with Fox Broadcasting in the fall of 1986, many new successful shows like "The Arsenio Hall Show" (below), "The Simpsons" (above right), and "Married with Children" (below right) have entered the Channel 29 lineup.

Bell Atlantic Corporation

I n 1876 something happened that would change the face of business and profoundly affect daily life: the telephone was invented.

Just over 100 years later, in late 1983, a sophisticated communications and information company known as Bell Atlantic Corporation was formed as a result of the breakup of the Bell System.

Today Bell Atlantic continues to change the way people live and work. Bell Atlantic defines the purpose of its business as meeting a broad, societal need: to improve the quality of life in the information age by providing products and services of the highest value.

Headquartered in Philadelphia, Bell Atlantic has evolved from a group of regulated telephone utilities serving the mid-Atlantic region into a major provider of communica-

Bell Atlantic is aggressively exploring information-age technologies to bring new services to customers and to build shareowner value. Currently its "world of potential" is limited by restrictions in the AT&T consent decree, the document that spelled out the terms for the Bell System breakup. Photo by Burk Uzzle

tions and information-management services and systems, with subsidiaries operating in regional, national, and international markets.

Bell Atlantic is one of the area's largest employers, with approximately 80,000 employees in the United States and abroad. Its 1990 revenues were $12.3 billion with assets of $28 billion. Bell Atlantic's common stock is traded on the New York Stock Exchange under the ticker symbol BEL. The stock is also listed on the Philadelphia, Midwest,

Boston, Pacific, London, Zurich, Geneva, Basel, Frankfurt, and Tokyo exchanges.

The company's core business is providing state-of-the-art voice and data communications to one of the fastest growing, most densely populated, and economically vibrant regions of the United States. Bell Atlantic's seven telephone companies serve customers with more than 17 million voice and data communications lines in a region that is home to the federal government and 75 of the nation's *Fortune* 500 companies.

Bell Atlantic has more than 414,000 miles of optical fiber in its network, and in 1990 the company invested $2.3 billion in its telephone network. More than 99 percent of Bell Atlantic's access lines are controlled by software-based technology that gives the company great range and latitude in customizing services.

Bell Atlantic's non-telephone subsidiaries are also in the forefront of technological advancement. In personal wireless communication, for example, Bell Atlantic Mobile Systems provides cellular service and equipment to serve the communications-intensive Northeast corridor. Bell Atlantic's software and systems integration companies offer business systems solutions to move and manage information. The computer services division, the nation's leading independent service provider, offers computer maintenance and

Clockwise from lower left: Raymond W. Smith, chairman and chief executive officer; Philip A. Campbell, vice chairman and chief financial officer (retired March 1, 1991); Robert A. Levetown, executive vice president and general counsel; and Anton J. Campanella, president. Photo by Burk Uzzle

C&P Telephone systems technician Ted Carroll, who installed microwave links to transmit video coverage of the 1987 U.S./Soviet summit worldwide, typifies Bell Atlantic's commitment to service. Photo by Mike Mitchell

cellular mobile network and building a public switched packet data network in Czechoslovakia.

Bell Atlantic is committed to improving the quality of life in other ways as well. A corporate leader in the fight against illiteracy, Bell Atlantic has sponsored the Family Literacy Project, in conjunction with the American Library Association, to help improve the reading skills of children and parents; the Science Institute, operated by the American Association for the Advancement of Science, to provide teacher training to help children, particularly girls and minorities, to get more out of science; and the National Literacy Awards, hosted by President and Mrs. Bush, to honor literacy volunteers and their students.

Bell Atlantic has also sponsored the Philadelphia Liberty Medal, awarded annually on the Fourth of July to the individual or organization demonstrating leadership and vision in the pursuit of liberty of conscience or freedom from oppression, ignorance, or deprivation. To date, medals have been awarded to Poland's Solidarity leader Lech Walesa and former President Jimmy Carter.

Bell Atlantic Corporation—like the industry's founder, Alexander Graham Bell, a teacher of the deaf—sees technology as a means for helping others.

comprehensive service and support for business systems and software.

Bell Atlantic International provides customers throughout the world with a range of operations support, software systems, consulting services, systems integration services, communications services, computer maintenance, and information products. From its headquarters in Brussels, Bell Atlantic International provides administrative support to its European operations. Bell Atlantic has entered the overseas market to provide better service to domestic customers with foreign operations and to provide new frontiers where the company can further explore the capabilities of its technology.

Bell Atlantic's recent foreign investments include the purchase with Ameritech of New

Zealand Telecom. In partnership with US West and the government of Czechoslovakia, Bell Atlantic is constructing and operating a

"Our reputation for quality depends on thousands of daily interactions with customers—each one a mirror of the values we stand for." Photo by Roger Foley

Producing and distributing goods for individuals and industry, manufacturing firms provide employment for many Philadelphia-area residents.

Photo by Rich Zila

Manufacturing

Wyeth-Ayerst

There are probably few medicine cabinets in the world that have not contained a Wyeth-Ayerst product at one time or another. Possibilities include a prescription for Inderal® for treatment of hypertension, or Ativan® for treatment of anxiety, Premarin® for estrogen-replacement therapy, or a container of SMA® infant formula in the kitchen.

As one of the world's largest makers and marketers of pharmaceuticals and other health care products, Wyeth-Ayerst has earned a reputation as a leader in the health care industry, largely due to its commitment to disciplined basic and clinical research and its development of quality prescription and over-the-counter pharmaceutical products.

Wyeth-Ayerst is actually composed of two companies: Wyeth-Ayerst Laboratories (USA), and Wyeth-Ayerst International. However they work together under the umbrella of their parent firm, American Home Products Corporation, to develop and market a wide variety of health care products for health care institutions and

consumers around the world. Headquartered in the Radnor/St. Davids area since 1955, it employs more than 3,500 people in the Delaware Valley and more than 24,000 people worldwide.

The roots of this research-based company stretch back to its founding in 1860 in Philadelphia by John Wyeth, a young pharmacist who opened a drug store with his brother, Frank, at 1410 Walnut Street. Unlike many other pharmacists of the time who were content to simply sell powders or

elixirs, John Wyeth was a pioneer in the production of compressed tablets—the form that is used today.

He also developed the system for increasing the efficiency of pharmacies. Instead of simply compounding a prescription when presented by a patient, Wyeth stocked an extensive line of frequently prescribed prepared drugs. This system laid the groundwork for the eventual large-scale manufacturing of labeled pharmaceutical products. Indeed, after a fire destroyed the

Right: The company employs more than 3,500 people in the Delaware Valley and over 24,000 people worldwide.

Below: Wyeth-Ayerst is headquartered in the Radnor/St. Davids area.

Walnut Street drug store in 1889, the Wyeth brothers sold the retail business to concentrate on the wholesale manufacturing of pharmaceuticals.

Through the years Wyeth has been a pharmaceutical pioneer, not only in developing new drugs, but in creating new ways to administer drugs. Its researchers are continuously looking for drugs that can treat or prevent serious health-related problems.

For example, Wyeth developed the first commercial production of penicillin in 1942; and following World War II, its researchers developed a tablet form of penicillin, which previously had only been available in an injectable form.

In 1960 the firm developed the processes required to make Dryvax®, a dried, heat-stable smallpox vaccine, and the bifurcated needle, used to deliver the vaccine. The bifurcated needle, a self-contained delivery system for which Wyeth waived patent royalties for needles made under contract with the World Health Organization, delivered an incredible 200 million smallpox vaccinations per year. These two products were acknowledged by the 33rd World Health Assembly in a declaration that smallpox had been eradicated completely.

A team of more than 2,400 scientists and technicians of Wyeth-Ayerst are focused on developing the most promising new drug candidates in Wyeth-Ayerst's research portfolio and on discovering new products for the treatment or prevention of a wide range of health-related disorders. The company has new chemical entities or biologicals under active study in various stages of clinical development.

In order to develop the most effective types of pharmaceuticals, the company has carefully nurtured the expertise necessary to focus on several major areas of health care therapy. These categories include female health care, infant nutritionals, cardiovascular drugs, psychotropic drugs, hospital injectable products, vaccines, and anti-inflammatory agents.

In addition, new therapies are expected to evolve from the company's scientific work in areas such as diabetes, asthma, senile dementia, and lupus erythematosus and other autoimmune diseases. Research is underway on anti-cholesterol compounds, drugs helpful in preventing rejection of organ transplants, and oral vaccines to prevent or eliminate hepatitis, AIDS, and respiratory syncytial virus in children.

These programs hold the promise of scientific breakthroughs and new therapeutic advances in treating some of the most widespread and serious health problems. Seeking the answer to many of the world's mental and physical illnesses is becoming increasingly difficult, but the scientists at Wyeth-Ayerst realize that today's research will ultimately result in tomorrow's most effective treatments.

Right: Through the years Wyeth-Ayerst has been a pharmaceutical pioneer, not only in developing new drugs but in creating new ways to administer drugs.

Below: Wyeth-Ayerst researchers are continuously looking for drugs that can treat or prevent serious health-related problems.

M.A.B. Paints & Coatings

The first can of paint bearing the M.A.B. label was sold in 1899 from a store operated by Michael A. Bruder. The significance goes well beyond the sale of a can of paint. Michael A. Bruder had introduced a new marketing concept—the selling of premixed paints. He also had set the stage for M.A.B. Paints & Coatings, one of the country's largest makers and distributors of painting products.

In those days, Michael Bruder not only sold bulk painting materials, but he also blended and stocked a large inventory of premixed paints. Painters no longer had to spend time mixing linseed oil, pigments, turpentines, and colorants. Instead, they soon relied upon the consistent quality and reliable color selection of Michael Bruder's premixed paints, which were ready for immediate use.

Right: Michael A. Bruder (behind the counter), founder, sold the first can of paint bearing the M.A.B. label in 1899.

Below: The exterior of the first M.A.B. paint store on the corner of 16th Street and Passyunk Avenue.

The only native born of several sons in an Irish immigrant family, Michael Bruder believed in providing a quality product and offering the customer personalized service.

His first store was at the corner of 16th Street and Passyunk Avenue. In 1926 M.A.B.'s expansion into New Jersey was fueled by the opening of the Delaware Bridge (now the Benjamin Franklin Bridge), which increased the flow of traffic between Philadelphia, Pennsylvania, and Camden, New Jersey. That same year Michael Bruder opened a new store in Camden.

One of Michael Bruder's sons, Tom, took an aggressive interest in the business. More determined than his father and a tireless perfectionist, Tom Bruder's philosophy was, "Make the best and you'll be the biggest."

Following his father's death in 1932 during the depths of the Great Depression, Tom opened more new stores, supplied by a small factory in downtown Philadelphia. In 1935, shortly before dawn on Sunday, June 9, smoke began billowing skyward over the factory. Despite fire fighters' efforts, M.A.B.'s supply turned to ashes. Instead of giving up, Tom Bruder set up shop at 52nd and Grays Avenue, which, to this day, remains the location of the M.A.B. Philadelphia plant.

Over the years, as M.A.B. expanded, so did the needs of its customers. In the first quarter of the century, the interiors of most homes were covered with wallpaper. Just prior to World War II interior wall paint was becoming popular. While professionals were

still hired to paint the exterior of the homes, often husband and wife weekend teams were taking over the interior decorating projects. And they sought out M.A.B. stores as information centers for the proper preparation and application of paint products.

The housing boom that followed World War II forced paint manufacturers across the country to formulate high-quality coatings for a variety of new modern materials. This presented a perfect opportunity for M.A.B., who welcomed the challenge to develop new products to solve complicated coating problems.

In the early 1950s as the suburbs sprouted, so did M.A.B. stores, opening throughout New Jersey, Pennsylvania, and south to Washington, D.C.

Simultaneously, the chemistry of coatings was undergoing significant changes. Latex, acrylic, and other more modern components altered and improved the character of paint. Lead disappeared. Silicone, epoxy, vinyl, polyester, and urethane coatings became commonplace.

M.A.B. has kept abreast of these changes through its research and development laboratory, staffed by innovative and experienced

The M.A.B. plant at 52nd Street and Grays Avenue.

M.A.B.'s colorful trucks are a familiar sight on the roadways around Philadelphia.

chemists. Its quality-assurance laboratory monitors each shipment of raw materials and each batch of coatings to ensure that the finished products meet all standards and specifications. Computers ensure batch-to-batch consistency of standard colors and make it possible to formulate custom colors requested by architects and designers for new projects or renovations requiring an exact color match.

Efficient production scheduling has also been an important element of growth. M.A.B. must be prepared for seasonal needs, unexpected large contractor requests, and trends in color preferences in order to maintain inventory levels. Because M.A.B. places a high priority on its commitment to customer service, M.A.B.'s own fleet of trucks make the scheduled deliveries.

The shelves of the M.A.B. stores are stocked with products for the home owner and the painting contractor. Rich-Lux is used for the interior, Sea Shore for the exterior, Timber Stain for decks and natural siding. M.A.B. has a full line of brushes, rollers, ladders, and drop cloths. In addition to its line of retail products, M.A.B. offers special-purpose products for industrial use, such as coatings that prevent rust and chemical corrosion and retard fire.

When Thomas A. Bruder, Sr., passed away in 1967, the board of directors promptly elected Thomas A., Jr., as president. At that time, M.A.B. finalized the purchase of Smith-Alsop, a paint manufacturer and distributor in Terre Haute, Indiana; this was followed by a new plant in Orlando, Florida.

Today these three plants produce and distribute M.A.B. paints and coatings for more than 300 stores in 18 states and the District of Columbia. The Bruder family still actively manages the business.

For nearly a century, M.A.B. Paints & Coatings have been used inside and outside of hundreds of buildings in the Philadelphia area. Bridges that span the Delaware River are maintained by M.A.B.'s high performance coatings. The oil refineries near South Philadelphia use M.A.B. to protect their steel pipes and tanks. Hotels, hospitals, museums, and colleges in the Philadelphia area all rely upon M.A.B. for beauty and durability.

Since its founding, M.A.B. Paints & Coatings has evolved into a Philadelphia institution. To wit, when a former employee was traveling internationally with M.A.B. key rings on his luggage, he was approached by a stranger in an airport who pointed at the employee's key ring and said, "M.A.B. You must be from Philadelphia."

Kraft Dairy Division

Move over Wisconsin. The midwestern state may be considered the heart of the country's dairy land, but the beginnings of the American dairy industry can be traced to the East Coast, specifically the Philadelphia area. This was the home of some of the earliest dairy distribution systems, and, more specifically, Breyers Ice Cream.

Breyers is one of the major brands of the Kraft Dairy Division, a division of Kraft General Foods. It is one of the mouth-watering products that is part of a long list of well-known dairy food brand names, such as Breakstone's, Light 'n Lively, and Sealtest, that are sold by the leading maker and marketer of frozen and refrigerated dairy products.

Today's Kraft Dairy Division was formed over the years through a combination of sev-

eral different dairy companies. In the early 1800s there was no dairy industry to speak of. Dairy farmers sold any extra milk, cheese, and butter to neighboring farms. A Philadelphia dairy farmer, Joel Woolman, is credited with starting the first distribution system when, in 1804, he carted his milk to other Philadelphia residents. His efforts are often considered the forerunner of the American dairy industry.

As refrigeration and milk pasteurization

Left: The Breyers Hot Air Balloon makes a regal appearance over the Philadelphia skyline. The aircraft competes in many area hot air balloon races.

Below: The Breyers Van is a welcome guest at Veterans Stadium, home of the Phillies, especially when free samples are handed out to an appreciative crowd.

the all-natural ice cream

were introduced to the industry, milk companies opened up in several major cities nationwide. Many specialized in a singular product, such as butter or ice cream. One Chicago entrepreneur, Thomas McInnerney, had a vision of a national dairy company. His vision became a reality in 1923, when he established the National Dairy Products Company and began acquiring milk companies around the country. The National Dairy Company eventually became Kraft General Foods. Along the way, one of the companies McInnerney acquired was Breyers Ice Cream Co.

Breyers Ice Cream was started by William A. Breyer in 1866 in his Philadelphia kitchen. He made the homemade ice cream in a hand freezer, insisting, even then, on using only the freshest ingredients—real dairy cream, real cane sugar, and carefully selected fresh fruits. That was his guarantee of freshness.

The ice cream was so popular with his neighbors that William Breyer started selling it from a wagon along the streets of Kensington and Frankford. In fact, he opened the first Breyer ice cream store in 1882 at 2776 Frank-

From the company's modest beginnings in 1866 in William Breyer's Philadelphia kitchen, the company has expanded to nationwide distribution.

ford Avenue. From the store, which also doubled as a manufacturing site, he delivered the ice cream from wagons brightly painted with a green sweet briar leaf. That green sweet briar leaf remains the Breyers trademark to this day.

William Breyer eventually opened six stores in various Philadelphia neighborhoods. Until ice cream production was consolidated at a facility at 43rd Street and Woodland Avenue, Breyers ice cream was still made in the much-expanded backroom facility at the first retail store on Frankford Avenue.

When William Breyer's son Henry took over the operation of the business, he continued his father's guarantee of freshness by signing a "Pledge of Purity" that stated, "I pledge that Breyers ice cream has never contained adulterants, gums, gelatins, powders or fillers, extracts, or artificial flavoring of any nature. Real cream, cane sugar, and pure flavorings

are used to make Breyers ice cream." Every package of Breyers ice cream still contains that pledge. In fact, the original pledge still hangs in the Kraft Dairy Division's offices.

Ice cream, once only a treat for European aristocrats and kings, was growing in popularity, and so was Breyers Ice Cream Company. In the early 1900s sales of Breyers had expanded into the Philadelphia suburbs, and in 1908 Henry Breyer and his brother Fred set up the Breyer Ice Cream Company. By then, Breyer was shipping ice cream by trolley, wagon, train, boat, and truck to major markets in Maryland, Pennsylvania, New Jersey, and New York. It became a division of McInnerney's National Dairy Products Corporation in 1926.

Since then, the Breyer brand name has expanded nationwide and appears on other dairy products such as yogurt, ice milk, and on one of the newest entries, Breyers Frozen Yogurt. And as Breyers Ice Cream Co. enters its 125th year in 1991, it is still made from fresh ingredients and is the oldest brand name in continuous use for any ice cream in the United States.

Boeing Helicopters

Boeing Defense & Space Group's helicopter division in suburban Philadelphia is a world leader in the rotorcraft industry. The company specializes in several key areas, including designing, developing, and manufacturing transport helicopters and tilt-rotor aircraft; designing and integrating advanced avionics and electronic flight-control systems for rotorcraft; designing, developing, and fabricating all-composite airframes and rotor blades; and manufacturing wing subassemblies for Boeing jet-transport airplanes.

Boeing Helicopters' manufacturing and administrative offices are located on 355 acres of prime real estate in Ridley Township, approximately three miles west of the Philadelphia International Airport. The company's Flight Test Center utilizes less-congested airspace at nearby Wilmington, Delaware, about 25 miles south of Philadelphia.

Boeing Helicopters is the largest employer in Delaware County, Pennsylvania, and is a major contributor to the economic vitality of the Delaware Valley. The company's workforce consists of 6,200 experienced craftsmen and professionals. Their technical and engineering skills combine to produce aircraft of ever-increasing reliability and productivity.

In the 1990s Boeing Helicopters is seeking to broaden its core business through long-

The Boeing-built CH-47D Chinook can transport the big M198 155-millimeter howitzer, its 11-man crew, and 32 rounds of ready ammunition.

term investments in advanced engineering, technology, facilities, equipment, and aircraft programs serving domestic and international customers.

During the previous decade, the company added nearly one million square feet of new facilities (an area equivalent to a 100-story office building), which raised the total of covered space devoted to a variety of manufacturing, engineering, and administrative activities to some 3.5 million square feet.

Important technology centers at Boeing Helicopters include a 470,000-square-foot, state-of-the-art Composites Manufacturing Facility, a whirl tower simulating a helicopter's drive system and permitting ground-based testing of rotor blades, and a V/STOL wind tunnel in which 100,000 pieces of information can be measured each second during an average test.

Boeing Helicopters is world famous for its production and unparalleled support of turbine-powered tandem-rotor transport helicopters, including the UH-46D and CH-46E Sea Knights, which are operated by the U.S. Navy and Marine Corps, and the CH-47 Chinook, which is flown by the U.S. Army and customers overseas. The Boeing 234 is a civil version of the Chinook; it is operated commercially in the United States and in Europe.

Boeing expanded the distribution of these helicopters through licensed production and marketing agreements. The H-46 and its civil variant, the Boeing 107, were built in Japan for customers in Asia, Europe, and the Middle East. Chinooks were built in Italy and sold to

military operators in the Mediterranean region. Today's latest version of the CH-47 is being coproduced in Japan to fulfill orders from the Japanese Defense Agency.

In addition to supporting Chinook coproduction in Japan, Boeing is continually improving the Chinook family of helicopters by remanufacturing and modernizing early model Chinooks to the advanced CH-47D and MH-47E configurations. The company is delivering modernized Chinooks to the U.S. Army at the rate of four per month. As of December 31, 1990, the Army had accepted 340 of the 472 CH-47Ds it had ordered through a combination of single-year and multi-year procurement contracts.

The company is also under contract to begin modernizing the Spanish Army's Chinooks to CH-47D standards, and it has been selected by Britain's Royal Air Force to rebuild its Chinooks to this equivalent.

Growing interest in the highly productive heavy-lift Chinook has resulted in Boeing's current fabrication and delivery of brand-new CH-47s to customers in the Pacific Rim. These aircraft are nearly identical to the CH-47Ds presently being shipped to the U.S. Army.

Boeing has begun building the U.S. Army's most sophisticated helicopter, the MH-47E Special Operations Chinook, which was developed to permit the Army to conduct long-range missions around the clock, at low level and in weather conditions that would keep conventional helicopters on the ground.

Production MH-47Es will be drawn from Boeing's Chinook remanufacturing/modernization line. These aircraft will undergo further modifications to complete them not as CH-47Ds but as MH-47Es. Included in these modifications are a fully integrated cockpit featuring a mission-management system having two color and two monochromatic multifunction displays, plus a mission-aids system that incorporates a forward-looking infrared sensor and multimode radar for terrain-following and terrain-avoidance.

Alterations that double the aircraft's normal fuel capacity, plus the ability to install internal auxiliary fuel tanks quickly, will enable the MH-47E to successfully complete extremely long-range missions. In-flight refueling will permit ocean-spanning deployments without sacrificing the ability to carry full combat loads.

A prototype MH-47E made its first flight in June 1990 and entered a flight-test program.

The Army plans to procure a total of 51 MH-47Es. Production deliveries are expected to begin in 1992 and end in 1994.

Boeing is teamed with Bell Helicopter Textron to build and flight-test six V-22 Osprey tilt-rotor transports under a $1.81 billion contract issued by the U.S. Navy. The multimission V-22 is being developed primarily for the U.S. Marine Corps; however, it is the first aircraft designed from the ground up to meet the needs of all four U.S. armed services. Four V-22s are currently operating: two at Bell's facilities in Texas and two at Boeing's Flight Test Center in Wilmington. A fifth V-22 will begin flight tests in April 1991.

In its vertical-flight mode, the revolutionary V-22 Osprey can take off straight up. It can also hover and descend vertically. In its horizontal-flight mode it can fly as high, as fast, and as far as the famous C-130 Hercules turboprop airplane. The V-22's remarkable flying qualities create new operational advantages and tactical capabilities extending beyond the narrow confines of ordinary helicopters and fixed-wing airplanes.

Another teaming arrangement involving Boeing Helicopters is the Boeing Sikorsky Light Helicopter (LH) First Team, which is proposing to build an advanced armed-reconnaissance/light-attack/air-combat aircraft for the U.S. Army. The LH is crucial to the U.S. Army's future war-fighting capabilities. Current plans call for at least 1,292 LHs to replace some 3,000 technologically obsolete and expensive-to-maintain light helicopters. The U.S. Army plans to award a five-year, $2

Boeing Helicopters teamed up with Bell Helicopter Textron to build and test the revolutionary V-22 Osprey tilt-rotor aircraft.

billion, full-scale-development contract in April 1991.

In addition to building military rotorcraft, Boeing Helicopters competes with other aerospace manufacturers for contracts involving production of major components for modern Boeing jet transports. These awards currently account for 25 percent of Boeing Helicopters' production base and include the fabrication of wing subassemblies for Boeing 737, 747, 757, and 767 airplanes. The division will begin deliveries of similar subsystems for Boeing's new 777 jetliner in 1993.

Progress Lighting

For most of the century, since 1906, Progress Lighting has been lighting American homes. Originally a maker of gaslights, today Progress manufactures an extensive range of lighting fixtures for interior and exterior uses. From crystal chandeliers that brighten elegant dinner parties to outdoor lanterns that welcome guests, Progress lights the entire home.

Progress Lighting is a Philadelphia company that has grown to be the largest producer of residential lighting fixtures in the United States. The company makes more than 10

The P4082-18 chandelier from Progress Lighting's extensive designer collection was introduced during the January market in Dallas. An elegant crystal chandelier with gray-cut floral decorations, the ornamental arms, candles, and column accents are in a choice of polished brass or silver.

million fixtures per year in its four manufacturing plants. Its Philadelphia facility at G Street and Erie Avenue, which also serves as Progress' headquarters, is the largest lighting fixture plant and distribution facility in the nation. Progress also operates distribution centers in Montreal, Atlanta, Chicago, and Los Angeles. Progress' manufacturing-distribution network represents one of the few vertically integrated lighting fixture manufacturing operations remaining in the country.

Progress is probably best known as the main supplier of lighting fixtures for the new residential construction industry. The Progress product line of lighting fixtures contains more than 1,800 items. The company's reputation for top quality and service has helped it to consistently maintain its leadership position in the industry.

Progress recognized that today's homeowners are investing in their existing homes

Progress offers outdoor lanterns for post, wall, ceiling, or chain-hung mountings. Finish selections include antique or polished brass, verde, and white or black powder-coated lanterns that provide superior resistance to chipping, color-fading, and even the corrosive effects of seaside salt air.

by remodeling and renovating. This usually includes replacing their old lighting fixtures with higher style, more fashionable designs.

Lighting has become a fashion statement as well as a functional necessity. People are seeking more stylized fixtures that blend with their homes' decor, be it contemporary or traditional.

Progress and its design department have been a leader in this developing trend, creating a broader selection of high-style, more decorative lighting fixtures. Some of Progress' newest designs feature the increasingly popular light sources such as halogen, compact fluorescent, and miniature incandescent bulbs. The company was also one of the first manufacturers to create authentic reproductions of Victorian-style chandeliers.

Progress sells its products through electrical distributors and their showrooms. Most recently Progress opened its first lighting showroom for the trade in the home furnishing center in the Dallas Trade Mart, which offers a full array of interior design products. Aside from a trade showroom in its Philadelphia headquarters, this Dallas showroom marks the first time Progress has displayed fixtures in a trade market center. Progress believes its new lighting showroom will augment its business by offering a wider range of high-style items to distributors who come from all across the nation to twice-yearly market showings.

As the twenty-first century approaches, Progress is dedicated to continue its commitment to lighting the American dream—in homes and business—for another 100 years.

Teleflex Incorporated

Teleflex Incorporated began in 1943 with a unique place in history. Indeed, the principal business of the company was to develop and manufacture a remote-control device for military aircraft, including the legendary Royal Air Force Spitfire fighter plane and other World War II aircraft.

Toward that goal, Teleflex produced a relatively simple though sophisticated push-pull helical cable that, in combination with a geared wheel, accommodated the Spitfire's control systems. The cable became the cornerstone of the company that was founded by M.C.C. Chisholm, who once said a mechanical control could be as simple as a piece of string.

Today Teleflex is known throughout the world as a company that solves engineering problems through the development and application of new specialized technologies in two distinct categories: technical products and services and commercial products.

The company's technical segment serves the aerospace, defense, medical product, and turbine-engine service markets—fields that require a high degree of engineering sophistication.

A stacked rotor coated with SermeTel process 5380 D.P.

The Teleflex Aerospace/Defense Group designs and manufactures control systems for military aircraft, helicopters, commercial jets and commuter aircraft, missiles, space vehicles, and naval vessels, with expanding applications in air-cargo handling systems. Sermatech International, also part of the Teleflex technical products and services, provides coating services and repair applications in the turbine engine service market.

With an eye toward the high-growth med-

The Teleflex TFX Medical Group manufactures and distributes a variety of disposable medical products for urology, anesthesiology, and gastroenterology markets. Here, a Teleflex technician inspects a Foley catheter.

ical products market in the 1990s, the Teleflex TFX Medical Group manufactures and distributes a variety of disposable medical products for urology, anesthesiology, and gastroenterology markets. In 1989 Teleflex acquired Willy Rusch AG, a 103-year-old privately owned company headquartered in West Germany that makes a broad line of disposable and reusable medical products.

The acquisition, Teleflex chairman L.K. Black indicates, will greatly strengthen the company's worldwide distribution system and add manufacturing capabilities, complementary products, research and development facilities, and new technologies to the present line of medical products sold through TFX Medical, now called Rusch International.

The commercial products segment services

Teleflex produces quadrant controls for commercial and military aircraft.

the automotive, pleasure marine, outdoor power equipment, and fluid transfer markets—development products that tend to be less complex and produced in greater volume. Products range from a Teleflex line of push-pull controls with engineered thermoplastic end-fittings for automotive controls to steering systems for upscale pleasure powerboats to cable controls for lawn equipment.

Teleflex, based in Limerick, Pennsylvania, enters the new decade with 5,000 employees in nearly 50 operating units worldwide. The company now manufactures products and operates in markets never envisioned in M.C.C. "Sandy" Chisholm's wildest dreams.

On January 24, 1945, Chisholm wrote to an English colleague, "To put the matter briefly, it seems that our venture in the United States will be a decided success, and present indications are that it may surpass even my wildest imaginings."

In short order, Teleflex took its aviation experience in high-performance control systems and capitalized on its growing technical and manufacturing capabilities through diversification into new and wider markets.

Today Teleflex Incorporated is universally recognized as a major supplier in every industry where precision remote controls are required. Its expanding presence in such diverse fields as medical disposables and gas turbine technology has positioned the company for even further growth in the new decade. Growth, in fact, that is still beyond Chisholm's "wildest imaginings."

The sophisticated technology needed for the aerospace and defense industries was easily adaptable for the manufacture of simpler mechanical cable-control systems for passenger cars, front-wheel drive vans, and light-duty trucks.

Herr Foods Inc.

James S. Herr and Miriam Herr pose proudly before the new Herr Corporate Center.

Few foods probably smell as mouth-watering as crisp, freshly cooked potato chips. That is the first aroma that greets visitors to the Herr Foods manufacturing facility in suburban Nottingham, Pennsylvania. But Herr's makes much more than potato chips. Pretzels, corn chips, cheese curls, and numerous other snack foods, are all manufactured under the watchful eye of Herr family members, who have managed the company's growth ever since the founder, James S. Herr, sold his first potato chip more than 45 years ago.

As one of the largest independently owned snack food companies in the country, Herr's has prospered by adhering to a simple operating philosophy that is communicated to all of its 900 employees. The company believes that quality and service are essential to its very existence, so every employee and every piece of equipment is dedicated toward producing the best possible chip or pretzel or cheese curl.

This philosophy is evident in the attitude of the employees who pack the potato chip bags or deliver the popcorn to the neighborhood grocery stores. And, perhaps because it is a family-owned business, all of the employees are embraced as part of the family. The Herr family is proud of its no-layoff policy, even if an employee's job would be phased out by a new piece of automated equipment. "We've never laid off anybody, and we never will," says James M. Herr, son of the founder. "We operate on Christian principles to help treat our employees better," he says.

Originally based in Lancaster, the operation moved to Nottingham more than 30 years ago and began expanding rapidly. James S. Herr, who oversees the company today as chairman and chief executive officer, remembers the early days of the business when he peeled and sliced potatoes by hand. In those days they used about 300 pounds of potatoes per week. That is a far cry from the sophisticated, automated manufacturing system employed by the firm today, which processes more than 2 million pounds of potatoes per week.

After the potatoes are delivered, they tumble into a darkened storage area, before making the trip to the washing and peeling machines. Special equipment slices the potatoes before they enter the huge cookers. As the chips wind their way through the maze of equipment, they are automatically separated by size before dropping into large or small bags. Along the way, quality-control staff and equipment monitor the chips for taste, texture, and imperfections, making sure the chips meet Herr's very high specifications. Only the highest-quality chips make it onto the store shelves. Freshness—or a lack of it—can make

or break a potato chip. Therefore in the mid-1980s Herr's installed a state-of-the-art computerized inventory and distribution control system. The computers track snack food sales item by item as they are loaded onto the delivery truck; which in turn directly deliver the snacks to the food stores.

Herr's makes potato chips, pretzels, corn chips, onion rings, cheese curls, and many other delicious snacks.

In order to more efficiently serve its market area, which includes Pennsylvania, New Jersey, Delaware, Maryland, Virginia, West Virginia, eastern Ohio, lower New York, and northern North Carolina; Herr's owns a string of distribution centers throughout the territory. Its main Philadelphia distribution center is located at the Eastwick Industrial Park, near the airport in South Philadelphia. Each day a fleet of trucks follow nearly 400 different truck routes to deliver the Herr's line of snack foods.

For many years potato chips were the only product Herr's made, but today Herr's manufactures and distributes eight different varieties of chips, along with pretzels, corn chips, tortilla chips, onion rings, popcorn, and cheese curls, producing more than 125 million packages per year. Herr's still has the number-one potato chip, based upon dollar and pound sales in Philadelphia.

That's one of the reasons why Herr Foods feels a strong commitment to the Philadelphia community. It has supported Philadelphia's sports teams for many years, as is evident by its billboard displayed in Veteran's

Above: **Every Herr employee is committed to the finest possible quality and service.**

Right: **Each day a fleet of trucks follow nearly 400 different routes to deliver the Herr line of snack foods.**

Below: **This sophisticated, automated manufacturing system processes more than 2 million pounds of potatoes per week and guarantees the freshness and excellence of Herr's products.**

Stadium, emblazoned with its well-known slogan, "Make Herr's Yours."

The company also has a special place in its corporate heart for children and has been a generous contributor to various children's charitable programs, such as the National Adoption Center and Easter Seals. The Herr family also supports the Philadelphia Leadership Foundation, which strives to give spiritual leadership to the disadvantaged.

In addition, it opens its doors to members of the community, offering free tours of its manufacturing facility. It recently built a new Visitors Center, with a goal of hosting 100,000 visitors each year.

The Herr family is proud of its growing operation and the quality of every chip or pretzel that is sealed into a Herr's bag. That's why Herr Foods Inc. expects Philadelphians will continue to make Herr's theirs.

SmithKline Beecham

SmithKline Beecham is one of the world's leading companies in pharmaceuticals and health care, over-the-counter medicines, animal health, and clinical testing. The company has 55,000 employees in 130 countries and sales of approximately $8 billion per year.

Strongly positioned in the United States, Europe, and Japan, SmithKline Beecham has a global marketing force of more than 6,000 and invests more than $600 million per year in innovative programs of research and development. The research and development of new health care products, especially pharmaceuticals, is the company's major mission.

SmithKline Beecham and a handful of other multinational pharmaceutical and health care companies lead the world in the search for new therapies. The company's commitment to research and development is clear—more than 5,000 people are dedicated to the task at major pharmaceutical research centers in the United Kingdom, the United States, and at its vaccine research center in Belgium.

To recover the costs of research—now representing a $231 million investment for each prescription drug that completes the journey from research to the market—pharmaceutical companies must discover major therapeutic breakthroughs and market them globally.

Research investment by the U.S. pharmaceutical industry has risen at an astounding rate, from $700 million in 1970 to $9 billion in 1990. The world trend is running at about the same rate.

The SmithKline Beecham research program is focused on six therapeutic areas, each with products in clinical trials: anti-infectives, for treatment of bacterial, viral, and fungal infections; gastrointestinal, for treatment of diseases of the digestive tract; cardiovascular, for treatment of heart disease and diseases of the circulatory system; mental health, for treatment of dementia and nervous system disorders; inflammation and pain, including treatment of arthritis; and vaccines, for prevention of bacterial and viral infections.

Many of the company's prescription pharmaceutical products are known worldwide—Tagamet®, for the treatment of ulcers and

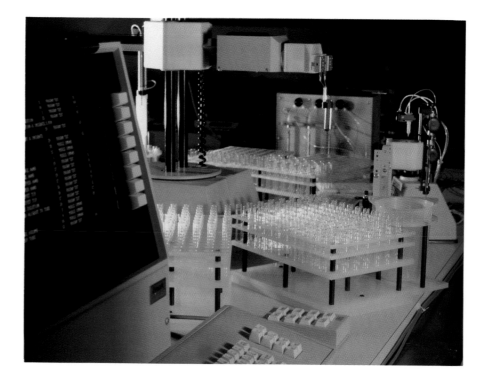

other gastrointestinal disorders; the antibiotics Augmentin® and Amoxil® for treating common bacterial infections; Eminase®, for treatment of heart attacks; Dyazide®, for the control of hypertension; Engerix-B®, a vaccine for the prevention of hepatitis B; and Reliflex®/Relifen®, for arthritis.

Its leading consumer brands are also well known: Aquafresh® and Macleans® toothpaste, the antacids Tums® and Setlers®, the Oxy® acne treatment line, Massengill® feminine hygiene products, Contac® and Beecham's Powders® cold remedies, and Sucrets® and N'ICE® for coughs and sore throats.

Cutting edge technology, like this robotic chemistry system, is a hallmark of SmithKline Beecham's pharmaceutical research.

Some 300 SmithKline Beecham brand products are sold in more than 130 countries, with the strongest market positions in the United States, Europe (including the United Kingdom), and Japan. The company's animal health business concentrates on the growing market for small animal pharmaceuticals. Its products are sold worldwide, with key markets in the United States, Europe, Latin America, and the Pacific Rim.

SmithKline Beecham Clinical Laboratories, which has its headquarters in the Philadelphia suburb of King of Prussia, is the leading clinical testing laboratory system in North America. In these laboratories, substance-abuse testing for industry and AIDS testing have doubled since 1988.

Created by the 1989 merger of SmithKline Beecham and Beecham group, SmithKline has long been identified with the Philadelphia area. The company traces its origin to downtown Philadelphia in 1830. From a small shop selling medicines and sundries, through the years it grew to become a major pharmaceutical firm. A leader in the 1940s and 1950s for its products used in treating mental and emotional diseases—including Thorazine, the first medication that could bring serious psychiatric illnesses under control—SmithKline Beecham in more recent years was the discoverer of the world's first H2 antagonist, Tagamet®, widely used in the treatment of ulcers

trointestinal disorders. The company has been strongly committed to the activities of the Greater Philadelphia community. Henry Wendt, chairman, points out that Philadelphia has been home to SmithKline for more than 160 years and that the company has been "deeply involved in Philadelphia's medical, cultural, educational, and civic life.

"Through its philanthropy," he adds, "we have supported many of the institutions in this city that are known and respected the world over."

Robert P. Bauman, chief executive, notes that some of the company's major operations are in the Philadelphia area, including its U.S. pharmaceutical business, its main U.S. pharmaceutical research and development center, and the headquarters for its animal health and clinical laboratories. He says the new SmithKline Beecham has a commitment to the Delaware Valley, and that "as part of that commitment we intend to continue playing a significant role in philanthropic support of the Philadelphia community."

Bauman says that the Greater Philadelphia area is a major center for SmithKline Beecham and "as our business grows and prospers, we fully expect our presence in Philadelphia to grow as well. We find the Philadelphia area ideally suited to the needs of the critical components of our world business."

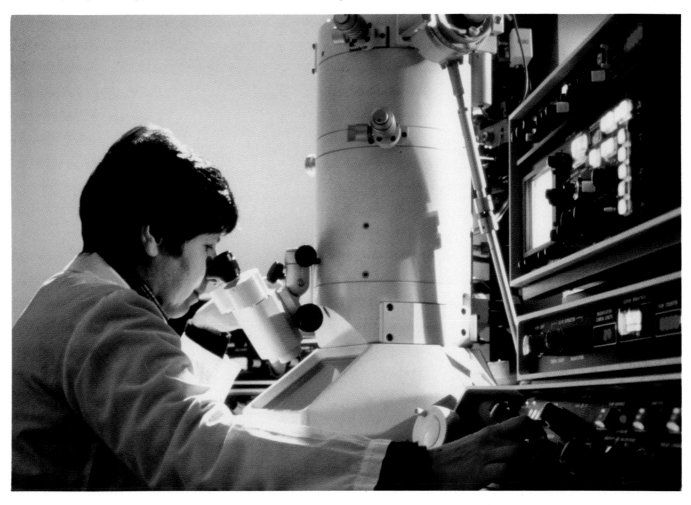

Philadelphia's solid financial base has provided a dynamic environment for economic growth and opportunity for both individuals and businesses in the community.

Photo by George Adams Jones

Business and Finance

CoreStates Financial Corp.

oreStates Financial Corp. builds upon 209 years of solid tradition to help define a vision of banking for the 1990s and beyond. Its roots reach back into the Revolutionary era of American history, when its origins intertwined with the momentous events that made Philadelphia the birthplace of a nation. Its branches touch the core middle Atlantic states and lend strength to the region's economic and community life.

The company's roots extend to the Bank of North America, which opened its doors at the beginning of 1782; the Philadelphia Bank, which officially opened for business at 9 a.m. on Monday, September 19, 1803, in a rented house at 104 Chestnut Street; and banks founded in 1804 in Trenton, New Jersey, and in 1810 in Lancaster, Pennsylvania.

Even its record of service to customers and fidelity to public shareholders ranks with the oldest in the nation: it still has customers whose relationships date to the beginning of the 19th century, and it has paid dividends on its common stock without interruption since 1844. Such a history notwithstanding, there is nothing musty about the way CoreStates does business with its customers.

New Jersey National Bank headquarters in Pennington, New Jersey.

From its base in Philadelphia, CoreStates offers wholesale and institutional banking services under the venerable banner of Philadelphia National Bank; retail banking services under the decades-old name of First Pennsylvania Bank; and trust and investment management services under the name CoreStates Trust and Investment Group.

The same services are delivered by the Hamilton Bank subsidiary in south central Pennsylvania and New Jersey National Bank throughout New Jersey, while CoreStates Bank of Delaware NA offers credit card services nationwide. And CoreStates also engages in factoring and commercial finance, merchant banking, investment banking, and international trade finance.

The services are as up-to-date as the latest technology of banking: CoreStates for many years has pioneered the kinds of banking technologies that directly address customer needs.

Thus a corporate customer can sit at a

First Pennsylvania Bank headquarters in Philadelphia.

Above: Philadelphia National Bank headquarters in Philadelphia.

Left: Hamilton Bank headquarters in Lancaster, Pennsylvania.

microcomputer anywhere in the world and tap into CoreStates' mighty mainframes in Philadelphia for up-to-the-second information on the status of the customer's accounts. Or the customer can even enter his own transaction, such as a wire transfer to Alaska or Singapore. Or a retail customer of a participating financial institution can slip a CoreStates-issued MAC ATM card into one of its MAC ICON Services(TM) self-service banking machines and cash his or her paycheck to the penny, day or night.

Such convenience-oriented innovation has made CoreStates a recognized leader among banking organizations for the use of technology to create value for customers—and fees for CoreStates itself.

But technology is only one ingredient of the management vision that has made CoreStates both a leader in serving its markets and a stellar financial performer.

The most important management principle is that people give CoreStates its competitive edge. CoreStates focuses great attention to the hiring, development, and recognition of its people for their critical role in the company's success, as well as continuous efforts to provide them with expanded skills and improved tools with which to work.

CoreStates and its people also reach out vigorously into community affairs, through both organized corporate efforts and employee volunteerism. The company added to its visibility in the Philadelphia region and nationally with its continued sponsorship of the CoreStates US PRO Cycling Championship, which is highly successful and increasingly significant in the regional economy.

Other basic CoreStates management principles include:
• Growth by building on existing strengths.
• Paying very close attention to the numbers—its capital strength and its profitability. As of December 31, 1990, CoreStates had total assets of $23.5 billion.
• Taking great care in structuring and managing the risks it undertakes on behalf of its customers, to minimize the disruption that can come, for example, from carelessness about credit risks.
• And, of course, using technology to serve customers better and operate more efficiently.

By such means, CoreStates has built itself into the largest and strongest banking organization based in the Philadelphia area, with a reach that is felt nationally and globally.

Like the historic city from which it operates, it is looking to a future that is full of challenge and opportunity.

Independence Blue Cross

Serving nearly 2 million customers throughout Philadelphia, Bucks, Chester, Delaware, and Montgomery counties, Independence Blue Cross is southeastern Pennsylvania's largest health insurance carrier.

The concept of prepaid health insurance was introduced to the community by Independence Blue Cross more than 50 years ago, as a means of assuring access to health care for the entire population. The company has evolved as the primary source of health care benefits for business and individuals alike, and has become a major force in the effort to hold down rising health care costs.

Furthermore, its role as an effective manager of health benefit dollars has made Independence Blue Cross a long-standing ally of business, commerce, and labor.

Through its relationship with Pennsylvania Blue Shield, Independence Blue Cross offers a full range of hospital, surgical, and medical benefits to all citizens, including individuals who could not obtain health insurance elsewhere. Independence Blue Cross is positioned for continued market dominance into the twenty-first century, through an impressive range of subsidiaries and affiliated companies: Delaware Valley HMO; Vista Health Plan, Inc.; American Health Alternatives; QCC, Inc.; Q-Care Insurance Company; TAO, Inc.; The Caring Foundation of Southeastern Pennsylvania; and the Southeastern Pennsylvania Health Education Institute.

The contractual relationship with member hospitals is an Independence Blue Cross hallmark. These unique agreements guarantee that hospitals are paid for the health care Blue Cross customers receive. At the same time, the agreements enable the company to purchase health care for its customers at a discount. Additionally, the hospital agreements are a means through which Independence Blue Cross introduces a diverse array of cost containment programs into the process of health care delivery.

The agreements make possible such innovations as mandatory preadmission review, the Quality Care Admission Review Program®, discharge planning, and Individual Case Management. These and other cost containment measures enable Independence Blue Cross to manage the health care of its customers as a safeguard against costly and

perhaps unnecessary health care. This is a continuing priority, because the forces that fuel this escalation show no signs of abating: a growing aging population, increasing utilization of health care services, continual breakthroughs in medical science and technology, and the costs associated with such relatively new diseases as AIDS.

Of particular concern is the extent to which life-style-related illnesses stemming from drug and alcohol abuse contribute to the health cost spiral. For this reason, Independence Blue Cross monitors these trends and includes detailed reports on life-style illnesses in the utilization studies it prepares annually for the business and labor communities.

While meeting the challenges presented by a constantly changing and competitive external environment, Independence Blue Cross is at the same time working on the internal front to streamline service and contain administrative costs. As a reflection of these efforts, nearly 95 cents of every dollar in rates goes toward claims payment. It's a financial stewardship that President and Chief Executive Officer G. Fred DiBona, Jr., describes thusly: "As the individual principally responsible for managing this corporation, it is my intention to operate Independence Blue Cross on a sound, businesslike basis.

"We are a billion and a half dollar enterprise with 1,600 employees," DiBona continues. "If this was a profit-making organization, it would rank near the top of the FOCUS 50. It must be run as a bottom-line business with the same sort of financial controls and administrative accountability of any other business."

Because of sound financial practices, Independence Blue Cross maximizes its investment policies. As a nonprofit institution, savings are passed on to customers, not shareholders. "Our true bottom line is more than a net profit figure. It's the prudent management of our customers' dollars which requires effective administrative cost control, stable reserves, and sound investment management," says DiBona.

New products and services are always at the forefront of Independence Blue Cross. In order to meet customer needs, cost effective pricing, improved claims processing procedures, and systems modernization are continually emphasized.

Always mindful of community service and its importance, the company regularly sponsors fitness walks, health fairs, and other activities designed to focus public attention on staying healthy.

A particularly visible demonstration of community concern was the establishment of the Caring Program for Children Foundation. Nearly 60,000 children throughout the company's service area are without health insurance, due to the inability of their families to meet basic needs, even though they may work. Under the Caring Program, Independence Blue Cross and Pennsylvania Blue Shield will match contributions to provide basic health insurance for these children at no cost to their families.

"We view the Caring Program as the type of creative initiative that, working together, we can make happen for the betterment of the entire community," says DiBona. "And that type of commitment stems from our historic social mission, founded in the depths of the Depression, to make sure that people in need have health insurance coverage. We're still operating on that principle today."

As for tomorrow, DiBona believes that a customer-focused approach is the only route to success and future growth. "Every fiber in our corporate being has to be geared toward providing the products and services that our customers want and deserve," he says.

At Independence Blue Cross, preparing for tomorrow is as big a job as serving its customers today.

Independence Blue Cross operations are centralized at the 1901 Market street headquarters in Philadelphia. The company offers a wide range of health insurance products, customer services, and managed-care programs to nearly 2 million Pennsylvania customers.

® Registered service mark of Independence Blue Cross.

The Mutual Assurance Company

A tree has often stood as a symbol of strength, longevity, and protection from the elements. In the same manner, The Mutual Assurance Company's Green Tree logo has come to represent an insurance company and a homeowner insurance program that has endured for more than 200 years, protecting homeowners' most important asset. The Green Tree is one of a few select companies in the United States that offers perpetual property insurance. While blooming trees are usually considered a thing of beauty, to the homeowners of Colonial Philadelphia, they posed an uninsurable fire hazard, which led to the founding of The Mutual Assurance Company in 1784. At the time there was only one fire insurance company in Philadelphia—an association of area residents organized by Benjamin Franklin and friends.

However, because fire was the most serious

The sign for The Mutual Assurance Company, circa 1856. The sign was designed by Collins West and is part of The Mutual Assurance Company Collection. Photo by Will Brown

and common hazard, that association stopped insuring homes with trees on the street facade. Trees were considered too much of a risk.

As a result, a group of disgruntled policyholders and disenchanted citizens banded together to form an insurance company that would insure homes with carefully pruned trees on the front facade, calling itself The Mutual Assurance Company for Insuring Houses from Loss by Fire. Since its early years,

The Mutual Assurance Company's first fire mark, issued between 1784 and 1785 to Archibald McCall, from The Mutual Assurance Company Collection. Photo by Will Brown

the company has been more commonly known as "The Green Tree" because of its leafy symbol.

Originally the insurance coverage was granted in the form of seven-year renewable term policies. In 1801 it seemed more practical to issue single-payment policies, eliminating the burdensome seven-year renewal cycle and recurring stamp taxes. It was at that point that the single-deposit perpetual insurance policy was created by the company.

Today The Green Tree perpetual insurance policy is essentially the same, but with contemporary features. Like in Colonial Philadelphia, when fire insurance was created to protect property, today's insurance is tailored to meet the needs and protect the assets of homeowners. In fact, perpetual insurance makes even more sense today as a hedge against inflation.

Perpetual insurance also works as an excellent financial planning tool. It allows a homeowner to significantly reduce the cost of his homeowners insurance and still have the benefit of comprehensive insurance coverage.

As with the typical one-year renewable homeowners insurance, perpetual insurance provides reimbursement for damage to a residence and for damage to or theft of personal property. It also provides liability protection should someone be injured on the property.

When a homeowner signs up for perpetual insurance, he or she pays a one-time upfront deposit and makes no annual premium

payments. The average deposit today runs about $5,000. The deposit is fully refunded when either party cancels the policy, no matter how many claims have been made against the policy over the years.

If a homeowner chooses not to pay the entire deposit up front in cash, The Green

The Green Tree Group Building at 414 Walnut Street.
Photo by Will Brown

Tree can arrange financing through a home equity loan. A 10 percent down payment is required, with the balance financed. Then the homeowner can deduct the interest on the loan to the full extent of the tax laws.

Because of this financing option, perpetual insurance is available to homeowners in all income brackets. Approximately 25 percent of The Green Tree's policyholders own homes with replacement costs under $100,000. Another 59 percent own homes with replacement costs of between $100,000 and $250,000.

Policyholders can choose from three different types of policies with a variety of special features, such as a built-in inflation-guard plan or a dividend-paying program.

Thousands of homeowners have taken advantage of The Green Tree's perpetual insurance, but the company believes more people need to be made aware of the oldest type of property insurance in America.

Consequently, in recent years The Green

"View in Third Street, from Spruce Street Philadelphia," hand-colored engraving by William Birch & Son, circa 1798, from The Mututal Assurance Company Collection. Photo by Will Brown

Tree has begun aggressively educating homeowners about the benefits of perpetual insurance in an effort to make it available to a greater number of people. The insurance is sold in Pennsylvania, New Jersey, and several other states through independent agents and brokers and by licensed Green Tree sales representatives. Today the company is the parent of The Green Tree Group, which offers several types of insurance in more than 30 states and employs more than 200 people.

The A.M. Best Company, the leading insurance company rating organization, has awarded The Green Tree an A+ rating for reliability and quality of service, the highest rating available.

That's one of the reasons The Green Tree has continued to grow and prosper for more than 200 years. And like the spreading branches of a tree, the company will extend its reach well into the next century.

Van Kampen Merritt

For nearly a century, the Heceta Head Lighthouse has been helping seafarers safely reach their destinations. This cliff-side, picturesque lighthouse is located 30 miles south of Newport, Oregon, and was built in 1894 for $180,000. That investment is still paying off today, because the Heceta Head Lighthouse remains the most powerful marine beacon on the Oregon coast, visible for 21 miles.

As a corporate symbol, the lighthouse speaks of stability, opportunity, vigilance, security, and above all, vision. Which is exactly why the financial firm of Van Kampen Merritt has adopted the lighthouse as its corporate signature—a symbol that represents the qualities foremost in Van Kampen Merritt's objectives for its investors, or as the Van Kampen Merritt slogan says, "Investing with a sense of direction."

Founded in 1974 and acquired by Xerox Financial Services in 1984, Van Kampen

Merritt has become one of the fastest growing financial firms in the country, with more than $250 million in capital, making it the 28th-largest investment banking firm in the United States.

A specialized investment banking firm and a Xerox Financial Services company, Van Kampen Merritt is a leading sponsor of quality investment products for the individual. In this regard, the firm currently has under its management more than $26 billion in assets and is the leading issuer of insured unit investments trusts.

Van Kampen Merritt, with principal offices in Chicago, Philadelphia, and New York, established its Philadelphia corporate base in 1980 to service the mid-Atlantic states.

The lighthouse at Heceta Head in Oregon is Van Kampen Merritt's trademarked symbol of "investing with a sense of direction."

Through brokers, dealers, and representatives, Van Kampen Merritt's Philadelphia operation has become a leader in promoting two distinct groups of the company's consumer products, namely unit investment trusts and mutual funds. Since the inception of the Pennsylvania Insured Unit Trust and the variety of Managed Mutual Funds, Van Kampen Merritt has invested billions in municipal bonds issued within the states represented by the mid-Atlantic group.

"The Van Kampen Merritt Investment Advisory subsidiary manages the mutual funds sponsored by the firm and assists pension funds and institutions in managing their fixed income assets," says John C. "Jack" Merritt, chairman and chief executive officer of Van Kampen Merritt and Xerox Life.

Merritt points to several factors unique to Van Kampen Merritt that distinguishes the firm from other financial groups. First, says Merritt, "We have always believed that re-

This scene was used to represent "vigilance," a quality Van Kampen Merritt considers essential to expert financial management.

search drives investment decisions. To supplement our own internal municipal research capability, in 1985 we acquired McCarthy, Crisanti, and Maffei, Inc. (MCM)."

MCM, a nationally recognized statistical rating organization, specializes in credit research relating to corporate debt obligations and fiscal/monetary policy to help select bonds for the unit investment trusts, mutual funds, and institutional clients. With innovations such as Yield Watch, Corporate Watch, and Currency Watch—three up-to-the-minute electronic information services that provide input on the corporate bond and currency markets—MCM has become one of the nation's premier financial research firms.

Second, according to Merritt, "closely linked with the strategy of being a major manufacturer of high-quality products has been the development and creation of Xerox Financial Services Life."

Van Kampen Merritt's sister company, Xerox Life, offers a variety of innovative market-sensitive insurance products that enable individuals tax-favored ways to accumulate money while enjoying guarantees with respect to safety of principal, current rates, and future income. Xerox Life experiences a number of operating efficiencies by using many of the resources of Van Kampen Merritt. For example, Van Kampen Merritt Investment Advisory Corp. manages the Xerox Life portfolio, providing a level of investment sophistication and expertise available to few insurance companies.

And third, Van Kampen Merritt is one of the leading issuers of precious metals certificates in the United States and has delivered millions of ounces of the very finest bullion to investors. The company offers gold, platinum, or silver bullion in the form of certificates, coins, bars, and numismatic coins.

For the future, Merritt sees a definite change in investors' needs and demands. "The real change that we are seeing today is going back to quality, being more conservative and investing over time versus the get-rich-quick scenarios," says Merritt. "We are well positioned to capitalize on this change with a full array of quality products that are consistent with long-term investment strategies."

During the last year as we move into the mid-90s, Merritt feels that U.S. investors will have to pay more attention to global investments. Most Americans, he feels, have tended not to invest in the foreign markets, as they were not familiar with them and were not concerned about a devaluating dollar. To this end, Van Kampen Merritt introduced its first short-term global fund and expects to expand its global product lines in the future. He feels that the managed fund concept is probably one of the safest ways for investors to gain exposure to the global markets.

As Van Kampen Merritt continues to grow, they need to expand on their equity product line, thus completing the firm's objective of being a major asset manager and provider of high quality products for individuals and institutions for the '90s.

Glenmede Trust Company

More than 30 years ago the family heirs of Joseph N. Pew, founder of Sun Oil Company, established a unique bank for their considerable assets.

As this organization developed, its officers were free to pursue an agenda unheard of in most investment circles. Indeed, their first order of business was simply to ask family members what financial services they desired. The second order of business was to provide those services.

Such was the beginning of the Glenmede Trust Company—a Philadelphia-area investment institution whose very name reflects a legacy and commitment to stability, quality, and a high level of personal contact. Although the company's business has changed over the years, its approach to service has not. The Glenmede Trust Company is committed to fulfilling each client's investment needs without the constraints of preconceived or predetermined service boundaries—exactly as it did in the beginning for the members of the Pew family. Quality of service remains Glenmede's primary concern.

In the early 1970s the company began providing services for selected institutions and eventually for individuals other than the founding family. More recently, Glenmede has evolved into a trust and investment company that provides a complete array of services for high net worth individuals. These highly personalized services include trust and investment management, custodian, estate planning, tax planning, and tax preparation for a limited number of clients.

Glenmede also provides a complete array of investment services for institutional clients, primarily charities, endowments, foundations, public funds, and middle market pension plans.

The name Glenmede is synonymous with one of the region's most benevolent and recognized charitable trusts. In 1987 the company was restructured into two separate divisions. The trust and investment division concentrates on providing management for individual and institutional clients. And the Pew charitable trusts division, which is staffed independently, focuses on the grants of the Pew charitable trusts, which in 1989 distributed more than $140 million to various

Overlooking Rittenhouse Square, the Glenmede Trust Company remains dedicated to providing the highest level of trust and investment services to its clients.

charitable institutions. In 1990 it is anticipated that more than $170 million will be distributed to various charitable institutions.

At the end of 1990 the Glenmede Trust Company had responsibility for the management of $6 billion in assets. And as a measure of its growth from its family-oriented beginning, the company reported that more than 50 percent of its total revenue now comes from non-Pew related accounts.

The Glenmede Trust Company continues to project an investment philosophy that is conservative, risk averse, and oriented to preserving capital in real terms. The results of a study by one of the nation's leading financial measurement firms has show the wisdom of this approach. Comparing total return over the most recent five-year period, DeMarche Associates rated Glenmede's largest account in the top 5 percent of more than 1,000 investment managers.

From its unassuming brick office building overlooking Rittenhouse Square, the Glenmede Trust Company continues to be a formidable financial organization. It remains dedicated to providing the highest level of trust and investment services to its clients, just as it did for the Pew family founders in 1956.

Chase Manhattan Corporation

When its regional banking office opened in center city Philadelphia in 1989, The Chase Manhattan Corporation had no instantly visible ties to a city where history and tradition are pervasive.

But tucked away in the biography of Chase is a historical footnote that does, indeed, directly link this venerable financial institution with the city founded by William Penn. And who better to tell the story than Anthony J. Drexel Biddle III, the vice president of Chase's Philadelphia regional banking office whose family names are synonymous with Philadelphia's financial institutions.

Chase traces its origin to the Bank of The Manhattan Company, founded in 1799. After New York City had passed legislation authorizing a municipal water company, Aaron Burr successfully lobbied for an amendment to allow the company to use capital not required in the water business in financial transactions and operations. The company's directors voted to establish an office of discount and deposit, and on September 1, 1799, the Bank of The Manhattan Company opened its doors at 40 Wall Street.

Another institution that would play an important role in Chase's history was founded on September 16, 1877, as the Chase National Bank. The bank was named for Salmon P. Chase, the secretary of the treasury who led the fight for passage of the National Banking acts of 1863 and 1864.

In 1955 the merger between Chase National and the Bank of The Manhattan Company created The Chase Manhattan Bank. Chase secured a national charter in 1965, and in 1969 The Chase Manhattan Corporation was formed as a one-bank holding company.

Sitting in an office that overlooks the business corridor to City Hall, Biddle is at once amused and delighted to add the missing Philadelphia story to the Chase saga.

Aaron Burr formed the Bank of The Manhattan Company to break the monopoly of Alexander Hamilton's first Bank of the United States, located along Fourth Street in Philadelphia. Nicholas Biddle, who was Anthony Biddle's grandfather's great-grandfather, was president of the second Bank of the United States in 1824, when Philadelphia was the financial center of the country and the bank was the largest corporation in the nation. Nicholas Biddle's financial dominance ended, however, after he and President Andrew Jackson disagreed over the ideals of currency; Jackson favored hard money, Biddle favored paper. After a long struggle that affected banking all over the country, the second Bank of the United States finally closed in 1841. The resulting panic triggered the closing of six other banks in Philadelphia, and the financial power-base of the country moved to New York and the Bank of the Manhattan Company, now known as Chase.

As of June 30, 1990, Chase had total assets of $102 billion, total capital of $12 billion, and common shareholders' equity of nearly $4.5 billion. With operations in more than 50 countries, Chase provides a range of services to wholesale and individual customers through 10 major business components. The four retail banking business units—Direct Response, International Individual, National Financial Services, and Regional Banking—offer loan and deposit products and trust and investment services to consumers worldwide, as well as financial services to the owners of small- and medium-sized businesses.

Chase's Philadelphia banking office is the first regional banking office that Chase has opened since 1982. According to Biddle, the bank has these distinct goals:

To provide a full range of corporate financing services to emerging *Fortune* 500 companies; to position Chase as a member of the community through corporate financing for middle-market companies; to provide domestic private banking and fund management, with related high-net worth financial services; and to provide specialized residential mortgage products and home equity services.

And due to "its sheer size, its access to capital markets, and its international expertise," says Biddle, "Chase brings to Philadelphia a level of sophistication in corporate finance and banking expertise that just simply isn't otherwise in residence here."

Photo by David H. Wells

Philadelphia's developers, property management firms, contractors, and real estate professionals work to revitalize and create the urban landscapes of today and tomorrow.

Building Greater Philadelphia

Strouse, Greenberg & Co.

When Strouse, Greenberg & Co. was founded in Philadelphia 75 years ago, this real estate office was known as the city's preeminent downtown retail leasing firm. But mention the words Strouse, Greenberg today, and a concept foreign to real estate during the company's early years immediately comes to mind—shopping centers.

For the past 30 years of its operation, Strouse, Greenberg has evolved as one of the leading shopping center developers in the country. Initially, shopping centers were open malls, with shops set in an urban street environment that was nonetheless suburban in location.

Today, however, the concept of shopping centers and shopping malls has resulted in the totally enclosed environment of shopping. And through shopping centers such as South-Park in Charlotte, North Carolina; Deptford Mall in Deptford, New Jersey; and Northpark in Dallas, Texas, Strouse, Greenberg has earned the reputation nationwide as innovative developers and redevelopers of this particular real estate phenomenon.

"We are one of the founders of the shopping center industry," says Samuel M. Switzenbaum, president and chief executive officer of Strouse, Greenberg. "Over the past 30 years we have managed in excess of 30 million square feet of shopping malls. It is, today, one of the mainstays of our business."

Switzenbaum, however, is quick to point out that Strouse, Greenberg is actually "three companies in one." First, Strouse, Greenberg is a property management firm, responsible not only for shopping centers but also 10,000 multifamily apartments and several million square feet of office buildings under its management domain.

Strouse, Greenberg is also a development firm for its own properties throughout Pennsylvania, New Jersey, and Delaware. And third, Strouse, Greenberg is also well known

Samuel M. Switzenbaum, president and chief executive officer. Photo by Sallie C. Brooke

as a brokerage, sales, and marketing company, specializing in leasing downtown office and retail space, industrial leasing and sales, appraisals and consulting, and real estate asset management services for financial institutions. The firm has directed the retail planning and leasing of such landmark urban mixed-use developments as Copley Place in Boston and Water Tower Place in Chicago.

"We plan to focus on pro-

viding a diversified range of highly professional services to major financial institutions, developers, real estate owners, and the industry," says Switzenbaum.

"And basically if someone had to ask me what they gain by an association with Strouse, Greenberg, I'd say we add value. By our presence and by the professionalism we bring to the table, we add value to that representation."

Scope of services:

- Development/redevelopment
- Asset management
- Property management
- Leasing & marketing

The Kevin F. Donohoe Company

I n 1983 a real estate development company was formed in Philadelphia that immediately captured everyone's attention when it announced that one of its first projects would be the largest renovation of an historic office building in the United States.

The Kevin F. Donohoe Company was instantly identified with The Curtis Center, a 1.1 million-square-foot property overlooking Independence Square.

The Philadelphia landmark, built in 1916, was once the headquarters of the renowned Curtis Publishing Company. After years of painstaking reconstruction and renovation that preserved the building's history and added virtually every contemporary business amenity, The Curtis Center is now occupied by many of the city's leading firms in law, architecture, insurance, and advertising. And the outstanding historic renovation has been recognized with awards by numerous local and national architectural and design organizations.

The skills required to master the challenges of scale and complexity of the $150-million reconstruction for The Curtis Center are evident in each of the diverse projects that comprise the portfolio of The Kevin F. Donohoe Company.

Operating primarily on the East Coast, The Kevin F. Donohoe Company is involved in the development, acquisition, and management of various office complexes, shopping centers, and hotels. The firm now owns and manages 4.3 million square feet of real estate. Since its premier Curtis Center development project, it has established a position in the industry as a firm committed to the highest level of quality in its every endeavor.

"There is tremendous pressure to compromise quality in today's world of fast-track construction and fast decisions," says Kevin F.

Above: The new Omni Hotel at Independence Park, Philadelphia, offers 155 luxurious guest rooms with park views. The 15-story hotel has been applauded for its architectural design that complements the historic neighborhood.

Left: The Curtis Center's beautiful Fountain Court Atrium plays host to many of Philadelphia's civic functions throughout the year.

Donohoe, the 40-year-old developer who is president and chief executive officer of The Kevin F. Donohoe Company. "But eventually that compromise for short-term gain results in long-term loss. I think people desire a level of quality in their environment, in the products they buy, and in the way they are treated. Incorporating that quality into everything we do takes time and effort, and we are willing to invest that time. We take a long-term view and feel absolutely sure that quality always pays off in the long term."

In addition to The Curtis Center, The Kevin F. Donohoe Company, Inc., has developed the Delaware Corporate Center, Wilmington, Delaware; Five Burlington Square and Seven Burlington Square in Burlington, Vermont; the Omni Hotel at Independence Park in Philadelphia; and regional shopping malls in Burlington, Vermont; Richmond, Virginia; Columbia, South Carolina; and Stroudsburg and Horsham, Pennsylvania.

Says Donohoe, "The corporate philosophy of The Kevin F. Donohoe Company is not just a statement of intent, but truly a guiding principle in the company's every endeavor—today and in the future. Our commitment to that philosophy will not be compromised as we seek new opportunities for growth and expansion."

Frankel Enterprises/Warwick Hotel

More celebrities, dignitaries, and guests of international renown have entered the ornate lobby of the Warwick Hotel than any other hotel in Philadelphia. And few hotels can boast the luxuries and ambience that the Warwick has come to symbolize ever since it first opened its doors in 1926 at 17th and Locust streets.

Upon its opening, the Warwick was clearly a hotel that catered to the very rich.

Designed by Frank Hahn in the fashionable English Renaissance style, the 22-story building featured such extravagances as elevators and steam heat. That is why the Warwick was barely touched by the 1929 stock market crash and the Great Depression.

At the time famous family names, which today are found in schoolroom history books, commonly appeared on the Warwick's guest register. Rooms were booked months in ad-

vance, especially for the annual Army-Navy football weekend. Banquets could only be described as lavish and bountiful. One dinner for 300 guests in honor of the president of Liberia took two weeks to prepare and included 1,000 hot and cold hors d'oeuvres, imported turtle soup, 300 pounds of fish, filet mignon, 48 heads of escarole, romaine, and Boston lettuce, and 96 pints of out-of-season raspberries and blueberries to top the lemon sherbet.

Above and Facing Page: Few hotels can match the elegant ambience of the Warwick Hotel.

No expense has been spared in decorating the public and private rooms. Plush wingback chairs, attractive paintings, and rare antiques were part of the everyday decor. In 1977 the hotel underwent a $17-million renovation and refurbishing to keep in step with its grand tradition.

Today the guest list at the Warwick still includes the names of the rich and the famous. It also caters to business groups and holds seminars and receptions in the several meeting rooms.

The Warwick, the only Philadelphia hotel to be awarded the prestigious Four Star rating by the Mobil Travel Guide for seven consecutive years, conjures up pleasant memories for guests from around the world and around the city.

Frank B. Hall & Co.

Dedicated to making a difference through distinctive service. That motto represents the quality of insurance services that Frank B. Hall & Co. has offered its customers ever since it was formed through a series of mergers and acquisition. And that's what the international insurance brokerage has sought to achieve in Philadelphia since it entered the market more than 30 years ago.

The Philadelphia office was formed in 1971 when the parent firm of Frank B. Hall acquired Parker & Co., already a major figure in Philadelphia's insurance community. Frank B. Hall was the first national insurance brokerage to open an office in Philadelphia. Today, as one of the more than 180 offices worldwide, the Philadelphia firm operates as a separate corporation, as set up by the parent company's regional management system.

Headed by William B. Churchman III as chairman and Edward Hollingsworth as president and chief executive officer, the Philadelphia operation today is the fifth-largest insurance brokerage in the city, enjoying significant growth each year. In fact, it is deemed as one of the flagship companies of the entire worldwide network of offices, and it serves customers in the five-county Philadelphia region as well as southern New Jersey.

As a publicly-owned firm traded on the New York Stock Exchange, Frank B. Hall prides itself on offering a unique brand of service that not only attracts new business, but also successfully cements long-term relationships with ongoing customers. Several companies, such as PPG Industries and Conrail, have been customers of Frank B. Hall Philadelphia for more than 35 years.

These types of relationships are important for an insurance brokerage because of the cyclical nature of the insurance business. Hall Philadelphia's quality of service helps it to remain competitive and aggressively seek out new business even when market conditions are less than favorable.

Frank B. Hall offers a complete line of insurance and related services. In addition to brokerage services, the Frank B. Hall Philadelphia office's property/casualty capabilities include claims management, loss control, engineering, and casualty actuarial services, as well as a specialized consulting unit known as Hall Administrative Services Company, which coordinates the activities among these and other service providers.

With a staff of more than 55 professionals, Hall Philadelphia provides coverage for most types of risks, including property/casualty,

group accident and employee benefits, aviation, and personal lines departments. In addition, Hall's Godwins, Inc., division offers

benefit consulting services. Major Hall clients include Hunt Manufacturing Company, PGW, Penn Central Corporation, First Pennsylvania Bank, American Refining, Commonwealth Land Title Insurance Co., Elwyn Institutes, Asplundh Corporation, Ursinus College, Bancroft School, and the City of Philadelphia.

Hall has always tailored its services to fit the needs of its customers and the overall market as insurance service requirements change. It believes in aggressively serving industry groups when others may hesitate. For example, Hall has developed the expertise for placing insurance for industries that others regard as too risky, such as day care centers. In that arena, Hall has become the largest insurance writer in the the world for institutions that treat the mentally disabled. Hall also believes in developing the insurance products and technical resources today that the future will demand. Recently Hall has positioned itself to market its expertise to four specialty areas—health care, financial services, energy, and environmental risks.

Hall's approach to the insurance and risk management service business is probably best summed up by a paragraph from the firm's Mission Statement that was created by all the members of the Hall team: "Our dedication to excellence will bring creative, competitive and professional risk management, insurance brokerage, and consulting services to our clients for the purpose of protecting their human, financial, and physical assets. We will bring the highest quality service available to our clients, remaining sensitive to their individual needs and expectations through an honest, open and credible relationship.

". . . In accomplishing this mission, we will be a positive force in each community we service, benefiting our prime stakeholders: our clients, associates, insurers, and our stockholders."

Jackson-Cross Company

The guiding force in real estate has traditionally been summed up in three words: location, location, location. The fortunes of real estate companies have risen and fallen based upon that premise. Location is important to Jackson-Cross Company, too; however, this real estate firm's wide range of activities are based upon a more innovative formula: information, information, information.

"Our stock and trade is information," says Dick Jones, president and chief executive officer of the full-service real estate company. "Our product is professionally communicated information and that, coupled with the skills of imparting the information correctly, is our service to our clients," he adds.

The roots of those skills stretch back to the 1876 founding of the firm by Joseph T. Jackson, when the real estate business was far simpler than it is today. Jackson merged his business with Edgar G. Cross' real estate firm in 1936, thereby establishing Jackson-Cross Company. Today it is one of the largest and most successful real estate firms in the Delaware Valley, and one of the oldest real estate companies in the country in terms of size and structure. But the firm has not achieved that status by simply brokering real estate. Its success has stemmed from a carefully planned management structure,

augmented by a keen sense of market direction and a savvy approach to the nuances of the real estate business.

Jackson-Cross believes that client companies expect real estate firms to provide high-quality service and accurate information in a responsive and timely fashion. Clients have also come to expect high-quality professionals. "The entire reputation of the company is directly related to the quality and capabilities of our people," says Jones. The ownership of the company has primarily stayed in the hands of the people who run the firm and know the Greater Delaware Valley. The framework not only focuses on strategic planning, but also fosters the entrepreneurial spirit.

This management approach has also lent credence to the firm's first regional real estate market report, which was launched in 1978. The company's Annual Real Estate Forecast Breakfast held each January and annual market report, released in the first quarter of each year to thousands of people, have become key barometers for assessing the regional real estate market. Companies have come to rely upon this market data—which analyzes real estate markets in the Pennsylvania, New Jersey, and surrounding suburban areas—for making real estate decisions.

However, Jackson-Cross also understands that real estate is becoming more global. Through its association with Oncor International, Jackson-Cross has the ability to conduct business through 29 associate firms in 108 offices covering 165 major markets in North America and Europe. Oncor International complements Jackson-Cross' broad range of real estate services, including real estate investment, appraisal and counseling, consulting, site acquisition, property management and residential.

As a major player in the Philadelphia real estate market, Jackson-Cross has achieved recognition through its day-to-day activities and highly visible real estate transactions. For example, Jackson-Cross conducted the largest appraisal project in real estate history when it appraised the entire Penn Central Railroad holdings. It also handled one of the largest and most complicated lease transactions in Philadelphia when it brokered the CIGNA lease for Two Liberty Place in Century City.

Those are the kinds of real estate transactions that put Jackson-Cross Company's name in the headlines, but the firm would not have had the opportunity to participate in those deals if it had not already earned its reputation as a high-quality, professional, and ethical real estate firm.

Below: The Philadelphia skyline

Inset: J. Richard Jones, president and chief executive officer of Jackson-Cross Company and chairman of the board for Oncor International.

Chapter Thirteen

T he professional community of Phila-delphia brings a wealth of service, ability, and insight to the area.

Photo by Rich Zila

Professions

Hoyle, Morris & Kerr

H oyle, Morris & Kerr is a relatively recent addition to the group of major Philadelphia law firms that emphasize providing excellent legal services to corporate and other business clients. Its named partners founded the firm on the premise that the best guarantee for enduring success is a commitment to provide its clients with innovative, cost-efficient, and high quality legal services. This commitment has proved remarkably successful, resulting in the firm's initial client base expanding rapidly through recommendation of satisfied clients and professional colleagues.

Founded in 1985 with a group of 18 attorneys from established firms and government practice, Hoyle, Morris & Kerr has grown rapidly to its present complement of more than 70 attorneys. Without acquisition or merger, this growth has been achieved by steady, selective recruitment and constant gravitation to the firm of talented attorneys from other firms. Among the college and law degrees earned by the firm's attorneys, more than half were awarded with honors; more than 20 of its attorneys have served in prestigious judicial clerkships, governmental, or prosecutorial positions. In addition to customary educational accomplishments, numerous Hoyle, Morris & Kerr attorneys have also earned additional postgraduate degrees. Its partners and associates regularly serve as lecturers at the University of Pennsylvania, Temple University, and Villanova law schools; at the Wharton Business School; and at continuing legal education seminars and professional meetings sponsored by the American Bar Association, National Law Journal Seminars, Defense Research Institute, Pennsylvania Bar Institute, Practicing Law Institute, and numerous other organizations.

The firm quickly outgrew its initial quarters in the Jacob Reed Building and now has its offices on the 47th through the 50th floors of One Liberty Place. The building, designed by the internationally acclaimed architect Helmut Jahn, was the first to surpass Philadelphia's decades-old height limitation. With a 50-mile view of the Delaware Valley in all directions, the firm's offices are a sought-after setting for the many charitable, political, and social gatherings hosted by the firm.

Hoyle, Morris & Kerr is primarily a commercial law firm, as reflected in the emphasis of both its litigation practice and its transactional business practice.

The firm's monumental staircase, designed by Daroff Design, Inc.

With a national practice, the firm's litigators are expert in pretrial, trial, and appellate phases of virtually every form of civil and white-collar criminal litigation. In addition to the traditional areas of commercial litigation, such as antitrust, securities, and contract, the firm's attorneys are particularly experienced in those forms of complex litigation which dominate commercial litigation today: product liability and toxic torts, environmental claims, and commercial insurance coverage.

In product liability, Hoyle, Morris & Kerr has served as national coordinating counsel for a major manufacturer of construction products in the asbestos litigation. The firm

developed, implemented, and managed a nationwide defense strategy for this client in the face of claims from building owners to recover costs resulting from the presence of asbestos-containing products in their buildings, including several class actions. In doing so, the firm focused especially on the mastery of a complex and rapidly evolving body of medical and scientific knowledge that proved instrumental in the successful defense of these claims. The firm obtained defense verdicts in the first two

Hoyle, Morris & Kerr's 48th-floor reception area, designed by Daroff Design, Inc.

In workout and bankruptcy proceedings, among the firm's clients are one of the nation's largest commercial real estate developers, a large Delaware Valley hotel developer, and a large East Coast shipbuilding company, in addition to numerous corporate borrowers and institutional lenders.

The firm's construction and surety bond clients include two major, multi-state general contracting companies for whom Hoyle, Morris & Kerr acts as regional counsel, and one of the nation's largest construction sureties, whom the firm represents and counsels with respect to projects nationwide.

The firm prides itself both on its ability to litigate aggressively and effectively and its commitment to the use of sound business judgment to help clients achieve results that are in their long-term best interests, whether this means litigation, settlement, or finding creative ways to cut defense costs or forestall future problems altogether.

Recognizing the responsibilities of lawyers to the community, the firm also encourages participation in community and professional activities and pro bono representation in a wide range of matters. The firm is especially proud that, in connection with these activities, the Philadelphia Volunteers for the Indigent program has awarded the firm the Justice William J. Brennan, Jr., Award for leadership and outstanding services to the indigent in 1987 and the Chancellors Award yearly since 1988.

asbestos property damage cases ever tried to conclusion before juries and continued to earn a successful win-loss record in the litigation thereafter. The firm's lawyers also utilized this medical and scientific knowledge in representing the company in associated legislative and regulatory activities.

The firm has transferred its experience in defending asbestos cases to numerous other products. For example, Hoyle, Morris & Kerr represents a *Fortune* 500 pharmaceutical company that has been sued in multiple jurisdictions in connection with a blood clotting concentrate administered to hemophiliacs that has allegedly been connected to the transmission of the causative agent of AIDS. Similarly, the firm has substantial experience in the defense of toxic shock syndrome and baby bottle cases. The firm is also actively engaged in defense of claims against a major cement manufacturer arising from cracking railroad ties.

Also in the field of toxic torts, Hoyle, Morris & Kerr has provided representation to chemical companies in connection with accidental releases of chemicals into the environment. Hoyle, Morris & Kerr has worked side by side with various companies to assist in the companies' internal investigation of the causes of the releases, and to develop comprehensive responses to complaints by residents of adjacent communities. When resulting litigation has been initiated, the firm has pre-

pared the defense, including development of the complex medical-scientific facts necessary to an effective defense. In environmental litigation, the firm also engages in the defense of Superfund litigation and in overseeing cooperative responses by clients to EPA and state agency cleanup mandates.

As a result of its practice in the defense of hazardous substance claims, the firm has also come to specialize in the representation of corporate policyholders in disputes with their insurance carriers over coverage for environmental, products liability, and toxic tort claims. The firm can also provide general risk management and insurance counseling for corporate clients interested in alternative insurance vehicles.

The firm's transactional commercial law practice covers a wide spectrum, including corporate, financial, securities, municipal bond, commercial real estate, taxation, and pension planning. Hoyle, Morris & Kerr attorneys are particularly active in three areas of commercial law: mergers and acquisitions, workouts and bankruptcy, and construction and surety bond law.

In corporate transactions, Hoyle, Morris & Kerr attorneys have served as counsel in corporate acquisitions and financing for a variety of manufacturing and communications clients.

The firm's reading room, designed by Daroff Design, Inc.

Environmental Resources Management, Inc.

Paul Woodruff founded Environmental Resources Management, Inc., (ERM) in October 1977 with two early partners, Phillip Buckingham and Kent Patterson, first operating out of Woodruff's study in West Chester, Patterson's dining room in Richmond, Virginia, and Buckingham's temporary home in Iran. They saw that the major environmental legislation being promulgated reflected the public's greater awareness and understanding of humanity's impact on the world. Companies and businesses that had never before been forced to respond to environmental and health and safety concerns would soon be challenged to do just that. The vision proved accurate: ERM is the founding member of The ERM Group, a multinational organization with more than 1,500 personnel working worldwide to solve and prevent environmental problems.

Woodruff's goals in 1977 are still the cornerstone of the company: to provide environmental services of high quality on challenging projects while saving clients money and improving the quality of life for everyone, and to have fun doing it.

The ERM Group's offices blanket North

Industrial and municipal water treatment is one sphere of ERM's expertise.

ERM's environmental services improve everyone's quality of life.

America, providing environmental consulting, construction management, analytical laboratory, and information management services from 52 locations in 31 states and one Canadian province. Environmental Resources Limited (ERL), which is based in London, provides a solid European presence with offices in Northampton and Durham, England; Milan, Italy; Madrid, Spain; and Frankfurt, Germany. Asian offices are located in Hong Kong, Taiwan, and India.

ERM's Exton office in Chester County employs about 450 people and realized $37 million in revenues in 1990. Its areas of ex-

pertise cover broad topics: strategies and engineering for site remediation; hazardous waste and solid waste management; hydrogeology; management consulting; industrial and municipal water and wastewater treatment; underground tank management; environmental science; air quality management; information management services; construction management; health, safety, and toxicology; and analytical laboratory services. Branch locations include offices in Pittsburgh, Pennsylvania; Princeton, New Jersey; Annapolis, Maryland; McLean and Richmond, Virginia; and Ann Arbor, Michigan.

According to Kent E. Patterson, chief of operations and managing partner of ERM, about half of the firm's business is involved in site remediation. ERM emphasizes that it is committed to solving a client's hazardous waste problems, not merely defining them. ERM works first to focus on the least costly, most technically appropriate solution to a waste problem and aggressively supports these solutions with scientific evidence, expert engineering, and regulatory expertise. Two innovative ERM on-site remedies—geotechnical sludge stabilization and the earth renovation method—have realized significant savings for clients faced with large sludge impoundment closures and soil-decontamination problems.

ERM not only helps clients manage past problems, it assists them in complying with present, and planning for future, regulations. The Management Consulting Group takes a proactive stance by helping clients recognize environmental risks before they become problems requiring costly remediation and by designing and implementing organizational structures and training programs that ensure ongoing compliance.

According to Patterson, the Management Consulting Group expects to "be a billion-dollar company in the next 10 years."

Paul Hertel & Co., Inc.

Paul Hertel and Company was established in 1908 as an insurance agency and brokerage firm. Paul Hertel, the founder, saw a need to assist commercial and industrial companies in minimizing their exposure to loss through property conservation and the purchase of insurance.

After all, Paul Hertel saw insurance as simply a transfer of risk that should be part of a company's overall risk management planning. And it was through an emphasis on loss control that Paul Hertel and Company succeeded in providing clients with higher levels of protection from loss—as well as lower insurance premiums.

Today the goals and traditions of the original founder are carried out at Paul Hertel and Company, where more than 75 employees continue to work from offices at Third and Chestnut streets, the very same Olde City Philadelphia neighborhood where the company began nearly a century ago.

Paul R. Hertel, Jr., is the third generation of Hertels to continue the business, which generates $5 million in revenues annually. More than 80 percent of the company's business consists of commercial property and casualty clients, primarily from the manufacturing, professional, printing, and transportation fields. According to Hertel, the company offers professional liability coverage for a wide range of design and architectural, financial, medical, and business professionals. Its list of 300 clients includes many who have been insured with Paul Hertel for more than 50

Jim McLaughlin reviews an insurance proposal with key members of his staff.

More than 75 Paul Hertel & Co. employees work from offices at Third and Chestnut streets, the same Olde City Philadelphia neighborhood where Paul Hertel & Co., Inc. started nearly a century ago.

years, and a greater number who have received uninterrupted services for at least 10 years.

The company's long experience and substantial size has enabled it to establish a number of specialized in-house capabilities. In the area of liability, Paul Hertel has negotiated sophisticated retrospective rating plans, large deductible programs, and captive studies. Through the risk management process, the company is able to tailor a program to the specific needs of the client. In addition, it has the capability to place unique coverages for directors and officers liability, fiduciary liability, and professional liability.

With respect to property, Paul Hertel and Company specializes in administering its Highly Protected Risk (HPR) programs. These carriers are able to provide high limits of insurance for relatively lower rates than are available in the standard marketplace, due to Hertel's engineering and loss control services. Hertel's published Loss Prevention Reports assist clients in identifying and controlling potential loss exposures. Hertel's staff also works regularly with carrier representatives and the client's personnel to ensure that loss control efforts are directed in the most efficient manner.

Critical to the company's success in arranging the most effective insurance program is access to the insurance marketplace. Paul Hertel and Company has represented most of the major insurance carriers for many years. Three of the company's principals are underwriting members of Lloyds of London, and the company has active correspondents in Tokyo, Brussels, and Hong Kong. These factors combine to give the company and its clients working knowledge and direct access to world insurance markets.

In addition to Paul R. Hertel, Jr., the principals of the company are James J. McLaughlin, Jeremiah A. Caron, James Gallagher, Sr., and Robert J. Bush. Paul R. Hertel III joined the company in 1990, continuing the family's history with the business. In addition to its Philadelphia office, the company has sales offices in Media and Feasterville, Pennsylvania.

For the future Paul Hertel, Jr., would like to see the company grow within five years to billings of $120 million, with $15 million in revenue. His strategy? "By just trying to be the best at what we do."

Mylotte, David & Fitzpatrick

Pictured here are (from left) Edward J. David, John A. Fitzpatrick, and Charles A. Fitzpatrick, III

Philadelphia witnessed an enormous expansion of its service during the past decade, and growth in the legal profession was no exception. Since its founding in 1979, Mylotte, David & Fitzpatrick has evolved into a medium-size, full-service law firm of more than 40 attorneys. For more than a decade the firm has provided its clients with a full range of expert and innovative legal services. It has grown successfully during this period in response to the emerging needs of existing clients and the addition of new ones.

Initially Mylotte, David & Fitzpatrick had an insurance-related litigation practice and presently maintains its forefront position with the insurance industry in the region in all aspects of insurance law. However, as the firm's clients have grown and broadened their

horizons, so too have the firm's own services and expertise. During the past decade it has handled tens of thousands of client engagements, from the smallest of matters to cases involving millions of dollars. Mylotte, David & Fitzpatrick renders advice to individuals, corporations, and institutions on a local, regional, national, and international basis. The firm actively represents and advocates its clients' interests when they are involved in litigation and acts as counsel and advisers with respect to the total range of corporate, commercial, and personal matters.

Because of the firm's size and managed growth it is able to provide a tremendous range of specialized resources—individual lawyers with experience in specific industries, legal issues, and practice areas. The firm's

attorneys include specialists in insurance services, health law, professional liability, product liability, toxic tort, environmental law, worker's compensation, employment law, commercial litigation, trusts and estates, and corporate law. Today the most extensive area of practice is litigation, and the area of estate planning continues to expand. The firm's litigation department, its largest, has an active courtroom practice. In recent years the firm has been involved in a variety of significant cases, including the representation of various claimants in their environmental and toxic tort claims, which have resulted in numerous multimillion-dollar recoveries; the defense of a major well-publicized antitrust case; acting as regional counsel in the defense of a major asbestos manufacturer with 5,000 cases in five states; and the defense of many department stores, supermarkets, and other retail establishments in their general liability and worker's compensation claims. Regardless of the type and size of the litigation, the firm's attorneys are trained and experienced litigators who will not hesitate to be on trial on the client's behalf when it is economically or philosophically appropriate to do so. Its litigators adopt an aggressive approach to each and every case and demonstrate throughout its handling a desire to prevail, but willingly search for early solutions and resolutions whenever warranted.

Chaired by Grahame P. Richards, Jr., the trusts and

Joseph P. Mylotte 1939-1991

For more than a decade Mylotte, David & Fitzpatrick has provided its clients with a full range of expert and innovative legal services.

Pennsylvania and all of central and southern New Jersey.

"We are in the service business," says Edward J. David, "and it is critical for us to find cost efficient ways to deliver quality legal services. Everyone in our organization, both lawyers and the staff, are requested to do the little extra things that enhance client relationships." Frequent seminars at the clients' facilities in which new developments in the law and risk management issues are addressed are part of the firm's commitment to providing its clients with individualized, high-quality service. In addition, many of the firm's attorneys are acknowledged authorities in their legal practice. Sponsors of these seminars include Defense Research Institute, Cambridge Institute, National Business Institute, Pennsylvania Bar Institute, and Pennsylvania Defense Institute.

estates department has grown dramatically during this period and is a leader in the preparation of sophisticated planned giving documents for donors and charities and tax and estate planning.

As an example of its approach, Mylotte, David & Fitzpatrick is implementing a firm-wide computer network. Every secretary, and also many attorneys and support personnel, has a desk-top terminal that provides word and data processing and other office automation functions. The system is compatible with many of its clients' software packages, enhancing communications and the sharing of resources. The firm's regional offices in Media, Hazelton, and Wilkes-Barre, Pennsylvania, and in Westmont, New Jersey, are linked to the system, which has greatly increased productivity for clients and already has contributed to the firm's expanded regional presence in eastern Pennsylvania and southern New Jersey. These regional offices, established at the request of the firm's clients, permit the firm to effectively handle client engagements throughout the eastern half of

In addition to providing its clients with individualized, high-quality service, the firm's lawyers use a team approach in solving a wide range of legal problems.

Arthur Andersen Worldwide Organization

Think straight and talk straight—with those words Arthur Andersen founded the professional services firm that bears his name, the Arthur Andersen Worldwide Organization, nearly 80 years ago. He dedicated himself and his future colleagues to providing creative solutions, backed by nothing less than integrity and candor.

It has served the firm well and has formed the foundation for the Philadelphia operation since it opened its doors in 1946. Since then, the firm has enjoyed the highest growth of any professional services firm in the city. This achievement has been made possible by an unfailing attention to a litany of fundamental values, which are best expressed through a series of commitments.

It goes without saying that the firm is deeply committed to its clients, incorporating innovation and productive change, when necessary. In a business climate peppered with questionable business practices, Andersen is committed to the most stringent standards of professional and business ethics. As the methods of conducting business have evolved, so has Andersen's commitment to research and new technology. To support these activities, the firm is committed to hiring the best people available and giving them the best possible training. And perhaps most importantly, Andersen's professionals are committed to each other, as reflected in the company's unique one-firm philosophy of worldwide operations.

From the beginning, the Arthur Andersen

Teamwork, dedication to their clients' success, and a standard professional approach ensures high-quality services from the Arthur Andersen Worldwide Organization.

Worldwide Organization has recognized that its success depends entirely on the success of its clients, so it has always put its clients at the center of all its activities. Consequently, the firm believes in building strong, enduring relationships with the executives it serves and on taking the initiative in bringing practical business opportunities to the client's attention. In addition, it seeks to provide services that give each client added value.

The Philadelphia operation serves all

major industries within the Delaware Valley. The firm's industry expertise allows it to understand the unique competitive environment of each of its clients and determine the best methods for improving each firm's competitive edge. Industry groups served include banking, health care, insurance, manufacturing, real estate, telecommunications, and utilities. This wide range of services is provided through two main strategic business units: Arthur Andersen, which represents accounting, auditing, tax, and business consulting services, and Andersen Consulting, which encompasses all aspects of computer-based information systems. Together, these units represent a full-service approach to meeting clients' business needs.

There are a number of specific operations that fall under the Arthur Andersen unit. In conducting its attest services, the firm's audit approach does not focus simply on the financial statements of an organization, but on the organization's business operations as well. This approach enables Arthur Andersen to offer knowledgeable and practical recommendations to management. The range of services include financial audits, transaction audit services, compliance audits, and information security services.

The cornerstone of Arthur Andersen's tax expertise is the firm's strong organization of

Arthur Andersen and Andersen Consulting invest heavily in the technical, business, industry, and functional training of professionals throughout their entire careers.

tax functional specialty teams. The services delivered reflect an in-depth understanding of not only current and emerging tax issues, but also the core business concerns underlying those issues. Specific services include tax compliance, corporate tax consulting, personal financial consulting, state and local taxes, international tax services, and compensation and benefits consulting.

In the area of corporate finance, Arthur Andersen offers its clients practical and creative advice on a variety of complex financial matters, including innovative financing tools, mergers and acquisitions, project financing arrangements, off-balance-sheet financing vehicles, and the creation of shareholder value.

In addition, Arthur Andersen's Specialty Consulting Services apply the firm's business, financial, and systems skills to a variety of focused consulting markets in the form of litigation services, government contract consulting, corporate recovery services, and business systems consulting.

Some business observers have regarded the accounting profession's move towards consulting as a fairly recent phenomenon. But that is not the case with Andersen Consulting. This division has been a leader in the information consulting business since the 1940s, when few

Technology and Andersen are synonymous. The firm not only helps clients use computer technology effectively but also uses technology itself to improve the efficiency and productivity of virtually all of its service lines.

others could see the advent of the so-called computer revolution. Through the 1950s and 1960s, Andersen Consulting continued along its innovative pathway in business computerization, and today it has become the world's leading management information consulting firm.

Andersen Consulting's primary services include strategic consulting, systems design and installation, system integration, change management, advanced information technology, software products and services, productivity tools and services, and facilities and network management. Collectively, these

Arthur Andersen's unique center for professional education is located in St. Charles, Illinois. In 1989 the firm invested nearly 8 percent of its annual revenue towards continuing education.

services allow clients to plan and implement ways to use the power of technology to enhance their competitiveness and profitability.

The Arthur Andersen Worldwide Organization is proud of its vast array of services and the achievements those services have allowed it to attain over the years, worldwide and in Philadelphia. However, it is also a firm noted more for looking forward than for glancing backward. Granted, Andersen's history and traditions are integral elements of its organizational culture, but history serves a company best when viewed as a series of ever-increasing benchmarks—not simply as a source of individual or organizational self-satisfaction.

As a result, the gaze of the Arthur Andersen Worldwide Organization is resolutely fixed on the future, where it will be developing new technologies and spotting emerging trends so it can promptly take advantage of them for its clients. The firm intends to continue in its mission to improve the value of service it provides to each client and build enduring relationships with those clients. Most of all, the Arthur Andersen Worldwide Organization intends to continue seeking excellence in all it does.

Towers Perrin

I t would be difficult to name a major Delaware Valley corporation that is not a client of the Philadelphia office of Towers Perrin, the leading independent managment-consulting firm. The client companies may require one or more of the vast array of services offered by any of the four operating groups that make up Towers Perrin: TPF&C, Tillinghast, Cresap, and the reinsurance unit.

TPF&C is the largest, and perhaps most well known, of the operating companies. TPF&C, in its current configuration, was founded in Philadelphia more than 50 years ago. However, its predecessor firms have been around the region for far longer, including the TPF&C firm that put together the country's first pension plan for Union Carbide in 1917. Since then it has expanded its range of consulting services to every aspect of personnel management, including employee benefits, compensation analyses, and performance appraisals. And the Philadelphia consulting office, which employs more than 1,500 people, still remains one of Towers Perrin's flagship operations.

Cresap, which became a part of the Towers Perrin family in 1983, offers general management consulting services. Tillinghast, a TPF&C unit since 1986, provides risk management and life and health insurance services. The reinsurance unit specializes in brokered insurance products.

Because of its wide range of services, coupled with its attention to quality and technical accuracy, TPF&C has earned a reputation as a leader within the Philadelphia corporate community. Its strengths lie in its integrity, and the depth of experience that each professional possesses. That helps explain why TPF&C consults with the majority of the *Fortune* 100 companies based in the Philadelphia area,

representing nearly every industry, including transportation, telecommunications, and heavy manufacturing.

TPF&C especially prides itself on a number of services it provides: actuarial, compensation consulting, internal communications, employee benefits, salary management, and human resource consulting. Its approach to every assignment is simple, yet direct. TPF&C believes in seeking out solutions to a company's problems that are flexible, yet practical. That is one of the reasons why TPF&C handles the pension plans for most of the 25 largest corporations in the Philadelphia area. Its clients include corporations such as SmithKline Beecham, Campbell's Soup, Scott Paper Co., and Bell Atlantic Corp.

TPF&C's long-term partnership with the Philadelphia business community has allowed it to play an integral role in shepherding the transition of Philadelphia's economic base from one focused on manufacturing to one focused on the service sector, and emerging companies including many "high tech" organizations with outstanding growth potential. TPF&C's involvement in the region and commitment to client services has fostered a series of surveys that delve into issues that affect the business community and keep track of current trends and patterns, such as wages and salaries and employee attitudes. For more than 10 years TPF&C has generated its highly respected Delaware Valley Executive Compensation Study that surveys the area's largest 100 companies.

The managers of Towers Perrin, who are all shareholders in the firm, believe the firm sets an example for other companies in the way it manages its business and the business of its clients.

Price Waterhouse

Within the past five years, there have been more global changes that affect the way business is conducted than in any other period in modern history. These changes are evident in Philadelphia and the surrounding community. The city's skyline is now punctuated by numerous high-rise office buildings. A major convention center is under construction and the airport is expanding dramatically. Philadelphia is, indeed, becoming an international city, having attracted millions in foreign dollars through investment and the establishment of international corporate operations.

Price Waterhouse believes it is vital for professional organizations to mirror the changes that are taking place in the surrounding business community. As a result, the scope of Price Waterhouse's operations and its thinking have taken on a whole new perspective, reflected not only by the reach of the firm's resources but by the resources of its clients. "We're attempting to think like our clients and be more global in our views," says Dean Markezin, managing partner of the Philadelphia office.

That is why Price Waterhouse, as one of the world's leading accounting and management consulting organizations, has redefined its role to one that goes well beyond its traditional function as auditors and accountants. The more than 400 professionals in the Philadelphia office are business advisers to their clients, offering new, specialized services that forward-thinking companies need to compete more effectively in the international marketplace.

The firm operates in four basic disciplines: accounting and auditing, tax, management consulting, and specialized counseling to emerging, growth-oriented businesses. Through these disciplines, Price Waterhouse offers services in areas such as risk management, litigation support, employee benefits, multistate taxes, mergers and acquisitions, personal financial planning, telecommunications, strategic planning, advanced information systems, technical space planning, and international taxes.

This broad range of services reflects a refined strategy that is simple and basic, yet responds to client needs. And nowhere is this strategy more evident than in the Philadelphia office, which could be called the Price Waterhouse prototype operation for the 1990s and beyond. As Dean Markezin puts it, "Price

Many Philadelphia-based companies are actively engaged in the international marketplace. Helping multinational clients manage globally is a priority for Price Waterhouse professionals. Dean Markezin has positioned the Philadelphia practice as a full-scope business resource so clients can gain the support they need to compete in the world arena.

Waterhouse is obsessed with client service, realizing that a global economy demands efficiency and follow through."

The firm also practices market selectivity, which is the overriding theme for its approach to a focused strategy. Financial institutions and multinational companies are growth market priorities. Future *Fortune* 500 companies, known as emerging businesses, are also a key focus. In addition, this strategy includes attracting and retaining the best and brightest professionals, by providing them with professionally rewarding experiences.

Clearly Price Waterhouse has taken its cue from the evolving Philadelphia business community, to which it is committed in its practice and in its presence. "We're an adviser and a sounding board, and we're able to interact with corporate executives whenever they need to bring in our experts," says Markezin.

Day & Zimmermann

Isn't that the company that built Veteran's Stadium? Didn't they do something on the Commuter Rail Connection? Aren't they the ones with a security force? Don't they supply contract engineering personnel?

Day & Zimmermann's diversification and 90-year tradition in Philadelphia often leaves people with the sense that they know the company, but can't quite remember why. They have seen the name, can frequently identify a project or service area, and can even remember a friend or relative who worked for the company. Yet there is also a sense that they don't quite know what the company does. Given the size and diversity of Day & Zimmermann, that isn't surprising.

In 1901 two young men, both graduates of engineering programs in Philadelphia, joined together to provide "modernizing engineering" services that helped industry keep pace with the rapid technological advances of the industrial revolution. From a shed on the grounds of their first client, Link-Belt, the two founders developed a reputation for creating operating efficiencies through equipment conversions, line layouts, and the implementation of the principles of scientific management put forth by Frederick W. Taylor, known as the "father of scientific management."

Today, from headquarters still located in Philadelphia, the company has grown far beyond the scope envisioned by its founders, yet it retains the drive for progress that inspired their efforts. Day & Zimmermann's 90th anniversary finds the company and its subsidiaries providing a broad range of services through some 30 separate operating units, each specifically tailored to respond to the unique requirements of its marketplace. Although organizational lines bundle these services into three fundamental management entities, the company retains the flexibility to draw on specialists with a remarkable diversity of talents from throughout the organization to resolve client needs.

At last count, more than 13,000 men and women in more than 60 offices worldwide supported total revenues in excess of $600 million. The firm's services, provided throughout the United States and in more than 75 countries, include multidisciplined

Advances in technology have fueled Day & Zimmermann's growth since its beginning.

engineering, design, and construction management; operating, engineering, training, technological, and logistics support for the defense industry; and a variety of management services that include program management oversight, contract temporary staffing, security, and data management systems. The company's fundamental corporate objective is to be a distinguished leader in each of the services it provides. Day & Zimmermann's growth and diversification are built on the solid foundation of loyal clients, dedicated

John Zimmermann and Charles Day, shown at a company outing in 1919, provided engineering and management counsel to a variety of clients throughout the world.

employees, and a strong set of values that guide the company leaders. Safety, quality, and integrity still form the core of every operating decision, as they did for the company's founders.

The company is also committed to remaining a contributing member of the community. Corporate sponsorship of events in Philadelphia during the bicentennial of the U.S. Constitution in 1987 represents that commitment, as does a leadership role with the Philadelphia Council of the Boy Scouts of America, with whom the company helped establish its Scouting for Food drive, and annual sponsorship of a corporate sports challenge to benefit the Cystic Fibrosis Foundation.

Civic commitment has included project support of Philadelphia's infrastructure, such as the Center City Commuter Rail Connection, for which the company received the American Society of Civil Engineers' national award for engineering excellence, and the ongoing project management responsibility for the expansion of Philadelphia's International Airport. Other local assignments have included transportation consulting for SEPTA and the Delaware Valley Regional Planning Commission, as well as serving as engineer of record for the Philadelphia Parking Authority and the city's Water and Sewer Authority.

For Philadelphia Electric Co., Day & Zimmermann and its subsidiaries provide services ranging from security force personnel at both the Limerick and Peach Bottom power generating stations, to engineering, maintenance, and repair support. Day & Zimmermann has been involved with helping Philadelphia cope with waste management issues for many years, first with the design of trash-to-steam facilities, and more recently with the construction and operation of a plastics-recycling plant in nearby Bridgeport, New Jersey.

One of the company's operating units has provided area taxing authorities with the systems and resources to establish equitable appraisal services. Others provide contract temporary staffing sources for clients seeking data processing, scientific, graphic arts, administrative, light industrial, engineering, and procurement personnel.

The region's growth in high-tech industries has led to greater involvement in engineering services for "clean rooms" for tight tolerance manufacturing, as well as the development of commercial scale facilities for biotechnical and pharmaceutical companies. Local food and beverage manufacturers also call on the firm to provide plant expansion, modernization, and new construction support.

In looking toward the future, the company is pursuing an expansion of dedicated partnering arrangements with its key clients. The pressure of global competition is forcing client companies to reassess their approach to retaining professional services, and Day & Zimmermann is there with creative solutions to the challenges of tomorrow.

Over its 90-year history Day & Zimmermann has stayed true to the vision of its founders. The company's purpose remains to help clients improve operations. Although the type and mix of services will change continually to keep pace with the evolving world of client requirements, the effort to be the best, whatever the endeavor, will fuel the company's growth and direction into the twenty-first century.

Above Right: Whether in professional engineering services or temporary staffing support, contract operation or security services, the story of Day & Zimmermann is written by employees who are dedicated to excellence.

Right: Day & Zimmermann professionals in engineering, design, construction management, and operation and maintenance teamed to complete the start up of a company-owned and -operated plastics-recycling facility—the first of several planned around the country.

Blank, Rome, Comisky & McCauley

At the law firm of Blank, Rome, Comisky & McCauley, the title "counselor" takes on new meaning. The term reflects a tradition of lasting relationships with clients. It means responding to the constantly evolving needs of businesses, professionals, and individuals. It pertains to the leadership role that Blank, Rome lawyers have taken in legal circles and in the Delaware Valley business, cultural, and civic communities. And it means understanding the nuances of city, borough, and township halls, state capitols, Washington, D.C., meeting rooms, and Wall Street trading floors.

The various roles taken on by Blank, Rome lawyers are perhaps the best expression of the firm's business philosophy. Because every client has special needs, Blank, Rome tailors its services to fit those needs. This approach is evident in the way the law firm serves all of its clients. Many of its

small- to mid-size client companies do not have in-house lawyers, so Blank, Rome lawyers step in to fill that void and operate

as an extension of the company's business. It is a true businessperson's law firm, striving to help a client company meet its business objectives.

"We work hard to uphold our reputation for success and our tradition of personalized service. It is what our clients expect from their lawyers—and it is the minimum that Blank, Rome lawyers demand of themselves," says managing partner David Girard-diCarlo. "The firm is young enough and strong enough to be flexible in our approach to the law. We constantly adapt and strengthen our resources to better serve the precise needs of our clients," he adds.

"We learn our client's business and the goals of management. We are able to understand a client's needs and fashion creative solutions," states firm Chairman Jack R Bershad. The approach focuses on overcoming the problem and finding the legal as well as the business solution. As a result, more than 2,000 public and privately held businesses, as well as many more individuals, depend on Blank, Rome for legal advice—counsel that stems from a deep knowledge of the law, an insider's perception of the marketplace, and concern for the client's well-being.

Compared with many of Philadelphia's other large law firms, Blank, Rome is quite young. Founded in 1945 to serve the "middle market" clients, Blank, Rome lawyers today counsel the *Fortune* 500 CEO, the high-growth company president, the entrepreneur, and the emerging company.

The firm's areas of practice include every major aspect of law: corporate, domestic relations, financial services, employee benefits, environmental law, health care, international, labor and employment, litigation, real estate, securities law, tax and estate, and personal planning. Blank, Rome serves virtually all sectors of the economy: the arts, banks and financial institutions, developers and construction companies, educational organizations, and major universities, entertainment companies, health care facilities and medical schools, hotels, manufacturers, municipalities, professional services, restaurants, retail, service companies, transportation, and wholesale suppliers.

Serving diverse industries has helped Blank, Rome grow steadily over the years, from a handful of partners and associates to more than 200 lawyers, including nationally recognized experts in virtually every major area of law. Throughout this successful growth period, Blank, Rome has retained the informality, flexibility, and intimacy that characterized it and its relationship with its clients in its early formative years.

"The firm's growth and expansion have been a direct result of our lawyers' commitment to identifying and fulfilling every client need," says the chairman emeritus and name partner Marvin Comisky. "We place a great emphasis on continuing legal education and adapting our services to match the ever-evolving corporate and professional climate," he adds.

Blank, Rome lawyers also understand that the firm's success is inextricably intertwined

with the vitality of the community that it serves, and they approach their civic and professional responsibilities with the same enthusiasm and creativity that they bring to clients. Blank, Rome lawyers serve on more than 125 boards of charitable organizations in the Philadelphia area, helping to shape the movements of regional organizations and enabling its lawyers to keep a finger on the pulse of the regional economy and business climate. In addition, Blank, Rome lawyers participate in nearly 700 business, cultural, and civic associations in the Delaware Valley.

Blank, Rome lawyers have held hundreds of leadership positions in local, state, and federal bar associations. These activities

Blank, Rome, Comisky & McCauley: Helping clients achieve their business objectives.

All photos by Brummet Studios, Philadelphia

have allowed them to be leaders in drafting the professional codes of practice and setting priorities for the legal community's agenda.

Blank, Rome, Comisky & McCauley lawyers are proud of their accomplishments in the courtrooms, boardrooms, and halls of government. As partners in progress with their clients and with the Delaware Valley, they ensure an expanding, exciting, and vibrant future for all members of the Philadelphia community.

Reed Smith Shaw & McClay

I t is not often that a major law firm is described as innovative, creative, or market driven. Yet those are terms that have been increasingly used to describe Reed Smith Shaw & McClay in recent years. As one of the largest law firms in Pennsylvania and one of the 30 largest firms in the country, Reed Smith has achieved that status through solid legal work and its ability to map its growth through a progressive management philosophy. The growth of the Philadelphia office, opened in 1978, is a prime example of Reed Smith's approach to practicing law and expanding its reach.

Reed Smith is one of the oldest law firms

Clockwise from left: Margery K. Miller, Stephen M. Lyons, III, Michael L. Browne, Ira S. Lefton, John E. Quinn, Richard H. Glanton, Michael T. Scott, and David C. Auten, managing partner. Photo by H. Mark Weidman

in the state, dating back to its founding in 1877 in Pittsburgh by two 24-year-old attorneys, Philander Chase Knox and James Hay Reed. What started as a firm focused on litigation associated with the mining industry has since grown to become a full-service firm, with nearly 400 attorneys in five offices. More than than 60 attorneys practice in the Philadelphia office, located in One Liberty Place. The Philadelphia office was formed by the merger of Reed Smith with the second oldest firm in Pennsylvania, formerly known as Townsend, Elliott & Munson.

Since its Philadelphia debut, Reed Smith's office has more than tripled in size. In doing so it has attracted to its partnership ranks some of the most respected legal minds in the region, who were eager to practice at a firm known for its innovative approach to the legal field, while growing in size and reputation.

Reed Smith has worked hard at making its presence known by its Philadelphia clients and peers. While other major firms are still hesitant at marketing their services in an increasingly competitive environment, Reed Smith was one of the first firms to institute an aggressive marketing program in the early 1980s, designed to call attention to its name and its legal capabilities. It is one of the few Philadelphia firms that conducts an ongoing advertising campaign, featuring the slogan "We Provide Solutions."

And some of the solutions are distinctly Reed Smith. For example, in 1989 Reed Smith introduced its TECHLEX practice group to Philadelphia. The concept is geared towards high-tech businesses and combines different areas of expertise in one practice group. TECHLEX goes beyond the intellectual property legal counsel usually offered by traditional law firms for their high-tech

clients, with the rationale that these companies simply need to protect their patents and ideas. Instead, TECHLEX is staffed by a group of corporate, tax, litigation, and estate-planning attorneys experienced in law and science, who work together with the intellectual property group attorneys. TECHLEX attorneys possess college degrees in chemical engineering, physics, electrical engineering, physical science engineering, and mechanical engineering. As a result, not only are they familiar with the laws that govern these areas, but the attorneys are also experienced and knowledgeable about software and artificial intelligence, robotics, electronics, biotechnology, and telecommunications. TECHLEX attorneys understand their clients' businesses, this forges a special relationship between the lawyers and the high-tech executives. At the same time, if a high-tech client requires the services of a big firm, those are available as well.

Reed Smith also offers a

broad range of other legal services. The litigation group spans the complete spectrum of client needs. This multistate litigation practice has handled major commercial litigation of all types, including environmental law, product liability, construction, insurance, banking, white collar crime, manufacturing, and small business and individual matters. The labor section lawyers represent employers, whether unionized or not, in all areas of labor and employee relations law.

Its real estate practice, as part of its business and finance group, focuses on all aspects of real estate, be it representing lenders with troubled loan situations or assisting developers and small firms with various real estate transactions.

Its corporate section handles a wide range of corporate transactions for clients, ranging

Clockwise from rear left: Louis M. Heidelberger, Norman M. Loev, S. William Richter, John Butterworth, Robert C. Podwil, Andrew J. Trevelise, Carl E. Esser, and Robert A. Nicholas. Photo by H. Mark Weidman

from large financial institutions to small family-owned businesses and nonprofit institutions. Legal assistance could include securities, insurance, utility, or zoning matters.

Reed Smith enjoys a prominent position in the municipal finance field, and is one of the few Philadelphia law firms qualified as nationally recognized municipal bond counsel. In addition to handling all varieties of municipal finance, the section includes a health care team, which regularly represents hospitals and other health care providers in corporate restructuring and financing.

Because the laws governing trusts and estates have become so complex, Reed Smith's trusts and estates group prides itself on possessing the skills necessary to untangle these complexities, and offer its clients careful estate planning services. The attorneys in the Philadelphia office have extensive experience in providing legal counsel to clients with substantial real estate holdings, closely held businesses, and valuable art collections.

The tax section handles a broad spectrum of tax matters at the federal, state, and local level, and works closely with attorneys in the other sections.

As a full-service law firm, Reed Smith Shaw & McClay has earned a reputation for developing legal services based upon the needs of its clients today, while keeping an eye on the needs of its clients tomorrow.

Delaware Group

Delaware Group is one of the nation's oldest and largest independent money managers, a full-service investment organization dedicated to investment excellence for more than 60 years. Through its knowledgeable and experienced portfolio management team, Delaware provides investment guidance to both institutional and individual investors, and manages more than $21 billion in assets.

Of this total, nearly $16 billion is managed for public and corporate pension funds, endowments, and other institutional clients through a separate division called Delaware Investment Advisers. Delaware currently manages the assets of more *Forbes* 500 companies than any other independent investment company. Some of the largest companies in America trust Delaware to make their pension funds grow so that they can provide for the retirements of their employees. Through these pension plans, Delaware is responsible for the retirement of more than 2 million Americans.

For individual investors, Delaware includes 16 mutual funds through which individuals can obtain professional money management. Delaware's mutual funds are responsible for $6 billion in assets for a total of nearly 450,000 shareholders. And Delaware Group is committed to making the American Dream come true for investors—with portfolio returns that provide for the home of their dreams, college educations for their children, comfortable retirements, and financial security.

By adopting a conservative, total-return

Above: Delaware Group's headquarters in One Commerce Square in Philadelphia.

Left: Delaware Group's trading desk where portfolio managers' investment decisions are executed. Photo by Ed Wheeler

approach to money management, Delaware has produced one of the top performance records in the asset management industry, with the firm's composite of all equity accounts outperforming the Standard & Poor's 500 stock index in 11 of the past 16 years.

Delaware Group says that discipline has been the cornerstone of its success. When Delaware first began managing money, its top priority was to establish realistic investment

goals and to adopt an investment philosophy with staying power. That philosophy was built on the belief that the best way to ensure long-term success was to protect profits in down markets.

Over the years Delaware has been faithful to this philosophy, avoiding any fundamental changes to its strategy. In both its mutual funds and institutional accounts, Delaware's portfolio managers follow established investment disciplines that guide them in buying and selling securities. The investment philosophy for its largest fund–Decatur–is a prudent one: Purchase high-yield stocks with current dividend returns greater than the average of the Standard & Poor's 500, and with an expected long-term return 300 basis points

Delaware Group is among the country's oldest and largest professional money managers. More than 60 years of experience stand behind the company's conservative, disciplined, value-oriented investment strategy. Photo by Ed Wheeler

above the yield available on investment quality corporate bonds.

Such philosophy has allowed Delaware to meet three important financial goals for its investors: beat inflation, beat cash, and outperform the markets over the long term.

This disciplined, conservative strategy can be traced to an investment counseling service founded in Philadelphia in the mid-1920s. In 1935 a group of investors from DuPont Company formed an investment club and two years later selected Delaware to manage their assets, a total of $800,000. A fund—the Delaware Fund—was created to protect this capital and Delaware Group joined the pioneering ranks of the mutual fund industry.

Delaware Fund remains one of Delaware Group's largest funds today. In 1988, responding to investor demand for more conservative equity investments, Delaware Fund became a balanced fund with three investment goals: growth, income, and preservation of principal. Delaware Fund has paid a dividend in every quarter of its 52-year existence.

Decatur Fund was added to the Delaware Group in 1957, and was named for Stephen Decatur who sailed the *United States* during

the War of 1812. Decatur now has net assets of about $1.6 billion. The Fund's dividend strategy was so successful that it later became the fundamental equity strategy for Delaware's investment advisory arm and the basis for Decatur Fund-Decatur II Series.

On several additional investment fronts, Delaware has been a leader as well. When the initial Keogh legislation was passed in 1962, Delaware was among the first to begin servicing personal retirement programs. Now Delaware handles more than 80,000 separate retirement plan accounts and continues to be an innovator in this arena. Delaware offers a

complete range of retirement plans, from individual retirement accounts to 401(k) plans.

Delaware became a leader in tax-free investing in 1977 when it moved to establish DMC Tax-Free Income Trust-Pennsylvania. DMC-PA is the oldest and largest single state fund in Pennsylvania and the oldest single state fund in the U.S. Since its first venture into tax-advantaged investing, Delaware Group has introduced two national municipal bond funds, the Tax-Free Fund-USA Series and its sister fund, the Insured Series; as well as a tax-free money market fund, Delaware Group Tax-Free Money Fund.

And on the cutting edge of the financial industry, Delaware introduced Cash Reserve in 1978. The Fund, which invests in money market instruments, was aimed at the average investor who needed relief from inflation, but couldn't afford to sacrifice either safety or liquidity.

The success of money market funds in the early 1980s opened the way for even greater expansion, and the entire decade proved to be one of outstanding growth for the mutual fund industry and for the Delaware Group. Assets under management at Delaware increased from about $4 billion to more than $21 billion including both institutional and mutual fund assets. Nine new funds were added to the family, creating an array of available investments.

Delaware is owned by the firm's key executives and by a limited investment partnership managed by principals of Castle Harlan, Inc., a New York merchant bank. The partnership, Legend Capital, purchased a controlling interest in Delaware in June 1988. In October 1989 a 10 percent interest in Delaware was acquired by Tokio Marine and Fire Insurance Co. And in September 1990 the group's Delaware Investment Advisers created an international subsidiary in London that will enable Delaware Group to offer global investment services.

Delaware's service areas employ more than 200 people who use state-of-the-art technology to serve shareholder and broker needs. Photo by Ed Wheeler

Medical and educational institutions contribute to the quality of life of Philadelphia-area residents.

Medical College of Pennsylvania, 228-229; Holy Family College, 230; St. Christopher's Hospital for Children, 231; Thomas Jefferson University, 232-235; Charter Fairmount Institute, 236-237; American College of Physicians, 238-239; Pennsylvania State University, 240-241; West Jersey Health System, 242-243; The University of the Arts, 244;

Photo by George Adams Jones

Quality
of
Life

Medical College of Pennsylvania

In the mid-1800s a small group of Quaker businessmen, clergy, and physicians, exploring a new frontier, established the nation's first medical school for women. The Female Medical College of Pennsylvania opened its doors on October 12, 1850.

In response to the barring of women from many of the city's hospitals, Ann Preston, M.D., a member of the college's first graduating class, founded the Woman's Hospital in the Fairmount section of the city. In 1862 the college moved to the same location as the hospital. In 1867 the school's name was changed to the Woman's Medical College of Pennsylvania. The college and hospital moved 63 years later to the institution's present location on Henry Avenue in the East

MCP recently acquired a 15-acre property on Queen Lane in the East Falls section of Philadelphia. This property, along with its existing 185,000-square-foot facility, is now MCP's Queen Lane Campus, designated for academic and research activities.

The Medical College of Pennsylvania Trauma Center entrance.

Falls section of Philadelphia.

The college became coeducational in 1969, and, to reflect its new status, changed its name to the Medical College of Pennsylvania (MCP) the following year. In 1981 MCP took over the management of the adjacent Eastern Pennsylvania Psychiatric Institute (EPPI).

In 1988 MCP formed a partnership with Allegheny Health Services (AHS), parent organization of Pittsburgh's Allegheny General Hospital.

Most recently, MCP purchased a 15-acre property with a 185,000-square-foot facility on Queen Lane in East Falls. This new campus will house MCP's academic and research programs, and will enable the institution to offer more student and faculty amenities. MCP's Henry Avenue campus will be primarily designated for clinical care with plans for a new ambulatory care center.

Thus from two rented rooms on Arch Street in 1850, MCP has grown into a 48-acre campus in Philadelphia with a second campus across the state in Pittsburgh, where third- and fourth-year medical students can complete their clinical rotations. The partnership with AHS supports the belief of both institutions that advances in medical education and practice depend on an environment that integrates education, research, and technology with the skills of experienced clinicians.

Today MCP remains the only medical school in the world with advocacy for careers

The entrance to MCP's Eastern Pennsylvania Psychiatric Institute.

for women in the biomedical sciences.

MCP's mission, simply stated, is to provide the physicians and scientists of tomorrow with the highest quality medical and scientific education available in a changing environment by supplying the appropriate tools of knowledge and experience. The foundation of this mission is based upon strength in research and clinical programs.

MCP Hospital provides advanced diagnostic services and clinical care in every medical and surgical specialty. It enjoys an outstanding national reputation for programs that combine the most current technology with a warm concern for human dignity. State-of-the-art programs are offered in cardiology and cardiothoracic surgery, neurosurgery, emergency medicine, perinatology, child development, oncology, trauma, infectious diseases, and mental health services. Facilities providing the latest in diagnostic services are available, as well as critical care units and step-down units. MCP also is designated a Level I Trauma Center. A variety of outpatient programs as well as a number of multi-specialty satellite facilities serve the many MCP communities.

More than 460 students are enrolled in the four-year program leading to the M.D. degree. Special programs leading to M.D./Ph.D., M.D./M.S., and M.D./D.M.D. degrees are offered for qualified students who wish to blend careers. MCP also enjoys many regional, national, and international affiliations, which broaden the medical school experience.

MCP's faculty includes approximately 800 physicians and basic scientists, many of whom are internationally known for their work in medical education, patient care, and research.

The college curriculum keeps pace with the rapid changes in medical science and technology through a variety of special programs. MCP's Teaching Program in Human Values in Medicine, which includes required course work in bioethics, has become a model for other medical schools throughout the world. The college participates in innovative work with the Standardized Patient Program, where trained volunteers interact with medical students to assist in the development of clinical skills. MCP was the first school in the country to offer a residency program in emergency medicine and a coordinated four-year curriculum in geriatrics and gerontology, the treatment and study of aging.

Approximately 280 physicians and dentists are engaged in residency and fellowship training in MCP's graduate medical education programs, which include studies in 14 specialty and subspecialty fields. In the Graduate School of Medical Sciences, approximately 100 students are enrolled in Ph.D. programs and in educational programs that lead to a master of science degree in medical technology or nurse anesthesia. In support of the belief that education is a life-long process, MCP also serves as a national center for continuing education in the health care professions.

As part of its academic health care mission, MCP is committed to providing the community with the tools for building a better quality of life through its public information services. MCP provides a speakers bureau network, community-based health fairs, Adopt-a-School activities and CHAPS, and teen parents and peer counseling programs.

To ensure that MCP will continue in its ability to fulfill its mission by improving its position in the academic health care arena, a number of institutional objectives have been established and form the basis of the institution's focus for the future.

The growing environmental changes facing all academic health care institutions represent an opportunity for MCP. To fully address the needs of the communities it serves, MCP has identified eight areas of concentration that best support its mission to educate physicians and scientists. An integrated, interdisciplinary approach is underway in developing the areas of cardiovascular disorders, cancer, geriatrics, mental health and neurological disorders, immune therapeutics, accidents and injuries, perinatal disorders, and education.

The front entrance of the Medical College of Pennsylvania.

Holy Family College

Holy Family College has a supportive campus atmosphere where warmth and friendliness are a tradition. Faculty members often are on a first-name basis with students, and some students have even been known to invite their professors to Thanksgiving dinner!

Such close relationships are not uncommon because Holy Family is a small college with a ratio of 13 students for every faculty member. That does not, however, mean the education process is easy. One continuing education student who took 13 years to get her degree described the relationship this way: "Teachers are demanding. There is no fluff. They accept nothing but your best. They set high standards and expect you to rise to meet them because they value the education they are giving." One of their important tasks is to teach students to think critically because not all the answers are in textbooks.

Holy Family College is the only four-year liberal arts college for men and women located in northeast Philadelphia. It was founded in 1954 by the Sisters of the Holy Family of Nazareth. Today its 50-acre campus at Grant and Frankford avenues, just a mile from the Academy Road exit of I-95, is populated by more than 1,800 full- and part-time students, day and evening, who commute from across northeast Philadelphia, south

Philadelphia, Lower Bucks and Montgomery counties, and nearby New Jersey. They include students beginning their education immediately after high school as well as the so-called "nontraditional" students—"empty-nesters," homemakers, and job-holders seeking to improve or change their careers. A significant percentage of graduates work within 20 miles of the college.

The college takes pride in its growing degree programs that are centered around an

Holy Family College offers its students a well-rounded education in an atmosphere of caring and support. More than 1,800 full- and part-time students attend classes at the beautiful, 50-acre campus.

extensive liberal arts core. The college offers a master's degree in education as well as undergraduate degrees in early childhood education, elementary and secondary education, and special education. A complete curriculum of business courses includes accounting, computer management information systems, marketing, and a distinctive program in international business. There is also an extensive program in the humanities, including literature, communications, language, history, and pre-medical and pre-law courses.

Students interested in the health professions may choose the college's highly-regarded nursing program, medical technology, or medical imaging.

Students also turn in excellent performances in athletics—men's and women's basketball, women's softball, and men's soccer. The Lady Tigers basketball team has won three consecutive district championships, while the men's basketball and soccer teams have won conference and district titles.

Whether it is academics or athletics, Holy Family College encourages students to reach their potential, to develop a commitment to community, and an appreciation of Judeo-Christian values. At Holy Family the care taken to provide a well-rounded education has earned it a reputation that lives up to its motto: "Family is Our Middle Name."

St. Christopher's Hospital for Children

There's probably nothing as precious as a child's smile, followed by a burst of laughter. Those moments of delight are even more heart-warming when the child has been very ill, but through the wonders of modern medicine has been made well again.

Those experiences are an everyday occurrence at St. Christopher's Hospital for Children, where every year more than 160,000 infants and children from the Greater Delaware Valley and from numerous foreign countries are treated by some of the best and most renowned health care professionals in the world.

Today those children receive their care at St. Christopher's new pediatric medical complex at Erie Avenue and Front Street, at the edge of northeast Philadelphia. The $100-million state-of-the-art facility is a far cry from the one-room dispensary at 522 East Dauphin Street set up by Dr. William H. Bennett in 1875.

The new, six-level hospital features patient room "towers," and is the focal point of the eight-acre campus. Convenient to I-95 and the Roosevelt Expressway, the complex also includes an 850-car parking garage and a three-story professional arts building, connected to the hospital by a dramatic atrium.

The hospital has 183 beds, compared to the 146 beds at the old facility, and a 30-bed neonatal intensive care unit, one of the area's most comprehensive.

The nonprofit, nonsectarian pediatric health care facility serves as both a regional referral center for youngsters and as the "family doctor" for children living in the north Philadelphia area. As the Department of Pediatrics of the Temple

University School of Medicine, St. Christopher's is nationally renowned for many of its specialized programs.

Some of the specialized services offered include a regional pediatric cardiology and cardiothoracic surgery program for infants and children; the only kidney dialysis/transplant program for children in the Delaware Valley and the only tracheotomy unit for infants and children in the region. St. Christopher's was a pioneer in the field of pediatric solid organ transplantation by establishing the first heart, heart/lung, and liver transplant programs for children in the region.

St. Christopher's is also the second-largest pulmonary center on the East Coast, and the third-largest in the country, for the treatment of cystic fibrosis and other pulmonary disorders. The pediatric Burn Center is the only unit on the East Coast located between Boston and Washington, D.C.

Combined with the new facility, the health care provided to the youngest patients at St. Christopher's can only continue to be offered in a warm and compassionate environment, designed to elicit those gratifying smiles.

Above Right: St. Christopher's Hospital for Children treats 160,000 infants and children from the Greater Delaware Valley and numerous foreign countries. Its staff consists of some of the best and most renowned health care professionals in the world.

Right: St. Christopher's Hospital for Children at Erie Avenue and Front Street, located at the edge of northeast Philadelphia. The hospital has 183 beds and a 30-bed neonatal intensive care unit.

Below: St. Christopher's is nationally renowned for many of its specialized programs in children's health care.

Thomas Jefferson University

P hiladelphia has long enjoyed a worldwide reputation as a hub for superior medical research, medical education, and patient care. Thomas Jefferson University, as one of the oldest and largest academic health centers in the country, has been a major contributor to that reputation, dating back to its founding as Jefferson Medical College in 1824.

As a budding medical school, Jefferson admitted its first students in 1825, and within a few short years the institution was operating a 125-bed hospital, one of the first in the nation that was affiliated with a medical school.

Students mingle at the statue of Samuel Gross, M.D. (Class of 1828), "the father of American surgery."

A school for nurses opened in 1891.

Today Thomas Jefferson University is made up of four major divisions that embrace all aspects of medical education, research, and patient care: Jefferson Medical College, Thomas Jefferson University Hospital and associated hospitals, the College of Allied Health Sciences, and the College of Graduate Studies. Together the academic health center annually treats more than 24,000 inpatients, more than 300,000 outpatients, and enrolls nearly 2,400 future health care professionals.

As the largest private medical school in the country, Jefferson Medical College has awarded more than 25,000 medical degrees since it opened its doors. It attracts students and scholars from all over the world who are eager to study with some of the world-renowned physicians who are among the more than 2,500 full- and part-time faculty members. Jefferson is proud of the faculty members it has attracted, many of whom are leading medical scholars in their respective fields. These physicians have been responsible for numerous major medical breakthroughs, including the discovery of the cause of yellow fever and the invention of the heart/lung machine that enabled Jefferson physicians to perform the world's first successful open-heart operation in 1953.

Because of Jefferson's commitment to excellence and a desire to provide the best patient care possible, patients from all walks of life, representing countries around the globe, travel to Jefferson to receive a diagnosis or treatment that may not be available elsewhere. In fact, faculty and alumni have treated 19 of the 41 U.S. presidents, from Thomas Jefferson to Ronald Reagan.

At the College of Graduate Studies, students striving to continue their medical studies with advanced training can receive

Jefferson Medical College—America's largest private medical school.

Ph.D. degrees in the biomedical sciences and master's degrees in the health professions. Doctoral degree programs are offered in anatomy, biochemistry, molecular biology, developmental biology/teratology, microbiology and immunology, pathology and cell biology, pharmacology, and physiology. Master's degree programs are offered in microbiology, nursing, occupational therapy, and physical therapy.

The College of Graduate Studies and the Jefferson Medical College form the core of the medical research programs conducted at Jefferson. At any given time, more than 700 medical research protocols are underway at Jefferson, all geared toward finding the "why" or the "how" for a vast number of diseases and therapies. Research efforts are focused on several different key areas, including genetics, cancer, neurology, cardiology, hematology, and rheumatology.

For example, in the area of neurological sciences, researchers in Jefferson's Multiple Sclerosis Center in the department of neurology are searching for new therapies to treat multiple sclerosis (MS), a disease of the central nervous system in which the immune system attacks normal cells. In the area of cardiovascular diseases, one focus of research at Jefferson's Center for Critical Care Research is seeking the cause, prevention, and cure for acute respiratory distress syndrome (ARDS), the failure of the respiratory system to function following events such as trauma, surgery,

More than 700 research projects are in process at Jefferson, the site of many medical advances including the world's first open-heart surgery.

In addition to M.D.s, the university graduates Ph.D.s in medical sciences and B.S. and M.S. nurses and allied health professionals.

or blood replacement, which frequently causes potentially fatal failure of multiple organ systems.

Scientists at Jefferson's Cardeza Foundation for Hematological Research are studying the potential benefit of the hormone erythropoietin in treating AIDS patients with anemia.

A broad spectrum of research is conducted at the Jefferson Institute of Molecular Medicine, which provides a truly interdepartmental forum for a vast range of research and teaching programs at Jefferson. The members of the institute have

made major contributions to the existing body of knowledge on the structure of collagen and the genetic basis of disease of the connective tissue. The institute's investigators have cloned human genes to establish the molecular basis for a series of genetic diseases that affect connective tissues in bones, joints, skin, and blood vessels.

Much of the ongoing research in connective tissue-related diseases is supported by three major project grants from the National Institutes of Health (NIH). More recently, the institute has received a $3.1-million grant to study the molecular biology of osteoarthritis, the most common form of arthritis in humans and the leading cause of disability, absenteeism, and loss of productivity in the workplace.

Jefferson faculty members are also

dedicated to the study of cancer. The Jefferson Cancer Institute is studying new techniques in patient care and treatment, such as the effectiveness of various therapies for treating advanced cancer. The National Cancer Institute of the National Institutes of Health is funding two-thirds of Jefferson's cancer research projects.

Both traditional and nontraditional students are attracted to the College of Allied Health Sciences' associate, baccalaureate, and master's degree programs in a variety of disciplines, including dental hygiene, diagnostic imaging, laboratory sciences, nursing, occupational therapy, and physical therapy. The college also operates a National Health Careers Information Hotline, a nationwide toll-free telephone service designed to provide information and guidance to individuals interested in health careers. The hotline receives more than 20,000 calls each year. Jefferson's School of Nursing not only graduates hundreds of nurses each year, but is also credited with more than fulfilling Jefferson's need for nurses, while other hospitals struggle to fill their nursing ranks.

The Health Services Division is designed to offer an extensive range of clinical services, led by the Thomas Jefferson University Hospital. The system also extends to Jefferson Park Hospital and Children's Rehabilitation Hospital, located in West Philadelphia, and the management of Methodist Hospital in

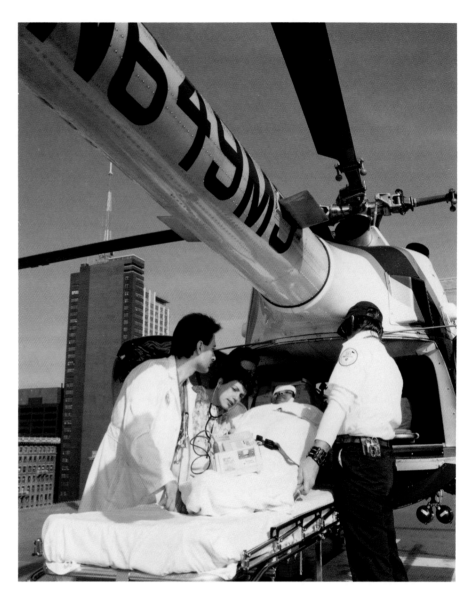

South Philadelphia. In addition, Jefferson is proud of its close clinical relationship with Wills Eye Hospital, the country's oldest and largest eye hospital, which serves as the Department of Ophthalmology; Magee Rehabilitation Hospital, which is a partner in the Spinal Cord Injury Center and is staffed by Jefferson's Department of Rehabilitative and Physical Medicine; and the Alfred I. du Pont Institute in Wilmington, which is a children's hospital and functions as part of Jefferson's Department of Pediatrics.

Of all the divisions, residents in the Delaware Valley are probably most familiar with the Thomas Jefferson University Hospi-

Jefferson is a major center for cancer diagnosis and treatment, including the area's largest mammography program.

tal and its vast array of services. Jefferson may have touched someone's life through the birth of a child or through one of Jefferson's preventive care screening programs. Patients come to "Jeff" because it is widely regarded as one of the best hospitals in the country. In fact, nationwide surveys of doctors in various national news publications in recent years have ranked Jefferson as among the best 40 hospitals in America. Perhaps that is because Jefferson offers a full range of medical care, on an inpatient and outpatient basis, from dermatology to neurosurgery to psychiatry. It has earned an especially excellent reputation for its cardiology, oncology, obstetrics, and injury-treatment programs.

For example, Jefferson is still a major center for cardiac surgery, but it has taken the treatment of heart diseases a step further. Working with the Division of Clinical

Pharmacology, Jefferson cardiologists employ state-of-the-art methods to develop the most effective means for using new cardiac drugs. Jefferson's Cardiac Catheterization Labora-

art radiation and radiation implants, or take part in a new intra-operative radiation program conducted by the department of radiation oncology and nuclear medicine, in conjunction with the department of surgery.

Ensuring the birth of healthy babies is important to Jefferson, and that is why its perinatology service offers the most extensive range of diagnostic services for the evaluation of possible maternal and fetal complications during pregnancy. As a widely recognized referral resource center, Jefferson's perinatology specialists collaborate with the investigators at the medical college to study the causes and prevention of a variety of birth defects. Every prenatal test in existence today is available at Jefferson, including amniocentesis, and tests for specific diseases, such as Tay-Sachs disease, muscular dystrophy, hemophilia, cystic

fibrosis, and sickle-cell anemia. Jefferson was one of the first hospitals in the country to offer chorion villus sampling, which allows physicians to diagnose fetal problems as early as eight weeks into pregnancy.

The treatment of accident victims is very complex and requires special expertise to handle the trauma, probably the greatest threat to human life. Jefferson is one of only four hospitals in the country that is both an accredited Level One Regional Trauma Center (designated as such in 1987) and a federally recognized designated Regional Spinal Cord Injury Center, in partnership with Magee Rehabilitation Center. This unusual dual status makes Jefferson one of the nation's leading centers of expertise in the treatment of accident victims.

In addition, Jefferson has made a major commitment to offer preventive and public health programs to the community. For example, its Dining With Heart program, sponsored with the Philadelphia Delaware Valley Restaurant Association, alerts restaurant patrons to health-conscious menu selections. And, to date, nearly 10,000 Delaware Valley residents have taken Jefferson's Cancer Test. By completing a detailed questionnaire on their health and life-style, residents can

Above: High technology plus attentiveness to patients puts Jefferson on many published lists of "America's best hospitals."

Right: Jefferson's faculty includes nationally renowned authorities in many fields.

tory, which opened in 1985, is one of the world's most advanced facilities.

Jefferson is also one of the leading cancer treatment centers in the Delaware Valley. Its Breast Imaging Center offers diagnostic expertise and prompt results in a setting designed for patient comfort and convenience—a crucial element for any possible cancer patient. Its Neurosciences Imaging Center combines sophisticated technology and skilled personnel to help with the detection of brain and spinal cord tumors.

Through Jefferson's Bodine Center for Cancer Treatment, the hospital has earned a reputation as a national leader in the treatment of pancreatic, colorectal, bladder, breast cancer, melanoma, and sarcoma. At the Bodine Center patients may receive state-of-the-

receive a free, personalized report on their main cancer risks and the most important steps to lower them. In order to meet the health needs of women and offer up-to-date information on women's health problems and concerns, Jefferson launched its Women's Health Information Line in 1989.

There's also Jefferson's Life is Fragile: Handle With Care program, which was designed to educate the public in accident prevention, especially young people. Experts from Jefferson's Trauma and Spinal Cord Injury Centers conduct regular sessions with Philadelphia and suburban school students. For adults, there's a "Guide to Accident Awareness," that also includes an awareness test to help people identify the personal behaviors that place them at the greatest risk of injury.

Charter Fairmount Institute

The grounds of the Charter Fairmount Institute, formerly known as the Fairmount Farms, resemble a restful countryside with flowering trees and shrubs as far as the eye can see. When the founders of the institution opened the private psychiatric facility in 1926 in the Roxborough section of Philadelphia, they were seeking a haven close to the city, yet rural and tranquil.

Today, the 25-acre site maintains its beauty, providing a peaceful setting for adolescents and adults who are recovering from mental illness or substance abuse. It is also part of one of the largest providers of mental health services in the world, the Charter Medical Corporation of Macon, Georgia, which purchased the Fairmount Institute in 1985. The Charter Medical Corporation operates 92 hospitals, 14 medical/surgical clinics, and 78 psychiatric and substance abuse treatment centers in the United States and Europe.

Charter Fairmount Institute is accredited by the Joint Commission on Accreditation of Health Care Organizations and is a member of the National and Pennsylvania Associa-

The 25-acre Charter Fairmount Institute is host to thousands of patients each year.

tions of Private Psychiatric Hospitals.

All of Charter Fairmount Institute's treatment programs are based on the philosophy that people who are suffering from mental illness or substance dependence have a right to professional treatment from specialists in the mental health field. Because of this philosophy, the staff uses a multidisciplinary team approach to treatment, providing a comprehensive daily program that includes individual and group therapy, family counseling, psychodrama, and allied therapies such as

music, art, and occupational therapy.

Patients are housed in comfortable dorms with a lounge area for each treatment team. In addition to the basic hospital functions, a wide variety of therapeutic activities such as basketball, volleyball, tennis, baseball, shuffleboard, Ping-Pong, and billiards is available.

The majority of patients at Charter Fairmount Institute are dually-diagnosed. They have mental health problems, such as depression or anxiety, that are complicated by dependence on alcohol or drugs. Two-thirds of the hospital's 169 beds are dedicated to adult treatment; one-third are reserved for adolescent care.

Free, confidential assessments are provided for adults and adolescents at Charter Fairmount Institute prior to admission to determine whether inpatient or outpatient care is needed. If hospitalization is recommended, patients may be referred to one of seven treatment programs at the institute.

Charter Fairmount offers inpatient treatment programs for adolescents, ages 12 to 17,

The adolescent program includes an on-site, accredited school program so that young people may keep up with their studies while receiving treatment.

The institute's beautiful, park-like grounds have an obvious therapeutic value.

who are suffering from emotional or behavioral problems, including substance abuse. An on-site, accredited school program is available to keep the young person up-to-date with his or her studies. The teenager's family is welcome to visit daily and encouraged to participate in the treatment process through family sessions and educational seminars.

The adult addiction treatment programs at Charter Fairmount Institute, for people ages 18 and up, espouse the principles of Alcoholics Anonymous (AA) and Narcotics Anonymous (NA), requiring patients to attend regularly scheduled AA and NA meetings. Recovering patients also receive one-to-one counseling and attend group therapy sessions while participating in a variety of activities designed to promote self-confidence, a sense of well-being, and sobriety.

Men and women in Charter Fairmount's adult services unit receive specialized team treatment for their emotional or psychiatric problems. For adults ages 65 or older, the senior adult treatment unit offers therapy that addresses psychiatric or emotional difficulties that may be encountered at that stage of life.

Prior to a patient's discharge, the treatment team prepares the patient and the patient's family for a smooth transition to home. The clinicians may recommend further therapy, either through support groups, community programs, or outpatient centers. Individuals may choose to continue treatment at one of Charter Fairmount's outpatient centers in Roxborough and Bensalem.

In addition to providing treatment for substance abuse and mental illness, Charter Fairmount has taken a leading health care provider role in promoting drug prevention in Philadelphia. In 1986 it was the only psychiatric institution to be a founding member of the Corporate Alliance for Drug Education (CADE). For the past three years Charter Fairmount, along with a number of major

Philadelphia corporations and the city's professional sports teams, has implemented school programs geared toward altering young people's perceptions of drugs and alcohol.

Community involvement is an integral part of Charter Fairmount's mission. Each week the facility provides free educational seminars for the public on topics ranging from identifying addiction in the family to improving self-esteem. In addition, the institute hosts monthly seminars for professionals in the mental health field. These conferences frequently feature prominent health care experts as guest speakers.

The facility's own Speaker's Bureau receives and fills many requests from local schools, parent/teacher organizations, professional groups, and businesses to provide clinicians to speak about mental health or substance abuse issues.

In emphasizing its commitment to quality psychiatric treatment and community education, Charter Fairmount Institute affirms its position as a leader in the Philadelphia health care field.

American College of Physicians

The American College of Physicians, which has made its home in Philadelphia since 1926, is the nation's largest medical specialty society. ACP also is one of the nation's most venerable medical organizations; in 1990 the college celebrated its 75th anniversary. Its mission is to improve health care by promoting excellence in internal medicine.

ACP's membership of approximately 70,000 doctors includes both internists and young physicians training to be internists. Physicians who specialize in internal medicine provide continuing, comprehen-

The college has been based in Philadelphia since 1926 and to this day remains dedicated to improving health care through excellence in internal medicine.

sive care to adults and adolescents and have long been regarded as medicine's master diagnosticians. Many internists also are expert in a subspecialty, such as cardiology or gastroenterology, or in a field related to internal medicine, such as geriatrics or occupational medicine. Although most of its members live in the United States, ACP also includes internists from all over the world and has chapters in Puerto Rico, Canada, Mexico, Central America, and Chile.

Internists who belong to the American College of Physicians receive not only the prestige of membership but an array of services. These services include continuing medical education, high-quality publications, technology assessment, representation in public policy arenas, and public education programs.

Helping internists keep abreast of advances in medical practice has always been a central ACP function. Executive Vice President John R. Ball, MD, JD, notes, "We would say that internal medicine is one of the most difficult medical disciplines, very much a knowledge-based practice. Internists are responsible for all dimensions of patient care and therefore they have to know a tremendous amount to care for their patients."

ACP's *Annuals of Internal Medicine*, first published in 1927, continues to be one of the world's premier medical journals, with a circulation of approximately 100,000 worldwide. It is one of the most widely cited journals in medical literature.

ACP is the internist's primary source for continuing medical education. The Medical Knowledge Self-Assessment Program (MKSAP), developed by ACP in the 1960s, is the first

Right: John R. Ball, executive vice president of American College of Physicians.

Below: Each year leaders of internal medicine share their knowledge with thousands of internists at ACP's annual session. Photo by Deng Jeng Lee

program of its kind in medicine. Updated every three years, MKSAP helps keep physicians informed of developments in internal medicine and its subspecialties. Other continuing medical education activities include the Annual Session, a national scientific meeting that features more than 300 presentations and is attended by thousands of internists; about 50 postgraduate courses offered each year in conjunction with major medical schools and teaching institutions across the country; and an audiocassette library of selected presentations from each annual session.

Through other educational activities, ACP is dedicated to making the internal medicine environment more attractive to medical students, in part by working to ensure that training received during residency remains relevant to the full spectrum of an internist's practice.

ACP recognizes that physicians must not overlook the importance of their input on public policy and health care issues. Advances in technology, changing patterns of health care delivery, and economic considerations make it necessary to re-examine and revise health policy on an ongoing basis.

Through its Washington, D.C.-based Department of Public Policy, ACP seeks to advance the development of national health care policies that place the highest priority on accessible, high-quality health care. The Department of Scientific Policy, located at ACP headquarters in Philadelphia, works with a wide network of physicians who bring their expertise to bear on pressing concerns affecting the practice of medicine and the broad health policy issues of the day, developing policy recommendations and medical practice standards.

ACP is clearly expanding its 75-year-old tradition of education into an agenda that reflects education, information, and the concerns of the public. Says Dr. Ball, "A major thrust for the 1990s is to attempt as a profession to represent the public interest. In the past medicine sometimes has been too focused on the interests of physicians. ACP's role as a professional society is analogous to that of the individual physician—to put the health of patients first. We are working to reform the health system to benefit patients as well as society. And we are addressing not merely the cost issue but access, quality, appropriateness, infrastructure, and human resources—the whole system.

"In the 1990s ACP will continue to be the internist's information and education resource, analyzing and distilling the torrent of information and making it understandable to physicians and adaptable to practice." Dr. Ball concludes, "Our unique representation of the professionalism of medicine will continue, supported by the information that makes us credible."

Pennsylvania State University

Driving around the Delaware Valley region, it is not unusual to see a Penn State sticker emblazoned on many cars. The distinctive blue-and-white Nittany Lion emblem might be displayed on a bumper sticker, a window sticker, or a Penn State alumni license plate. Not only are those car owners Penn State fans, but you can be sure that many of those cars carry people who are students or alumni of one of the three regional Penn State campuses: the Delaware County Campus in Media, the Ogontz Campus in Abington, or the Graduate Center at Great Valley.

Simply put, Penn State's presence in the five-county area is impressive, easily dwarfing other regional centers for higher learning. Its three regional campuses conduct classes at 58 locations in the area and enroll 6,500 credit students annually, ranking the regional campus system as the ninth largest among the 80 degree-granting institutions in the region. With an annual operating budget of more than $19 million, the campuses maintain a total of 13 major buildings on 136 acres and

employ more than 600 people.

But Penn State's impact on the region goes beyond the education of students, or even the employment of a great number of area people. The regional campus system has played a leading role in building Greater Philadelphia's reputation as a center for academic excellence. Penn State has been able to respond to the expanding economic development activity in the region by supplying local businesses and industries with well-educated, well-trained employees through formal undergraduate and graduate programs and through informal continuing education training. Of the 58 classroom locations, many of them are arranged at the request of employers. In addition, the full-time faculty is further supported by hundreds of experts from area businesses, industries, government agencies, and the arts who teach on a part-time basis. Many of these experts participate as instructors in the campus system's continuing education program, which is one of the largest in the world. More than 10,000 local residents enroll in noncredit continuing education programs at the three campuses annually.

The Ogontz campus in Abington is located on the site of the former Ogontz School and Junior College, situated on 45 wooded acres. It became a Penn State campus in 1950, opening its doors to 225 students. Even though Ogontz is the largest of all of Penn State's campuses throughout Pennsylvania, it is known for its friendly, small-college atmosphere. The campus is home to 2,000 full-time students and 1,500 part-time students. Most students entering Ogontz are taking the first step toward a baccalaureate degree in any of the more than 160 available majors. The most popular programs among traditional, full-time students include business administration, the liberal arts, engineering, and science. The campus is also host to the largest continuing education operation in the Pennsylvania State University system, and one of the largest in the state.

More than 1,950 full- and part-time students enroll in classes at the Delaware

Above and Facing Page: Great Valley campus is surrounded by a corporate park and offers a wide range of graduate and continuing education programs tailored to the needs of the area's business, industrial, and service organizations.

County campus in Media each year. The campus is spread over 100 acres, just four miles west of the borough of Media. The main classroom building and the new, $3.9-million athletic center/student commons building give no hint to the campus' humble beginnings. When it opened in 1967, the classrooms occupied two windowless floors of a former fish market and dry goods store in Chester, Pennsylvania. The top floor of the building housed a still-operating roller skating rink, and the 236 students were frequently distracted by the roar of steel-wheel roller skates and the blasting of a Wurlitzer. The faculty and students endured the roller rink until the first major building at its present site in Media was completed in 1971.

Today students can roam the sprawling campus, taking part in numerous extracurricular activities, including athletics, clubs, and various cultural programs. In addition to the wide choice of available major programs, students can enroll in two-year associate degree programs in electrical engineering technology, business, letters, arts and sciences, and telecommunications technology.

The Graduate Center at Great Valley in Malvern is not only one of the newest in the Penn State system, but it is possibly the most

The Penn State Delaware County campus, spread over 100 acres, has more than 1,950 full- and part-time students. This campus has come a long way since its beginnings in 1967 as a former fish market and dry goods store.

unique campus in the country. When it opened it 1988, it marked the first time a university had constructed a new facility in an existing corporate park. The 81,000-square-

foot building is located at the entrance to the Great Valley Corporate Center along Chester County's Route 202 high-tech corridor. Surrounded by numerous corporate neighbors,

this prototype campus offers a wide range of graduate and continuing education programs geared towards the needs of the area's business, industrial, and service organizations. More than 1,200 adult students are enrolled in upper-division and graduate-level courses on a part-time basis. Graduate degrees are available in education, engineering, philosophy, and management, including business administration, contract management, general management, health care administration, and public administration.

As the home to more than 38,000 Penn State alumni, the Delaware Valley and its residents, businesses, and industries have clearly benefited from Penn State's responsive and wide-ranging regional campus system.

The Ogontz campus in Abington became a Penn State campus in 1950. Located on 45 wooded acres, on the site of the former Ogontz School & Junior College, it is the largest of all Penn State's campuses and hosts the largest continuing education operation in the Penn State system and in the state.

West Jersey Health System

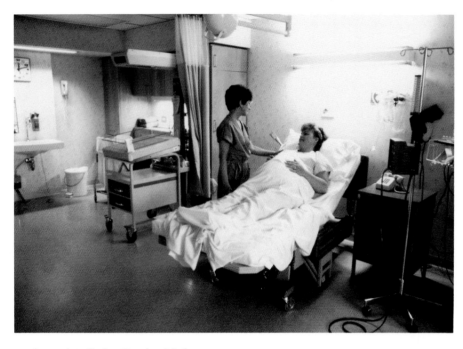

odern medicine was in its infancy when Dr. E.M. Howard, one of Camden's leading physicians, found the help he needed to establish the city's first operating hospital. The facility, called the Camden Homeopathic Hospital and Dispensary Association, was incorporated on February 5, 1885.

Today that organization has grown into West Jersey Health System, the state's largest not-for-profit, multihospital organization. West Jersey's four hospitals contain 763 beds and bassinets and are staffed by some 3,700 employees who work in conjunction with the system's nearly 1,000-member medical staff.

As a major multihospital system, West Jersey serves a broad geographic base that focuses primarily on Camden, Burlington, and Gloucester counties. This tri-county area encompasses nearly 1,400 square miles occupied by a population that exceeds one million.

To serve the citizens of South Jersey, West Jersey's health professionals offer a multitude of important medical services. In the most recent calendar year, more than 45,000 patients were admitted to West Jersey's acute

West Jersey traces its roots to 1885 and the city of Camden. Today the system's Camden Hospital is a cornerstone of health care delivery in Camden and surrounding communities.

care hospitals in Berlin, Camden, Marlton, and Voorhees. Another 91,000 sought care in the hospitals' emergency departments, while 87,000 more called upon West Jersey for outpatient diagnostic testing.

While these statistics speak to the breadth of services offered by West Jersey, a closer look at several individual programs reflects the depth of the system's expertise in delivering vital health care services to the region.

Among West Jersey's showcase services is

With 5,000 deliveries each year, West Jersey's Scarborough Center for Women and Children is one of the region's largest and most comprehensive birthing facilities.

the William and Elizabeth Stretch Center for Arthritis Treatment, housed at West Jersey Hospital-Marlton. Located on the third floor of the facility, the center combines a 39-bed inpatient unit with a full range of education and outpatient programs.

Especially noteworthy is its Total Joint Replacement Orientation Program for candidates for delicate hip and knee replacement surgery. This unique program provides a plethora of information regarding the procedure and the recovery process. It is extremely valuable for the hundreds of patients who undergo this surgery at the Marlton hospital each year.

The center also offers a host of support programs for arthritis and lupus sufferers that focus on topics such as exercise and nutrition. While in the hospital, patients can count on sensitive, compassionate care from a team of nurses specially trained in the needs of individuals with arthritis.

In the Stretch Center for Arthritis Treatment at West Jersey Hospital-Marlton, patients are assured of high-quality, compassionate care from a team of skilled physicians and nurses.

Since 1987, when West Jersey consolidated all of its maternity and pediatric services at the Scarborough Center for Women and Children at West Jersey Hospital-Voorhees, a growing number of South Jersey families seeking the finest in maternity and pediatric care have called on the center. Each year the staff in the center witnesses the beginning of approximately 5,000 lives—by far the largest number in all of South Jersey.

For women with high-risk pregnancies, the Scarborough Center offers the expertise to detect and skillfully manage difficulties that may occur before and after delivery. In the center's Antenatal Testing Unit, a comprehensive range of critical diagnostic procedures are performed to pinpoint problems. And for infants born with complications, neonatologists in the center's Neonatal Intensive Care Unit provide sophisticated medical attention.

To treat many of these patients, the center draws upon its affiliation with St. Christopher's Hospital for Children. In an office on the Voorhees campus designated the St. Christopher's Center for Children at West Jersey, subspecialists provide care critical to the good health of youngsters with special needs.

In the area of emergency care, West Jersey has distinguished itself through its Mobile Intensive Care Unit (MICU) Program. Initially a one-vehicle service, the MICU fleet now numbers nine vans and provides prehospital emergency care to more than 13,000 South Jersey residents each year. The MICU program has also extended its geographic reach through a cooperative agreement with Atlantic City Medical Center, Shore Memorial Hospital, and Burdette Tomlin Hospital. As a result, the program now serves shore communities in Atlantic and Cape May counties. West Jersey is also home to Southstar, one of New Jersey's two Med-Evac helicopters. The aircraft is housed on the campus of West Jersey Hospital-Voorhees.

In addition to its commitment to providing quality health services, West Jersey understands the need for health education. At the Helene Fuld School of Nursing in Camden County, which is located on the campus of the Camden hospital, students prepare for nursing careers. The hospital is also home to the system's School of Radiologic Technology. In the area of medical education, West Jersey offers residency training programs in family practice and general practice dentistry.

To assure easy access to medical care, West Jersey offers a computerized Physician Locater Service. Area residents that call the service can select from the more than 500 West Jersey doctors who belong to the service. Participating physicians represent the full range of medical specialties.

With this commitment to the community, South Jersey families can be assured that the West Jersey Health System will continue to offer innovative and sophisticated health services and programs for many years to come.

Situated in one of the fastest-growing portions of Camden County, West Jersey Hospital-Voorhees is the largest of the system's four acute care hospitals.

The University of the Arts
Philadelphia College of Art & Design
Philadelphia College of Performing Arts

In the purest sense The University of the Arts trains, coaches, and educates dancers, singers, musicians, artists, actors, artisans, and designers. Located in the heart of Philadelphia's artistic community, it is the only university in the country that is devoted to education in design, the performing arts, and the visual arts.

But this commitment to the arts goes beyond painting a picture or executing a pirouette. Under the leadership of President Peter Solmssen, The University of the Arts has embraced the technology of the business and scientific worlds and has incorporated it into all aspects of its curriculum. The university believes its students need a multidisciplinary awareness of art in all areas of study. That's why the curriculum is based upon a realistic assessment of business and industry's future needs. This approach is particularly evident in the design field, be it architectural studies, graphic design, illustration, or industrial design. Because all design fields have been so profoundly affected by the computer, this technology has been integrated into the learning process. Much of this educational effort has been developed through the school's industrial design department, seeking to encourage the incorporation of sound design in the planning, development, and marketing of products sold to consumers and other businesses.

For example, industrial design students learn how to design products that fit the needs of an evolving industry and society's anticipated lifestyle. There's an emphasis on designing products that fit into our environment, and make it better and more efficient. One student group created a computer package that makes it possible, through the telephone, for a person to call home and program a videocassette recorder.

By adding an artistic slant to a seemingly technical field, university graphic design students can produce designs that incorporate good technical judgment with an artistic flair.

This multidisciplinary approach prepares students for more than 150 career paths in the arts and related fields. The University of the Arts includes the Philadelphia College of Art & Design, the Philadelphia College of Performing Arts, and the Shubert Theater.

As a major player in the Philadelphia arts community, the university also has embraced

Above: University of the Arts students are at the center of a dynamic educational environment.

its role as an ambassador for Philadelphia, attracting students from all over the country and from more than 30 foreign countries. The university is also serving as an anchor for the Avenue of the Arts. And when it's not stirring up the creative juices in its students, the university is involved in community concerns.

Like its students, The University of the Arts is a creative force in Philadelphia.

Below: Haviland Hall, the historic focal point of the campus at Broad and Pine streets.

Chapter Fifteen

Philadelphia's retail establishments, service industries, sports teams, and accommodations are enjoyed by both residents and visitors.

Photo by George Adams Jones

Marketplace

Philadelphia Phillies

Grover Cleveland Alexander, Chuck Klein, Ed Delahanty, Robin Roberts, Steve Carlton, Mike Schmidt, the Phillie Phanatic.

It may seem strange to see the Phillie Phanatic listed along with some of the Philadelphia Phillies' all-time greatest players, but since the Phanatic arrived on the scene in 1978, his swaying oversized belly and protruding furry beak have become as much a part of the Phillie folklore as the Hall of Famers. In fact, during some Phillie seasons, the Phanatic has even been able to rally the fans who may not feel like rallying much.

He entertains at each of the Phillies' 81 home games, and can usually be spotted dancing on top of the dugout with some unsuspecting female fan or racing his Honda four-wheeler around the field during the

Right: Mike Schmidt, during his career, held or shared 14 major league records, 18 National League records, 24 Phillies career records, and 11 Phillies season records. Photo by Al Tielemans

Below: The renowned Phillie Phanatic entertains at each of the Phillies 81 home games. Photo by Al Tielemans

seventh-inning stretch. Regardless whether the Phillies win or lose, the Phanatic can always guarantee a chuckle from the crowd.

Unfortunately the Phanatic wasn't around when the Phillies played their first game on May 1, 1883. The Phillies lost that day to the Providence Grays by one run, but the event still goes down in the history books as the start of the first National League franchise. The early days were rocky, but led by a young pitcher named Grover Cleveland Alexander, the Phillies captured their first National League pennant in 1915.

That win was followed by a long dry spell, sprinkled with a few refreshing moments offered by sluggers such as Chuck Klein, who blasted 186 home runs in his first five years. The Phanatic would have loved it.

A second pennant eluded the Phillies until 1950, when young players such as Del Ennis, Richie Ashburn, Andy Seminick, Robin Roberts, Curt Simmons, and Granny Hamner combined to form the "Whiz Kids" who snatched the pennant away from the Brooklyn Dodgers.

After that season, the Whiz Kids seemed to lose their zip, and the Phillies—and their fans—suffered through several disappointing seasons until left-handed pitcher Steve Carlton arrived from the St. Louis Cardinals in 1972. In his first year as a Phillie, Carlton won 27 games, and even though the team placed last in the league, the Phillies knew they had a promising future. That year Carlton won the coveted Cy Young Award as the most valuable pitcher in the National League.

Carlton formed the core for a new group of developing "whiz kids"—Greg Luzinski, Larry Bowa, Bob Boone, and Mike Schmidt. The Phillies were ready to become serious contenders. In 1974, they finished in third place. The next year, they finished in second place. And in 1976, the Phillies won the first of three straight Eastern Division titles. Yet the World Series title continued to elude the struggling Phils.

Then came 1980, a year that still evokes smiles on the faces of Phillie fans. Even the Phillie Phanatic, a member of the Phillie franchise for a mere two years at the time, still performs a special wiggle at the mere mention of that year. On the strength of

Steve Carlton was the first left-hander to strike out 3,000 batters in the history of baseball. He retired in 1988 with numerous awards and honors, including four Cy Young Awards.

Mike Schmidt's bat and relief pitcher Tug McGraw's arm, the team earned another division title. After battling the Houston Astros in the play-offs, the Phillies earned a third World Series appearance in the team's 98-year history. And on October 21, 1980, McGraw struck out Willie Wilson of the Kansas City Royals to give the Phillies their first World Championship. The Phanatic turned cartwheels.

The bright lights faded a bit the next year, but received a new jolt in 1982 when William Y. "Bill" Giles headed a group that bought the Phillies. The team repeated its league championship performance in 1983, but lost to the Baltimore Orioles in the World Series.

In recent years the Phillies have been unable to rekindle the drive that produced the whiz kid teams of earlier times. Yet the Phillies have probably produced more thrills and excitement than many teams and have entertained millions of fans both on and off the field.

Steve Carlton, the first left-hander to strike out 3,000 batters in the history of baseball (he ended his career with 4,136 strikeouts), earned numerous awards and honors, including four Cy Young Awards. He retired in 1988, and is a shoe-in for baseball's Hall of Fame when he becomes eligible in 1994.

Mike Schmidt, whose 548 career homeruns place him seventh on the all-time homerun hitter's list, was one of the greatest players in baseball. When he announced his immediate retirement in a tearful press conference on May 29, 1989 in San Diego, Schmidt held or shared 14 major league records, 18 National League records, 24 Phillies career records, and 11 Phillies season records. He's expected to join the Hall of Fame when he become eligible in 1995.

Through the years the names of Phillies players, as well as the Phanatic, have also been connected with a variety of area community and civic organizations. And for several years the Phillies' Wives have raised thousands of dollars for research support for Lou Gehrig's Disease.

That's yet another reason for the Phillie Phanatic to kick up his oversized heels.

John Wanamaker

There are probably few business establishments that represent Philadelphia more than John Wanamaker. Since its founding in 1861, the retail chain, usually referred to as Wanamaker's, has emerged as Philadelphia's premier merchandiser of clothing, housewares, home furnishings, and other home and personal accessories. Anyone who has grown up in Philadelphia holds fond childhood memories of lunching at the Crystal Tea Room, listening to the Wanamaker organ during the annual Christmas light show, and setting up numerous shopping trips that started with "Meet Me at the Eagle."

When John Wanamaker opened his first store on the corner of Sixth and Market streets, he also started a tradition of quality and integrity that his successors have carried through to today. He was committed to serving the public and is credited with introducing several retailing innovations, which were certainly daring at the time, but are now commonplace.

For example, in 1865 he introduced the notion of a moneyback guarantee, saying, "Bring back any article that doesn't please the folks at home, and we will refund the money." Wanamaker's held the first "white sale" in 1878, when it advertised a "sale of muslins below cost." Other merchants quickly copied this annual event. The country's first "bargain room" opened in 1880, which was the forerunner of department store bargain basements.

But Wanamaker's reputation is based on much more than historical milestones. The store has always been known for offering high-quality merchandise, backed by a dedication to service. Like customers of a century ago, today's customers have come to trust Wanamaker's. Innovation and retailing savvy are still its trademark, which is indelibly stamped on the 15 Wanamaker stores scattered around the Delaware Valley.

As a division of Woodward & Lothrop, Wanamaker's has continued to evolve into a store that is sensitive to its customers' needs, making it one of the leading retailing establishments in the region. Not only are the stores stocked with a broad array of quality high-fashion, high-tech merchandise, but they also offer consumers a pleasant shopping experience, thanks to ongoing in-store display renovations. This evolution is probably most evident in the dramatic renovation that has

The 10-foot majestic bronze Wanamaker Eagle, installed in the Grand Court in 1911, has come to symbolize the Wanamaker's shopping experience.

been underway at the flagship store, originally built by John Wanamaker in 1861.

Even though the layout and design of the national historic landmark department store sport a new, updated look, the flavor and ambience that have always characterized a shopping excursion to downtown Wanamaker's are still the same. The massive, multimillion-dollar building renovation, started in 1989, was carefully crafted to preserve the distinctive touches, such as the Ionic columns and the majestic chandeliers, that have always been part of Wanamaker's heritage.

Yet, for the generations of Wanamaker shoppers to come in the twenty-first century, this continuing process will mesh together classic traditions with contemporary merchandising techniques. And these shoppers, too, will probably "meet at the Eagle."

The Oliver H. Bair Company

A historical event took place one day in 1908 when a Philadelphia funeral director named Oliver H. Bair opened the doors of his new venture at 1820 Chestnut Street. Inside, according to stories passed along by the Bair family, was the first funeral home in America built with that particular intention in mind—an exquisite and extravagantly decorated landmark with Corinthian columns, coffered ceilings, marble floors, and a monumental staircase. The very sight of the building's lobby brought hushed tones to visitors.

This funeral home ushered in a new era, one developed by Bair to replace the need for conducting funerals in the residences of the deceased. The Bair funeral home concept was financed by another new entrepreneurial

Pennsylvania, Oliver was the youngest of nine children of Isaac and Elizabeth Baldwin Bair. He studied in public schools and with private tutors, and in 1875 he came to Philadelphia and started his career as a funeral director while employed by his oldest brother, Andrew J. Bair. Nearly two years later, Oliver Bair founded his own business at 18th and Filbert streets, where he remained for 20 years. In 1908, after several interim moves, he built his memorable funeral home at 1820 Chestnut Street.

Before Bair died in 1923, he had long established the company's philosophy of never turning anyone away because they could not afford a funeral. Mary A. Bair, his daughter, succeeded her father as president of The Oliver H. Bair Company and

Above: The Oliver H. Bair Company's elegant brick Georgian Center City funeral home.

Below: One of the other five Oliver H. Bair Company funeral homes.

venture conceived by this Philadelphia businessman and civic leader. In 1902 Bair had created a successful, before-need funeral arrangement program known as the Oliver H. Bair Benefit Bond, which furnished a complete funeral for as little as five cents per week. The bonds were issued from 1902 to 1937, and they helped thousands to prepare for the inevitable from the monthly household budget.

Today The Oliver H. Bair Company and its affiliates are dedicated to providing the finest in funeral care and service to all. And the company that continues to bear his name has retained the spirit of the founder and his commitment to excellence in funeral service.

Born on July 4, 1854, in Chester County,

maintained these same ideals. And the Bair legacy was passed along to Maytor H. McKinley who purchased the Bair company in 1962 and chose to continue the business with its highly respected name intact. Mary Bair was succeeded as president in 1962 by John R. Camp and he was followed by Jesse R. Pebley in 1976.

From 1963 to the present, The Oliver H. Bair Company has made numerous funeral home acquisitions and expanded throughout the Delaware Valley. In 1980 the company moved from its historic headquarters to 1812 Sansom Street, and more recently to an elegant Georgian-style brick building located at 1920 Sansom Street.

In addition to providing for traditional

funeral needs, the Bair organization began in 1984 to implement a "funeral trust plan," which means that, through a trust arrangement with an area bank, Bair can guarantee the price of a funeral today regardless of funeral costs in the future. According to Oliver H. Bair Company officials, thousands of families throughout the area have recognized the wisdom of planning ahead and taken advantage of a program that is now widely accepted throughout the funeral industry.

In retrospect, the contemporary funeral trust plan is not unlike the pre-need sales program that Oliver Bair started in 1902 to help the public plan in advance for one's funeral. And like the company he founded, the goals and contributions of Oliver H. Bair have flourished.

Hotel Atop The Bellevue

It is known, affectionately, as The Grande Dame of Broad Street, a hotel that opened on September 20, 1904, and immediately captured the hearts and allegiance of Philadelphia's elite.

Today the historic Hotel Atop The Bellevue combines the grandeur and style of a hotel of yesteryear with every modern amenity befitting its recent rebirth as an exclusive, 170-room European hotel.

The Bellevue, a National Historic Landmark, recently underwent a $100-million renovation by owner and developer Richard I. Rubin & Company. The facelift turned the 19-story French Renaissance building into retail shops, prestigious office space, restaurants and, on the top seven floors of the building, the Hotel Atop The Bellevue.

The results are breathtaking. The hotel's magnificent ballrooms, original woodwork,

The Hotel Atop The Bellevue offers the most modern amenities in a setting of historic grandeur and style.

high ceilings, elliptical staircase, mosaic tile floors, and marble columns have been preserved. A few architectural details that were once hidden have been brought back to life, including two sets of spectacular, floor-to-ceiling oval windows located on the 19th floor in what is now the hotel's formal dining room and the Barrymoore Room. Many of the hotel's guest rooms overlook the new interior sky-lit atrium and palm court that blends perfectly with the building's historical appointments.

Located at Broad and Walnut streets in the heart of downtown Philadelphia, The Bellevue is rich with historical footnotes. The original Bellevue was built for $8 million by one of the most successful men in hotel history, George C. Boldt, who was hired in 1898 by the Astor family of New York to run the famous Waldorf Astoria. In 1902 Boldt decided to open a hotel of equal opulence and splendor in Philadelphia. What was then known as The Bellevue Stratford opened in 1904 with more than 1,000 rooms.

The suites were designed with colonial, French, Italian, and Greek decor to suit the tastes of each individual guest. The hotel housed an internal power plant that produced enough electricity to make the building self-sufficient; more than 700 employees were hired, including 50 cooks. The rooms contained everything from electric curling irons to coal-burning fireplaces, and the hotel engaged the services of typists and stenographers to cater to "men of affairs." In the lobby there was a stock board and a broker's office.

From the beginning, the rich and the famous—including royalty, movie stars, and politicians—slept and dined there in rooms filled with mahogany woodwork and glistening chandeliers. Much of the

Part of the Bellevue building $100-million renovation project focused on bringing the hotel's elegant ballrooms and dining halls back to their original lustre.

authentic lighting inside the hotel is reputedly the work of the hotel's original electrical contractor, Thomas Edison. Franklin D. Roosevelt was nominated for president in 1936 in the Hunt Room, and Harry S. Truman reportedly got the nod for the 1948 presidential nomination in the hotel. And local Philadelphians, the developers say, have always had a special fondness for the Bellevue, which managed to survive when other grand hotels along Broad Street closed after the Depression. Families have long turned to the hotel for weddings, receptions, bar mitzvahs, and the annual Assembly, the oldest society ball in the nation.

During the 1940s and 1950s, however, the rich and decorative architectural style was considered offensive and overpowering, and so began an attempt to modernize the total image of the hotel. However, the new austere decor, air conditioning, and other attempts at rejuvenation succeeded only briefly. By the late 1960s the hotel was only a shadow of its former self. After a final charity gala on November 18, 1976, the hotel was closed and the property was put up for sale.

Two years later, Rubin Associates agreed to buy the building for $8.25 million—the same amount paid for the entire construction of the original Bellevue. On June 21, 1978, about 15 feet of legal documents were signed, and Rubin Associates was the new owner of the former Bellevue Stratford. The Hotel Atop The Bellevue and the $100 million mixed-use

The landmark hotel boasts plush, luxurious decor and state-of-the-art services such as help with travel arrangements, theater tickets, and restaurant reservations.

renovation of the entire building is the third attempt by the new owner to bring this famous landmark back to its original glory.

The luxury hostelry is now under the management of Cunard Hotels and Resorts. Gone are the hot curling irons and coal fireplaces, which have been replaced with state-of-the-art services and plush decor. The hotel's European style concierge service can handle almost any request, including travel arrangements, theater tickets, restaurant reservations, and sporting event bookings. Guests can enjoy a boutique shopping experience on the first floors of the buildings, where

distinct shops by Polo/Ralph Lauren, Gucci, Alfred Dunhill of London, and others have opened. There is also the Sporting Club at the Bellevue, a full-service health club where guests can maintain a fitness regimen. The hotel's restaurants offer everything from a very proper afternoon tea to casual and formal dining experiences. And Philadelphians are once again donning their evening attire and coming to The Hotel Atop the Bellevue to dance and dine in the city's most beloved and elegant ballrooms.

"We are giving The Bellevue back to Philadelphia," Ronald Rubin, managing partner of the Rubin Company, says. "I would think that it's not overstating to say that most Philadelphians are involved emotionally with the Bellevue. It's an important part of the fabric of the city."

The Hershey Philadelphia Hotel
"The Hershey Philadelphia Hotel will become the Philadelphia Hilton & Towers in September, 1991."

Ever since it opened its doors in March 1983, The Hershey Philadelphia has catered to the interests of vacation visitors and business people alike. Its guests have ranged from professional teams in all major sports to opera singers to members of the U.S. House of Representatives.

For some guests, The Hershey Philadelphia Hotel's attraction is its close proximity to the city's major cultural attractions. For others, it is the only hotel (and warm retreat) located on the route of the annual New Year's Day Mummers Parade. And others like the hotel's convenience for convention and meeting business. Whether it is for business or pleasure, the hotel's guests enjoy the comfort of a familiar name.

The Hershey Philadelphia Hotel's roots go back to its founder, Milton S. Hershey. Milton Hershey believed that a business had a responsibility to help the surrounding community to thrive.

In 1927 Milton Hershey established Hershey Estates, predecessor to Hershey Entertainment and Resort Company (HERCO), the manager and operator of The Hershey Philadelphia Hotel. Milton Hershey used Hershey Estates to manage and develop the town of Hershey.

The Hershey philosophy has been evident since the first guest set foot into the four-story atrium lobby of The Hershey Philadelphia Hotel. The modern concrete and glass hotel rises 25 stories above Broad and Locust streets, the heart of Philadelphia's cultural district.

Across the street is the elegant Academy of Music, where The Philadelphia Orchestra, world-famous musicians, dancers, and performers have entertained for decades. Around the corner is the Forrest Theatre that has thrilled audiences with its Broadway shows. So it is not surprising that The Hershey Philadelphia Hotel's 428 guest rooms have housed ballet, opera, and theater stars when they perform in Philadelphia. The hotel also has held numerous special events and programs in conjunction with the ballet and legitimate theater.

The hotel's cultural focus will be further heightened once Philadelphia's Avenue of the Arts becomes a reality. Still on the drawing boards, the Avenue of the Arts is a grand plan

Above: The Hershey Philadelphia Hotel rises 25 stories above the intersection of Broad and Locust streets, in the heart of Philadelphia's cultural district.

Left: Because of its central location, the hotel is one of the best parade-watching sites in Philadelphia.

to tie together all of Philadelphia's major cultural attractions, and The Hershey Philadelphia Hotel will play a pivotal role in that plan.

The Hershey Philadelphia Hotel is a good sport, too. Due to its central location, the hotel, in traditional Philadelphia sports style, has hosted numerous major-league baseball teams when they visit Philadelphia to take on the Phillies and several professional football teams, who choose to relax at the hotel when they are not battling the Eagles.

On New Year's Day crowds line the

Above: Corporate executives who choose to stay on the limited-access concierge floor frequently conduct informal meetings in the sitting areas of the executive suites.

Right: The relaxed atmosphere of the mezzanine Cafe Academie restaurant caters to families and business guests.

streets, and guests flock to the rooms to watch the annual New Year's Day Mummers Parade, a sometimes cold and snowy Philadelphia tradition that is made much cozier by the hotel.

All of the hotel's guests receive the same caring service as espoused by Milton Hershey. Thousands each year take advantage of the Hershey's 24,000 square feet of meeting space and its mezzanine Cafe Academie restaurant that overlooks the atrium lobby. Many frequent business travelers also enjoy the special Executive Privileges® frequent-traveler program.

"Upon check-in, every guest receives a Hershey chocolate bar," says a hotel spokesperson. The hotel gift shops always carry a large supply of Hershey chocolate candies, and every restaurant patron receives chocolate Hershey's Kisses chocolates with the check. It is The Hershey Philadelphia Hotel's way of giving every visitor the warmest welcome in Philadelphia.

ARA Services

The bright red ARA sign glowing atop the ARA Tower at 1101 Market Street may be relatively new to the skyline of Philadelphia, but the international service-management company headquartered at this address has played an important role in the city for 30 years.

From a regional firm with 1,000 employees and $24 million in revenue, ARA Services has grown into a $4.6-billion international diversified management company. More than 130,000 ARA people deliver a wide range of services that improve the quality of life for millions of individuals in all 50 states and five foreign countries.

Joseph Neubauer, ARA's chairman and chief executive officer, led a management buyout which took the company private in 1984 and guided its subsequent growth and development into the nation's leading provider of quality services. Today nearly 11,000 employees enjoy the benefits of stock ownership.

ARA has had only two other chief executive officers: cofounders William S. Fishman and David Davidson. Fishman was a driving force in ARA's expansion and extensive diversification. He was also prominent in Philadelphia's business, civic, and cultural affairs. Davidson guided ARA's growth from a small, regional company into a national leader.

Today ARA is the country's leading provider of quality food and refreshment services to more than 7,000 business locations,

350 hospitals, 250 college campuses, and more than 175 school districts across the country.

The company also has a fine dining division which operates gourmet restaurants, and its ARA/Cory division provides refreshment services to 175,000 people daily.

ARA, through its Leisure Services division, also serves many of the country's major sports stadiums, arenas, convention centers, and airports, as well as state and national parks, including the nation's newest, Ellis Island.

The company's reputation was put to the supreme test in Mexico City in 1968 when ARA was asked to be the first professional food service company to serve the athletes at the Olympic Games. ARA has since served 13 more Olympic events and is gearing up for the 1992 Games in Barcelona, Spain.

ARA has long been operating in the international arena. Its affiliate, VS Services, is the largest food service company in Canada. ARA also has significant operations in Japan, Great Britain, Belgium, and Germany. It was among the first companies to move into East Germany when the barriers came down.

In the United States, the company provides a wide range of other services including uniform rental, periodical distribution, child care, and health care.

ARA's ARATEX division is the country's largest uniform rental company. It offers customer uniform programs to help create unique corporate identities or meet specialized environmental needs, such as static control or flame retardance. ARA-TEX's 150 centers across the nation also provide an array of other products, including walk-off mats, mops, shop towels, rest

Below and Right: ARA provides a wide range of employee dining services. The company has served 14 Olympic events since the 1968 games in Mexico City and is gearing up for the 1992 games in Barcelona, Spain.

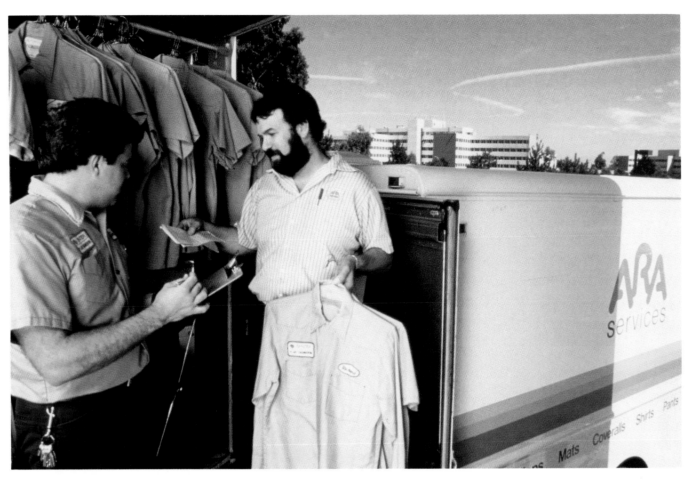

room supplies, and linens.

ARA's Magazine & Book Division is the industry leader, distributing some 500 million newspapers, magazines, and paperback and hardcover books annually to more than 22,000 retail outlets.

The company also provides long-term health care through its ARA Living Centers division. More than 23,000 residents in 13 states live in ARA's 240 facilities, which pro-

vide care for the elderly, the developmentally disabled, and for those with special needs such as Alzheimer victims.

ARA also is the leader in providing early childhood education at its 470 Children's World Learning Centers. The company cares for more than 60,000 preschool and school-age children, providing professionally planned and supervised social development.

The company also provides specialized management services for nearly 500 hospital emergency departments through its Spectrum Emergency Care division, and it is the nation's leader in correctional health care, serving 111 institutions in 18 states through

its Correctional Medical Systems division.

And ARA's Environmental Services division provides quality housekeeping and maintenance to educational, health care, and corporate facilities.

ARA Services looks to the future with confidence. It plans to maintain its leadership role in meeting the ever-increasing needs for diversified services around the country and around the world.

Above: ARA's ARATEX division offers customer uniform programs to help create unique corporate identities or to meet specialized demands such as static control or flame-retardant materials.

Right: ARA's Children's World Learning Centers care for more than 60,000 preschool and school-age children.

Left: ARA's Periodicals Group is the leader in the industry, distributing some 500 million newspapers, magazines, as well as paperback and hardcover books annually to more than 22,000 retail outlets.

Wawa Inc.

A convenience store by any other name just wouldn't be Wawa. To people who want to grab a cup of coffee on the way to work, a sandwich for lunch, and maybe a family hoagie for dinner, Wawa has come to mean a special kind of convenience.

That's not exactly what the founding family members had in mind, however, when George Wood decided to branch out from the family's textile mill business into the dairy farming business in the 1890s. For them Wawa was the name of the town in rural Delaware County where the family spent its summers. Eventually it became the location of George Wood's dairy farm and milk processing business. It's still the location of the company's corporate offices, called the "Red Roof" as a reminder of the red tile roof that graced the original family house.

For many years, Wawa built its reputation by selling its milk door-to-door while still operating the textile mills. The Wawa Dairy Farms milk wagons were a familiar sight around the region. After decades of steady growth, however, by the 1960s the textile operation had shut down and demand for door-to-door delivery of Wawa's milk was slipping. It was no longer necessary to have milk delivered in order to guarantee freshness, so milk drinkers were choosing to buy their milk at the supermarket rather than have it delivered to the back door. It was simply more convenient.

That development was not lost on Grahame Wood, grandson of George Wood, so he decided to buck the supermarket trend. In April 1964 he opened the first Wawa Food Market in Folsom, Pennsylvania. His intention, as Wawa's pledge to its customers succinctly spells out, was to offer caring service, clean stores, and quality fresh foods. Known as Store Number 1, that shop quickly became a success and signaled the beginning of Wawa's rapid expansion into a chain of more than 500 stores that operate today throughout Pennsylvania, New Jersey, Delaware, Maryland, and Connecticut. It also represented a philosophy at Wawa that has become the hallmark for all its stores today.

Wawa sees itself as a viable alternative to the supermarket by providing the same kind of selection, freshness, and quality of food at comparable prices. The company, today led by chief executive Dick Wood, great-grandson of the founder, has taken great pains to discipline itself to not simply follow the pack by offering videocassette rentals or lottery tickets, but stick to an approach that has served it well, and more importantly, has served its customers well.

That approach has been evident in the vast array of innovative services and product lines that are available in every Wawa store today. Wawa believes in providing food service, not just food. One of its first food service innovations was the introduction in

1975 of its award-winning coffee, which is offered in a never-empty coffee pot. Its deli department, which is separate from the cash register, offers customers a broad selection of fresh meats, cheese, and salads. And if a customer is not in the mood for a cup of coffee, the self-serve soda fountain is just as convenient.

In addition to this long line of so-called "perishable" items, every Wawa Food Market stocks more than 3,000 items including bread, groceries, tobacco, and candy. And most stores are open 24-hours-a-day, seven days a week.

As life-styles have changed, so has Wawa's mix of food service and selection. After all, many people don't eat breakfast at home, can't enjoy a leisurely lunch, and have to rush to prepare dinner. So breakfast sandwiches and bagels have become a staple on Wawa's menu, along with deli sandwiches, hoagies, and Lite Bite salads.

Most recently Wawa has focused on the dinner hour with a line of hot soups, stews, chilis, and hot sandwiches.

When Wawa isn't expanding its food service, it is concentrating on people—those who work for the chain and those who depend upon the Delaware Valley corporate community for its support. Wawa prides itself on the loyalty of its employees, many of whom have worked for Wawa since it opened its first stores. That loyalty is apparent in the store clerks, known as associates, who are not only friendly, but are eager to please.

Wawa also operates its Wawa Charities Fund, which is supported by the employees and the corporation. The company matches every dollar contributed by its associates, and donates the funds to dozens of United Way and other charitable organizations in the five-state area. Wawa also supports numerous other area organizations, such as Children's Hospital and the Sunshine Foundation through acts of caring and support.

Considered a stellar performer by industry observers, Wawa is commited to continuing its growth rate, relying upon the same discipline that has served it so well for so many years. Since the first store opened, Wawa has averaged opening 30 stores a year, concentrating them in its five-state market area. And as long as people are hungry, Wawa will continue to offer them innovative and fresh food selections.

Patrons

The following individuals, companies, and organizations have made a valuable commitment to the quality of this publication. Windsor Publications gratefully acknowledges their participation in *Greater Philadelphia: Into the Future*.

American College of Physicians*
ARA Services*
Arthur Andersen & Co. and Stephen M. Smith, Andersen Consulting*
Bell Atlantic Corporation*
Blank, Rome, Comisky & McCauley*
Boeing Helicoptors*
Charter Fairmount Institute*
Chase Manhattan Corporation*
CoreStates Financial Corp.*
Day & Zimmermann*
Delaware Group*
Environmental Resources Management, Inc.*
EZ Communications*
Focus: Metropolitan Philadelphia's Business Magazine*
Frank B. Hall & Company of Pennsylvania, Inc.*
Frankel Enterprises/Warwick Hotel*
Glenmede Trust Company*
Harron Communications Corp.*
Herr Foods Inc.*
The Hershey Philadelphia Hotel*
Holy Family College*
Hotel Atop the Bellevue*
Hoyle, Morris & Kerr*
Independence Blue Cross*
Jackson-Cross Company*
John Wanamaker*
The Kevin F. Donohoe Companies*

Kraft Dairy Group*
KYW-TV*
M.A.B. Paints & Coatings*
Medical College of Pennsylvania*
The Mutual Assurance Company*
Mylotte, David & Fitzpatrick*
The Oliver H. Bair Company*
Paul Hertel & Co., Inc.*
Pennsylvania State University*
Philadelphia Business Journal*
Philadelphia Electric Company*
Philadelphia Newspapers Inc.*
Philadelphia Phillies*
Philadelphia Suburban Water Company*
Price Waterhouse*
Progress Lighting*
Reed Smith Shaw McClay*
St. Christopher's Hospital for Children*
SmithKline Beecham*
Strouse, Greenberg & Co.*
Teleflex Incorporated*
Thomas Jefferson University*
Towers Perrin*
The University of the Arts*
Van Kampen Merritt*
Wawa Inc.*
West Jersey Health Systems*
WFLN-FM*
WTXF-TV Channel 29*
Wyeth-Ayerst*

*Participants in Part 2, "Greater Philadelphia's Enterprises." The stories of these companies and organizations appears in chapters 9 through 15, beginning on page 149.

Bibliography

BOOKS

Bookhouser, Frank. *Our Philadelphia: A Candid and Colorful Portrait of a Great City.* Garden City, N.Y.: Doubleday & Company, Inc., 1957.

Bowen, Catherine Drinker. *Miracle at Philadelphia.* Boston: Little, Brown and Company, 1966. Reprinted 1986.

Burt, Struther. Philadelphia: *Holy Experiment.* Garden City, N.Y.: Doubleday, Doran & Company, Inc., 1945.

Clark, Dennis. *The Irish in Philadelphia.* Philadelphia: Temple University Press, 1973. Reprinted 1984.

Collingswood Centennial. Collingswood, N.J.: The Borough of Collingswood, 1988.

Harding, John J., ed. *Marsh, Meadow, Mountain: Natural Places of the Delaware Valley.* Philadelphia: Temple University Press, 1986.

Longstreth, W. Thacher. *Main Line Wasp.* New York: W.W. Norton & Company, Inc., 1990.

Lukacs, John. *Philadelphia: Patricians & Philistines 1900-1950.* New York: Farrar, Straus & Giroux, Inc., 1981.

Meyerson, Martin, and Dilys Pegler Winegrad. *Gladly Learn and Gladly Teach.* Philadelphia: University of Pennsylvania Press, 1978.

Miller, Frederic M., Morris J. Vogel, and Allen F. Davis. *Still Philadelphia: A Photographic History, 1890-1940.* Philadelphia: Temple University Press, 1983.

Oakley, Amy. *Our Pennsylvania: Keys to the Keystone State.* New York: Bobbs-Merrill Company, Inc., 1950.

Summers, Anita A., and Thomas F. Luce. *Economic Development Within the Philadelphia Metropolitan Area.* Philadelphia: University of Pennsylvania Press, 1987.

——. *Local Fiscal Issues in the Philadelphia Metropolitan Area.* Philadelphia: University of Pennsylvania Press, 1987.

Webster, Richard. *Philadelphia Preserved.* Philadelphia: Temple University Press, 1976.

Weigley, Russell F., et al., eds. *Philadelphia: A 300 Year History.* New York: W.W. Norton & Company, Inc., 1982.

Wolf, Edwin, II. *Philadelphia: Portrait of an American City.* Harrisburg, Pa.: Stackpole Books, 1975.

Wolf, Stephanie Grauman. *Urban Village.* Princeton: Princeton University Press, 1976.

MAGAZINES

Applause
Focus
Fortune
Meetings & Conventions
New Jersey Monthly
Philadelphia Magazine
Plants, Sites and Parks
Real Estate Forum

NEWSPAPERS

The Courier-Post
The New York Times
The Philadelphia Inquirer
The Philadelphia Daily News
The Philadelphia Business Journal
The Welcomat

Directory of Corporate Sponsors

American College of Physicians, 238-239
Independence Mall West
6th Street at Race
Philadelphia, PA 19106-1572
215/351-2400
John R. Ball

ARA Services, 256-257
The ARA Tower
1101 Market Street
Philadelphia, PA 19107
215/238-3000
Harry Bellinger

Arthur Andersen & Co.
    and Stephen M. Smith, Andersen Consult-
    ing, 214-215
1601 Market Street
Philadelphia, PA 19103
215/241-7300
Joseph G. Reichner

Bell Atlantic Corporation, 166-167
1600 Market Street
31st Floor
Philadelphia, PA 19103
215/963-6070
Cynthia Ciangio

Blank, Rome, Comisky & McCauley, 220-221
1200 Four Penn Center Plaza
10th Floor
Philadelphia, PA 19103
215/569-5500
Robert Wert

Boeing Helicopters, 176-177
Route 291 and Stewart Avenue
Ridley Park, PA 19078
215/591-3575
H. Robert Torgerson

Charter Fairmount Institute, 236-237
561 Fairthorne Avenue
Philadelphia, PA 19128
215/487-4003
Stephen Chesney

Chase Manhattan Corporation, 195
8 Penn Center
16th Floor
Philadelphia, PA 19103
215/893-9500
Anthony Bittle

CoreStates Financial Corp., 186-187
P.O. Box 7618
Philadelphia, PA 19101
215/973-3100
Paul Kistler

Day & Zimmermann, 218-219
1818 Market Street
Philadelphia, PA 19103
215/299-8151
Karen Lautzenheiser

Delaware Group, 224-225
One Commerce Square
40th Floor
Philadelphia, PA 19103
215/751-2954
Charles W. Carr

Environmental Resources Management, Inc.,
    210
855 Springdale Drive
Exton, PA 19341
215/524-3657 & 524-3562
Dorothy C. Buffington

EZ Communications, 154-155
Two Bala Plaza
Bala Cynwyd, PA 19004
215/667-8100
Michael B. Marder

Focus: Metropolitan Philadelphia's Business
    Magazine, 160-161
1015 Chestnut Street
Philadelphia, PA 19107
215/925-5295
Gary Dvorkin

Frank B. Hall & Company of Pennsylvania, Inc.,
    202-203
Cigna Plaza II
1622 Arch Street
Philadelphia, PA 19103
215/568-1700
Edward Hollingsworth

Frankel Enterprises/Warwick Hotel, 200-201
1845 Walnut Street
Philadelphia, PA 19103
215/751-0900
William Frankel

Glenmede Trust Company, 194

229 South 18th Street
Philadelphia, PA 19103
215/875-5843
J. Thomas Dunlevy

Harron Communications Corp., 150-151
70 East Lancaster Avenue
Frazer, PA 19355
215/644-7500
Mike Mahoney

Herr Foods Inc., 180-181
P.O. Box 300
Nottingham, PA 19362
215/932-9330
Dina Warren

The Hershey Philadelphia Hotel, 254-255
Broad and Locust
Philadelphia, PA 19107
215/893-1600
Felix Rappaport

Holy Family College, 230
Frankford and Grant streets
Philadelphia, PA 19114
215/637-7700
Frank Avato

Hotel Atop the Bellevue, 252-253
1415 Chancellor Court
Philadelphia, PA 19102
215/393-1776
Suzanne M. Epps

Hoyle, Morris & Kerr, 208-209
One Liberty Place
1650 Market Street
Suite 4900
Philadelphia, PA 19103
215/981-5700
Ellen Briggs

Independence Blue Cross, 188-189
1901 Market Street
Philadelphia, PA 19103
215/448-5529
Nelson Fellman

Jackson-Cross Company, 204
100 North 20th Street
Philadelphia, PA 19103-1443
215/561-8900
Michele McKinney
John Wanamaker, 250

Woodward & Lothrop
11th and F streets N.W.
Washington, D.C. 20013
212/879-8703
John T. Buckley

The Kevin F. Donohoe Companies, 199
Curtis Center, Independence Square West
Suite 700
Philadelphia, PA 19106
215/238-6400
Laurie Wolfe

Kraft Dairy Group, 174-175
1635 Market Street
7 Penn Center
Philadelphia, PA 19103
215/587-1749
Mike Ginley

KYW-TV, 152
Group W Television, Inc.
Independence Mall East
Philadelphia, PA 19106
215/238-4964
Joanna Calabria

M.A.B. Paints & Coatings, 172-173
600 Reed Road
Broomhall, PA 19008
215/353-5100
Mary Ruff

Medical College of Pennsylvania, 228-229
3300 Henry Avenue
Philadelphia, PA 19129
215/842-7000
D. Walter Cohen

The Mutual Assurance Company, 190-191
414 Walnut Street
Philadelphia, PA 19106
215/925-0609
Daniel F. Crough

Mylotte, David & Fitzpatrick, 212-213
1800 John F. Kennedy Boulevard
Philadelphia, PA 19103
215/751-9450
Edward J. David

The Oliver H. Bair Company, 251

1920 Sansom Street
Philadelphia, PA 19103
215/563-1580
Maytor H. McKinley

Paul Hertel & Co., Inc., 211
N.E. Corner Third and Chestnut streets
Philadelphia, PA 19106
215/925-7656
George E. Mansfield

Pennsylvania State University, 240-241
Delaware County Campus
25 Yearsley Mill Road
Media, PA 19063
215/565-3300
R.D. Nargi

Philadelphia Business Journal, 163
718 Arch Street, #6N
Philadelphia, PA 19106
215/238-1450
Mary Huss

Philadelphia Electric Company, 158-159
2301 Market Street
Philadelphia, PA 19101
212/841-5664
E. Martin Shane

Philadelphia Newspapers Inc., 156-157
400 North Broad Street
Philadelphia, PA 19101
215/854-5515
Gari Brindle

Philadelphia Phillies, 248-249
Veterans Stadium
Broad Street and Patterson Avenue
Philadelphia, PA 19101
215/463-6000
William Giles

Philadelphia Suburban Water Company, 153
762 Lancaster Avenue
Bryn Mawr, PA 19010
215/645-1017
Jerry A. Sacchetti

Price Waterhouse, 217
30 South 17th Street
Philadelphia, PA 19103-4094
215/665-9500
Irene H. Korsyn
Progress Lighting, 178

Erie Avenue and G Street
Philadelphia, PA 19134
215/288-1200
Fredrick Martin

Reed Smith Shaw McClay, 222-223
2500 One Liberty Place
Philadelphia, PA 19103
215/851-8186
Sheryl B. Levin

St. Christopher's Hospital for Children, 231
United Hospitals, Inc.
Erie Avenue at Front Street
Philadelphia, PA 19134-1095
215/663-5400
Terese Vekteris

SmithKline Beecham, 182-183
P.O. Box 7929
Philadelphia, PA 19101
215/751-4000
Thomas M. Landin

Strouse, Greenberg & Co., 198
1626 Locust Street
Philadelphia, PA 19103
215/985-1100
Lydia Panulas Zelinsky

Teleflex Incorporated, 179
155 South Limerick Road
Limerick, PA 19468
215/948-5100
Mary Pilcicki

Thomas Jefferson University, 232-235
111 South 11th Street TJU
Suite 2024
Philadelphia, PA 19107
215/928-8051
Carmhiel Brown

Towers Perrin, 216
Center Square West
1500 Market Street
27th Floor
Philadelphia, PA 19102-2183
215/246-6000
Robert Gore

The University of the Arts, 244

Broad and Pine streets
Philadelphia, PA 19102
215/875-4800
James Merlihan

Van Kampen Merritt, 192-193
2 Penn Center Plaza
Suite 1600
Philadelphia, PA 19102
215/972-0555
John C. Merritt

Wawa Inc., 258-259
Red Roof, Baltimore Pike
Wawa, PA 19063
215/358-8000
Howard B. Stoeckel

West Jersey Health Systems, 242-243
Mount Ephraim and Atlantic avenues
Camden, NJ 08104
609/342-4000
Barry D. Brown

WFLN-FM, 162
8200 Ridge Avenue
Philadelphi
a, PA 19128
215/482-6000
Richard Tedesco

WTXF-TV Channel 29, 164-165
330 Market Street
Philadelphia, PA 19106
215/925-2929
Denise Rolfe

Wyeth-Ayerst, 170-171
555 E. Lancaster Pike
St. Davids, PA 19087
215/688-4400
Audrey Ashby

Index

Photo by Rich Zila

This book was set in 10/14 Goudy
and Franklin Gothic
composed on a Macintosh II.
Printed on Mead 70lb. Offset Enamel
and bound by Jostens Printing and Publishing Company
Topeka, Kansas.